I LOVE A ROOSEVELT

I Love a Roosevelt

by Patricia Peabody Roosevelt

1967

Doubleday & Company, Inc., Garden City, New York

008 038 310

To my husband

Foreword

The best of a book should be the last, I suppose. But this part is more fun. Especially with the best behind me. Hopefully the Roosevelt family will read this best effort. If I could afford it, I would send them each a copy of my book. It was written because I had an insatiable urge to tell many people of *my Roosevelt* and our wondrous love. Yet Elliott is part and parcel of a great family, whose personal inclinations and desires have always been submerged by their humanitarian feelings toward helping their fellow man. It may be true that they are strong and never accept fear . . . Yet what a relief it would have been to them if their troubles had been a private family affair.

It is difficult to take your place in such a controversial and well-known family. Uncertainty and awe add to insecurity which destroys lines of communication. You find yourself trying too hard. You learn to feel fear and loneliness. You set new standards, most of them foreign to what had gone before.

Yet above all you are a Roosevelt, and you suddenly feel pride coupled with all this insecurity. The world turns faster, there is more to do and less time. Soon, if you love and believe, if you wish hard enough, everything will come true because you are a part of this great clan.

It seemed to me appropriate that I should write a book about the Roosevelt clan because books have always been important to

them. All the Roosevelts are readers, some of them very rapid
and knowledgeable readers. (FDR himself was one of our first
leaders to make use of the benefits of speed reading.)

I hope if my candor is too direct it will be understood. I want
this new family to stop and know me, to let me share with them
my pride in their name. I hope to do them honor in my
endeavors. I want them for my friends, most of all.

Friends are hard to describe, difficult to thank. Freddie Peterson, who asks no questions, but believes and is always near.
Martin Jones, who accepted and protected me. Charlie Whited,
who is my writer, my teacher and my friend. (I hope to write
another book with him.) Pauline Hevia, Eunice Seidler . . .
Their loyalty is only exceeded by their devotion.

Ford was my runner . . . Gretchen my critic and David
brought me ice-cream bars throughout. Ruthi Hillman was my
reader. Her husband, Dr. Dan, didn't believe I was serious.
Better friends will be hard to find. Nancy and Stanley Colbert
were always ready to listen . . . To say nothing of Jim Bishop.
Drew Pearson and Jeane Dixon encouraged me, always providing inspiration.

But best of all was Elliott . . . "His Eminence," my husband.
The end and the beginning . . . My love. I hope that he likes
my book . . . I wrote it for him.

Contents

I LOVE A ROOSEVELT

1

The End and the Beginning

The rain had stopped, but there was no sunshine to dry the soggy ground or warm the backs of those who stood in the rose garden. A light breeze had risen out of the valley of the Hudson behind them. It swept up, up over the bluffs of brown grass and hardwood trees, to play in the eaves of the gray fieldstone mansion at Hyde Park and ruffle the coattails of the people arrayed so solemnly by the plain marble tombstone. Floral sprays of chrysanthemums, gladioli and lilies rose behind the stone. Upon its face was engraved the words, FRANKLIN DELANO ROOSEVELT, 1882–1945, and on an identical stone next to it, ANNA ELEANOR ROOSEVELT, 1884–   . Today was November 10, 1962, and soon a stonecutter would fill in the rest of the date, chipping away alone after the crowd had left.

Dr. Gordon L. Kidd, a white-haired, distinguished figure in white vestments and black surplice, had not delivered a eulogy during the funeral at Hyde Park's tiny, crowded St. James Episcopal Church. At the request of the family, the committal service also embodied the simplicity of the Book of Common Prayer. But now, he looked at the lowering sky and gathered his thoughts to speak briefly of the person who was dead. "In the death of Eleanor Roosevelt," he said, "the world has suffered an irreparable loss. The entire world becomes one family orphaned by her passing."

Peeking out through my black veil, I looked carefully around at the mournful ritual taking place here in the drab garden of the Hyde Park estate. The surrounding tall yew hedges glistened from the recent rain, much as they had seventeen years before when a nation weary from war had paused to bury one of its great Presidents. Now the four sons and one daughter of Franklin D. Roosevelt stood together again to grieve for their mother, Eleanor Roosevelt, a woman who had overcome her fright and insecurity to achieve world greatness of her own. The Roosevelt heritage was in their hands, to be given new luster or frittered away and lost forever.

To my right stood Jimmy, tall, baldish, handsome in an owlish kind of way; an enigma to those close to him, but a pleasant enigma. Beside him was his third wife, Irene. During most of the service Jimmy stood stock-still with his hands clasped.

To my left was Johnny and with him, Anne: he with his fists tightly clenched at his sides, she looking bleak and stony-faced. They were not easy people to get to know, Johnny and Anne, perhaps in part because of the shocking tragedy they had endured just two years before this, when they stood at the grave of their teenage daughter, Sally, killed in a fall from a horse.

Then there was Anna; the spare, and to me, awesome-looking, eldest of the Roosevelt children. Today she wore her old Persian lamb and stood pulling a pair of black gloves from one hand to the other. At Anna's side was her husband, bespectacled Dr. James Halsted of Birmingham, Michigan. Her marriage to the doctor gave her and her brothers a closer picture of their mother's illness, as he tried to translate the medical terminology for them.

And beyond Anna was Franklin, Jr., the personable man who bore such a striking resemblance to his father, but whose political attainments thus far had fallen far short of his ambitions. Franklin kept thrusting his hands into his pockets and taking them out again, which caught the attention of his wife, Sue, a tall, well-dressed, reserved-looking blonde. Her face showed sadness.

Characteristically, I stood violating the etiquette of public appearances by holding the hand of my husband, Elliott Roosevelt, the complex and controversial second son of FDR. Elliott's stormy marital past and personal involvements had kept him in the gossip columns for most of his adult life. Just three years prior to this funeral I had become his fifth wife, at a time when Elliott was destitute, hounded, and sick at heart. In our brief time together we had already endured reversals, family rejection, and deep personal loss; but out of this was growing a rich store of love and affection, and a strong marriage.

The woman we had come to mourn, who now lay in the plain oaken casket beneath a covering of pine boughs, had made it plain to me that an outsider in this strong family had to earn acceptance. My own clashes with some of these in-laws had already been bitter and emotional, and there would be more. Even now, as I was clutching my husband's hand while a battery of TV cameras whirred and flashbulbs popped from a platform beyond the marble monument. I was still an intruder to this family in which bloodlines were more binding than marriage. I felt a kinship with Eleanor Roosevelt, who had begun her own married life as an outsider, caught between a domineering mother-in-law and a pampered husband.

It was this Eleanor Roosevelt who had inspired the man to rebuild himself after polio had ravaged his body, rebuild until he became one of the great figures in world history. Joining us now in mourning were living symbols of the immensity of her achievement: three Presidents of the United States and a Vice-President, American and foreign dignitaries of the highest credentials, and beyond the wooded acreage of the Hyde Park estate millions of ordinary people speaking many native tongues who had come to revere her leadership and humanity.

At the southwest corner of the tombstone stood the young President who would be martyred in precisely one year and eleven days.

The breeze off the Hudson ruffled the tousled brown hair of John Fitzgerald Kennedy, and passed over the head of the man standing one pace behind him who would be catapulted by an assassin's bullet into the Presidency, Vice-President Lyndon Baines Johnson. At Kennedy's shoulder, looking gray and drawn, was the man who had taken up the massive burdens of Franklin D. Roosevelt in the midst of war, Harry Truman. Beside Mr. Truman and his wife Bess stood General Dwight D. Eisenhower, who as President had failed to reappoint Mrs. Roosevelt as a delegate to the United Nations.

Bareheaded in the cold stood New York's Governor Nelson A. Rockefeller, Chief Justice Earl Warren, Associate Justice Arthur Goldberg, later to become Ambassador to the United Nations, UN Ambassador Adlai Stevenson, and such figures from the New Deal days as FDR Cabinet members Frances Perkins, James A. Farley, and Francis Biddle, and the late President's friends, Samuel I. Rosenman, Ben Cohen, and former New York Governor Herbert Lehman. The former Anna M. Rosenberg, who had served as Assistant Secretary of Defense in the Truman Administration, stood weeping at the side of her husband, Paul Hoffman.

Feeling the touch of Elliott's hand, my thoughts strayed back to the advice a close friend, Mary Jim Bagley, had given me in Minneapolis: "Patty, your husband is a public figure and it just isn't proper to display affection out where people can see you." As a TV camera swung our way I tried to pull my hand away. Elliott's grip tightened. I stopped pulling.

The voice of Dr. Kidd intoned the eulogy. The breeze sighed, a dreary and lonesome sound. And I, Patty Peabody from Seattle, a former divorcée who had left home for the first time at age thirty-six with four children, was part of it. For better or worse, these five Roosevelts with whom I mourned were relatives-by-marriage now. I fervently hoped that our future paths together would be smoother than the past.

As for myself, it was incredible that it had happened at all. Seattle, and all those frustrating years leading to this day and this place, now seemed unreal. Life in Seattle, for all its sometime turbulence, had been comfortable upper middle class. Our home was one of those large, traditional residences on a quiet, well-shaded street. It was filled with heavy antique furniture, white curtains, potted plants, and all the trappings of Catholic respectability.

Family connections were secure, sometimes financially but always by bloodline. Dating back to pioneer days we were in the *Blue Book* every year. My father, who begrudged secretly what he considered a good but incomplete education, had a substantial interest in the family's Black Ball Ferry Line and owned and was president of the United Fuel Co. in Seattle. Our cousin, Endicott Marshall Peabody, had been a governor of Massachusetts. Mother, Eunice Ford Peabody, descended from an old line Iowa family which pioneered in the settling of Seattle. Her father had been president of the Great Northern Railroad.

I was a proper young product of a proper old school. The Sacred Heart Convent was one hundred years old, very expensive, the kind of institution which turned out future wives of bank presidents, doctors, lawyers, and executives. A diploma from the Sacred Heart means not only that you knew your catechism, but also that you could featherstitch, pour tea, and speak French. As an adult you would be accepted by the Women's Club and the Junior League.

I attended the convent for twelve years, with mixed emotions. Part of it was resentment of the school's authoritarian regimen, symbolized by such things as the bloomers and long black stockings of gymnasium class. Part of it was an inborn rebellion.

Childhood for me was constant rebellion. I had an insatiable urge to do things of which my parents disapproved. Paradoxically, my friends were mostly adults, contemporaries of my mother and father. With people my own age I tended to be bossy, spoiled, and uncertain. The adult influence gave me an air of maturity, so that my sisters credited me with having more sophistication than they.

A diary of those years would be filled with the bizarre happenings which seemed to befall me.

Dear Diary: Trouble again. Visiting my grandmother's farm, I failed to saddle a horse properly and the cinch slipped, spilling me to the ground. The horse backed up and stepped on me, gashing my face and right arm. The animal had been rope burned which I knew caused the accident but I didn't tell anyone. Later, my sister Lee mounted him and he threw her against a sharp-edged water trough after becoming frightened when he became tangled in a clothesline. In addition to my being laid up with injuries, I was punished by being ordered not to leave the property for three months. Oh, woe.

At the Sacred Heart, demerits came every Monday morning at Prime. All the nuns and student body assembled to hear the good and bad news of the Prime read. Mine was usually bad. My two sisters, Lee and Nina, seemed to get along much better in school. When Mother and Daddy went on a trip we were put in

boarding school which I dreaded. I looked forward to the summers, with carefree days of sailing and horseback riding.

Lee was nineteen months younger than I, a sentimental,
heavy-set girl who cried so easily we accused her of having her
bladder too close to her eyes. The contrast between her, whom
we called "Loads of Love Lee," and Nina was striking. Nina, the
youngest in the family, was precise and prim, inclined to be short
of humor. I think she inherited these qualities from my father, or
perhaps from Uncle Alexander.

Daddy had grown up in a family of thirteen boys and his
home life had been extremely strict. My impression of him was
of a man intellectually insecure. Socially he sought out people
mentally inferior to him, and seldom seemed at ease with his
peers. Thus, Daddy might bring home a group of hockey players,
and fill the house with loud, joshing talk which ill-suited him,
but which he professed to enjoy hugely. He doted on my sisters.
They sang beautiful duets together. At parties, no matter what
the hour, they were summoned from their beds to sing for the
guests. I would sit off in a corner to listen in a pout, telling
whoever was in earshot, "I can ride a horse."

Uncle Alexander Marshall Peabody had my father's round
brown eyes, with the addition of a little clipped mustache, but
there the resemblance ended. Uncle Alexander was the lord high
administrator of the family, its principal mediator and maker of
money. Of the thirteen brothers, five of whom died in childhood,
he was third eldest and most competent in business matters and
general self-assurance. In time Uncle Alexander became so lordly
that he nearly lost all relationship with his brothers.

To me he was an ogre; but he did a splendid job of building
the estate. One of his major coups was the sale of the Black Ball
Ferry Line to the State of Washington. He retained four vessels
which formed the nucleus of a new operation, the Puget Sound
Navigation Co., Ltd., in Vancouver, British Columbia. This he
ultimately sold to the Canadian government and made a fortune.
He retired, with homes in Malibu and Seattle.

The person who exerted greatest influence on me as a child
was my grandmother, Lillie McCauley Peabody. She was an
elegant person, short, heavy-set, with lovely gray hair and im-

maculate fingernails. To me she was a dowager duchess. For years she complained of being lame with arthritis, a device, I think, to make Uncle Alexander treat her more kindly. She had a bell for summoning servants, and sat with a cross little Pekingese in her lap.

I spent days at a time in "Da's" house. She treated me as a grownup, spoiled me and taught me. She was a fiend at crossword puzzles, and it became my task to look up the more troublesome words. When it wasn't crosswords she entertained herself at endless games of Russian Bank. In the quiet of that huge house, filled with mahogany furniture, Oriental rugs, silver and bric-a-brac, her bracelets jingled and her rings twinkled as she played the cards over a red velvet-topped table. "Da's" death in 1943, after I had had my first child, came as the first great shock of my life. They brought her coffin to the big house and it sat in somber splendor in the dark parlor, while people gathered about talking in whispers. I went out and picked a bouquet of flowers in the park, then stole into the room like a child again and placed them on her coffin. It was the kind of thing "Da" would have appreciated. Years later I was to see this repeated by Aunt Polly.

> *Dear Diary:* Some young people across the lake, older than we, invited the three Peabody sisters to a party. There were kegs of beer, food and dancing. Lee imbibed beer and food and came home deathly ill. She got sick on her bed. We thought we heard someone coming in the hall. I bundled up the blanket and tossed it out the window. It landed on Daddy's head. Another three months of punishment for me. Oh, misery.

That same year, Daddy gave me permission to take flying lessons, on condition that neither of us would say anything to Mother, who might worry. Lee Clark, a friend of mine who lived across the lake, drove me to the Lake Union Flying Service for regular lessons. I wound up taking fifty hours of training, including solo, and delighted in buzzing our house. One evening Mother complained at dinner: "I really don't know what's happening these days. The planes keep coming over so low." As it turned out, she refused to sign the papers for my private pilot's license. Since both parents' signatures were required, my flying training went down the drain.

> *Dear Diary:* A new romance shattered. Tom Bell, twenty-eight, a graduate of Cal Tech, has speedboats and money. Daddy thinks I'm too young. Tom went to Daddy one time, asked if I could go to a houseparty with him. Daddy blew a gasket. "Get off this property, young man," he thundered. Secretly I suppose I was just using him. I'm forever bringing young men home for dinner so Daddy can sit across the table, glaring and finding fault with their manners. Boys are such a problem for me. For years I've been smothered with the company of girls. I don't know how to act with a date. I trip on my high heels; and on double dates the other girl usually ends up with my beau. Mother always said, "Nice girls don't go around kissing boys." She scared me to death by saying I would never see them again if I let them get fresh. It's so embarrassing. What will I do?

At eighteen I graduated from the Sacred Heart Convent and told Daddy I wanted to attend the University of Washington. But again, I found school life dull and too strict. Other things seemed far more interesting. Besides, it did not seem fair for the college to continue treating young women as if they were kindergarten students. I endured it until the first quarter of my second year, then dropped out.

While at the university I began dating a boy, Westervelt Barker, whose name was far more elegant than he. In eight months we were engaged, although for the life of me I don't know why. Then conveniently the war came along and he was sent to North Africa, from where he wrote long, dreary letters. Grandmother Peabody had been righteously indignant about the whole affair. "That boy has nothing," she would say, with a withering sniff. "He's certainly not the man who can make you happy." I could see that, but engagement to Wes did provide me an excuse for having a ring, even though its stone was so tiny you needed a magnifying glass to see it. The engagement provided emotional support, too, when I left college and went to work in the Boeing plant as a clerk, working for the first time on my own.

I couldn't type but drove a cart around the plant, for the most part, delivering memoranda. Boeing was making B-17 bombers and I was making money. Uncle Alexander said I was vastly overpaid, and said I should keep $50 a week, which I was worth, and send the rest back to the government. With the Boeing job I soon forgot all about Westervelt Barker and was dating Navy fliers from Sand Point. I left the airplane plant after a year to work for a while as a record librarian in Providence Hospital, a Catholic institution. I was fired when a nun saw me in a drugstore with one of the interns. Socializing between employees of the opposite sex was against hospital rules. Then came a job in a women's shop.

And then came Milton Whitehead.

He was dark, attractive, and twenty-three years old, two years older than I. In May 1943, he was a second lieutenant in the Army Air Corps, and I met him on a blind date at the Officers' Club. He was a quiet Texan from Dallas who let me do most of the talking; and at the time I did not realize that his taciturnity was from acute shyness. He was socially minded and I represented social improvement, a bargain which I did not find unacceptable. As usual, I was clumsy and ill at ease, but we managed to kiss after four dates. Two months later we were ready to be married, and Mother and some friends made arrangements for the wedding to be held in St. Joseph's parish house. Daddy had a fit. Not only did he refuse to give his consent but vowed he would not even attend the wedding. One evening he took Milt out and had a man-to-man talk, which consisted mostly of Daddy's angry monologue. "You can't marry her. I won't permit it. She won't stay with you. She's in love every week, etc, etc, . . ." I must say, in Milt's behalf, he stood up like a rock and returned just as firmly resolved to go ahead with our plans. Then Daddy turned his wrath on me.

"You can't get married," he shouted. "You'll never come back into this house if you do."

"I don't want to come back here. I will marry Milt, and there's nothing you can do to stop us."

It ended in a bitter impasse, while Mother and the others went ahead with arrangements for the caterer, flowers, and all the rest. With little money to go on, I borrowed a dress from a friend. This, on the eve of the wedding, broke Daddy's determination. "She can't get married like this," he said at last. "After all, Patty is our eldest daughter." So he relented and became the benign "Father of the Bride," then turned up to give his daughter away in marriage, even with serious misgivings.

We spent a brief honeymoon in Victoria, British Columbia, then were together six weeks before Milt went overseas for three years. I went home pregnant. After seven months, I fell on the steps of the neighbor's house, broke my pelvic bone in two places and found myself in the hospital for a week. They took me home by ambulance with orders to sleep on a board for two months. The experience shattered me. I was terrified of the day when I'd have to deliver the baby, Jimmy. I trembled and cried at times, and unburdened my fears to Mother. "Patty," she said sternly, "the most important thing a woman has in this world is self-control." (Years later, she finally confessed that she was an even bigger coward about pain than I am.) Jimmy was on time, and his delivery came with surprisingly little trouble. But afterward, the doctor said I was too nervous to nurse him, so he was bottle fed. He wouldn't eat, and could keep little on his stomach. He turned out to be a skinny little thing, spoiled by his grandparents and hovered over by his mother. Daddy, whose regard for Milt had warmed not a bit in long absence, resented my even sending a picture of the baby overseas.

The war ended at last, and one day Milt called me long-distance from England, saying he was coming to Dallas to be discharged from the Army and asking if I would meet him there. It was like talking to a stranger on the phone, a stranger for whom I had lost all feeling. Daddy took the receiver. "I'm sorry, she is not coming to meet you and is certainly not bringing this baby with her," he announced. But I did both. I got on a plane, with my three-year-old in a baby harness, and flew away to Dallas. It was a sobering experience for us both.

Milt looked fit and greeted us affectionately. We were like hundreds of thousands of couples being reunited after agonizingly long separations, in which each had forgotten what the other was like as a person, and in countless instances one of the persons—or perhaps both—had changed to the point where there could be no real reconciliation.

We stayed with Milt's parents five days, and then fled to the comparative quiet of a hotel. In all, we remained in Dallas ten days. Then he was given his discharge papers and we went back to Seattle.

Milt enrolled in Seattle University in Business Administration, under the GI Bill, and got a part-time job to supplement his government income of $110 a month. Daddy did not believe in providing any financial help for his children, or giving them anything until he died. But he harped constantly about our handling of money. "You are foolhardy and a spendthrift. You don't know how to manage what you have."

We had a small apartment on the lake, and there were some good times in the early stage of married life. Both of us were excited about beginning our new home, and there was so much to learn about each other that war and circumstance had not given us time for before. But it wasn't long until I began to feel there were differences between Milt and me which could never be bridged.

Later on, to earn money, I became editor and publisher of the Seattle Social *Blue Book*, and also executive secretary of its entire Board of Directors. There were several criteria serving as a basis for listings, but chief among them was one that the socially chosen also buy the *Blue Book*. The house began to resemble the aftermath of a ticker tape parade. I'd never realized before that an editor and publisher had to do much envelope stuffing and licking. It is a wonder I didn't come down with glue poisoning. When friends dropped by, they soon found themselves on hands and knees, stuffing envelopes.

The gulf between us widened. We were completely different personalities with little basic rapport to bind us to each other. I had married Milt, I knew now, to get away; so we had gotten away together to a one-bedroom stucco apartment with a balcony on the lake, sparsely furnished but with the makings of a fine set of built-in problems. When we moved to a slightly larger place, we took the problems along. Somehow, they tended to grow with each new child.

Our second son, Ford, was born in June of 1947. He had a multiple cystic condition of the right lung. Caring for him put an added strain on our relationship. It meant shots every four hours, an oxygen tent at hand for three years. During the first year Ford was in the hospital thirteen times. Milt, of course, was busy holding down a job as assistant bank loan officer and studying. At night he was tired and wanted to rest, which I resented. Ford became my complete responsibility, and so I looked upon him as belonging entirely to me. The doctor bills put us $10,000 in debt, with no hope of climbing out. When the baby began gaining strength and was over the worst of it, I fell apart physically and emotionally, which did nothing for the marriage.

With the coming of the Korean war, Milt went back into the service with the rank of captain and was stationed at McChord Air Force Base at Tacoma. Perhaps a separation would have done us more good, for even as he returned to uniform we were talking about divorce. There was a quarrel which ended with me announcing, "I'm leaving!" and stalking home to Mother and Daddy. They begged us to patch it up. "You've made your bed," Daddy said piously, "Now lie in it." We went back together and took a second honeymoon to Victoria. Result: Gretchen, born in March 1952.

While I was pregnant with Gretchen my parents separated. The news came abruptly in a telephone call from Mother. "Patty, your father is leaving me for another woman." She had been an old flame of Daddy's, several times married. Mother refused to give Daddy a divorce. In the State of Washington you live apart five years then you are granted an automatic decree. Daddy had a long time of separation to go, technically still married. For reasons which, I'm sure, were purely selfish, I was bitterly angry at Daddy. I began spying on him, following when he left his apartment and calling Mother when he went to the other woman's home. She would arrive in high dudgeon and there were violent quarrels. Sometimes when Daddy took his friend to a restaurant, I would sneak into the parking lot like a very pregnant thief and let the air out of his tires.

But I couldn't stay angry forever. My own marital troubles were pyramiding much too rapidly. Milt and I separated again and this time Mother alone tried to reconcile us. The experience, however, was giving me a much better understanding of how a marriage could go wrong, so quietly I began to see Daddy again. Some evenings I would go to his apartment and we would talk for hours. Before leaving I always fixed his coffee for breakfast the next morning. He promised that he wouldn't remarry, even when the divorce became final, and this salved my moral indignation somewhat. But when Mother found out about my visits, she was hurt, feeling I was disloyal to her.

As it was to turn out, Daddy waited exactly two days after the divorce became final before marrying the other woman. The impending nuptials were again announced by Mother, who had her private pipelines for news. Almost casually, she said one day, "Are you going to the wedding on Friday?" "What wedding?" I inquired. "Why, your father is being married in Vancouver. Didn't you know?" This time it was my turn to feel betrayed. I telephoned him in Vancouver.

"I hear you're getting married on Friday. You promised me, Daddy, that you wouldn't."

"What are you talking about?" he said coolly. "Who told you I was getting married on Friday? I most certainly am not."

"Well, are you getting married at all?" I gasped.

"Yes," he answered, "but on Thursday."

Feisty as I had become, I aimed a nasty blow by bringing up her four previous husbands. "Frankly, Daddy, I can't see you being such a fool as to marry a woman with four sets of references. I'll never speak to you again." And I hung up.

I didn't hear from him for six months. Then he called from Vancouver inviting me to come and have dinner. I told him I didn't want to see his wife. "You're being unfair, Patty," he said. "She is a good woman and a good wife. I'm very happy." It was true, of course. I relented, and I was not sorry.

The rift between Milt and me continued to grow. We had a siege of flu with the children, which kept everybody but Milt cooped up in the house. The flu took its toll of my patience. Frustrated and exhausted I packed up the children and moved out to a friend's house. Mother and Daddy communicated through their attorneys, and their messages were relayed to us. By this rather ridiculous means, we tried still another reconciliation. We were together just long enough for me to become pregnant a fourth time. This baby was David, and he was born December 25, 1957.

Milt had been working at the bank since his separation from the service after the Korean war. But he was not happy. One day he quit his job and announced he was going to Phoenix. "You can come," he said, "if you want to."

Life in Seattle had grown stagnant. With both parents angry at me, and four children to care for, I decided now might be a good time to make a change. Phoenix, then, it would be.

It was raining in Seattle, a cold April rain that seeped through our heavy coats and into our bones. The rain sluiced down from a thick gray sky, putting a sheen on the concrete runways and parked planes. Tiny droplets clung to our coats and eyelashes as we hurried into the airport terminal.

My father shook out his soft blue wool topcoat and ushered me and the children past the ticket booths with a grand sweep. Even this morning of parting was a sad one for us all, and the weather had done nothing to lift our spirits, Folger Peabody always had style. It was a kind of consolation.

I had $1500, four children as traveling companions—the youngest, David, slung like a papoose at my side—and a future which was uncertain at best. Milt had urged us to come to Phoenix. We owed it to the children to make one more try. Now, leaving the family and friends I had known for a lifetime, and not even being certain my husband would be waiting in Arizona, I felt condemned.

"Honey, you just be your own sweet self and don't try to keep up with the Joneses," Daddy said. "You'll be all right." He drew up, a full six feet, one inch, and put his arm around my waist. Beneath his neat, roll-brimmed hat the hair had grown grayer in recent months: the lines had deepened around his brown eyes, those eyes which could be so warm and frank at one moment, cold the next. I looked into his face and wondered what had gone haywire with our family.

There he stood, broken from my mother and married again, regarding me as his last close link with the family; a man criticized by his two other daughters, and not heartily approved of even by me, despite my own marital troubles. Perhaps this was the thing that drew us together, for we were both lonely and frightened and out on a limb.

There wasn't time to think for long. So many friends of long standing had made the effort to bid us farewell at the ungodly hour of 7:30 A.M.—Marly Holm brought traveling books and games for the children—Maggie Randall had reading material for me—Nancy Franck donated candy. They clustered around me and the children, raising a babble of voices, pressing their gifts, and last-minute goodbyes upon us. My sister Lee was there, too, having shed her determination not to come to the airport. A flurry of tears and quick kisses, then we were trooping to the plane, my eldest son Jimmy, then thirteen, in the lead, followed by Ford and Gretchen, with David in my arms. On impulse, I ran back to kiss Daddy again, then boarded with his last words still fresh in my ear: "Don't worry, honey, everything will be all right." We crowded into our seats, the doors slammed shut and the four-engine airliner roared down the runway, pointed its nose skyward and lifted toward a line of rugged gray clouds which hung just above the hilltops still climbing, we banked toward the south.

I was scared.

2

On My Own—And Scared

From the door of the airplane I took one look at Phoenix, one deep breath, and said, "Oh, my God." Beyond the airport the desert stretched away toward a range of craggy mountains, as bleak a view as I had ever seen. The houses squatted in fierce sunshine. Heat rolled up and into the plane. In our northwest woollies, we were soon prickly and perspiring and out of sorts. I wanted to get back to my seat and return to Seattle.

Milt, looking tanned and cocky, was waiting with a motley looking secondhand car. We piled in after perfunctory greetings and as we rattled along he told us about his new job as assistant cashier in the Valley National Bank. He had found a motel in the commercial part of town, two rooms with no air conditioning. We stuffed six hot bodies in there for the night and quietly roasted. Next day at the swimming pool the children suffered second-degree sunburns and we had to take them to a doctor.

It was an inauspicious beginning to a new life in Phoenix.

Day after day we drove around in a car full of kids looking for an apartment. Finally we found one, stayed in it about a month, then moved to a house. It was clear that there would be no more patching up between Milt and me. He had already managed to find interests outside the home, and our times together were chilly endurance tests. Milt wanted us to remain married with each living his own life. This offended my Catholic upbringing. "Milt, I just want to live by myself and reconstruct myself," I told him. "I want a separation."

Within three months, we were living apart again.

For all our domestic troubles, our first house in Phoenix was unique: a two-bedroom flat-roofed adobe once owned by Rudolph Valentino. It was now the property of a widow from Seattle and friend of my parents, Mrs. Ralph Fleming, who would come down from time to time for a vacation. She let us move in with the understanding we would trim the trees and lawn and pay a small rent.

One of the main features of the house was its rooftop solarium where the Sheik of the silent screen used to sunbathe in the nude. It was reached by a secret staircase in a closet by the fireplace, presumably hidden so that he could escape any hordes of feminine admirers who might drop in. Surrounding the house were six acres of orange grove; and from its location along Phoenix's main highway, Camelback Road, it commanded a splendid view of Squaw Peak Mountain. As a bonus, the house was fully furnished in mostly Spanish style, with Mrs. Fleming's Persian rugs, wall hangings, and *objets d'art*.

One morning the children opened the door and screamed, "We're going to drown." The yard and surrounding fields were knee-deep in water. Nobody had told us that the local method of irrigation was simply opening flood gates and letting the water pour across your property. We called the fire department, the sheriff, the newspapers, and finally got an explanation.

My big break in Phoenix came in a small way, and I almost backed out on it. The Junior League had their monthly meeting at Paradise Valley Country Club. Joanie Register, whose husband's family owned a large furniture store and whose sister I'd known in Seattle, invited me to go with her. I dressed up in a new silk suit, hat, furs, and white gloves, which is the way we used to attend Junior League meetings in Seattle, only to find when I got there that everyone else was in shorts and bathing suits. One who took pity on me was Mary Helen McGinn, who worked for Russ Lyon Realty Co. She took me under her wing, and I was grateful.

Life in Phoenix so far had been one of sickening loneliness for me. I hungered for friendship. I was writing long, nostalgic

letters home every day—so many that Milt finally issued an
ultimatum that I could write only one letter a week. When
Mary Helen invited us to dinner three days after we had met,
my spirits soared. But Milt, not knowing them, was not anxious
to go, so I told her we couldn't make it. Mary Helen persisted,
and we therefore went and spent what turned out to be a
thoroughly miserable evening. The next day Mary Helen called
me. "Patty, it's none of my business," she said, "but you're a big
girl. Why don't you get a job?" I shook my head at the telephone,
told her I would be terrified, and shook my head some more . . .
"You've got a fine personality, Patty. Why don't you try selling
real estate?" Within a week, she took me to meet Russ Lyon. We
chatted, and the following day he called to tell me I was hired
as a saleswoman if I could pass my real estate exam. I spent an
evening memorizing the book, and scored 98 out of 100 on the
test.

On a Sunday, the day after receiving my license, Russ sent
me to sit as the firm's representative in a rambling, $98,000
ranch house which was for sale. The place had ornate model
furnishings and I spent several hours by myself, going from
room to room, sitting. Finally a young couple from California
came in. The house was just what they'd been looking for. I
didn't even know how to write up a contract yet. I took it to
Mary Helen. My commission that day: $2500.

That Monday I walked into the office crowing. "Gosh, there
is nothing to it. This is a cinch." The response was chilly. "Be-
ginner's luck," somebody said, with a sniff. Mary Helen con-
gratulated me, but offered cautious advice. "Selling runs in
cycles, Patty. You'll hit a couple, then go for weeks with a big,
fat nothing. I wouldn't be surprised if you sold another this
week." Three days later I did just that. This house was a $60,000
job, and afterward I returned to the office so elated my feet
didn't touch the ground. This time, even Mary Helen, who had
always been the top seller, greeted me with restraint. I was
quickly losing popularity around here.

The second week on the job I was going through the listings
of homes for sale when I came upon one bearing the name
"Elliott Roosevelt." I asked Tom Jackson, the office manager,
about it.

"That's not *the* Roosevelts, Tom? The President's son?"

"What's so great about it?" he asked.

"I mean, one of *those* Roosevelts?"

He gave me a fishy stare. "Yeah."

I had read in the papers that Elliott Roosevelt was heading for a divorce. I'd also lined up prospects for such a house, a prominent rock-ribbed Republican, but rich. On the telephone, I told them about it. "I have just the place for you. The Elliott Roosevelt house." He reacted as if I'd hit him with a rattlesnake. "I would never move into a Democrat's house," he said icily, "especially a Roosevelt Democrat."

That evening I began calling the Roosevelt number to arrange to see the house myself. After several tries the maid finally answered.

"Is Mr. Roosevelt at home?" I asked.

"No ma'am, he's gone. He's at the ranch."

Next morning I hopped into my three-year-old Ford convertible and drove over, strangely excited. The house was a large, rambling affair with a circular driveway, set in a grove of citrus trees. It had a heavy double-shake roof and an inner court arrangement, with a guest house around by the swimming pool. They were asking $150,000 for it, but I knew I'd be lucky to sell it for $90,000.

I rang the bell and a woman's face appeared at one of the windows, which turned out to be a front bathroom.

"Yes? Who is it?"

"Uh, I'm Patty Whitehead from Russ Lyon Realty. I've come to look at the house."

"Just a moment, I'll be right with you."

She opened the front door and hurried back into the house, calling over her shoulder, "Now be sure and look at the master bedroom, it's divine. I designed it myself." This had to be Minnewa.

My first impression of her was fleeting: large boned with fine, almost austere features and excellent carriage. Her hair was blond, worn short, with little curl. There was a bigness about her, but not fat, and she walked lightly.

The living room led into a hallway, past a guest room and linen closet. The master bedroom was indeed large and spacious, furnished heavily but with taste. A king-size bed jutted out from one wall. I walked around it and into a corner dressing room which led to the bath. A bathrobe was hanging there, near a closet filled with dresses and gowns. There was a vanity in one corner. Only after I had stepped into the dressing room did I hear the water running in the shower. From behind the frosted glass a dripping arm reached out for a towel. Then the master of the premises emerged, saw me standing by the vanity and bellowed like a wounded buffalo: "Get the hell out of here!"

I stampeded back through the bedroom, tripping over the king-size bed, and scurried down the hall to the kitchen. Breathless, I burst through the kitchen door to find myself face-to-face with Mary, the maid. My eyes were glazed, mouth dry, but I recovered quickly and pretended nothing had happened. It suddenly dawned on me that the Roosevelts weren't away as I had thought.

"Is Mr. Roosevelt here?" I asked Mary.

She was hard of hearing. Cupping one ear, she said, "What?"

"Are the Roosevelts here?"

"Oh, the master is in the bedroom, I think. I'm not sure, but I think he's in the bedroom."

Mary was a kindly soul and offered me a cup of coffee. It calmed my nerves enough for me to continue my tour of the house. As I walked back up the hallway toward the living room, my host emerged again, freshly dressed and relaxed. "Hello," he said. "I'm Elliott Roosevelt."

I took his outstretched hand and, mustering all my dignity, replied: "How do you do, Mr. Rockefeller."

As it turned out, my buyer's political prejudices overcame his wife's enthusiasm for the house and they did not buy. But in trying to sell them I made several visits, in the course of which Minnewa gave me a key and exclusive listing of the property. I also got some intimate glimpses of life with the Roosevelts.

The day I brought my clients to see the house, I was introduced to the Roosevelt style of hoisting a highball. While we chatted in the living room, Elliott moved to the bar and asked: "What'll you have?" I was not unaccustomed to liquor and being thirsty, I asked for a scotch and water. He mixed one, handed it to me, and I inhaled enough to wet my dry throat. It got only halfway. So strong was the drink that my throat locked tight and I gave a deep, convulsive cough. Tears streamed down my face. Finally I managed to gasp, "Would you give me some water, please?" Elliott obliged, and delivered a brief lecture on the art of imbibing. "Mrs. Whitehead, you don't know how to drink," he said. As if to demonstrate, he downed his own whiskey and water in rapid, man-size gulps. "If you can't be a two-fisted drinker, you shouldn't drink at all."

The clients dickered for weeks, at one time offering $75,000 for the place furnished, before the deal fell through. It wasn't until that September 1958 that I finally found a buyer, through another broker, who paid $85,000.

Two months after the sale, Elliott called me saying he wanted to buy a lot to build another house. "Where do you want it?" I asked. "Squaw Peak Mountain," he replied. As an afterthought he added: "I don't know yet if I'll build it by myself or with her." I suppose he assumed automatically that I knew what he meant. At any rate, my Seattle connections came in handy. A wealthy developer named John McChesney was married to an old school friend of mine, and had bought acreage on Squaw Peak on which to build custom homes. My only experience in real estate so far was a couple of lucky sales, but I sought out John McChesney—the hard way.

The road to McChesney's office ran along an irrigation ditch. Thunderheads boiled in the western sky as I drove out of town. Soon the rain came down in huge, splattering drops. It quickly developed into a downpour, so heavy I could hardly see to drive. Water rose swiftly in the ditch, until it became a torrent. Unable to drive farther I pulled off the road . . . into the ditch. I sat there fuming, my car awash, until the rain stopped as suddenly as if someone had shut off a faucet. Half an hour later I walked into John McChesney's office carrying my muddy shoes, wearing a sodden cotton dress, my hair streaming. I looked like I had survived a shipwreck.

"John McChesney," I announced, "I've got a tremendous customer for you."

"For what?"

"For a lot, one of those expensive lots on Squaw Peak."

"Who's the customer?"

"Elliott Roosevelt."

"You must be kidding. I've heard all about him. He has wild parties and throws furniture off balconies and things."

"When you meet him, you'll like him. Take my word for it."

Grudgingly, he said he'd think about it, fixed the price at $25,000 and pushed back from the desk. "Come on, I'll take you up to look it over. Don't bother to put on your shoes."

It was like visiting an eagle's nest. The "lot" was actually a rock shelf about 400 feet high, overlooking Paradise Valley. Mc-Chesney had blasted a road through solid granite for a distance equivalent to about two blocks. From there the route dwindled to a mountain goat trail, studded with potholes and jagged boulders. Puffing and streaming perspiration, I made the last hundred yards on hands and knees.

"If this doesn't make you a real estate woman, nothing will," McChesney panted. He grabbed a rock outcropping for support and stood blowing like a spent ox and dripping sweat. "Yes, indeed, you've got to" (*puff, puff*) "get right down to the" (*puff*) "root of it."

The view was magnificent. Behind us, the gray, inhospitable granite of Squaw Peak swept upward, as remote and forbidding as it had been in the days when this was the windswept domain of vultures and Apaches. Even now, looking down upon the broad sweep of Paradise Valley and the tiny white houses, strewn across the valley floor as if tossed out in some colossal crap game, I was overwhelmed by the awesome emptiness of the place, the majesty of the high and remote world which would endure long after the little houses had crumbled once again, and become part of a desolate waste, of mesquite and scorpion and rattlesnake.

We did not stay long. McChesney told me something about how you built a house on such a spot, with pilings and can-tilevered architecture and pointed out the sights of Scottsdale and Phoenix in the distance. Then we went down again and I put in a call to Mr. Roosevelt. I told him I had a lot on Squaw Peak for him to see, but it would be better to wait until the road was a little better. His voice crackled with enthusiasm. "I want to see it tomorrow." We agreed to meet early at John McChesney's office.

This time I was decked out in shorts and boots for rough, hot climbing. Mr. Roosevelt arrived on time, wearing Western shirt, whipcord trousers, and a fine pair of hand-made black boots with red trim. I introduced him to John. "How do you do," John managed to say, then lapsed into a clammy silence.

"Well," I said, nervously, "Heh, heh. I'll just take Mr. Roosevelt up. We'll be back down shortly."

"Okay," McChesney snapped.

We drove the car to the end of the road, then started hoofing. Elliott ate up ground with the long, easy stride of a rancher, making small talk.

"I hope this is a high lot," he said, skirting a boulder.

"Oh it is, Mr. Roosevelt, it's very high. You have to climb for miles."

"Good," he said, "I always wanted to build a house high enough so I could look down on Barry Goldwater."

He gave me a small half-smile. At this point I didn't know whether to laugh or not to laugh, so I played it safe and merely simpered. I didn't know, of course, that Elliott was going through a period of agonizing insecurity. He was a man afraid to commit himself fully to a joke, lest the listener laugh at him instead of with him. I had no way of knowing, either, that Barry Goldwater was not only a friend but his locker mate at the Phoenix Country Club.

A dry, hot wind blew across the desert. As he stood on the brink of the shelf, it ruffled his long brown hair. His face squinted in the sunshine, baked brown as it was from long exposure to weather. I stood beside him and stole a glance as he looked directly down on Goldwater's house, the first roof he could see.

"Ah," he said . . . and he stared down the mountain.

On Christmas Day, Elliott and Minnewa bought the lot for $25,000.

3

Real Estate and Roosevelt

Bill Goodheart was a phenomenon. He came into my life at the precise time I needed him most. Fifty-seven years old, short and pigeon breasted, he had snapping brown eyes, a mind like a machine and a habit of licking his mouth when he looked at you, rather like a nervous squirrel. One of the original founders with Jules Stein of Music Corporation of America and a retired vice-president of NBC, he knew Russ Lyon from the old days when my realtor boss had been a band leader playing the dance circuit. Goodheart had been Russ's agent then, and a good one, but later they had gone their separate ways. By the time he retired from business, Bill was suffering from arthritis and general poor health. But the peaceful life on a farm in Ohio almost drove him crazy. So he came to Phoenix, established domicile in the posh Cadillac Apartments, and one day walked into Russ Lyon Realty Co. as an executive vice-president in charge of commercial sales.

The Arizona land boom was riding a crest. Big out-of-town investors—men like John F. Long and Ralph Staggs and Dave Murdock—were buying up 200 and 300 acres at a time to develop whole cities. The system was to pay 10 percent down and the rest when you catch me, and fortunes were being made. It was good times for the shrewd land buyers, and to make a killing you had to think big and fast. Bill Goodheart fell into it like a man made for the action, and from our first meeting he liked me and the way my own thought processes moved in wind sprints. But by the end of the year, with six months of hard work behind me, I was beginning to despise residential selling.

Long since separated from Milt, I had moved into a development house I had bought for $21,500, with a pool, an acre and a half of land, fenced, and no trace of landscaping. With the children in the care of Pat Gundy, a maid I'd had in Seattle who joined me in Phoenix, my work became a full-time passion. I was out at sunup and seldom home before dark. Russ Lyon was parceling out some of his own clients to me, so that I was selling two or three houses a month. Selling houses, however, always meant toting a supply of hardware in the car, signs, nails, hammers and such: it meant tramping around in muddy new developments and knocking yourself out for clients who often-times crawfished at the last minute. But this was the kind of thing my boss expected in his sales personnel.

Russ Lyon liked success. He was a big man, attractive, at home on the golf course; a gentleman real estate operator who wanted you to belong to the local clubs and have social connections. The key to Russ's success was the people with whom he surrounded himself, people with energy and dash.

My own key to success turned out to be a dentist from Seattle named Paul Chilton, who had seven children, a portfolio of blue chip stocks and bonds, a supply of fluid cash and a zest for financial adventure. Paul would fly down for the day and call me up, saying, "Patty, I'm looking for some nice property. What have you got?" At first, it was a frustrating experience. With Mary Helen McGinn helping me, I tried to engineer a deal for Paul to buy the Cadillac Apartments. The deal collapsed. Then I attempted to purchase the Doris-Heyman Furniture Store for him. The building was owned by Arnold Becker and Herman Chanen, the builders, and leased to National Furniture Co. It was a prime piece of property, located on North Central Avenue, the main north-south artery in Phoenix. But Becker and Chanen demurred and refused his offer.

Russ Lyon watched my failures from the sidelines and felt badly. He knew I had worked hard and was disappointed. One

day he called me in and said, "Patty, I've got a good deal for
your friend, Dr. Chilton."

"Oh really, Russ, which one?"

"Our building, right here on Central Avenue."

So I sold Paul Chilton the real estate office out from under
us for $300,000. It was a small office, and I had the feeling Paul
was getting the short end of the bargain, but he paid and didn't
even flinch.

Billy Goodheart had seen me tackle the commercial prospects
for Chilton and liked my enthusiasm. Over the Christmas holidays he presented me with a chance to switch entirely from
residential to commercial selling. I hedged.

"Billy, I'm terrible. I'm dumb. I don't know anything about
commercial property."

"You think about it and let me know in a week. Here's what
I am offering . . ."

He spelled out a proposition to me. I had three alternatives:
share 50–50 with him any commissions we earned jointly on a
sale; go on straight commission, working only his clients with
two-thirds of the commission going to me and one-third to him;
or take a $500 monthly salary and 10 percent of the sales. For
four days I searched my conscience, fearful of blundering in over
my head upon an unknown field. Finally I decided on the 50–50
arrangement. I let him know on New Year's Day. It was 10:00
A.M. and I had been out until 2:00 A.M. seeing the New Year in.
My head was full of cobwebs, my mouth felt like a bird cage.
But Billy was jubilant.

"I'm going to give you your first sale, Mrs. Whitehead," he
chirruped, "start you out with a symbol of success. I want to start
off the New Year by buying the Praying Monk. Can you get it
for me?"

The Praying Monk is a famous landmark of Phoenix. It was a
figure in sandstone, dominating the countryside: a monk, kneeling in prayer to the eternal gods of desert and wind and hot
blue sky, rising from the heights of Camelback Mountain. The
legend of the monk goes back to the times of the early Spanish
settlers, when the good abbots made a perilous crossing of the
mountain under God's protection, but with orders not to look

back. One monk, in a moment of doubt, did look back and, in the manner of Lot's wife, turned to stone.

The tract was seventy acres, owned by my friend John McChesney, a slick trader in any league, who had bought it for development. I went to McChesney and we settled on a price of $78,000.

Billy paid his earnest money, the contract was signed, and a week later we discovered a rather embarrassing technicality that McChesney had forgotten to reveal. Goodheart had no ingress or egress to his property. Unless you happened to be an eagle, legally, the only way you could get there was by helicopter. For the time being, at least, he had $78,000 worth of nothing. But Billy seemed satisfied, and the transaction gave me starting momentum. Ultimately it was favorably settled for us.

I now went into real estate with feverish intensity, concentrating on commercial property: who owned what, who might sell, who might buy, and how I could get them together? Day after day I was on the road at 7:00 A.M., exploring, visiting, talking. The main roads of Phoenix and adjoining Scottsdale form a huge H on the map, with Scottsdale Road and Central Avenue forming the two sides and Camelback Road the cross bar. Central, the main business street, is where real estate exchanges made money. On a huge roll of butcher paper, I made a map of Central Avenue and each piece of property, noting the owner's name, address, and telephone number, a description of the property and whether it was for sale. I went to each owner and asked him under what conditions he might bargain. Ultimately I ended up with a number of "Pocket" listings. This is a real estate slang expression, and not too flattering for the salesman. He is supposed to share all listings with the office so the other employees can have a crack at selling the property. The term "Pocket" listing is self-explanatory. In my case, however, it was a little different, as none of the owners really wanted to sell. However, I had made it my business to find out whether or not they would be interested in a good sale, and on what terms. It was sometimes months before I had just the right buyer for a certain property, but I knew in advance the requirements of the seller.

While I performed the legwork, Goodheart brought in valuable potential buyers, old friends in the entertainment world such as Guy Lombardo and Ted Fiorito and others. My job was to show the real estate and work both sides for a sale. We split the commissions.

As our connections and business grew, I was working full-tilt, having no social life, and losing weight. Goodheart decided a trip would do me good and sent me off to Chicago and Gary, Indiana, to locate the owner of a piece of Central Avenue property and talk him into selling. For all the wheeling and dealing I'd grown accustomed to in Phoenix, in Chicago I felt like a waif cut adrift. I was a grown woman with four children and making my first trip alone.

My introduction to the Blackstone Hotel put me on edge. The Blackstone, as legions of lost souls from out-of-town have discovered, is a maze of hallways so intricate the management even contrived a color-coding process to try to simplify matters, painting each section of the hotel a different hue. But even with this, I am sure there are helpless guests who have vanished into the fourth dimension. My troubles began when my zipper got stuck as I was dressing to go out the first evening. Seeking help, I went down several hallways and became thoroughly confused. In one corridor, a man came out of a room and said, "Honey, what's the matter, can I help you?" I fled, babbling incoherencies, finally found a fire escape and backed down. Looking pale and disheveled, I finally found my way to the lobby. A woman at the front desk zipped my zipper. I knew now how explorer Livingstone must have felt.

That night I had another introduction to the wonders of Chicago: a night club mind reader. A couple who were friends of my parents took me out to dinner and entertainment. The feature attraction was a clairvoyant. I have always been a sucker for mind readers, dabblers in the occult, and signs of the zodiac. The mind reader's assistant singled me out and intoned: "Here's a lady sitting with two friends. What is her name?" The mind reader, a lean, Swami type with an ascetic face and nicotine stains on his fingers, clutched the bridge of his nose in concentration. "It begins with a P," he said. "Pat. I think it is Patricia." The aide asked him what business I was in. "She is in Chicago to buy real estate." I almost flipped. Not wishing to be disillusioned, I did not press my friends to find out if they had given him the information. As in a good sales approach, sometimes half the fun is concealing how much you don't know.

The investor I sought was John Anderson, a charming entrepreneur of eighty who owned the Ansco Windshield Wiper Co. in Gary. I taxied to Gary and was confronted at the plant by security guards and an elaborate system of checking in and out, a holdover from the war years. I wondered if perhaps these windshield wipers might also be our secret weapon. Mr. Anderson soon put me at ease, however. Shortly after I arrived in his office, he summoned in all of his vice-presidents for a luncheon of lamb chops and cole slaw and pastries. After an hour of pleasant talk, he signed the contract I carried and assigned his chauffeur to drive me back to Chicago. I returned to Phoenix next day, refreshed as if I had taken a trip to some foreign country.

The real estate business began to mushroom; and with it, my life was rapidly becoming peopled with colorful, off-beat types who might have been provided by Central Casting for a Hollywood production about saints, sinners, and tycoons.

By now, Bill Goodheart and I were successfully handling restaurants, service stations, and other commercial properties, and word had spread about our sales. I studied for my broker's license and got it. Shortly afterward, the work of building syndicates began.

One of my clients was wealthy young Tom Fifield, who flew his own plane in from California two or three times a week, shopping for Phoenix properties. Through Fifield I met Ted Nelson and Jack Hart, who owned the Royal Packing Co., a thriving business dealing in sugar beets, lettuce, and tomatoes. Nelson and Hart had made a small fortune in produce and were anxious now to leap into real estate. They were high-pressure people. It didn't take much persuasion to sell Ted on the idea of pooling his capital with other investors in a syndicate.

Bell Properties was baptized in January 1959. Ted Nelson and associates bought a $2,500,000 tract for a development as a subdivision, with me as broker. Billy Goodheart and I split a commission of $250,000. The closing came after weeks of grueling, secret maneuverings. Six pieces of property were involved, and our job was to nail down options on each without letting the other owners know what we were doing, for fear they would hike their price. I was elated. I also had to hire an accountant.

As time passed, syndicate-type business dealings gave me valuable inside savvy about real estate operations. At the same time, they gave Ted Nelson some lessons about people—particularly rich dentists from Seattle.

By March, Nelson had a number of other investors allied with him bankrolling a syndicate which had grown to $3,500,000. In a year, the group would swell to twenty investors with holdings worth $50,000,000. Of the twenty, I was to enlist eight backers, among them Dr. Paul Chilton. My dentist friend's appearance belied his bankbook. Thin, short, and uninspiring, he went about in Bermuda shorts, knee socks and a sloppy untucked shirt. Nelson, already fancying himself a full-fledged tycoon, scoffed. After their first meeting, the produce prince pulled me aside and whispered. "Patty, if that man's got the nickels to rub, I'll be surprised. Why waste time on small change like him?"

"Just wait," I said. "You'll see."

A week later, Paul Chilton's first check arrived for deposit in the syndicate account, $160,000. It not only was the largest single investment up to that time, it was the springboard that launched the entire investment enterprise.

I was rapidly finding out, meanwhile, that there is no sure thing in real estate. The successful broker or salesman must constantly ride herd on the paperwork. Sloppy habits in the unglamorous pick-and-shovel field of contracts and deeds can undermine a transaction quicker than a plague. I learned that when you got a buyer's signature on a contract, you did not rest until the seller, too, had signed. You never left the papers with him overnight, for a man pondering dollar signs is tempted to vacillate. When the deal was signed at last, I would hand-carry it to the title company processing it through from desk to desk and personally seeing to the title search, escrow accounts and other details. I worked as often as possble with the Phoenix Title and Trust Company. I had gotten to know people in its many departments and small courtesies and thoughtfulness paid off when I needed instant service from any of them. Ed Juliber, a vice-president of the company, was alert to any and most of my requests. It brought in much more business for them when I could finish one sale, and go on to the next. Instead of having to wait for as long as six weeks, and risking in the process the loss or misplacement of papers in the title office, I would often get a closing on the property in two or three days. It also meant quick money in the hands of the seller, quick claiming of the property by the buyer, and repeat business from both for all of us.

One of the colorful figures in Arizona land speculation was O. L. Becker. Most of his interests were in Cedar Rapids, Iowa, where he had multi-million dollar holdings in grocery stores, subdivisions, and general commercial property. A tough, seasoned land buyer, he visited Phoenix annually to play golf with Jackie Gleason, who had a home there at the time, and shop for good deals. Every year Becker bought and sold a million dollars worth of property, carefully timing his transactions to take maximum advantage of capital gains taxes. Each morning after golf he would make a round of the major real estate offices. Russ Lyon was always last on the list.

In midwinter, a tract of desert land in the middle of nowhere came on the market. Aptly named Gila Bend, its only selling point was the fact that it lay along the route of a planned federal highway. I have never visited Gila Bend, and frankly don't see why anybody would want to go there. But for a brief period, it turned out to be a very hot property for me.

O. L. Becker strolled into Russ Lyon's office with his customary perfunctory greeting. "Mrs. Whitehead, what have you got to-day?"

"Mr. Becker, I've got a wonderful piece of property for you. Yes, sir, just wonderful. Gila Bend."

"How's that again?"

"Gila Bend. Wonderful piece of . . ."

"How much?"

"Only a hundred dollars an acre, Mr. Becker."

"Too much." He cocked his head and gave me a sly look. "Ed Post just offered it to me for eighty."

I figured the matter was closed, but I had neglected to count on the resourcefulness of O. L. Becker. A few days later he returned with the announcement that he had a chance to buy 1200 acres of Gila Bend for $35 an acre.

"I can't buy it through you because I've already given my

commitment to this other broker, Mrs. Whitehead," he said, "but I'll tell you what I'm going to do. I'm going to let you buy it from me for forty dollars an acre. I'll give it to you for that and take the five-dollar profit because I want to see you get ahead."

While he talked, I did frantic mental arithmetic, trying to figure out what 1200 acres would cost me and what the chances were for a sale. As usual, I stumbled on the math. However, I was afraid to become a buyer in real estate, even though I could have scraped together a down payment on the $48,000 needed. I shook my head.

"Look, I'll make it safe for you," Becker said. "If you don't sell this property in six months I'll buy it back for forty dollars an acre, and give you a six months escrow to prove it."

I still wouldn't buy. Becker promptly put the property back on the market, with me holding the exclusive listing. That afternoon I sold it for $40 an acre. The next afternoon I sold it again for $50 an acre. A week later, another sale: $75 an acre; the week after that, $100, and the week after that, $125. In all, I sold Gila Bend five times to various speculators, made money for each one —except the last—and became so engrossed in trying to calculate my commission earnings with Patty Whitehead's terrible arithmetic that I got a headache. But after that, there was plenty of money for aspirin.

Another favorite client of mine was Mr. Galdamez of the chemical company named Galdamez and Yeaton. On our first meeting I found him to be a man of many talents. His private office was covered with family photographs. There were hundreds it seemed to me. The group poses showed my client, his wife and nine children. Wishing to establish immediate rapport with this new found prospect I chirruped, "Oh, Mr. Galdamez, you must be a Catholic—such a lovely large family?" This enigmatic fellow didn't bother to look up from his desk. No smile—nothing— merely a nod of the head and his answer, "No ma'am! Just a sexy Episcopalian." What a way to be a real estate woman!

That year, I was to make $150,000 in real estate, the highest earnings of any woman broker in Arizona. It won me, in addition to a tidy bank account, an award from the real estate association.

Private life by now had been pushed into the background. I felt guilty about having so little time for the children, but they understood and did not complain. Besides my faithful Pat Gundy who had moved down with me from Seattle, was in constant attendance and had a mother's love for these little people. My divorce from Milton had become simply a matter of formality. Typically, the day of our court hearing brought unforeseen problems. Jimmy woke up with a raging toothache. I drove him to Paul Chilton's office. He took an X ray and announced, "It's got to come out. There is a serious abscess here."

"Can you do it, Paul?"

"No, I don't do this kind of work. Jimmy needs to go to an oral surgeon. I suggest you go to this man." He wrote down the name of Bill Baker. I explained to Paul that this was the day for my divorce hearing. "Okay," he said, "I'll pick Jimmy up when he's through, and take him home, don't worry."

At the oral surgeon's office, I had to explain again why I was dropping my son and leaving. "I have such an important engagement downtown," I said. "It's been six months, and if I don't do it now I'll never get it done."

"What do you have to do that's so important?" Dr. Baker asked.

"Get my divorce."

"Oh!"

The following day, after the successful tooth extraction, the surgeon called me about Jimmy's condition. He called again the next day, and the next. The third time, he advised me to bring Jimmy to the office for a check-up. That night he called again. Jimmy by now had healed so well he could have eaten a ton of peanut brittle and never said "Ouch!"

"How is he?" Dr. Baker wanted to know.

"Fine, Doctor. Perfectly fine. Why do you want to know?"

"I wondered if you'd like to go to a movie with me."

For the eight months I had been separated from Milt I had never gone out on a date for fear of disrupting the divorce. Actually, it had been fifteen years since I had had a date with anyone other than my husband. Nervously, I accepted. Then I had a talk with Jimmy, a worldly-wise fourteen.

"Jimmy, your dentist called, Dr. Baker."

"So?"

"Know what he wants me to do?"

"No, what?"

"He wants me to go to a movie with him."

"Okay, go to a movie."

"But what'll I talk about? What'll I say to him?"

Jimmy looked at me patronizingly, "Mom, just be yourself," he said. "Just be your own sweet self."

Less than a year before, my father had given me the same advice.

My parents refused to communicate with me at all, now. I was a divorced woman, working and leaving the children in the care of a servant. They assumed the four were running wild, which was not true. Surprisingly, the experience was giving the children, especially the older two, a sense of responsibility and maturity.

After this first date it did not take long for me to get back into social circulation. I went out with Tom Fifield now. A successful sugar beet grower, he still flew in frequently from El Centro, California. Separated from his wife, he was dark and good looking, but too short for me. I had a new Thunderbird and had added an extra bathroom to the house, complete with a sunken tub.

At the office, I was snowed under with work, and took in, as an assistant, Al Lustbader. A graduate of the University of Illinois, he was methodical, smart, and above all, young and energetic. I looked to him to keep me from making stupid mistakes. I also discovered he had common sense.

One day a salesman arrived carrying a Frieden Calculator, and launched into me with glee. "Mrs. Whitehead, you're a successful businesswoman and no successful businesswoman ought to be without one of these fine machines. Calculates like lightning. Post your bills, add, subtract, keep accounts. Look at that, isn't she a beauty?" I was impressed. The machine came with a ten-day free trial, and I decided the first thing to do was master it. So for ten solid days I sat at the desk trying to work the Frieden Calculator. While I punched buttons and rang bells and made whirring noises, sales tumbled to zero. If we had kept a chart, the curve for that week would have made a hole in the floor. Al Lustbader watched with agonizing patience. Whirr, chink, buzz, click. Damn! At last, Al could contain himself no longer.

"Patty," he said, "when I was in college we had this skit about the successful comedian. All he had to do was stand up and open his mouth and people roared. Made a fortune. One day, though, he decided to find out the secret of his success. 'My God, what makes people laugh at me?' he said. So he went to a psychoanalyst and spent days and days on the couch and finally came away with complete understanding. But nobody ever laughed again. That's like this machine. You learn how to work this you'll never sell another piece of real estate."

That did it. I sent the thing back.

While all this was going on, there was also developing rivalry of sorts between my colleagues, Billy Goodheart and Ted Nelson.

For my birthday, Billy Goodheart told me to go to Goldwater's Department Store and pick out an alligator bag by Lucille of Paris, with shoes to match. I was delighted. But the gift put Ted Nelson out of joint. He was determined to top it. On the great day I walked into Nelson's office and was told, "Patty, there's a contract on the desk in the other office. Bring it to me, will you?" I asked why he didn't send the secretary. He lost patience. "Don't argue," he snapped, "just bring it." I walked into the other room and there on the desk was a cage containing a live alligator. I'm terrified of alligators, so Nelson had his secretary deliver it to my home. By the time I arrived there that evening, Ford had collected $2.50 in admission charges from neighborhood children to see the alligator. Also waiting to greet me was another gift, from my former husband, Milt: a live monkey. This was an insidious gesture on his part. For years I had spoken of having one monkey as a pet and yet he paid no mind to my request—now, knowing it would be a scourge rather than a pleasure, "Dennis the Menace" (monkey) came into my life. He thought the living room was a jungle, and enjoyed swinging from drape to drape. It was months before we could finally get rid of our unwanted animals by giving them to a pet shop.

Bill Goodheart had his heart set on scoring a real estate coup, one that would give Phoenix something to talk about. His eye lighted on Cudia City, the most sought-after property in town. Owned by peppery octogenarian and restaurateur Sam Cudia, the 40-acre tract spread between Camelback Road and the mountain, a location which made it perfect for development—residential, commercial, or both. A rugged, boulder-strewn area of typical desert, Cudia City had been used for years by movie companies shooting Westerns. It even boasted a sun-bleached Western "town," consisting of a dusty main street, hitching posts, and buildings with false fronts. The moviemakers leased the area from Mr. Cudia, who took in a handsome annual profit.

"Patty," Bill Goodheart said, "I want to buy Cudia City."

"Buy Cudia City? People have been trying to buy Cudia City forever, Billy, you know that. Mr. Cudia won't sell. He won't even talk about it."

"I want to buy Cudia City."

"And even if he could be persuaded, he'd probably insist on taking income off of it for the rest of his life, and setting a ridiculous price."

"I want to buy Cudia City."

I shrugged. "Okay, I'll try."

Mr. Cudia's office was in a cluster of buildings on the property which included a nice restaurant that he also owned. I piled the four children into the car and turned up unannounced at his door looking like the harassed housewife on a day's outing. At my knock, he opened the door and peered at me, his face squinting in the sunshine.

"Mr. Cudia, I'm Patty Whitehead. I hate to bother you but I've heard so much about you I just had to drop by. My children have always wanted to see a movie studio, and we were wondering if they might . . ."

"Come in, come in, young woman," he said. "Don't stand out there in the hot sun."

He led me into his office and we sat down. Sam Cudia, I discovered quickly, was a garrulous old man who enjoyed people, especially if they were women. While Gretchen and Ford went out into the town to watch the filming of a horse opera, we chatted amiably about weather, children, and Phoenix. Carefully, I steered the discussion to Cudia City. "Gosh, this is a wonderful piece of property. It must be wonderful to own. But I'll bet the taxes are high. Are the taxes high? You really ought to build something on it, Mr. Cudia, shouldn't you?"

"I'm too old," he said. "By the time I started getting a return on the investment I'd be molding away in my grave."

He asked if I had ever seen his restaurant. I said no. "Then please join me for dinner tonight." I accepted.

With Sam Cudia, dinner was always an occasion. Each evening he appeared in his restaurant in full dress, with white tie and tails, usually alone. He always sat at the same table and dined with candlelight and wine. I had hurried home, deposited the children, put on my basic black dress and returned. After the initial shock of Mr. Cudia's formalities, I sat back and enjoyed myself. By dessert, I had impressed upon him the point that I was a struggling housewife with a brood of four children trying to make a living in this big, cruel world, but didn't know how to go about selling real estate. "If I could possibly get a client interested in Cudia City, do you think you might be interested in selling?" Then I told him, as if blurting out a confession, that I did have a friend who would like to buy but was afraid to approach a man of Mr. Cudia's standing. The old face lit up.

Perhaps it was the wine and candlelight, or perhaps Sam Cudia had been available all along. He leaned back in his chair, took a sip of water and said, "Well, young lady, if this friend is serious you tell him to send over the money and we just might make a deal."

Next day I hot-footed back with Billy Goodheart's $25,000 earnest money—10 percent of the $250,000 selling price. Deliberately I had made the contract tough, so we would have to work backward. It took two days to sign, and as I had predicted Mr. Cudia indeed insisted upon continuing to take income from the property as long as he lived.

The sale hit every newspaper in Arizona. Overnight, Goodheart became a kind of real estate wizard. From being merely too busy to keep up with business, we suddenly became overwhelmed. Patty Whitehead was real estate woman of the year.

4

More Roosevelt—Less Real Estate

After selling the mountain lot to Elliott Roosevelt I did not see him again for several months. Then one day he called me at the office. "Mrs. Whitehead?" The voice was brusque and business-like. "I have something for you, I want to list it with your firm."

"Yes, sir."

"Let's talk about it tomorrow morning."

"Will you come down to the office, Mr. Roosevelt?"

"No. I prefer that you come to the house. I have some important calls. I'll have all the maps here and can explain it more fully."

Despite our recent real estate transaction, Elliott Roosevelt to me was still a remote, awesome personality; a picture seen occasionally in the newspaper; a name relished by gossips who spoke animatedly of vague but deliciously scandalous Roosevelt-isms, a tall man across the room at parties.

The new house was not yet built, and he and Minnewa had rented another on Squaw Peak Mountain. The following morning at nine sharp I was greeted at the front door by a cool, mannish-looking woman in blue jeans, moccasins, and loose blouse. "Yes?" She inspected me with the indifference one accords a bit of lint. I blurted out something by way of identification, and drew a "How d'ya do. Won't you come in?"

This was my introduction to Minnewa's private secretary. "Do you have an appointment with Mr. Roosevelt, dear? What was it you wanted to see him about? . . . Do sit down." For the next quarter of an hour, I underwent a highly skillful grilling. Guilelessly, I answered all questions, volunteered everything I could, and apparently convinced her—and, I am sure, Minnewa— that I was a harmless, hard-working boob and no threat to the household.

Elliott arrived late, explaining he had been playing golf. I had expected him to start unrolling maps and giving me details of a real estate plan with force and precision. Instead, we sat on the couch engaging in desultory talk while I carefully kept my feet and knees together, sitting as a lady in approved convent fashion. He did manage to explain that he had forty acres south of the airport, in ownership with some other men, which he was interested in selling. The land was planted in cotton. The information thus conveyed, he then lapsed into uncomfortable silences.

That afternoon Billy Goodheart and I drove out to see the property. "I have the most awful time talking to that man," I told Goodheart. "I get all tied up in knots, I'm so awed by him. I just can't think of anything to say." Bill cocked one eye at me and puckered his mouth. "He's no different from anybody else, Patty," he said. "He puts on his pants one leg at a time."

As a divorcée I was handy as an extra girl at parties, and this was the usual basis for an invitation. When the Roosevelts' new house was completed on the mountain many months later, Minnewa called me. They were having a celebration, warming the new house. "I've got a perfectly divine date for you, my dear," she cooed. "Do come."

It was a glittering, sophisticated crowd. Barry Goldwater's brother Bob was there, along with people from places like Las Vegas and Palm Springs. Ice tinkled in the glasses, smoke and the scent of expensive perfumes mingled in the living room, conversation was "in," neatly cutting out the stranger ignorant of the names and personalities being discussed. The laughter had a brittle sound. The fact that I arrived alone did not strengthen my confidence. As soon as I walked in, however, Minnewa peeled away from a group and introduced me to Claude Smith.

My date was handsome but overweight, rich, a devotee of the pro-am golf circuit, lived in California and had a sick wife. There was about him an air of confidence and dash, especially in the company of women, and he owned an Eldorado with a fur rug. We chatted easily, getting acquainted. In a group nearby, Elliott Roosevelt turned and watched us. I smiled and nodded. During the rest of the party, our host seemed always near my elbow or joining our discussion. Smith said, "Shall we go out to dinner?" I accepted. As we were leaving, Elliott was at the door to say good-bye. He peered at Smith and said: "Claude, you be nice to this girl. She is a very nice girl. I don't want anything to happen to her." It was the first indication that his feeling for me was anything beyond casual cordiality.

I saw Smith for three months, off and on. The children were crazy about his Eldorado.

The Phoenix boom continued. Speculators swapped parcels of land as if they were pocket knives. Land hunger even went long distance, so that while working as a Phoenix broker I managed to sell two pieces of property in California. The investors lived in Phoenix and Chicago.

It was during this period that Elliott was arrested one night, precipitating another newspaper scandal and a legal battle which was to be resolved finally by the Arizona courts.

The policeman had found him sitting in his car asleep, parked at the curb. Elliott was awakened, ordered out and frisked. The police said the keys were in the ignition and the car in gear. Under Arizona law, he was charged with drunk driving. Elliott hired as his attorney Dick Kleindienst, who later was to become manager of Barry Goldwater's presidential campaign. Arguing that the arrest and charge were a sham, Kleindienst fought it to the highest court and won a reversal which was to set a precedent for all future cases of this sort.

At the height of the nationwide publicity, Daddy, whom I had told about selling the Squaw Peak Mountain plot, sent me a caustic telegram: AREN'T THERE MORE OUTSTANDING CLIENTS FOR YOU IN THE STATE OF ARIZONA THAN ELLIOTT ROOSEVELT?

I had not seen Daddy since leaving Seattle two years before. When he made a trip to San Diego, I invited him to come on to

Phoenix. "No, I'm too old and too tired," he said. "You pick up the children and come over here."

"But there are five of us and one of you."

"You'll just have to come to San Diego."

I left David, still a toddler, in Phoenix and took Jimmy, Ford, and Gretchen. We checked into the El Cortez Hotel, and that afternoon Daddy gave them each five dollars to spend and suggested, probably for the sake of his own peace and quiet, that they go to see the town. He was to rue the impulse to dispense such largesse.

"These children are too young to go out by themselves," I protested. "They've never been in San Diego. Neither have I."

"Nonsense," Daddy said. "They'll get along quite well."

"We can handle it, Mom," Jimmy said.

Handle it they did, to the chagrin of Daddy, the hotel elevator operator, the desk clerks, and ultimately even a couple of airline stewardesses.

While Jimmy and Gretchen spent their money going to a movie and buying candy and popcorn, Ford visited a novelty shop. Soon after the children returned to the hotel I walked into my bedroom and let out a shriek. There was a patch of vomit by the bed. Ford doubled up laughing. It was made of rubber. I was furious. Daddy chuckled. "That's just a little boy trick," he said, patronizingly.

"Nothing to get upset about." Then he walked into his own room. Another yelp, this time over a blob of ink on his bed. It was disappearing ink, of course, but this time Daddy was livid. Then a patch of doggie-do turned up in the hall. By now we were standing about hurling threats of life and limb down upon the head of my mischievous second son.

The next day, the elevator operator said to me, "Madam, is *that* boy yours?"

"Which boy?"

"The one with glasses."

"Well . . . yes."

"Please tell him to keep his dog out of the elevator."

In the lobby, too, the help was unhappy. Gretchen and Ford had teamed up to harass the desk clerk. While Ford pretended to retch, Gretchen had cried, "Oh, oh, my poor brother. Please bring paper towels!"

The staff of El Cortez Hotel was very glad to see us leave.

On the airplane flying back to Phoenix, I was placidly reading when I heard Gretchen's voice from behind, "Oh my brother, my poor brother!" Before I could get things in hand, here came the stewardesses, running with paper towels. I buried myself in *Time*.

In Phoenix, meanwhile, life may have taken some bizarre turns for Elliott Roosevelt, but it was never dull. Publicly he was regarded as something of a middle-aged rakehell who liked his liquor and whose men friends were, more often than not, carousers and philanderers. People gossiped that he had been banished from a country club after getting drunk and hurling chairs from the balcony. Paradise Country Club blackballed him on the vote of a single member, author Clarence Buddington Kelland, whose only announced objection was that he did not wish to be in a club with a Roosevelt. After that, Barry and Bob Goldwater proposed him for membership in the Phoenix Country Club and Elliott was accepted unanimously.

Elliott enjoyed twitting the Goldwaters, but actually held the family in high esteem and was a close friend of the Arizona senator. The Goldwaters understood his impatience with the lifelong silent enemy, anti-Roosevelt sentiment, for they too had felt the sting of prejudice. There was the famous story of the day Bob went to the exclusive Los Angeles Country Club. At the first tee, he was politely informed by the manager that the club was restricted. Bob laughed. "Surely you won't mind, then, if I just play the front nine," he quipped. "I'm only half Jewish."

After the separation, the Roosevelt mountain house went up for sale. Minnewa designated me as exclusive agent and gave me a key. This meant it was necessary for me to accompany any salesman or broker showing the property to a prospective client. One day in May of 1960, a salesman from Ed Post Realty made an appointment to take some prospects up the mountain. Minnewa had gone to the ranch in Meeker, Colorado, and I assumed Elliott was in California. He wasn't. I walked in and found him in the living room talking business with a fat man with a bulging briefcase. While the salesman and his clients went off to explore the house, Elliott introduced me to Mike Lorenzo, a representative of the Aimee Semple McPherson Church enterprises.

Lorenzo was a mountain of a man with curly reddish-blond hair and nervous hands. The hands fluttered as he talked, like twin birds. In the course of our chat, he gave me to understand that he was the broker for Aimee Semple McPherson's considerable real estate holdings. Elliott had interested them in financing development of an All Seasons Club on his Colorado ranch. This project was to provide a year-round private meeting place for executives of major corporations, suitable for hunting, skiing, hiking, camping, meetings—a kind of Aspen in the rough. I was to become intimately involved with it all later on, but for now I was more concerned with my jitters at finding Elliott Roosevelt there. I also had misgivings about Mr. Lorenzo, especially when he informed me that the bulging briefcase contained all of his files and he never went anywhere without them.

The salesman and his clients wandered through, then were gone, and Elliott was suggesting that I go get the children and bring them up for a barbecue dinner. "Oh, no thank you, sir," I said. "We're going to barbecue at home. I use a pot roast that I marinate for several days, and it's all ready—we've been planning—I really couldn't . . . Well, just one drink."

I went to call the children to tell them I would be late. While I was using the phone, Mike Lorenzo got up to leave. I returned, saying, "Oh no, Mr. Lorenzo, you can't go and leave me here alone with him." Lorenzo and Elliott laughed. "My dear," said Elliott, "what do you think I'm going to do with you?" I stammered something about nothing, nothing at all, and Lorenzo walked out, waving, the huge briefcase bumping against his leg. I sat gingerly on the edge of a chair, sipping the drink my host had handed me and making small talk. Somehow the words kept sticking in my throat, because my mind was a jumble of the stories I had heard about him being a feisty, rambunctious man who took his pleasures where he pleased and damn the consequences. It was six o'clock on a Friday evening on a mountainside with the nearest neighbor two miles away and the sun going down.

"Ahem, Mr. Roosevelt, heh, heh, how's your wife?"

"I have no wife."

"Of course you do, Minnewa's up in Colorado."

"We're separated, and in the process of getting a divorce."

The divorce was news to me. I could think of nothing else to say, so I stared into my glass and wondered how I could gracefully get out to my car and off Squaw Peak Mountain.

"Mrs. Whitehead, do you mind if I call you Patty?"

"Certainly you can call me Patty, Mr. Roosevelt."

"Will you go out to dinner with me tonight?"

My mouth dropped open. "Go out to what?"

"I didn't ask you to jump off the cliff, for heaven's sake, I merely asked if you would have dinner with me. There are several things I would like to discuss with you."

Well, I couldn't possibly go to dinner, I told him. Not possibly. The children . . . the barbecue . . .

"If you can't have dinner with me, would you do me a favor?"

I tried to keep my voice from shaking. "It all depends."

"Could we go for a swim?"

Alarm bells were clanging inside my head now. I started to give a flat "no," then hedged. I said I had no bathing suit. He suggested I wear one of Minnewa's. I couldn't do that. Well, I might just have a bathing suit in the car. I'd look in the car. Of course, I did not tell him I always carried one in the car. I went outside. The sun shone like copper, glistening against the rocks of Squaw Peak Mountain. A vulture wheeled in the sky. My little green Thunderbird looked forlorn. I wanted to hop in and make dust down that mountain. But there was something overpowering about this man. I felt that he had a desperate need to talk, and for someone, someone, to listen to him. I didn't want to go back into the house, but something propelled me back on an invisible wire.

The pool was surrounded on all sides by the house, which opened into it through glass doors. An overhanging roof formed a covered patio, and there were lounge chairs, wrought-iron tables and huge bath towels for guests. Sunshine came in at a steep slant now, and the sky seemed to descend so closely you could reach out and touch it. In my nervousness, I wrapped myself in one of those bath towels, only tossing it aside as I slipped into the pool.

Elliott already was splashing around like a whale, diving, sputtering, and then swimming end-to-end with great lumbering strokes. He practically filled the pool all by himself. Then we stopped swimming and, gulping air from exertion, tried to talk. Water streamed down the crags of his face and dripped off his chin.

From somewhere, a small black shape exploded down upon us, skimmed an inch above the water, wheeled sharply skyward and swooped down again, a flapping dive-bomber.

I shrieked. "A bat!"

Elliott charged out of the pool, shouting, "I'll get it. I'll get it, honey!" and began flailing at our attacker with a bath towel.

"Mr. Rockefeller, do something!"

"I am doing something! Don't worry. I'll get him!"

Trapped in the pool enclosure, the poor bat was as panicked now as we were, wheeling and diving, aiming for my head. With each pass I went under, taking in great gulps of chlorine water. Elliott whipped the towel once more, then his bare feet went flap-flapping for the kitchen. He returned waving a broom and bellowing like a wounded bull. Finally, with a last rush, the bat found flying space into open sky and vanished across the roof.

Still sputtering, I climbed out of the pool, collapsed on a lounge chair and started to shake. Tears of fright made mascara stream down my face. Out of breath, Elliot sat down beside me. In a few minutes we recovered. He began to talk, and dropped his hand lightly onto my knee. A jolt went through me.

"Take your hand off my knee!"

He removed it, laughing. "What's the matter?"

"Nothing. I just don't like to have anybody put their hand on my knee."

Elliott lit cigarettes for us both and took in deep gulps of smoke. The cigarettes made a fierce glow in the twilight. He had turned the lights on inside the house, and they suffused us with a soft glow. He sat there with a towel around his shoulders, his hair long and wet and falling over his forehead, talking, talking. I was impressed by the feeling of great bulk about him, of hugeness almost. He smoked in quick, hard puffs, his lips making a soft popping sound. His fingers were heavily stained with nicotine. Conversation was halting, desultory, the conversation of two people unsure of themselves and each searching the other.

"I want to see your children again," he said. "I want to see you again. I want to know you better."

"Why?"

"You'll see."

I told him about my family in Seattle, my alienation from them and their belief that I was not properly raising my children. We talked about dogs, which he loved (at this time, he owned two basset hounds), and the ranch in Colorado where he ran five thousand head of cattle. He discussed his hopes for developing the All Seasons Club at the ranch, which was surrounded by the Sleepy Cat Mountains and was within easy packing distance to some 240 virgin lakes stocked by the Colorado Game and Fish Department. He had had a survey made for an 18-hole golf course, and a ski slope with gondola lifts. After an hour, I accepted his invitation to dinner. From home, my houseman drove up with the clothes I would need for dinner, a basic black dress, black pumps, evening bag and a long strand of pearls, the kind I could twine around my fingers. Finally dressed and still fearful I went off for one of the strangest and most exhilarating evenings of my life.

Elliott's choice of restaurants was Mountain Shadows, a plush, sophisticated resort hotel club in Scottsdale with a magnificent view of the mountains. It had a T-shaped pool surrounded by leaning palm trees hung with colored lights. A booth was waiting for us, low, softly upholstered and stylish. The crowd was lively. A small orchestra played.

Elliott did not waste a lot of time on preliminaries. Barely had our second round of drinks been served than he came right to the point. Gripping his glass with both hands, staring intently at me with those bright blue eyes, the soft wall lighting playing about his face, he said:

"Patty, I know this sounds silly and you won't believe me but I've been in love with you from the first time we met. I want to ask you to marry me. Seriously."

"Marry you? What do you mean, marry you?"

"I love you."

"You couldn't possibly . . ."

"I love you."

"Mr. Rockefeller, listen, I've heard all about you. My father and mother would die if they thought I even went out with you."

"I don't want to just go out on a date, I want you for my wife and I want those four children to be mine."

His grip tightened on the glass. His fingers fluttered nervously. I felt crowded in a corner, mesmerized. I was afraid the people in the next booth would overhear.

"You drink too much," I said.

"I don't drink too much at all."

"You have a bad temper."

"Who says so?"

"Well, everybody. Everybody says so. I couldn't possibly marry you. I don't want to get married again. I've been married and I don't want to go through that again. And you, you've been married four times."

"I've made mistakes, I know," he said. "You are the person I could be happy with, Patty."

"Please don't talk like that. You don't know what you're saying."

He was holding my hand now. I was perspiring. My hands were clammy. I pulled away and wiped them on a napkin. He asked me to dance. I thought anything would be better than this. As we walked toward the dance floor, however, I had doubts. How could such a big man maneuver me around that crowded floor? I had visions of my nice black pumps being ruined. Our first few steps proved how wrong I was. Elliott Roosevelt danced like a bird. The orchestra did a sprightly rendition of "Little Things Mean a Lot." I tripped and stumbled, but his expression never changed, and we never missed a beat. From around the circular dance floor I could catch the furtive glances. In Phoenix, this man was a walking conversation piece.

We returned to our table. With a start I recognized the people in the next booth, my friends Mary and Ted Nelson and Al Lustbader from the real estate business, Betty Lee Lundin and her husband Mac, and Phyllis and Paul Chilton.

Betty Lee was a lifelong friend of mine from Seattle who wintered in Phoenix and sold some real estate.

A friend of mine came over and asked me to dance. I accepted and left Elliott sitting alone. My partner was very impressed with himself and his opinions and had had a couple of drinks. While we danced he said I was an idiot for jeopardizing my business career by being seen with a man like Elliott Roosevelt. "Patty, you've got a great future."

"Listen, he happens to be a very nice guy," I said, "and you shouldn't talk like this without even knowing him."

"I don't want to know him any better than I do now," he grumbled. "But I do know this, he's not for you and you're for the real estate business."

When we returned to the table Elliott's face was like a thundercloud. It was my first glimpse of his intense and some-times uncontrollable jealousy. The notion startled and, I must admit, excited me. He said that Betty Lee and Mac had invited us to a small party at their home, which Elliott understood was on the way to my house. "I want to meet all of your friends," he said. "I want to know more about you."

"That's fine," I replied, "but I don't want to go to the Lundins."

By now the others were leaning over the booth listening. "Oh come on, Patty," they said, "be a sport." Betty Lee said Janet Dwyer would meet us there with her date, and Mary Jane and Phil Garrity—Betty Lee's sister and brother-in-law—were visiting from Tucson. I relented, and about 11:30 in the evening we left Mountain Shadows and drove fast up the darkness of Camelback Road.

It was a convivial crowd, with light conversation and good drinks. It was nice to see Janet again. She had given me a lot of advice about trying to hang onto my marriage with Milt. Sophisticated, breezy, with platinum hair and a fondness for low-cut gowns, Janet was a divorcée herself. She lived and loved the fast life and had grown cynical. Before Milt and I finalized our divorce, she would come down and visit me from her home in Los Angeles. "Patty," she would say, "why the hell do you want to get a divorce? You've got four children, honey. No-body's going to marry you." I told her I much preferred a clean break to living the pretense and sham of an unfortunate marriage.

Now, when I walked in with Elliott Roosevelt, her eyes widened and her mouth made a small o.

The word obviously had arrived before we did and now everybody wanted to see for themselves if it really was Elliott squiring me. He was all protectiveness and endearments, with his arm at my waist and constant little courtesies ("Baby, can I get you a drink? . . . Let me light you a cigarette . . ."). I had never received such attention from any escort before. All the women were trying to corner me in the bedroom for whispered conferences.

"What's going on, Patty?" came the breathy queries.

"Nothing."

Eyebrows lifted, lips gave me knowing smiles.

Finally I confided in Betty Lee that he had asked me to marry him. She burst out laughing. "Are you out of your mind. He's already married."

"But he's getting a divorce."

"I don't believe it. You're not very cagey about men, Patty. Don't let him hoodwink you."

We danced, ate, drank. Elliott regaled them with stories of his life as the son of the President, and soon had the crowd laughing until tears streamed down their faces. Talk got around to dogs, and Mary Jane mentioned that she had always wanted a toy female white poodle. Elliott announced in lordly fashion that he had a kennel full of poodles. He would bring one around tomorrow morning. "I'll be back here at nine-thirty."

We left at 4:30 in the morning and drove to my house, fifteen minutes away. It was almost daybreak when we pulled up in front and parked. He insisted on telling me again how he felt and was adamant in his stand that he wanted to marry me. I did not believe him any more than I had many hours before and still was not even convinced he was getting a divorce.

Daylight came and we were still sitting there. This was a street of small houses and close neighbors, and I could feel eyes peering out from behind the venetian blinds. I suggested to Elliott that since he was going to deliver that poodle in a few hours anyway, he might just as well sleep in the children's playroom. With three household employees living there and a houseful of kids, I had no compunctions. We skulked into the house, I got sheets and blankets to fix his couch and said good night.

"Could I kiss you good night?" he said.

"No, please. I really think I'm dreaming. I just want to get a good night's sleep and think it over."

He laughed. "You really don't have time for a good night's sleep, but go ahead and think it over."

I went to my room and fell into the deep sleep of complete exhaustion. At nine o'clock I awoke to see five pairs of eyes looking at me: Jimmy, Ford, Gretchen, David, and . . . Elliott. "Wake up, wake up," they were saying, "you've got to get up, Mom." My mind was fuzzy at first. It was difficult to focus thoughts. Then I realized what was happening, jerked the covers over my head and said, "Oh, please—please go away." Gretchen shooed everyone out so I could get up and dress. Elliott too, I learned later, had a rather bizarre awakening in the playroom, with four strange children staring at him. Jimmy, speaking as the man of the house, had said politely, "Pardon me, sir, but what is your name?" Elliott replied pleasantly, "I'm Elliott Roosevelt." Jimmy smiled a thin smile. "Sure," he said, "and I'm Harry Truman."

As we drove away from the house, this time in glaring Arizona sunshine, he said, "Patty, I'm going to marry you and be the father of those children." In the full light of day it seemed now so incredible that I choked back a laugh and changed the subject quickly by asking how far it was to his kennels.

He didn't have any kennels, not around Phoenix anyway. We were on our way to buy a toy white poodle, female, for $125. What's more, it was Elliott Roosevelt's last $125, which I wouldn't have believed either. Very soon he would be in hock for more than half a million dollars, right down to and including his clothes. But all this I was to learn later, when it was my income alone that was to tide us over while Elliott tried to unsnarl his financial affairs and get back on his feet.

The poodle was white, squirmy, and three months old. We bought her in South Phoenix from a woman in a housetrailer, and went to Betty Lee's house, where Mary Jane and Phil were staying during their visit. Mac was surprised to see us. "Uh, well, hello again, Mr. Roosevelt."

"We brought the poodle for your sister-in-law, Mary Jane," Elliott said.

"Uh, fine. She's in Betty Lee's bedroom having coffee." Our host seemed on edge, and we were quickly to learn the cause of his discomfiture.

Together, Elliott and I proceeded down the hallway leading to the bedrooms. I was holding the poodle in a towel. The dog was squirming and wet. I was concentrating on her and failed to see the man solidly planted in the hallway ahead of me until we collided with him. I looked up and, astonished, recognized my former husband, Milt.

Elliott had stopped beside me, and now stood quietly looking down from his 6-foot, 3-inch vantage point. The encounter left me completely flustered.

I turned to Elliott, who still had not offered a word, and said, "Oh, Milt, this is Elliott Roosevelt."

Elliott said pleasantly, "How do you do, Milt."

We walked on into the bedroom and gave Mary Jane her new puppy.

Later, the Lundin cleaning woman, May, spirited me off to the bedroom for a word of advice.

"Miz Whitehead, no matter what happens, ma'am, you marry that man Roosevelt, even if it's only for sixty days. It'll stand you in good stead all your life."

5

Roosevelt and Romance

May's words were more than prophetic. For Patricia Peabody Whitehead, life took on a new vibrancy. That first day, I could feel the gears shift. Suddenly we were hurtling down a broad open road, and the man at the wheel had big hands and a massive frame and a face like the northern exposure of Squaw Peak Mountain. This was a man who dashed into living and poured on the gas, and didn't always stop to sleep. Life was there for the asking, if you had the nerve and the drive; and the greatest human waste was boredom.

The following afternoon Elliott decided to have a barbecue and swimming party at his house on the mountain. He went up, and I bundled the children into my Thunderbird and picked up Janet Dwyer, who was invited along with the Lundins and the Garritys. Janet still clucked her tongue at me, "Patty, you're not seriously going around with a creep like Elliott Roosevelt. Are you out of your mind?" At the house we walked in and I said, "Janet, have you met Elliott Roosevelt, the creep?" Then I left her there, facing him. Furious at me, she spent the rest of the afternoon making a play for him.

While we fixed cheeseburgers, hot dogs, and potato chips, the four children flopped on the floor of his bedroom in front of the color television set. When it was time to eat I ordered them outside. Elliott was impressed. "Most mothers don't care," he said, "whether their children eat standing up or lying down." We spent part of the afternoon playing bridge. That evening, when the others had gone, Elliott came down to my house and I fixed a Caesar salad with romaine and croutons and bacon. The children, especially the three youngest, were warming rapidly to him. Elliott chatted on all sorts of subjects, and enchanted Ford especially with his tales of the wild West and adventures as a rodeo rider. Jimmy, the eldest at fifteen, kept his distance. As the man of the house, it was his responsibility to keep track of the others, the state of their hair, fingernails, and teeth. He looked upon this male newcomer as a potential spoiler. After the children went to bed, Elliott and I argued over his persistent marriage proposals. "I can't marry you until you get a divorce anyway," I protested. "You don't even know what you want to do yet."

During the next three weeks we saw each other sporadically. He was busy hopping around to his Colorado offices of Elliott Roosevelt Enterprises in Denver and Grand Junction. The thing smacked of uranium and oil wells and ranching; he owned an airplane and land and houses, and money seemed to drip from his pores. I would have laughed at anyone who said Elliott Roosevelt was on the verge of bankruptcy. He went to Denver for a few days and planned then to fly down to Dallas. Three times a day there were long distance phone calls for me. The man was begging me to bring the children and meet him in Dallas. "Elliott, I'm working for a living," I tried to explain. "I can't just pick up and leave." Secretly I dreaded what people would say about me flying all around the country with a married man. Besides, I had only known him a few weeks, and his stability as a person was a vast unknown quantity. But I relented, called some old acquaintances in Dallas, Glenn and Martha Justice, and asked if I could come and visit them. In Phoenix, my friends Phyllis and Paul Chilton knew what was happening. I told them Elliott was asking me to marry him. "Go ahead and marry him," said Paul. "He must be a terrific guy to have courage like that." It was good to hear someone say something nice about Elliott for a change. Phyllis and I went on a shopping spree. For the first time in my life I got everything coordinated; black silk suit for daytime wear, black cocktail dress, black and white linen, light colored silks. Having no furs or exceptional jewelry anyway, I did not have to worry about accessories.

Elliott was waiting at the Dallas airport. When I stepped off the plane he gave me a bear hug and a noisy kiss. I was flushed with embarrassment. (Later I was to learn that such display of affection is characteristic of the Roosevelt brothers; when one meets the other, even after a week's separation, they hug and kiss. I've grown to love Elliott's demonstrativeness, and think it is the kind of thing I've needed all my life.) He drove me to the Justices' home, where Martha greeted us both warmly. Elliott was accepted immediately, at face value. It was good to have loyal friends.

The business in Dallas involved continued efforts to get the All Seasons Club project launched. Elliott had discussed the ranch plans there with Paul Cain, a promotions and public relations man. Glenn Justice perked up his ears and began asking for more details. Glenn was a mortgage banker, and this type of thing interested him greatly because Martha had grown up in the Colorado hills. They decided to fly to Meeker, so Glenn could look over the ranch. Elliott had flown down from Denver in his Beechcraft. The four of us piled in for the four-hour flight to Meeker. Much of the trip was a monotony of rugged hill country, desert and plains, scoured by erosion. Then ahead rose the Rockies; first a purplish smudge beneath a line of ragged clouds, then pine-fringed foothills, going bald as the altitude increased, and finally the immensity of the mountains themselves, rampart upon rampart and jagged, snowy peaks. It was an awesome landscape, splotched with high virgin lakes, shimmering orange in the sunlight. In the crisp, thin air, haze vanished and one could see seventy-five miles in any direction. The sight put a catch in my throat as Elliott dipped his left wing and descended for landing at Meeker airport. Fearful that I would run into Minnewa, I stayed in town shopping with Martha while Elliott and Glenn toured the ranch. After three hours they returned, picked us up, and we flew back to Dallas. Glenn was enthusiastic over the All Seasons Club now. The following day Elliott flew me to Phoenix, then continued on to Denver.

What followed was probably a new high-water mark for romantic pursuit by telephone. Day after day, sometimes hour after hour, Elliott Roosevelt was on the phone long distance. It got so I could almost recognize his ring by its urgency. The conversation followed a pattern.

"Patty? How are you doing?"

"Fine. I'm fine."

"That's good. Do you miss me?"

"Yes."

"How much do you miss me?"

"I miss you."

"I'm in love with you, Patty. Do you love me?"

"Elliott, I've told you, I don't know . . ."

"You must love me. Nobody could feel as I do without being loved back. I think you love me and you're going to marry me."

"Elliott . . ."

"You must love me."

"Elliott, this just isn't real. I mean, things like this just don't happen."

On and on it went, day after day. Finally, in desperation, I blurted out: "All right, I do love you. Yes, I think I really do love you."

Elliott tried to jump through the phone.

"I knew it. I knew it! When can we get married?"

"Not until you get a divorce. Do you want to be a bigamist?"

That weekend he flew back to Phoenix. He wanted to move out of the Squaw Peak house and take an apartment near where I lived. My houseman, Tex, helped him pack his things over to the Phoenix Manor, an older resort hotel. Tex complained about having to do such heavy work. Later I was to rue the impulse to volunteer his services, for the trouble he made for us was terrible.

After committing myself this far with Elliott there was no alternative but to tell him that I would marry him. I did not believe in free love; if I was in love, then I must be married. We began making plans. This was June. Elliott had been talking with the lawyers, his and Minnewa's, and thought the divorce might be final in August. She had filed suit in Meeker, charging mental cruelty. At this point, it appeared that a settlement could be reached. Excited as teenagers going steady, Elliott and I sat for hours by the pool talking about where we might live (he suggested the ranch in Colorado) and what splendid lives we would have together. He dropped quiet words of caution about publicity, warning that we were fair game for the press; a bad press would reflect on me, my family and the children. Avoid reporters, he said. Don't give interviews. My only exposure to the press had been society editors and women's news writers, and they had never done me harm. So unfortunately his advice went out my other ear.

We had been going together for a month when the bubble burst: Minnewa would not consent to a divorce.

A sledge hammer could not have hit us any harder. But Elliott told me to be calm, things would work out. Meanwhile, I planned to take the children and go away for a vacation during the month of July. We were going up to the northern part of Arizona to a dude ranch so we could ride and swim. I particularly looked forward to some cool weather. Elliott intervened in our plans however by convincing us that a place called Redstone Lodge in Colorado would be more fun. Besides, he said, it would give me a chance to know more about my new home state, and it would also mean we could see each other as it wasn't too far from Denver. Reservations were then made for us at the Redstone Lodge. Just before we were to leave, Elliott told me he had to attend the State Democratic Convention at Durango, Colorado, as a delegate. John and Bobby Kennedy would be there trying to line up votes, and Elliott was to help them. Could I go along? I jumped at the chance. We flew to Durango and taxied in beside the Kennedy plane, the *Caroline*. It sat there looking too big for the runway. Two of Elliott's men from Grand Junction, Jack O'Connor and Dave Cross, met us with a car. They made no acknowledgment of my presence, greeting Elliott with a poker-faced "Hi boss." Even after having to browbeat the harried hotel manager into making a single room available to me, they asked no questions and we volunteered nothing.

The Grange Hall of Durango was teeming with delegates, tough, weathered ranchers for the most part, wearing Western jeans and chewing tobacco. Spittoons were as numerous as Stetsons. Old acquaintances greeted one another with guffaws and bone-crushing whacks on the back.

When Elliott walked in, Robert Kennedy steamed toward him

with a face like a raincloud. "Elliott, why the hell are you so late?" snapped the lean, mop-haired field general for the JFK campaign. "You haven't been here to do your homework. If you don't get elected a delegate to the national convention we could lose Colorado." Elliott shook hands and grinned. "Don't worry," he said.

Now for the first time I watched the Roosevelt political magic turned on full blast. Elliott went through the Grange Hall like a roller skater, pumping hands, patting shoulders, grasping forearms for urgent, whispered conferences. There were greetings and cattle talk, sheep talk, hog talk, "Hello, George, haven't seen that boy of yours in a long time . . . Hi, Sam, how's the pen-feeding? Mary, did your husband get back from overseas? . . ." It was a natural, inborn geniality, without sham; a phenomenon of warmth and smiles and laying-on of hands. It was person-to-person, nose-to-nose. This was Elliott Roosevelt, rancher, in a slate-blue Western suit and cowboy boots. That night he was elected by an overwhelming majority on the first ballot, and Bobby Kennedy sat there with his mouth sagging. Jack, Teddy, and Bobby spoke to the delegation, after which Bobby came over to congratulate Elliott. Elliott shook hands, but he has never quite forgiven Bobby Kennedy for thinking he could not win the vote even though he was a day late.

That evening as we all sat in the Caucus Room of the hotel, I asked about the time of my return to Phoenix, in order to drive the children back up for our month at Redstone. Elliott's face suddenly lit up with an idea, "Honey, I will have my man, Alex Baldo in Grants, New Mexico, fly back tonight. He can pick up my car in Phoenix. I need it in Denver anyway, and gather up the nurse and the children. Jimmy can drive your T-bird and they can motor up in tandem." Besides it would be a good thing for Jimmy to have such a responsibility, he told me. Being in somewhat of a quandary, and not really knowing my own geographic location, I consented. Elliott spoke to Jack O'Connor about making the arrangements. I phoned the children and told them their ETD for Redstone would be at 7:00 A.M., the next morning. Trusting fully, they asked no questions and said they would be ready. Elliott and Jack estimated their driving time, and we made plans to meet them in Cortez, Colorado, the next evening.

I slept restlessly that night. Life had not only assumed a new perspective for me, but also had given me my first taste of being dependent on another person. I had fought my own battles for so long that I marveled at Elliott's ability to take away my headstrong lead. Somehow it was a relief and almost peaceful. The next day the convention was ended and we had nothing to do, so he suggested we fly to the ranch at Meeker so I could get a good look at it.

"That's a wonderful idea," I said.

"Good. We'll take a picnic."

"Fine."

Holiday magazine had carried an article not long before about private flying clubs, and how they organized picnics and skiing and fishing trips. The magazine published menus so appetizing you could eat them off the page. With the cooperation of the Durango hotel chef, I arranged for a beautiful picnic hamper, stocked with fried chicken in foil, a lovely salad, French garlic bread, a bottle of dry white wine and linen napkins. When it was done, the chef peered at me and asked again, "Going on a picnic by airplane, madam?" I nodded. He shrugged.

Thunderheads gathered to the southwest as we took off. Gaining altitude, we headed for Meeker along the edge of a squall line. Around us the sky gradually turned purple and billowing clouds vomited lightning. Soon rain was lashing the windshield and visibility dropped to zero. Elliott clung grimly to the controls as updrafts and downdrafts bounced us around the sky like a toy. Perspiration popping out on my forehead, I grasped my rosary beads, shut my eyes tight and started whispering Hail Marys. Into my mind flashed visions of us piled up dead on a mountain peak, never to be heard from again; and on the floor behind us, the picnic hamper bounced around violently, filling the cabin with the odor of fried chicken, garlic bread, and wine. Flying by grit and luck, Elliott got us to the ranch and made several passes over it, explaining between sickening lurches, "Here's the house . . ." (*zoom*) ". . . Down there's the barn . . ." (*roar, crash*) ". . . See those cows" (*lurch*) "grazing? . . ." Then he looked over, saw my eyes tightly shut and my lips moving, grumbled, "Hooey!" and started searching for a place to land. We couldn't make it into Aspen, or Meeker or Steamboat Springs. Finally, with the gas tank almost empty, he made an approach for the little runway at Cortez. The plane settled to within three feet of ground when something bounded into our path. Elliott swore and zoomed upward, brushing the antlers of a full-grown deer. On our second attempt we bounced in safely. I stepped down from the cabin, my face a ghastly white and knees buckling. The airport attendant ran up, took one look and said, "Jeez, lady, you look like you seen a ghost!"

We arrived in Cortez, ahead of the children. Still bushed from the plane trip, I took a nap and was awakened by the sounds of shouts and laughter. It was a treat to watch them pile out of the cars, all talking at once about their experiences on the drive from Phoenix. Three of the children had ridden in my green Thunderbird. David and the nurse drove with the patient Alex Baldo. The cars were rolling trash piles full of chewing gum wrappers, crushed soda crackers, bits of jelly bread, bottle caps, and whatnot. Diagonally across one side and back fender ran a purplish smear that had not been there before. I asked the nurse. It took some explaining. To simplify David's diaper problem, she had placed his potty chair in the seat beside her and let him ride sitting on it. When nature called, the potty was ready. The nurse then would empty it out the window. There was a rush of wind to carry it away. Every few miles they stopped at a service station for soft drinks, refreshments, and David's favorite thirst quencher was grape pop. All that grape pop does surprising things to one's insides. The purple swipe on my beautiful green car, it turned out, was there to stay.

Early the next morning the children and I drove out to wave good-bye to Elliott, as he soon became a speck in the distance to Denver. After picking up the nurse and Mr. Baldo, we resumed our trip to a wonderful month's vacation.

Redstone Lodge was a magnificent, columned place set in the mountains and surrounded by quaking aspen trees. July was the month of full bloom, and the high country was a gaudy mass of color. The nights were delightfully cool, the days warm.

The children and I rode horseback, swam in the numbing cold of a raging mountain stream and enjoyed movies after dinner.

We had three rooms with a balcony overlooking the river. In the mornings I walked out onto the balcony, breathed fresh, pure air and was glad to be alive.

Elliott called three or four times a day. He was lonely for me and I for him. The rumor started around the lodge that Elliott Roosevelt had been there and was coming back. One of the servants, I discovered, was a gossipy soul and helped them spread, even to the point of supplying new material. The second weekend Elliott flew up to join us. We went horseback riding together, and he almost fell off laughing at me posting on a Western saddle. Always before, I had ridden on an English saddle. When we returned the nurse ran out to meet us. "Mrs. Whitehead, you had a very important call. There's been a death."

Billy Goodheart, my old friend, the man who had made so much possible and given me the start I needed, was dead in Phoenix.

I was sick at heart. Before we left for the Durango convention I had taken Elliott to see Billy and tell him of our plans for marriage. He accepted this with mixed feelings, hating to lose my services as a real estate saleswoman but wanting me to be happy. I think he knew that Elliott was the one man capable of bringing me real happiness. Billy had a sixth sense about people. We used to call him the Chess Player, because he would move his people—knights, bishops, pawns—into position to where they were either all fighting or all happy. I knew that Billy had maneuvered me into a position where I would be self-sufficient and perhaps find the man I wanted. His feelings toward Elliott were charitable enough, even friendly. Our last hours with him had been, as always, a pleasure; but he appeared tired. His conversation had lost some of the old keenness.

"I'll fly you right down there," Elliott said.

A few hours later we left Redstone Lodge for Phoenix. As the familiar bulk of Camelback Mountain loomed below us, I remembered how Billy had sent me out to buy the Praying Monk.

With the drone of the Beechcraft's twin engines, thoughts of this good man continued to fill my mind. Although it seemed presumptuous, I sensed that Billy may have hung onto life a little longer in order to see me come into a period of happiness. He had been in failing health for so many years, and never told anyone about it, that the idea was not entirely illogical. Later I was to learn that he died of a reactivated tuberculosis, the same illness that would kill Eleanor Roosevelt in just two more years.

I went alone to the funeral. Elliott, who had not known Billy well, did not think it becoming for him to attend. There was a very large crowd. Afterward, Elliott went with me to visit Billy's widow, Marybelle. A year before she had undergone major surgery for cancer, but the doctors said they had removed it all. Now she was shattered by grief. "Billy wanted you to know," she told me, "that he is happy for you and wishes for your happiness."

Marybelle could not live without him . . . Three months later she died in her sleep.

Elliott was still trying to find some workable settlement for the divorce, flying to Denver, Phoenix, and Dallas for talks with lawyers and advisers. In Phoenix he hired a lawyer. As a result of the divorce settlement Elliott was to assume some $625,000 worth of debts, and had to sign over to the bank as collateral everything he possessed. Elliott pinned all his hopes on developing the ranch into the All Seasons Club for executives. Of the 29,000 acres there, 5000 still belonged to him, at least until the final settlement with Minnewa.

A month later I brought the children home from Redstone Lodge and he asked me to join him in Dallas again, where he was talking with Glenn Justice about the All Seasons project. They were going to California to line up a syndicate with the Aimee Semple McPherson people to buy the property; but the key to it now was to secure an option to buy the adjoining 10,000 acre ranch owned by a sheepherder named Charlie Snow. In the middle of Mr. Snow's property was a natural site to dam up a stream emptying into the White River. It could make a lake about eight miles long for fishing, water skiing, swimming, and building waterside cottages for club members.

"Let's send Patty to talk to Mr. Snow. They don't know her out there. If anybody can get that option, she can."

"Sure. Let's send Patty." It was agreed.

I arrived in Meeker alone, wearing dark glasses and trying to look casually inconspicuous. In a town where everybody knows everybody, this is like being a turnip in a petunia patch. I was "Helen Daniels," representing a syndicate in Arizona, here to buy land. In a restaurant where I stopped for coffee, I almost wished I was Helen Daniels. The main topic of conversation was Elliott Roosevelt, his divorce from Minnewa, and Patty Whitehead. "He was living in Mexico with this woman," said a man in the next booth. "They got illegitimate children. Whole bunch of 'em."

Renting a car, I drove fast out to Charlie Snow's. The speed not only helped ease my jitters, it also got me past the Roosevelt ranch, Minnewa's stronghold, in a hurry.

Charlie Snow had one tooth, a face like parchment, a stubble of tobacco-stained beard, an ancient shirt, frayed pants held up by suspenders, one good shoe and one with the sole half off, and a pair of incredibly dirty socks. He slept in a lean-to summer and winter, furnished with a blanket and a rug, and definitely smelled of sheep. A deeply rutted dirt track led to his abode. My car lurched crazily on the old road while a pack of rangy dogs yapped as if they had never seen company before. Charlie Snow looked at me in silence for a time, and then he smiled that one-tooth smile and said, "How do?" I looked up behind him and the bowl of the mountains formed a natural amphitheater. Sheep grazed on the high slopes.

We talked about land. I told him about the syndicate and said they were interested in buying the Roosevelt property but wanted his, too. They were prepared to pay $90,000 for his acreage. I hunkered down beside him while we talked. Charlie Snow catered to the idea. He was getting old and didn't have any folks to leave this land to anyhow. "It might just be a good idea." There, with sheep nuzzling us, we drew up an option for my syndicate to buy it at that price, no money down.

There was a house on his land, and the people who lived there had a sick dog. Charlie Snow rode up there with me, to see the dog. The tenants had worked for the Roosevelts.

"Have you seen her, this Whitehead woman?" Charlie Snow asked.

"Naw," they said. "We heard she took off."

"Took off where?"

Again there was discussion then about me going to Mexico with Elliott while Minnewa was sick.

From there we drove into town to get a legal description of the property for the contract and Charlie Snow invited me to lunch, a rare gesture for this man. A lawyer joined us to work on the papers. The place was attached to a fishing camp and crowded with ranchers and herdsmen. I fished a cigarette from my purse and offered one to the sheepherder.

"No thank you, lady. Never smoked one of those ready-made things in my life, and I ain't gonna start now. Here"—he handed me a cloth sack of Bugler and some cigarette papers—"you take one of mine, little girl."

It took me fifteen minutes to roll one cigarette. Tobacco spilled into my coffee and over the tabletop. I tried to jerk the string taut on the tobacco pouch with my teeth, the way Gary Cooper used to do it in the movies, and almost lost a filling. When I fired up the cigarette there was an acrid stench of paper. I was coughing, choking, spilling tobacco, and singeing my eyebrows. Finally I got it started, inhaled a small glob of smoke, coughed, wiped my eyes and said, "Mighty fine."

After lunch, my head was spinning so I almost wrecked the rented car. But I had the option. After spending the night in Meeker, I took off the next morning for Dallas. Elliott and Martha Justice met me at the airport. In the Sheraton-Dallas Hotel I proceeded to unpack and get things in order. Elliott and Martha sat on a couch watching me. Carefully I put my things out on the bed, filled my little steam iron with water and plugged it in.

"Honey," Elliott said, "what are you doing?"

"I'm pressing my clothes, they're all wrinkled."

"Haven't you ever heard of the valet service?"

"Yes, I've heard of it, but I'm just not in the habit of using them if I can do it myself."

"You just put the little iron away and we'll get the valet service to finish the clothes for you."

This was one of my practical lessons in adopting the ways of the man I was engaged to marry. It brought home to me the fact that Elliott Roosevelt lived life with certain services and prerogatives, things he had always been accustomed to and would remain so, regardless of his financial condition. This was one of the sharp distinctions between him and others I had known, and a characteristic which endeared him to me.

That morning we went to Glenn Justice's office for a meeting and I handed over the option papers. The men were elated, Glenn signed as the buyer so Elliott's name would not appear. The plan was going together well. Estimates were complete for construction of a ski lift, golf course, shooting range and clubhouse. Paul Cain had had beautiful drawings and layouts prepared. In the hotel that evening we all gathered for drinks and celebration. With the option in hand, it seemed to be all but buttoned down. Suddenly, I had an urge to call Seattle and inform my mother that I was going to be married. Martha Justice came into the bedroom with me while I placed the call. I had not talked with Mother for months, because we were still at a standoff. I recognized her voice on the telephone.

"Mother, I want to tell you something."

She started to cry. "I don't want to talk to you," she said, and dropped the phone.

"Mother! Mother, what's the matter?"

Another voice came on the line. It was my sister, "Loads of Love" Lee. "My mother doesn't care to talk to you," she announced.

"*Your* mother! She's my mother, too. What's the matter with you?"

Lee told me in a disdainful voice that the day before the New York *Times* had called, asking Mother if she had a daughter, Patricia Peabody Whitehead. "Yes," Mother had said, "but she isn't here." They knew she wasn't, the reporter said, but they wanted to confirm a story they had heard that I was going to marry Elliott Roosevelt. Mother fainted.

Afterward, Lee had come over to spend the day and night, taking care of Mother and putting cold compresses to her head. The disgrace of it all: Not only had I divorced, I was marrying a Roosevelt, and out of the Catholic Church.

"Well, Elliott happens to be a fine man," I told her.

"Don't tell me," Lee retorted, "I know all about whom you're marrying. We don't approve of it and never want to see you or hear from you again."

"What are you talking about, Lee? You can't be serious."

"I certainly am serious."

"You don't even know which Roosevelt he is."

"Oh, yes, I do. I looked him up in the *World Almanac*."

With that, she hung up. (The *World Almanac*, I discovered later, carried about five lines on Elliott, mostly reciting his occupations and the names of his various wives.) Even today I still send Lee an annual gift of this publication.

With August upon us, the marriage seemed imminent. In Dallas, I was still blue over the loss of Billy Goodheart. Elliott and Martha Justice decided a good way to cheer me up was to send me shopping for a trousseau. As Martha and I headed for the Neiman-Marcus store, Elliott called Stanley Marcus and asked him to personally supervise my buying spree and make sure I got everything I needed. It was a wonderful, kind gesture, and he didn't know I wouldn't let him pay for my purchases.

To my surprise, waiting to greet me was an old friend, David Hughes, a Neiman-Marcus executive who for years had been with I. Magnin in Seattle. He and his wife had lived across the street from me there. David plunged into the task of finding something suitable for my wedding. We looked at dress after dress, but nothing really appealed to me except one green chiffon—a Galanos original for $750. Stanley Marcus, meanwhile, ordered his various departments to bring to my dressing room bras, girdles, slips, hats, gloves, shoes, everything. Most of the time he hovered on the sideline, smiling and clasping his hands, while David rushed around matching accessories to costumes.

The flurry in Neiman-Marcus was hardly spontaneous. For weeks the newspapers had carried running stories with bold headlines: ELLIOTT SHEDS FOURTH WIFE; ENGAGED TO SOCIALITE FROM SEATTLE. Now a salesgirl went out to get another pair of gloves and returned with a look of surprise.

"Oh, Mr. Marcus, there are photographers and reporters out there and they want to see Mrs. Whitehead. Shall I bring them in?"

"No!" I snapped.

"No," said Stanley. He glanced at me. "I'll handle it." Then he vanished through the curtain. Martha and I waited, nervously burning up cigarettes. I had to go to the bathroom, but there wasn't one in the dressing room. After a quarter of an hour, Stanley came back and shrugged. "There is nothing I can do, Patty. They picked up your trail and know what's happening.

They're not going to leave until they talk to you. Can you get hold of Elliott?"

"I have no idea where he is."

Martha said she would go make a few calls.

My need became more acute. I whispered to Stanley Marcus, "Look, I have to go to the powder room."

"You can't."

"But I've got to."

"There's no way for you to get out to the ladies' room from here without going past those reporters."

I tried to force my mind to other things. I stood on one foot and then on the other. I smoked. I tried on dresses and suits.

The shoe man came in and took a sample of the dress material. The gown was stunning, the colors ranging from pale olive green to mint green to blue with a skirt of chiffon that billowed in those hues when I walked.

We stalled and talked: I groaned and smoked. Stanley Marcus said Elliott had ordered me a set of luggage as a wedding present, but that I would have to select a monogram. The luggage was beautiful, red leather and with so many pieces you would need a truck to carry them all.

After two hours, the bells finally rang signaling closing time. To me they sounded like the chimes of heaven. In disgust, the reporters and photographers trooped out of the store and went their separate ways.

I set a new indoor record sprinting to the ladies' room.

Stanley made us remain in his office another half hour, just to be safe. Then I sneaked out a side door in dark glasses, like Mata Hari.

The following day I left Dallas but I had ordered the clothes sent to Elliott's hotel in Denver, the Mayflower. We decided to put the children in school in Denver, where we would be living after our marriage. Elliott arranged an apartment for me in the Gotham Hotel. When we were married he would move over from the Mayflower. In Phoenix, meanwhile, Paul and Phyllis Chilton rented my house for six months while a new one of their own was being built. They offered to keep my furniture, to save putting it in storage.

In Dallas, I had hired a Negro maid, Lily Belle Hays. She came with excellent references, and this allowed me to discharge the gossipy servant. During the next six months, Lily Belle was to share a strange and, at the last, fearful life with us.

September came. We completed the move to Denver. At the Gotham, Lily Belle and the children and I settled down to apartment living to await what would happen next. Denver was a whole new experience for us. Unlike Phoenix, the winter would be cold. Already the air had a bite, and cold winds moaned out of the Rockies.

The lawyers wrangled over details. Elliott grumbled and pounded tables and then stepped back, rocking on his heels.

By bits and pieces I was gaining some idea of the extent of Elliott's troubles. Financially, they amounted to disaster. The wonder of it was that he could even keep his sanity, much less accept these incredible setbacks with such a kind of gentlemanly equanimity. Watching him now, plodding inexorably toward ruin, I could see something almost quixotic about this man I loved, with all my heart.

The All Seasons Club project could have pulled him out. It was good, the bank was willing to relinquish hold on Elliott's 5000 acres if development became a reality, and we had the option to buy Charlie Snow's adjoining ranch. But then the Aimee Semple McPherson group had a change of heart and pulled out. Next, the Florida multi-millionaire, J. N. McArthur, expressed interest, through Land Vice-President Bob Prince.

There was a plan for McArthur to buy both the Roosevelt and Snow places, then sell the sheepherder's 10,000 acres to the State of Colorado for a state park. I was sent to dicker with the state game and fish people. They would pay $200,000 for the Snow land. Subtracting the $90,000 we were to pay the sheepman under the option, this would have left us $110,000 with which to develop. Then McArthur backed out, with no explanation. With that, the All Seasons Club collapsed. Eventually the state did buy Snow's ranch for $90,000 and built the dam, creating a fine lake. To this day Elliott is convinced the All Seasons Club would have been a success.

Now he was being buffeted on all sides. Not only did he stand to wind up half a million dollars in debt by divorcing his fourth wife, but he took out a loan which locked up his share of his mother's estate near Hyde Park, worth $225,000. In less than six months of 1960, he took a $750,000 beating. When our married life finally did begin, if it had not been for continuing income from my real estate business, we wouldn't have had cigarette money.

This all started in the early summer. Elliott figured he needed $20,000 to meet expenses. For a loan, he sought the help of his mother in New York. She asked Johnny for advice and then called Elliott back. "Dear, you call Johnny," she said, "he thinks he can work something out."

Johnny arranged a loan against Elliott's remaining half interest in Val-Kill, Mrs. Roosevelt's country home. It was payable in sixty days, or about mid-September. Elliott couldn't raise the money and lost the property. Mrs. Roosevelt's property consisted of about 250 acres along Highway 90, two miles south of the village of East Park.

When the $20,000 loan was arranged, in June of 1960, officials of the Colorado National Bank were furious. They were impounding all of Elliott's assets pending the divorce settlement, and now saw $225,000 worth of Val-Kill property pledged to secure a $20,000 loan. The bank tried desperately to recoup this interest. As the sixty days dwindled away, bankers attempted to prevent the note from falling past due.

The divorce picture, meanwhile, grew darker with each passing week. Minnewa refused to budge from her terms. Elliott would have to stand good for $625,000 in accumulated debts. During the six months the divorce was pending, including feed bills at the ranch, salaries for the help, veterinary services, and other expenses amounted to $75,000. Into the hopper would go all of Elliott's personal assets: his clothes, his furniture, the ranch, Elliott's one-fifth of the family's share of royalties from the play Sunrise at Campobello, oil wells in Colorado and Nebraska, mining interests, real estate holdings, everything.

The attorney Elliott had hired in Phoenix came to Denver and told him, "You can really fight back on this thing." Elliott said he did not want an open court fight. In September the final property settlement was presented for signing. In it, Elliott was to agree to all of Minnewa's terms. His lawyer was abashed.

"I'm going to sign."

The lawyer resigned from the case.

Elliott was handed the final terms in the office of Minnewa's attorney in Denver. I was at home in the Gotham Apartments and had sent the older children off to school. Elliott called me.

"Honey, would you mind coming down? I need your advice."

He was standing by the drinking fountain in the hallway outside the lawyer's office. When I walked up, he came right to the point.

"I wasn't going to tell you before, but this is your decision too. It's only fair that I ask you what you want to do. This is what she said she would agree to . . ."

"Don't do it," I said. "Fight. Don't let them do it to you."

"It is not a gentleman's position to sue a lady," he said. The words had a ring of eighteenth-century courtliness which, under the circumstances, seemed oddly refreshing. "No, if you want to marry me, these are the only conditions I will accept."

"I'll marry you no matter what the conditions, and accept half the liability."

It really did not matter then or later, but it was to take us four years just to pay off the personal bills. Even Elliott's $240,000 cash inheritance from his father's estate eventually released from a family trust fund at his mother's death, would go into the Colorado National Bank.

The die was cast even as we stood there by the water fountain outside the lawyer's office in Denver.

Elliott took a long drink from the fountain. Then I drank. Patting his mouth with a pocket handkerchief, he turned on his heel and flicked me a little wave.

"'Bye, love."

"See you later."

6

"Mud Packs" and *Marriage*

For Elliott, the signing of those papers put an end to any immediate hope of rising from the morass into which he had been pulled. A man's life has many demands, and in only the shallowest of personalities can one ambition satisfy them all. Thus, while I offered him new love and a family and stability, on yet another level—the financial level—he had become a ruin. In four turbulent marriages and a series of bad business risks, he had lost not only his existing fortune but had hocked the future as well. It was more than any man could bear. So now, this human being with whom I had cast my lot began to sink into depression, silent, brooding, bereft. With quiet desperation, I tried to reach him; but the thing was not of my making, so his recovery would have to come from within. The news that his divorce was, at last, finalized in Rio Blanco County, Colorado, came as an ironic climax to all he had tried so hard to achieve in recent months.

There had to be some way to jar him out of this limbo. I could not call his mother or brothers, for that would have been crude audacity. I decided instead to appeal for help from one of his children. On one occasion I had met his daughter, Chandler, when she visited Elliott and Minnewa in Phoenix. Beating down nervousness, I called her in Texas.

"Your father is very depressed," I said. "He needs you."

She and her husband, Henry Lindsley, flew to Denver in their small plane and checked in at a motel near the airport. Knowing that Elliott did not want any of his four children to become involved in his personal crisis, I kept their arrival from him. Making arrangements with Jack O'Connor to have Elliott at my apartment that afternoon, I picked up Chandler and Henry in my car. When we all walked in, Elliott hugged Chandler and kissed her. This was followed by several hours of conversation, mostly inconclusive. Elliott told Chandler he loved me, and that we were going to be married. Her response was, "That's nice. I hope you'll be happy." I made excuses to go across the hall to see about the children. Elliott finally persuaded me to go out to dinner with them, and I sat at the end of the table feeling isolated. Resentment to Chandler gnawed at me, although I knew that were our places reversed I would have acted in the same way—and in fact had done precisely this during the breakup of my own parents. The following day they returned to Texas, and I knew I had done the right thing. For a change, Elliott was able to give me an honest smile.

In our discussion of the wedding we had tentatively decided on having it in Sante Fe, New Mexico. While still in the real estate business, I had visited the town and had fallen in love with its quaint Spanish charm. Arrangements were being made by a man in Paul Cain's office who lived in Sante Fe. Then to our dismay we discovered that Paul, a publicity man to the core, had invited the press. For us, this put the lid on it. I called Daddy in Vancouver and told him of our predicament. "Why don't you come up to Eagle Crest?" he said. This was a lovely resort near Vancouver. The thought of a wedding there delighted me. What I could not tell Daddy was that our finances had dwindled so the trip would slash deeply into our tiny reserves. We decided to go anyway, and set the date for the first of November. Getting out of Denver, however, was not going to be as easy as I had thought.

To make certain that all the arrangements would be in order, I made plans to go to Vancouver four days ahead of Elliott. Jack O'Connor arrived at the Gotham to drive me to the airport. He came to my apartment and announced, "The lobby is full of newspaper reporters." Somehow word had leaked that we were going out-of-town to be married. The press had set up camp, waiting for me to come out. My heart jumped. Slipping on a pair of sunglasses, I went down the fire escape in modern day Juliet fashion and ducked into the waiting car.

"Hey!"

As we sped away, a photographer managed to snap a shot of our back bumper.

This, I thought, was getting ridiculous.

In Vancouver, Folger Peabody was jubilant. Already he had mentioned to friends that his daughter, Patty, and Elliott Roosevelt were coming to be married. He discovered that the name Roosevelt in Canada had immense prestige. Elliott was, among other distinctions, a Commander of the Order of the British Empire. Daddy fairly romped into preparations for our visit. "I'm going to handle all the arrangements," he had told me over the phone. "You just leave everything to me." He was waiting to meet me at the airport, and I was almost overwhelmed by his high spirits. After a flurry of hugs and kisses, I was whisked out to their home. It was lovely, the carriage house of a fine old English estate in Vancouver. Surrounded by flowers and ivy and stone walls, the carriage house smacked of elegance and landed gentry, on a small scale.

Some of Daddy's enthusiasm dwindled when I announced that I wanted to take out a quiet marriage license. Under Canadian law, one has the option of keeping the license secret. He looked hurt. "Why on earth would you want to do that? Why don't you be like everybody else?" I explained Elliott's distaste for publicity and his warning that the press would not be kind. "Well, who gives a damn about your getting married or not getting married? This is ridiculous, Patty."

The following morning at seven the doorbell rang. I went down to answer it, and there stood a reporter and photographer from a Vancouver newspaper.

"Good morning, madam. We would like to see Mrs. White-head."

I kept a straight face. "I'm sorry, you must have the wrong address. I don't know anyone by that name."

He asked me if this was not 1647 Angus Drive.

"Yes, but there is no Mrs. Whitehead here."

"Isn't this Folger Peabody's residence?"

"No it isn't."

They went away. I woke Daddy and told him. He snorted in disbelief. Then the telephone rang. It was the newsman, calling from a drugstore on the corner. Daddy answered.

"Sir, is this the home of Folger Peabody?"

Daddy scowled, "It most certainly is not!" and slammed down the receiver.

Uncle Alexander and Aunt Marie had an apartment in Vancouver which they kindly offered for Elliott's use. I had the kitchen stocked with coffee, juice, and other breakfast supplies, and placed fresh flowers around. Elliott called me from Denver, asking about the press in Vancouver. He was worried that he might be trapped at one of the airports. The day of his arrival was drizzly and cold, which probably helped him slip through unnoticed.

Daddy and his wife insisted on having a reception for us. Elliott was strongly against the idea, but realized that it was unbecoming to protest too loudly, since we were guests under their roof. When Elliott walked into the house, his meeting with the stanch Republican who was to become his father-in-law had a decided coolness.

"How do you do, Elliott."

"How do you do, sir?"

"Yes, well . . ." (*clearing of throat*) ". . . heh, heh, how was your trip?"

On the sidelines, my stepmother tried frantically to make conversation. I just watched the men eye each other like a pair of roosters, thinking of how long it had been since Daddy had said similar words to Milt and devoutly wishing that he and Elliott would establish a better relationship. My wish was already getting results, for Daddy was acutely aware of the Roosevelt prestige in Vancouver. The preliminaries soon ended, and Daddy took Elliott on a tour of his office at the Black Ball Ferry Line Terminal to show off his future son-in-law. That night Daddy and his wife had a dinner for us at the Vancouver Club and invited about twenty of their close friends.

I was walking around in clouds. It was beyond belief, this thing that was happening: elation poured over me like sunshine, so powerful I could almost taste it. Never had the world been so beautiful, or the sky so blue; never had birds sung so sweetly, or had the touch and smile of another person been so close to the sublime. This feeling, this sheer joy of living, lifted us as human beings into yet another order of existence. We turned into ourselves and focused upon ourselves, and all of our sense of surrounding life was in terms of each other. For me, a woman with four children and a past life which somehow had never been complete, love opened into a new dimension.

The morning after Elliott's arrival, I met him at his apartment and we went for a walk in a nearby public park. The leaves had long since fallen, leaving black branches that clashed in the wind; the grass had turned brown, and the park benches were empty and forlorn. At the pond the water was black and still as glass, and white swans drifted. But then the sun came out, splashing the light over the pond and the swans. Overhead, the clouds broke into light, scudding wisps, throwing moving shadows across the earth. Elliott and I locked hands and walked, and looked into each other's faces and spoke our minds.

"I love you. I love you. I love you."

Daddy was into everything, part of all the arrangements. He wanted to see the dress I would wear. When I unpacked it, and the folds of color spilled down over the edge of the bed, he said to his wife, "What do you think of that dress?" She said it was lovely.

"Why don't you wear a white dress?" Folger Peabody asked.

"I can't wear a white dress, Daddy. I've been married before."

About two hundred people were invited to the reception and cocktail party at Daddy's house. There was a receiving line including Daddy, Elliott, and me. This soon became a joke as all the guests made a beeline for Elliott and had scant time for all of us. In his lapel he wore the little button denoting the Commander of the Order of the British Empire. The Canadians were delighted. Daddy stood off to one side, feeling ignored. Finally he sounded off, "Hasn't anybody ever heard of Folger Peabody?" and did a little tap dance. At first glance it seemed a joke, but a closer look at Daddy's face showed me that it wasn't a joke. He was jealous.

The morning after the reception we left for Eagle Crest.

Longest leg of the trip was a four hour ferry boat ride from Vancouver to Nanaimo, on Vancouver Island. The boat was my family's, part of the Black Ball Ferry Line. As soon as we cast off, Daddy took Elliott by the arm and began talking nautical talk. Elliott, who had spent his life on and around boats and the sea, nodded and smiled. Daddy took him to the wheelhouse and introduced him to the captain and crew. "This is my future son-in-law, Elliott Roosevelt." Delightedly, the crew crowded around Elliott, shaking hands and elbowing Folger Peabody out of the way.

We had drinks and lunch in our cabin, then took a tour on deck. The weather was superb, beautiful, crisp and sunny and cold. Around us spread Juan de Fuca Strait, a dazzling blue fringed in the distance by land and deep forests of evergreen trees. A breeze spanked the strait, and the prow of the ferry kicked up white spray.

Daddy insisted on impressing Elliott with his knowledge of seamanship.

"Well, of course you don't know much about navigation, Elliott, I'm sure."

Elliott, an expert navigator in both planes and ships, replied mildly, "I know a little bit, but it's been awhile."

"Now I was in the Navy in World War I and took a course in navigation. It's something that will always stand a man in good stead. Someday if we have a little more time, I'll . . ."

It was too much. I interrupted. "Daddy, if you're going to teach Elliott how to box the compass, don't bother. He already knows."

My father had that look again, as if someone had let out the air from his tires.

To reach Eagle Crest, you get off the ferry at Nanaimo and drive about thirty miles through hilly country to Qualicum Beach. Elliott and I rode in the back seat while Daddy drove pointing out sights of interest. Just before Qualicum, we turned off the main highway into a narrow, smooth dirt road cutting through heavy woods. We passed barns, fields surrounded by beautiful white fencing and the houses of tenant farmers. On the rolling hills Hereford cattle grazed in fine herds. We took a curve, topped a rise, and there stood Eagle Crest before us.

Once the home of the late Sir General A. D. McCrae, Eagle Crest was sold after his death to Leonard Boultbee, president of the Boultbee-Sweet Real Estate Co. in Vancouver. He had turned it into a small guest resort, with a capacity of about thirty people. Mr. Boultbee also had owned the estate where Daddy lived. They came to Eagle Crest twenty or thirty times a year for a weekend of relaxation. As our car moved along the driveway, I heard the familiar swishing sound of tires on the crushed brick they used for paving, and looked up at the magnificent ivy-covered main house, with its red brick exterior and leaded casement windows.

As the doorman unloaded our luggage, the housekeeper led us into the huge living room which they called the Great Hall. Rich with woods and dark furnishings, the room had a very high ceiling and balconies all around. Drapes, sofas and chairs were in lovely flowered linen covers. There were large traditional tables and chairs, and an immense walk-in fireplace, big enough in which to roast a steer.

The Great Hall opened into a dining room with refectory-type tables. A double stairway led to the upper floor; but the house also had downstairs suites, off a long hallway. Here was the Queen's suite, where a year before the visiting Queen Elizabeth had slept. This was where I would stay. It had an enormous bedroom and sitting room, with a fire in the fireplace, thick bear rugs and wood floors polished to a deep luster. Prince Philip had occupied a similar suite across the hall. With all that room in her suite, I could never understand why the Queen and the Prince had to have separate accommodations. At the far end of the house was a large book-lined library, furnished with massive pieces covered in bright Scottish plaids.

Elliott was impressed by Eagle Crest. He walked around admiring everything. "Honey, this is magnificent." I knew that secretly he was jittery and out of sorts, here to be married among strangers without even calling his mother or any member of his family. Elliott's reasons for this were his own and I did not question them, but I had hoped he might at least send a telegram. His nervousness was apparent to me where it would escape the notice of anyone else. Under such stress, he usually falls asleep. The usual pattern is for him to take a book into a corner and hide, then nod off. He had napped during most of the ride from the ferry to Eagle Crest, and probably would have slept on the boat if Daddy had not insisted on conversation.

That night we had an appointment to visit the Congregationalist minister who was to marry us. Daddy drove us the ten miles to his house. The minister, a genial, talkative man, was a great admirer of the Roosevelts. He asked about Elliott's parents. He also asked other questions, mostly routine: Why did we want to marry? What about the children? Then he said he would come to Eagle Crest to perform the ceremony the following afternoon at five. A former Army Air Force man, he had heard about Elliott's war record and they chatted briefly about military service, buddy-buddy talk. Then we drove back to Eagle Crest, had a nightcap and went to bed. Half an hour later the telephone rang in a booth down the hall. I put my robe on and went to answer it. The minister was on the line.

"I can't marry you," he said.

"Why? What do you mean, you can't marry us?"

"Did you know he's been married before?"

"Of course I knew it."

"Why didn't you tell me?"

"Because I thought you knew."

"Well nonetheless," he said in his deep Scottish brogue, "I refuse to be a party to this marriage."

Dropping the phone, I rushed to Prince Philip's suite and banged on the door. "Elliott, Elliott, something terrible's happened. We can't get married!"

Mopping sleep from his eyes, Elliott barreled into the hall and grabbed the phone. They talked for nearly a quarter of an hour, Elliott's voice rising and falling like crashing waves. In the end, the minister gave in and agreed to marry us.

Actually, neither Elliott nor I could be angry at the man, for his misgivings had come from a sincere desire to do what was best and, if necessary, try to protect me and the children from a terrible mistake.

The day of our wedding dawned fresh and clear. I was up at seven o'clock for breakfast in my room, and about an hour later joined Elliott for a walk on the beach. Officially, the resort was closed for the season. It had been reopened for our wedding, at

Daddy's request. Now, the ocean and the wind and the salt air made a large and empty world that was all ours. Hand in hand we went down the steep, rocky path to the beach, then along the edge of the surf where the water packed the sand hard, making a firm footing. It was much too cold for swimming or even wading, but the sun was warm enough for me to wear walking shorts.

Daddy had the old-fashioned idea that bride and groom should be kept apart on their wedding day until the ceremony. But at Eagle Crest, there was no one else I could talk to but Elliott. I had a tremendous need to be with him; and, being a complete stranger, he had even more need of my company. Trotting along with us were a pair of Irish water spaniels owned by the Boultbees. Large, frolicsome dogs with long, dark, curly hair, they kept bounding into the surf to retrieve sticks and bits of bark we threw.

From the beach we walked up into the rolling pastures of the Boultbee farms. The stock was mainly Herefords, and there were several very good bulls. We hiked up a hill and climbed a rail fence into a pasture. A herd was grazing there, and to me it seemed very large, but Elliott said this was probably just a sampling of the ranch animals. He walked up to the herd and failed to see a strong, surly bull standing in the middle. Suddenly the herd exploded, and down upon us thundered a half-ton of horned fury. I bounded like a rabbit for the fence, barely touching ground. Elliott took off in another direction. The fence, which I had climbed easily enough coming in, was too high going out. Blocked, I swarmed up a large, bushy tree and hung from a top branch like a piece of laundry. The bull pawed the ground a few times, gave a disdainful toss of his horns and stalked away. Elliott finally was able to maneuver me from the tree to safety outside the fence. Moments later, we met Mr. Boultbee, who was showing some people around the farm, and he offered us a ride to the main house. Puffing and perspiring, we accepted gratefully.

We changed in time for cocktails and a leisurely lunch. Daddy twitted me about the possibility of the bridegroom backing out, and offered toasts to our happiness in case he didn't. It was a gay table. Afterward, my Aunt Marie was busy picking flowers and keeping me from seeing the wedding cake, a surprise from the pastry chef. She made me go to my room, saying, "Rest, so you will look radiant." I took a bath and washed my hair, setting it as best I could with hair curlers. Instead of a manicure, I simply removed a layer of polish I had put on two days before; my hands would look better today without bright fingernails. I gossiped with Marie, who assured me that my hair would come out of the curlers beautifully.

Marie brought me a facial mask to apply. I was totally unfamiliar with the mud pack, and neglected to ask her how to remove it. Smearing it on liberally, I lay down for about fifteen minutes. When it had hardened to the consistency of stone, I decided it was time to begin removing it. My face was beginning to shrink. I tried water. Nothing happened—if anything, the mask grew harder. Marie had stepped out of the room. Wrapped in a sleazy robe I had found in the closet, my hair a mass of curlers, I dashed into the hallway and . . . collided with Elliott.

"Elliott!"

"What in God's name has happened to you? Is this something you're supposed to wear for the wedding?"

"Yes . . . That is, no! I was looking for Marie . . . You see, this facial pack . . . Oh, hell." I dashed back into my room and slammed the door. Aunt Marie came to the rescue with a lotion to remove the facial.

It was 3:15 when I began the final preparation: a little powder, mascara, and lipstick; removal of the curlers and many brush strokes. Aunt Marie zipped up my dress and adjusted my veil. We struggled with my new kid gloves, which I had neglected to break in earlier. Marie gave me a little pearl pin to hook onto my necklace to make it hang higher. This was "something borrowed." For "something blue," I used a blue handkerchief, pinned inside my dress; "something old" was a handkerchief of my own, in a little bag, and "something new," my beautiful dress. I pinned a corsage of green orchids to the bag, glanced in the mirror and was ready to . . .

Someone came rushing down the hall. "Where's Elliott?"

"What do you mean, where's Elliott?" I said. "He's in his room, isn't he?"

"No. We can't find him anyplace."

"He must be there!"

"He isn't."

"But it's time to go. The minister, Daddy, everyone's ready."

My hand went to my mouth. "Oh, my God, you don't suppose he's left?" I started looking. "Elliott." He wasn't in Prince Philip's suite. "Elliott?" He wasn't on the terrace. "Elliott, where are you?" In the library, stretched face down on a huge couch, I found him—the man who went to sleep when he was nervous. He was still in his walking-around clothes. I leaned over and kissed him. "Darling, wake up. It's time for us to get married." He opened his eyes, and they were blue and full of sleep. "Honey," he said, "I'm sorry."

While Daddy entertained the minister, Uncle Alexander went off to help Elliott dress. In fifteen minutes he appeared, grinning, wearing a dark suit and a carnation in his buttonhole. He looked splendid. He looked like the old dream I dreamed of a husband. Uncle Alexander stood beside Elliott as his best man. I walked into the living room on my father's arm. Afternoon sunlight streamed through the small leaded window panes. Daddy, caught up in the spirit of the moment, kept whispering, "My little girl."

The ceremony was surprisingly brief. Elliott held me for a brief full minute after the minister had pronounced us man and wife, the Eagle Crest employees came over to congratulate us. Some of the women dabbed their eyes with handkerchiefs. Afterward they served a lovely champagne supper, and the minister and his wife remained as guests. During the meal the minister looked at me as if thinking, "What have I gotten her into?" But I knew his attitude was weakening. One look at our faces was enough to shake the most confirmed skeptic. Clearly we were two people in love. If anything, Elliott was the personification of a man being married for the first time, not the fifth. He was everything a bridegroom should be: gentle, naïve, gracious, and nervous. Looking at him, I knew that whatever his reversals had been in recent months, from now on he would not have to stand them alone; our marriage provided a new strength. Both of us were determined to profit from the past by making the future into something real and something good—a new lifetime.

Supper over, we sat around talking and smoking. Suddenly

it occurred to me that all these guests were going to stay overnight, and there was no place where Elliott and I could truly be
away by ourselves. The only possible seclusion was in our room,
behind a locked door. With a show of sophistication, I dropped
hints to Elliott to cut short this friendly chit-chat. In his usual
manner, he was listening politely to what was being said, showing great interest. Finally, it fell to Uncle Alexander to make
the first move. He stood up, glanced meaningfully at us and
announced, "Well . . ." The word hung in the air while a flush
crept slowly up my face. Uncle Alexander bestowed upon us
something between a smile and a leer. "I think it's time." From
around the room came winks and giggles. But it broke the impasse so that we could make our exit in a spirit of fun. I gave
silent thanks to my waggish uncle.

As we went into our room, Elliott tried to close and lock
the door. It refused to close. After a couple of tries, he gave the
door a mighty slam. This time it closed. It also jammed so
tightly we could not open it again.

"Now you're a prisoner, Elliott Roosevelt, in my bridal chamber."

"Damn!"

"Darling, what a thing to say." His arms made any other remark impossible.

The jammed door did not give us real concern until later,
when Elliott decided to get a glass of milk. Grabbing the knob,
he pulled and huffed and swore. We tried the doors leading out
to the terrace. Locked for the winter. I thought of those old
Western serials, when the heroine was trapped in the abandoned
mine with a fuse of dynamite sputtering. What did they do?
They made you wait 'til next Saturday to find out.

"Elliott, we could call the fire department."

"Humph."

"Do you know, dear, that in less than twelve hours we have
been chased by a bull, I almost lost my face in a mud pack, you
went to sleep at one of the crucial moments of your life, and
now we're locked in our honeymoon suite? What I'd like to
know is, how did you go through those other four marriages and
survive?" He shushed me with a kiss, then by using the telephone, we were finally able to alert a maintenance man, who

came and unwedged the door and showed Elliott how to close
and lock it properly.

After such a keyed-up wedding day, my batteries suddenly
drained. I wanted to crumple like a rag doll and sleep for a week.
At the very least, we should be able to look forward to a lazy
morning lying in bed until eleven and having a languid lunch.
No such luck. The sun was barely up when Daddy was banging on the door. "You'll have to get up early. We're driving to
Victoria."

"Who's we?"

"You and Elliott and me. I've arranged for two suites in the
Empress Hotel."

I dragged myself over to the suitcase, muttering, "Egad."

During the ninety-mile drive, Elliott and I missed all the
scenery. We were fast asleep in the back seat.

Victoria is one of the picture-book cities of Canada. The influence of British architecture, style and taste is apparent everywhere. People of Victoria have a zest for pomp and ceremony.
You see British colonial manners and conservatism, but without
so much old-school snobbery.

The Empress is the fine old hotel in this famed city, sitting
across the street from the bustling harbor and commanding a
magnificent view. Liners, tankers, and freighters, plying the
coastal trade routes, put in regularly at its doorstep. There they
disgorge every type of cargo from the smelly tinned kippers
Britishers so dearly love to coils of tarred rope and flocks of
sightseeing visitors. Tourists off the ships prowl Victoria's quaint
streets and shops, and annually leave a rich pile of American
dollars in its cash drawers. This city of the great Northwest is the
kind of place which, once visited, draws you back again and
again.

The management of the Empress welcomed us with fuss and
fanfare. My tiredness vanished as we walked across the carpeted lobby, a place of high ceilings, potted plants, massive lamps,
and period pieces. Elliott and I had a corner suite looking out
onto the harbor, with flowers and champagne from the powers
that ran the establishment; Daddy was in an adjoining room.
When the luggage had been brought up and we were alone
again, at last, Elliott carefully locked the door between the two

1. June 1961. Mrs. Roosevelt on her first visit to us in Minneapolis receives a plaque from the Police Benevolent Association with a medallion of President Roosevelt in the center. She is wearing a silk print dress and the necklace I remembered from my first meeting with her after Elliott and I were married. (*Chic Photos*)

1a. June 1961. Mrs. Roosevelt holds court in our garden. Ford, top left, Gretchen, far right, and little David at Granmere's knee. (*The Minneapolis Star and Tribune Co.*)

2. June 1961. The Director of the Minneapolis Institute of Art, Carl Weinhardt, chats with his honored guest, Mrs. Franklin D. Roosevelt, at the dinner preceding the reception opening the Rooseveltiana Art Show. (Frank Agar, photographer)

3. Same occasion. Reception at Minneapolis Institute of Art. In the receiving line are, left to right, Elliott Roosevelt, Ford Roosevelt, Gretchen Roosevelt, the authoress, Mrs. FDR (honored guest) and Mrs. Carl Weinhardt. (Frank Agar, photographer)

4. Elliott and I watch Eleanor Roosevelt greet one of the guests. (*Frank Agar, photographer*)

5. June 1963. The Roosevelt children on one of the few occasions they were together after their mother's death. This was taken in Hyde Park the day John and Anne's daughter Nina was married. From right to left, Elliott, Jimmy, Anna, John, and Franklin. (*Jay Te Winburn, Jr.*)

6. July 1963. Elliott teaching David to handle himself on a horse. David's comment, "Haven't you got anything smaller?" *(Nat Harrison)*

7. October 1963. The "Eleanor Roosevelt Commemorative Stamp" ceremony in the Rose Garden at the White House. Elliott and I were thrilled that President Kennedy asked us to stand on his right. Postmaster General John Gronouski is making the presentation and on his left is Ambassador Adlai Stevenson, close friend and admirer of Mrs. Roosevelt. In the background are Walter Reuther, Congressman James Roosevelt and Mrs. Anna Rosenberg among others. *(Cecil W. Stoughton)*

8. Same occasion, the "Stamp" ceremony after the presentation. President Kennedy is congratulating Elliott and me on our Florida tan. Unfortunately we were not close enough for Jimmy (right rear) and Anna Halsted (extreme right rear) to hear what we were talking about. (*White House Photo*)

9. November 19, 1963. President John F. Kennedy, on his last visit to Miami Beach shortly before his death, was honored at a Democratic party dinner. Senator George Smathers is on his right. Elliott was directly behind him on the dais. (*Edgar R. Ron*)

10. March 1964. Elliott was the guest speaker at an Israel Bond dinner held in Kansas City, Missouri. Our good friends, the former President and Mrs. Harry S. Truman were honored guests, and we had a wonderful visit with them in their home in Independence, Missouri. President Truman is on Elliott's left and Mrs. Truman on his right. I am at the far left-hand corner of the picture. (*Mo-Bee Photo Service*)

11. April 1964. This was publicity earned when Elliott was a candidate for Democratic National Committeeman for Florida. We visited the new Seaquarium in St. Petersburg Beach, and spoke personally to each "mammal" guest in the establishment—some of them not too eager to shake hands.

12. May 1964. Our beloved David Grey, who is Eleanor Roosevelt's uncle, spoke in behalf of Elliott's candidacy for Democratic National Committeeman by saying, "If you want quality in the man you elect, look to one like my nephew who has it bred into his bones." This took place at a Democratic women's luncheon in Sarasota, Florida.

13. May 1964. Former President Harry S. Truman along with Mrs. Truman, Elliott and me, inducting us into the rigors of campaigning.

14. December 1964. A family affair—Elliott Roosevelt in one of his all too few periods of relaxation as a family man. He is completely happy when he surrounds himself with young people. Clockwise: Gretchen, Ford, Harpur Evoy, Mom, David, and Daddy in the middle.

15. Decmber 1964. "What is so rare as a" Gingerbread House? Gretchen Roosevelt and her mother make this an annual affair as a Christmas centerpiece.

suites, uncorked a bottle of champagne and set out two glasses. Then we sat together on the couch, Elliott's arm around me. "How wonderful this is, honey," I was saying. "I can't believe it is really happening . . ."

Suddenly the hall door opened and in strode Daddy. There had been no knock. "Can't understand it," Folger Peabody said, "somebody locked that door between the suites."

Daddy had big plans for our day. First a sightseeing tour of Victoria for Elliott, then a press conference . . .

"A press conference?"

"Certainly, the papers are dying for an interview."

Elliott remarked that after we had gone to so much trouble to take out a quiet license and have a private wedding, he did not see why he should have to be exposed to the press now.

"But you're married, now," Daddy said. "You're married."

"That doesn't make any difference," Elliott said. "The press will find us soon enough, on their own. They don't need our help. I rather think we should relax, and not waste this little time we have together in staging press conferences."

I could sense my father's terrible disappointment. His scheme sprang, I felt, from deeper motives than the simple desire to keep the public informed. Folger Peabody wanted to take charge, conduct the press conference, play the benign but strong mover of people and famous sons-in-law. In the past it had always been this way; in the past, Daddy made decisions for those around him. He had been able to influence my former husband, Milt. Under his stern and patronizing guidance, my mother had been rendered so self-insufficient she could not even be depended on to ride the bus alone. Now, he was becoming aware that Elliott was much more knowledgeable than he, about such things as press conferences; that Elliott had his own mind and will and intended to use it, and did not intend to remain a sideline spectator if Daddy attempted to work his overbearing way with me.

A short time later we went to the dining room for a formal lunch. The room was gigantic, with a soaring ceiling, snowy tablecloths, and chairs upholstered in cherry-red velvet. Waiters and captains wore English livery, with knee breeches and white stockings, buckled shoes, white shirts and livery coats. For dinner, they donned more formal tailcoats. Each piece of table linen was immaculately clean and freshly pressed, and the entire dining room seemed to shine with reflected light from silverware. In the old-world style, the maitre d'hotel and captain made frequent inquiries about the quality of the service, bowing first and asking permission to speak. With each service, the waiters bowed low from the waist. I had seen this type of thing before, but rarely: Elliott knew the ritual thoroughly from his many trips to England and the Continent, and handled all the formalities for us. Daddy watched my new husband take full command of the luncheon and said nothing.

That afternoon, at high tea, another male companion of mine was not nearly so skilled. An old friend from Seattle, Marly Holm, had a son, Chuckie, in private school in Victoria. Chuckie was a boyhood friend of my son, Ford. I called the school and asked if he could be permitted to come out with me. Even over the telephone, I could feel a ripple of excitement go through the "Why, of course, Mrs. Roosevelt. Chuckie would be delighted."

Chuckie was delighted. His first words were, "Gosh, Aunt Patty, do you know who I just finished a paper on today?"

"Who, Chuckie?"

"Your brother-in-law."

"I don't have a brother-in-law that you might read about."

"I mean your brother that was President."

"Chuckie, he would have been my father-in-law."

"Gee, I thought you married his brother."

High tea was served every afternoon in the lobby of the Empress. We went through all the ritual of pouring, and guests took their tea in fine porcelain cups, with little napkins, crumpets and English muffins. Chuckie attacked the goodies like a ravenous wolf. Crumbs dusting his chin, jacket and the carpeted floor, he stuffed crumpets into his mouth with both hands and went at the muffins as if he hadn't had a meal in three weeks. I was wishing I had taken him out for steak instead of high tea. While the other guests politely looked away, Chuckie told Elliott about his school paper. Elliott explained patiently that Franklin D. Roosevelt had been his father, not his brother. "I think you should get that paper back and correct it, Chuckie," he said. "An error of that nature might shock a few of your teachers."

We spent three days in Victoria, and each day my gratitude to

Daddy grew for thinking of such a honeymoon. While it was terribly brief and far from private, the days were idyllic. Elliott's spirits soared as we wandered through cobblestone streets, poked into antique shops, and went clop-clopping over the city in a rented pony cart. Granville Street was so cluttered with antique shops you wondered if there could be any fine porcelain, crystal or silver pieces left in Europe or England. We found that our tastes complemented each other's. Elliott has a passion for antiques, especially inlaid woods and silver; my fancy runs more to porcelain and crystal. The things we each contributed to our home later on would prove to be astonishingly compatible.

The ferry boat to Seattle docks across the street from the Empress. On our fourth day of married life we boarded her for the eight-hour ride to my home city. Although the sea breeze had a cutting edge of cold, the day sparkled with sunshine. We arrived in Seattle fresh and invigorated.

The Camlin Hotel was owned by friends of my family and was a favorite stopping place for Daddy. We drove to the motor entrance. The manager was waiting to greet us, looking worried.

"You will have to come in the side entrance," he said. "The lobby is full of photographers and newsmen."

Elliott turned green.

We scurried in like thieves. By now, however, the prospect of a news conference was beginning to intrigue me. I have always found interviews exciting, and love the give and take of sharp questioning.

"You just don't know," Elliott said, "what these newspaper people can do to you."

"What can they do? We're married. We have nothing to be ashamed of. After all the bad publicity we've had, I think it's time we started getting a good press for a change."

"Honey, just take my word for it. You don't want to see the press. Let it die down. Later on, perhaps . . . My God, in a year or so we won't be news any more."

Again I found myself on the fire escape, avoiding newsmen. This time we climbed the inside stairway of the motor hotel. At the second floor we got on the elevator. Again there were adjoining suites, one for us and one for Daddy. As we walked in, the telephone rang. I answered.

The society editor of the Seattle *Post-Intelligencer*, Laura Emory Gilmore, was begging me for an interview. I had known her for years. Not only that, Elliott's sister Anna had given her her first job on the paper when John Boettiger, Anna's second husband, was publisher. She was waiting in the lobby, and thought she should have an exclusive with the bride and groom. I told her I would talk it over with Elliott and call her back. "No," Elliott said.

The phone rang again. This time it was Dorothy Brant Brazier, society editor of the Seattle *Times*. I had worked closely with her when I was editor and publisher of the Seattle Social *Blue Book*. Dorothy was sputtering. "If you give Laura an exclusive, I'll never forgive you, Patty. After all, I did a great deal for you while you were in Seattle. I've always been good to you."

By now, Elliott was too tired to argue. "All right," he said, "tell them to come up one at a time."

The papers hit the street that afternoon, and the phone started ringing off the wall. Old friends and acquaintances who, I knew, had cut me to pieces in the past, suddenly had become paragons of warmth and congeniality. We must come see them . . . dinner party . . . the club . . . just an afternoon get-together, dear . . . What it really amounted to, I knew, was a concerted pitch to lure Elliott Roosevelt into the salons of Seattle. Publicity in the society pages for a change, instead of two columns of lurid type on the front, had magically given us respectability.

During our two days in my hometown, we kept it down to small social gatherings with people who had been, and still were, my friends; people who, knowing me, had reserved judgment about my romance with Elliott Roosevelt until all the evidence was in. Most of them had no strong feelings at all, except perhaps their surprise and delight at the charm which my new husband could display in our host's living room, or over drinks and dinner. With a catch in my throat, I remembered Billy Goodheart's assessment of this fascinating man: "Elliott Roosevelt puts his pants on one leg at a time." As host or guest, he had the touch which puts people at ease, and makes them laugh.

For all the publicity and the new mood of Seattle acceptability, there was one home in which I was not welcome: my own. Mother, I knew, would not receive me. She did not call. My sisters made no attempt to reach me. Except for Daddy and Uncle Alexander, my immediate family no longer recognized that I existed. It gave me pain. I debated whether or not to call, and risk rebuff and more hurt. Under the curcumstances, my call could serve no purpose. The next move was theirs.

Elliott and I left from the Seattle airport November 10 on a flight to Denver. So much had happened in the three years since I had last gone away from Seattle on a plane, with children and gifts, lonely and uncertain and scared. The future offered no more certainty now than it had then, but for the first time in my life the present had an anchor. But mercifully, life keeps tomorrow hidden from us; if I had known what lay ahead, I might have been tempted to look backward.

Beside me, my anchor put his head back and soon fell fast asleep. He was my love, now and forever.

7

Roosevelts, Rockefellers, and Santa Claus

Most newlyweds manage to set up housekeeping in small quarters
with reasonable tranquillity. Not so the new family of Roosevelts.
Our venture into domestic life in Denver was nearly as hectic
as our courtship. Unlike most bridegrooms, Elliott had taken on
a full family, and at low tide in his financial life. The entire
crowd, Elliott and me, the four children and our maid, packed
into a furnished apartment in the Versailles, a building owned by
Cuban dictator Fulgencio Batista. We had a living room, two
bedrooms, library, dining area, kitchen, two baths and four closets. People were spilling over one another. Tempers quickly
frayed. Elliott made an heroic show of outward calm, with magi-
cal success.

Our bedroom was cramped and had a tiny half-bathroom attached. The children, accustomed to living alone with me, would
come bursting in at will, which nettled Elliott. In his first official
crackdown as master of the house, he made each youngster knock
ten times at the bedroom door while he sat inside repeating,
"Come in." The children have never again entered unbidden.

Reaction to our marriage, meanwhile, was coursing through the
Roosevelt family, mostly in shock waves. Nobody knew much
about me beyond the wild rumors which had circulated during
the months before our wedding. One juicy morsel was that Elliott
and I had lived together illicitly in Mexico. This was preposterous.

I think many of the relatives pictured me as a seductive vamp in spangled tights who had lured him into a matrimonial trap. Some people expressed the view to Mrs. Roosevelt that Elliott was highly disturbed and guilt-ridden, grasping desperately for security. An old friend of hers from Seattle described me as "completely unstable."

My first social exposure to "family" as the new wife was dinner with Elliott's son Bill Roosevelt, then twenty-eight, and his wife Karyl in their beautiful big house in the Cherry Hill section of Denver. Bill, the son of Elliott and his first wife, Elizabeth Donner, was an heir to the Donner fortune. He shared with other heirs their grandfather's estate valued at many millions of dollars.

Despite the happiness we shared as newlyweds, Elliott was going through a private kind of hell, trying to recover from the financial shellacking he had taken. He wrote to his mother that during the summer I had sacrificed to help him get on his feet. "We have begun to see daylight, but nothing startlingly successful." He assured Mrs. Roosevelt that despite reports he was not drinking heavily, or even lightly.

"There is nothing you can do to alleviate my situation," he told his mother. "Don't feel sorry for me, because this is a great challenge. I think I can lick it, and if I do it will make a great difference for the future of not only myself but all connected or interested in me . . . I do hope that fate will give me a chance of seeing you in the not too distant future, as I do love you with all my heart. I know I'm terrible about writing or communicating, but when one is fighting with one's back to the wall it is hard to write and wrong to share those difficulties . . ."

Mrs. Roosevelt replied with a poignant letter in her wavering handwriting, by now, because of her failing health, all but illegible. She said it was tragic that apparently the only way she could help any of her children was to die and leave them her estate, but that lately she had been in very good health so this, too, seemed remote. Unknown to the family, she already had the beginnings of a bone marrow deficiency which was to lead to her death in less than two years.

One day in Denver, I sat beneath the hair dryer and poured out my heart in a letter to this overwhelming woman whom I had never met. I told her that her hopes for Elliott were mine, too, and that I would work very hard to make him a good wife, and give him the security we all needed for happy and rewarding lives. ". . . The other thought I have in my mind and my heart for you in this letter is my promise to you that all of my life I will spend every thought and every action on making my dearest Elliott the happiest most contented person alive. He has given me so much love and understanding in our short time together that my only fear is our years as husband and wife are too short to give in return what he so richly deserves. I can only try to do my best each day. I know that without him, and his love and care I am nothing. He is my life and my only love . . . I don't want you for a minute to feel you must make any move, as a result of this letter. I merely wrote because of the joy I feel in telling Elliott's mother of my love for her son."

I was delighted and grateful to receive a letter from Mrs. Roosevelt, dated December 21, in which she thanked me for writing and said it was a sweet thing to do. She mentioned that with Bill, Karyl, Tony, and Joanne, I had already won my place because of their new-found relationship with their father which they felt had come about because of me. She told me Elliott loved children and would be a good father to all of my little ones and that with David, especially, because of his age they would have a close relationship all of their lives. She said that it had always been difficult for Elliott to stand alone and that she was so glad I was with him because she felt from my letter that I intended to make him happy. She cautioned me that this could not be so unless he made me happy but she felt this he had done and her hopes and prayers went to us both. She finished by telling of her meeting in Denver in the spring and the hope that she could see us both then. She closed with her deep gratitude for my letter.

Elliott was quick to get a taste of domestic crisis and I was amazed to see how rocklike he was when it came.

Shortly after Thanksgiving we decided to take the children to Canon City, Colorado, to visit little Jimmy in the Benedictine School. The morning we were to leave Ford was in the kitchen fixing his own breakfast and accidentally spilled a frying pan of hot grease down his leg. In the panic, I went to the bathroom looking for Vaseline. The maid offered some of her hair grease. I decided not to put anything on it, but instead dumped him into a bathtub of cold water. Elliott took charge, rushed Ford to the doctor's office and held his head in his lap while the burn was being treated. The doctor said our quick action and the cold water probably saved the boy's leg from being terribly scarred and shriveled. Ford then insisted on making the three-hour trip to Canon City to see his brother, riding in the back seat with his leg propped up.

A month after our marriage, Elliott and I went off on an idyllic honeymoon to the Ozark Mountains retreat of the Winthrop Rockefellers. It was to give us a glimpse into the private life of this fabulously wealthy, personable and troubled man which few but the most intimate associates ever see.

It all began when I learned that Win Rockefeller's wife Jay was coming to Denver to lecture on mental illness for the Junior League. She was a member of the National Board of Mental Health. I had known her in Seattle as Jeannette Edris, whose father owned the Olympic Hotel. Winthrop Rockefeller, one of the five Rockefeller brothers, was her fourth husband. Winthrop's previous wife Barbara had been the celebrated Bobo Sears, the coal miner's daughter who received from him one of the biggest divorce settlements in history.

When she arrived in Denver, Jay returned my telephone call. She told me she had read the gossip columns which said we had been living in Mexico before our marriage, and sympathized. "Don't worry, Patty, people love to gossip. Just hold your head high and rise above it." She said that she and Win had run the same gamut of an ugly press, and lived to laugh about it. My own feelings and heart were still too bruised by our publicity barrage to really understand her advice. Seeing my deep distress, Jay who is a wonderfully warm person with a great deal of empathy, suggested that we get away and forget our problems. "Come up to Win-Rock for a week and play with us." We accepted, and a week later took off in our Cessna for Arkansas.

Win-Rock was atop Patechek Mountain, about fifteen minutes' flying time from Little Rock. It wasn't on the navigation charts. To find the place, you flew into the vicinity and searched for his private airfield. Looking down from a sky clear as glass, the panorama of Arkansas hills rolled away on all sides, splashed with the breath-taking colors of fall. The hollows had a darker cast, bringing up the hilltops in sharp three-dimension. Meandering over the slopes were thin brown cattle trails and tracks cut through the woods by the Forest Service as fire lanes. Here and there in the distance there rose a thin curl of blue smoke, as farmers and woodsmen burned first against the autumn chill.

Elliott found the field in early afternoon and we banked off for an easy descent, nosing finally onto the end of the runway for a landing. We saw a cluster of outbuildings, a hangar, a windsock billowing in the light mountain breeze. Parked off to one side was the Rockefeller private twin-engine Beechcraft in which Jay took the wives of Win-Rock employees twice a week for shopping in Little Rock. Across the field raced a bright red station wagon, kicking up a trail of dust. It braked to a stop beside our plane and Jay climbed out, tall, tweedy, with bold features, a prominent nose and eyes made dominant by strong glasses. "Hi, how was your flight?"

We unloaded the plane and stashed our luggage in the wagon, then Jay drove over a road that looped through rolling high pastureland and patches of woods. Grazing in the fields were the famous Rockefeller herds of Santa Gertrudis cattle, a breed of cattle developed in Texas by the world-renowned King Ranch. Winthrop Rockefeller had bought a complete herd of pure-breds, and now ran nearly four hundred head, including mother cows and bulls for an artificial insemination operation.

"I'm giving you my studio cottage. I think you'll be comfortable there," Jay said.

We passed a number of houses as we drove, all built on the highest level of the ranch and commanding a superb view of the Ozarks. There were guest houses, Jay explained, built of native stone, with shake roofs and the high-peaked style of many houses in the Pacific Northwest. Win-Rock was a popular place for students to become experts in animal husbandry. They came here from all over the world to inspect Rockefeller's livestock and modern breeding techniques. Each week two or three groups arrived and on occasion several hundred were here at a time.

Win-Rock covered approximately some 1200 acres, surrounded by cast-iron pipe fencing which, alone, cost about $500,000. The ranch had its own fire department with two engines, its own telephone exchange and directory, plus an elaborate security system with roving guards and police radio monitoring.

Jay's "studio cottage" made me catch my breath. She ushered us in and, while a houseman unloaded the station wagon, took us on a quick tour. You walked in on the second level. Downstairs was her studio, with a kiln for her ceramics and pottery and easels and oils, provided all an artist could need. This area was small. The rest of the "cottage" had thirty-foot ceilings and a solid wall of glass looking out over the Ozarks; in the distance, we saw the gaudy display of fall color blend into a line of blue hills. The floors were marble, the couches enormous, the rooms done in persimmon highlights. In the bedroom, a bar was filled with every kind of liquor and cocktail mix from gin-and-tonic to old-fashioneds. The room was the size of a double tennis court. The bed was actually two king-size beds made into one. I took one long look at that beckoning comfort and said, "Well, this is the end of me."

"What do you mean?" Elliott said.

"I'll never get out of that bed. I'll sleep for a month."

Jay laughed. "Win wants you to see the farm in the morning," she said.

The bathroom was another shock: it was as large as a normal-size bedroom, all pink and white, with fur rugs. Two toilets were set into frosted-glass cubicles and equipped with telephones, so that one could talk under any circumstances. A wall-to-wall vanity was fully stocked with electric razors, soaps and mouth washes, plus lotions, notions, powders and creams in every fragrance Elizabeth Arden makes. There was a sunken bathtub, approximately ten by fifteen feet and sloped at one end. It had a tiled aperture in the wall which contained a round sponge the size of a gymnasium medicine ball. We never found out what that sponge was for. If the thing was ever filled with water, it could drown you. Later on we threw it at each other. The velvety towels were as large as sheets; a closet was crammed with pure linen sheets and thousands of down pillows.

Elated by our surroundings, we went on another inspection tour. Jay had suggested I wear dinner slacks so we changed and drove over to the main house a quarter of a mile away in a car which had been provided for us. Set like the other houses on the brow of the mountain, the main structure was built on several levels, semi-modern with a high-peaked roof. Bright moonlight pierced the darkness and spotlighted the front door. The living room was an impression of low lights, broad couches, antiques, and wide plank flooring brought to a glassy polish. The Rockefellers were waiting.

I had never met Winthrop Rockefeller, but Elliott had been introduced to him a few times. He was tall and heavy set, a bit inclined to overweight but handsome, his hair thinning and brownish. The face that came smiling toward me had a freshly scrubbed look, the eyes were lively and interesting, the handshake firm. "We're very glad you could come," he said. "Congratulations on your marriage. I hope you will be very happy."

Elliott knew Winthrop's brother, Nelson. He did not consider Winthrop as gregarious as either the New York Governor or David Rockefeller, but felt he rather tended to be more like John D., III. We had cocktails in the living room, exchanging polite small talk. Then as we prepared to go to the dining room, Rockefeller picked up a telephone at his elbow and said, "This is Mr. Rockefeller. I am going from the living room to the dining room." Elliott and I exchanged quizzical glances.

Winthrop Rockefeller, we were to learn, had an obsessive fear of a member of his family being kidnaped. Lately, he had received threats, causing him to hire extra security guards and mount regular patrols on the property. The fact that a few years before his ex-wife, Bobo, had taken their son, Winthrop, Jr., off the ranch, stirring a great legal fuss, did not make him feel any more secure. Now, this man of vast material riches feared to move from one room to the next without notifying someone. To go from the bathroom to the bedroom, he would pick up the telephone and call the guard. "This is Mr. Rockefeller . . ." They knew precisely how many steps it was between the two rooms, and that the boss would call back in exactly X minutes with the word he had arrived safely.

To reach the dining room we went outdoors over a kind of footbridge, crossing a chasm with a waterfall. The dining room was enormous, with refectory tables to accommodate five hundred. Our table stood ready off to one side, a magnificent but lonely looking thing of linens and silver and crystal, attended by a butler and two waiters in dark livery. There was a sterling silver serving cart, domed dish covers, a silver warming oven. Our voices echoed as we took our places. Beyond us stood ranks of silent dining tables. It was like having dinner in an empty gymnasium. The six-course meal included a bouillon soup, Win-Rock beef carved into thin slices with creamy horseradish sauce, brook trout, delightful salad, a dessert of fresh strawberries with whipped cream. There were wines with each course, champagne with dessert, coffee and liqueurs. Elliott and Winthrop talked cattle, Jay and I talked old times in Seattle. The service was swift and silent. I felt pampered, served, spoiled, and guarded. The clamor of our Denver apartment, the nagging worries of money and the future, faded away and Patty Peabody Roosevelt reveled in long forgotten splendor. After dinner we drove slowly back to the guest cottage, feeling giggly. A full moon rose over the Ozarks in a cluster of light clouds.

Next morning we slept late, then spent the rest of the time lounging, looking out the window, and taking baths in that fabulous bathtub. I tried most of the cosmetics. We spent nearly an hour searching for a huge eight-foot bolster which had been on the bed the afternoon before. The thing had vanished.

We never saw a servant, and yet lunch appeared at noon, fresh linens were brought out, dirty dishes removed. I had the strange feeling we were being cared for by a ghost. In the middle of the afternoon Jay called.

"Are you two all right?"

"Yes, we're fine. We can't find the bolster."

"The what?"

"That big bolster on the bed. It's vanished. A ghost took it. Where do they hide a thing that size?"

Jay laughed. "That's a secret."

"Do you want us?"

"No. We have some agricultural people here, so we will dine with them. Have a good time, we'll see you tomorrow."

We went to the main house for dinner, but did not see the Rockefellers. Elliott and I ate together in the huge dining room. I felt ridiculous, using all that space.

On the third day we were up early and Jay and Winthrop met

us at eleven o'clock in his office at the main barn. On the way
Elliott turned on the radio monitor in our car and heard the
now-familiar voice: "This is Mr. Rockefeller, I am going from the
veterinary's to the office . . ."

The Rockefeller barns were communities within themselves,
modern, fully equipped, spotless. There were aluminum watering
troughs, tiled hallways, an animal hospital done in antiseptic
green with a full-time veterinarian. Even the straw looked expensive. Winthrop's "office" was more like a living room, with
soft couches and leather-topped desks. He showed Elliott his files
and discussed problems of shipping semen throughout the world
and having it retain its potency.

Each year Rockefeller put out a catalog of his cattle sale,
and from five hundred to a thousand buyers would come to Win-
Rock. The master of the ranch used the opportunity to recoup
some of his expenses: if the visiting buyer wished to eat or drink,
he bought it from the Rockefeller concession.

We spent two hours in the office, finishing with a lunch of
sandwiches, then Winthrop took us for a tour of the ranch, the
show barn, the fire house, the pens and training area. Win was
tripling the size of his security force and fire department, and
rebuilding part of the biggest barn, which had burned.

The training area sickened me. Here, cattle with rings in their
noses were hooked to a long, winch-drawn cable. This was to
train them to walk around the show ring. When they fell, the
cable kept pulling, dragging the bellowing animal through the
dust until it regained its footing. At the end of the course, some
cattle would be bleeding from scraped knees and torn noses.

In the laboratories and clinic, technicians wore starched white
coats and the veterinarian sported a refraction light strapped onto
his forehead. We might as well have been in the Mayo Clinic.

Winthrop explained to us the artificial insemination process.
Containers similar to milk cans were packed with dry ice, to
store vials of semen for shipment. Nearby was a place where they
brought the bulls to collect it. The equipment there consisted
mainly of a dummy cow built onto a saw horse, complete with
ribbons on the cow's head and a special spray to arouse the bull.
Elliott looked at me and grinned. I blushed.

On the fifth day we left Win-Rock, with Jay waving at us from the runway, and headed back for Denver by way of Tulsa. There we made a two-day stopover to visit another old friend of mine from Seattle, Anne Smith, who had married a lumberman named Dewey Bartlett. Her husband later was to be governor of Oklahoma.

Back in Denver, the children gave us a boisterous welcome, and the cook had a very special dinner ready for Elliott. "Oh, God," I said, "we're home."

In my heart, of course, I was delighted to be home. Christmas was coming on, and it would be our first together as a new family. The children were ecstatic. David in particular had assumed a trance-like appearance, rather like one of the Seven Dwarfs. Christmas was not only Christmas but his birthday as well.

Even at age three the commercialism of the holiday had gotten him and he knew that Santa Claus would bring presents not only for Christmas but for his birthday. I had always celebrated this double event with both Christmas and birthday trees. We later changed his birthday celebration to coincide with that of his daddy on September 23.

A particularly amusing and yet heart-rending incident introduced Elliott and David to their new roles of father and son. Our little boy was all man at three years of age and had been toilet trained for over a year—with nary a slip—however, with the fever and excitement surrounding him, this control had occasion one night to vanish. We heard a very forceful knock on our bedroom door one morning—a week before Christmas. Elliott thundered, "Come in!" Jimmy, Ford, and Gretchen confronted us with the statement, "Daddy, David wet his bed last night." Again, a peal of thunder from Elliott. "David did what?" he barked. At this point, from the foot of the bed peered a little face streaked with tears. David said, "Me did, Daddy, me wet my bed." With that the tears changed to a torrential rain and he came closer, wearing the evidence. I looked at Elliott in horror for he issued one terse command and started to get out of bed.

"David, come here, young man," he said with convincing finality.

In our cramped quarters, there was little place for David to run and hide. With convulsive gasps and a world of entreaty in his voice, he stumbled over to Elliott and managed to gulp, "Yes, Daddy."

"Take down your pants, young man—this instant—and bend over!"

All of a sudden he assumed the new visage of a not so kind and understanding husband. My mind scrambled away from the horrible thought that he might be thinking of a spanking. It just as quickly ran back with the knowledge that a spanking was already in progress—three hard whacks. Elliott's hand more than covered the area he was aiming for and this darling youngest child of mine nearly crashed into the wall from its force. At this point, David wasn't the only tearful one. I couldn't believe my eyes. Elliott had loved this little baby so intensely—to think he would turn on him with no other explanation but "bend over and take down your pants." What I didn't know, of course, was that David and Elliott were in complete accord as to the reason for the punishment and each respected the other for his tolerance. Elliott let him cry for two or three minutes and then said in a more gentle fashion. "All right, David, that's enough crying now. You've felt sorry for yourself long enough. Stop the tears right now." Gulping in carbon dioxide and little oxygen, David woefully managed to pick up his pants and limp painfully from the room, promising in a rasping aside, "me won't do that any more, Daddy."

The day continued in its usual hectic way and I had my hands full with Christmas thoughts and Christmas giving so that the incident of the morning escaped my memory. It was to be brought back only too vividly the next morning at about the same hour. This time we were awakened with only a small knock, and again the thundering command, "Come in!" To my horror once again appeared the little tousled birthday boy saying in grave and lucid tones, "Me did it again, Daddy, me sorry." Before Elliott had a chance to collect his thoughts, David took down his little pajama pants and bent over in front of his father. He had not only accepted the realization of why he was punished yesterday, but today recognized that another rebuke was in store for him. Elliott gamely reached over and gave him three hard whacks. David pulled up his pants and looked at Elliott with drowning brown eyes.

"Thank you, Daddy."

This brought an end to this chapter of David's babyhood.

Elliott had so many names on his Christmas list that the prospect of finding something appropriate for them all gave me the jitters. To begin with, they were people I had never met and, for the most part, harbored no feelings for me but polite hostility. I set my jaw and did my best, following, with Elliott's advice, the gift-giving patterns established long before I came upon the scene. For Mrs. Roosevelt, I bought an assortment of Elizabeth Arden products which I had heard she enjoyed using. There was, also, a Miss Laura Delano whose name meant nothing to me . . . she traditionally received a bottle of Chanel ⅝5. For Anna, who was a birdwatcher . . . a bird book; and so on through Johnny and James and Franklin, Jr., and their wives and children. I had had three of Elliott's children to buy presents for whom I still did not really know—Tony, Chandler, and David—and suddenly I, also, had eight grandchildren. In addition, there were my parents and two sisters, none of them really close to me any more but with whom I would continue to preserve the amenities.

At a delicatessen, I noticed a sign advertising caviar for $38 a pound. What a fine gift for Elliott, I thought, and ordered a pound delivered to the apartment. When I got home I asked the maid if the caviar had been delivered.

"Caviar? I didn't see no caviar."

We searched and finally found it in the refrigerator, where she had placed it. Small wonder she failed to recognize the expensive delicacy. The pound of caviar was contained in a tiny waxed ice cream carton. I gift-wrapped it as best I could for presentation to my husband Christmas morning.

Mrs. Roosevelt, who shopped for her huge family all year round, sent a big box to us. For Elliott, there were shirts from Brooks Brothers, ties, socks and sweaters, all individually wrapped by his loving mother. This should have given me an indication of her nature for it had been traditional all my life to spend hours, even months, wrapping sometimes insignificant presents in beautiful, stylized fashion. Yet from Mrs. Roosevelt there were boxes with plain little knobby bows with large Christmas cards suspended from them, and the messages of love and cheer in her handwriting. I am sure the paper had been used over and over as there were creases showing the size of another package and another gift. For the children, she sent a sweater apiece, each a size too small, for me, a pair of black kid gloves, a size and a half too large, and three pairs of stockings, two sizes too small.

Our own Christmas was frugal, of necessity, that year and yet never were presents exchanged more lovingly. David received from his daddy a large stuffed horse on wheels, which he has to this day. For Jimmy—boxes of Ivy League clothing desperately desired for his new life at boarding school. For Ford there was a sled and a pair of thick mittens. For Gretchen—a sled and pretty embroidered mittens. For me there was a beautiful simply mounted ring Elliott had had made of some stones given him by his mother many years before. It was my first gift of jewelry.

Despite the miscues, Christmas 1960 was one of the happiest I had ever experienced. Some of Elliott's grandchildren visited us and, with none of the antipathy of grownups, accepted their grandfather's new wife at face value, with love and affection. We visited friends around the city. We cooked a big turkey and the new Roosevelt family sat down together to enjoy it.

Mine were mixed feelings, joyous and at the same time wistful. Looking around at the faces in our little Denver apartment, at Elliott's and the children's, a sudden awareness crossed my mind:

We were all displaced persons.

8

"So, You're the Latest One?"

Life had begun afresh for me. The doors were opened into a breath-taking world. The love I shared with Elliott Roosevelt had a depth and maturity I had never thought possible. Each of us was old enough and wise enough now to know that you build love on kindness, day by day, with respect and concern. Petty things so upsetting to the very young or insecure were to be fought against, selfish pride swallowed. The reward was a new awareness of love, complete and self-assured. For me, and for Elliott, there could be no greater security than this. But as the glorious days and weeks of new marriage unfolded, another less comforting realization also worked at the back of my mind. Soon I would face the test of being introduced formally into the Roosevelt family as Elliott's fifth wife.

In the public eye, our courtship and marriage had no luster, no softness. Following so closely the noisy breakup of Elliott and Minnewa, it had made grist for sensation hunters, columnists, and parlor gossips. Awakening at night in the darkness with my husband beside me, the prospect of having to carry such a handicap while trying to win spurs in a family of great reserve and strong-minded personalities, sent a chill down my back. By his example during my first meeting with his son and daughter-in-law, Bill and Karyl, Elliott had made clear the ground rules. He would give moral support, but I had to pull my own wagon.

This was actually a fine compliment, for it reflected his conviction that I could handle myself. His confidence served to rein-
force my own to some degree.

Like a fighter in training, I was given some preliminary opportunities to spar. There came an evening with Harry and Ginny
Coombs, who had been mutual friends of Elliott's and Minnewa's
and also knew Mrs. Roosevelt and Franklin, Jr. We went into
that one with Elliott in a surly mood, carrying a chip at the
thought that they would reject me. Ironically, his grouch was the
only damper on the evening. The rest of us got along splendidly,
so splendidly indeed that it was decided the Coombses would
go with us to New York for my Roosevelt debut shortly after
Christmas.

We were making this a combination trip, a family dinner in
Mrs. Roosevelt's Manhattan apartment, then a visit to Washington for the inauguration of President John F. Kennedy. The
die was cast. New York lay under the pall of winter. As we
drove in from Idlewild Airport, the rising mass of city was
forbidding and gray. Rushing past the dirty brick apartment com-
plexes of Queens, through the tunnel and into the windy canyons
of downtown, I longed for sunshine and open spaces, for greenery
and distant mountains. But here, my mountain was the Pan Am
Building, soaring above the dirty mausoleum of Grand Central
Station; my greenery the seven dollars Elliott handed the cab
driver at our Park Avenue hotel, and my sunshine the hard
fluorescent light of a steel elevator, whisking us high up to our
suite in the hotel.

I had brought enough clothing to stay for a year. Not knowing
what to expect, I crammed my suitcases with fifteen outfits. Included was a formal gown designed by a couturier in Denver for
me to wear to the inaugural ball. The material I had gotten
many years before in Seattle always thinking it would become
part of a famous event. The Inaugural was famous to me, and
the dress was later to become famous in the *Women's Wear
Daily*, a fashion trade journal, as being one of the outstanding
seen at the ball.

As we readied ourselves for the evening at Mrs. Roosevelt's
my nervousness increased. I kept changing dresses and fussing.
"This won't do . . . I look terrible in this . . . What will be

right?" Harry Coombs was the soul of sympathy. "Patty, now just be yourself," he said, "and everything will be fine."

"What will they think?" I said. "How should I act?"

"Let them do the talking. Smile, and keep smiling."

"Harry, but I look terrible. What'll I wear?"

"Wear basic black, a good basic black."

"They'll probably expect me to be in spangles and sequins." I took Harry's advice and put on the old standby, simple black with two strands of pearls. It was a combination that seemed to fit anywhere.

Like the condemned mounting a gallows, I could take some comfort in the fact that it couldn't last forever. In this instance, Mrs. Roosevelt had thoughtfully provided an afterdinner escape: tickets to the musical *Camelot*. Not only would this put a definite time limit on my discomforture, I would be able to see my first Broadway show.

Shortly after dark we arrived at Mrs. Roosevelt's narrow brownstone apartment building at 21 East 72nd Street. From outside, it resembled a thousand other brownstones in New York, five stories high, two windows wide, a short flight of steps leading to a heavy front door. Mrs. Roosevelt occupied the second and third floors and rented out the first and two top floors. My knees turned to jelly as Elliott rang the bell.

Most of the guests had already arrived. Walking in, my first impression was of people in the confinement of a small apartment, made smaller for the overabundance of furnishings and knickknacks, high ceilings and red drapes. I sensed that the person who lived here never threw anything away.

Mrs. Roosevelt came forward to greet us, a somewhat shapeless figure, stooped, with a crinkly-eyed smile and rather prominent teeth. The teeth were surprisingly white, and I found out later she had just had them capped. She had a motherly peck for Elliott, a handshake for me. "It's so nice to see you, my deah. Did you have a nice trip? . . . How delightful . . . I do hope you like New York . . ." Small talk, practiced small talk, the kind you use with strangers. The others peered at us from a distance, tall men and well-groomed women, in expectant little groupings. I felt like the Avon lady, breaking in on the reading of somebody's will.

Smile, Harry had said.

"My deah, you have a lovely smile."

The voice was the familiar one I had heard so often on radio and TV, the high register, the cultivated tone, the careful diction. The face and the person I might not have recognized so easily, she had aged so. The face had a puffiness about it, the shoulders were drawn down, the proud head no longer held erect. Her dinner dress was something in bluish-purple, dropping to the middle calf. A modest strand of beads together with a simple chain and pendant, adorned the bodice. This necklace of purple stones I would soon come to recognize as one of Mrs. Roosevelt's trademarks. On her wrist was a small gold watch set with inlaid diamonds. Her hair was combed soft and high, and she wore a trace of lipstick and pink nail polish. If there was anything striking at all about Eleanor Roosevelt it was her hands. They were slender, tapered, exquisite, and she was quite vain about them. She wore a plain gold wedding band, a solitaire diamond engagement ring and, for the right hand, a small sapphire dinner ring. Her shoes were plain black low heeled pumps— very utilitarian. The over-all impression was of plainness, an extraordinary plainness, almost to the point of monotony.

Barely had we started the handshaking when Elliott was summoned into a corner to take a long-distance telephone call. It was from Sheldon, Iowa, where he had just become involved in a promising business venture. In months to come, it was to plunge us into the middle of a small town's financial disaster, triggered by embezzlement, deceit, and stock swindles. For the moment, however, the call was simply a small crisis for Patty Peabody Roosevelt. With Elliott on the sidelines, my anchor had been temporarily cut and I was adrift in a sea of Roosevelts.

The apartment resembled an oversize corridor. The floor we were on had a sitting room at one end, a long hallway, and the dining room and kitchen at the other. In a tone one would direct at the troop of Brownies, Mrs. Roosevelt announced: "Now, children, let us join our guests in the sitting room for cocktails." We all dutifully filed along to where the other guests had assembled. I needed a cocktail badly to settle my quaking stomach. However, I was in for a disappointment. Mrs. Roosevelt, who had the sentiments of a teetotaler, served only Dubonnet wine.

The women guests were gathered at one end of the room, sipping wine but the men separated to provide their own libations. The Roosevelt boys had long known of their mother's dislike for alcoholic beverages. By unspoken agreement therefore, one of the boys would always make sure that there was a bottle of scotch or bourbon hidden away behind some books or in a drawer for their liquid enjoyment.

Fifteen people were milling around in the sitting room now. All of the Roosevelt offspring were present but Jimmy and his wife Irene. I was introduced to Johnny and Anne, Franklin, Jr., and Suzanne, Anna and her husband, Dr. Jim Halsted. Also present were the Coombses, Ellie Roach, FDR's niece, and her husband George, and Senator William Benton of the Encyclopaedia Britannica. The reception I received gave me goose-bumps. No one made much pretense at being cordial. My mother-in-law was polite but distant, as if she were talking to a stranger on the street. There was no warmth about her. I was surprised, wondering if this could be the same person I had read so much about, whose public image was one of goodness and charity.

Being naïve and unsure of myself with strangers made this evening no easier for me. I had honestly thought that my letter to Mrs. Roosevelt, in which I poured out my heart to her about our common love for Elliott, would magically open a flood gate of warmth and welcome to her new daughter-in-law. This was to be only the first of many disappointments. When I looked back on this bizarre occasion I was to realize that it was only by a monumental effort on her part that she could have been as cordial as she was. This display was to stand me in good stead when I had to face a similar situation with my son, Jimmy, and his new bride.

Elliott hung on the phone forever, talking and blowing kisses at me. "Don't worry sweetie, I'll be right there, right there." At one point, I heard him rumble at his caller, "You say Kistner's left town? Well, get him back. Get him back whatever you do." Desperately I tried to make small talk with my in-laws, thinking of things we might have in common. With Anna and Johnny I tried horses, because the Roosevelt children had always ridden at Hyde Park. But there's only so much you can say about horses, especially in a sitting room sipping Dubonnet wine. I talked to

Anna about the time she had lived in Seattle and we were neighbors. "That's strange, dear," she said, "I don't remember a thing about it. I don't remember ever seeing or hearing of you before." With Franklin, Jr., who had the Jaguar distributorship in New York, I made a game try at automobiles, telling him about how interested my son Jimmy was in them. I received a thin smile for my efforts. "That's fine," Franklin said wearily, "we'll have to take him for a ride sometime."

Ellie Roach and I had something in common though. We had both been married only a short while. Her first was even stormier than mine—her second produced the same bliss. Instinctively I was drawn to her, and felt her response. What a warm feeling—an oasis in a desert of glaciers—both of us had found happiness. Yet hers was to be taken away by sudden and tragic circumstances. Mine still lives.

While this was taking place, Senator Benton was carrying on with Mrs. Roosevelt, at length and in volume, about Faye Emerson and the old days when she was Elliott's wife and a star part of the family. It gave me a sinking feeling. They all seemed to have so much in common and my spirits did another flip. How do you make friends with people who don't want to be friendly. Nothing ventured—I approached Senator Benton and struck out on the subject of encyclopedias and the necessity for them in a child's life. His superior smile as he said, "Do you have children, Mrs. ——, ah Mrs. ——?" made me gasp as though I had been hit. He knew, but wasn't talking.

All around there were quick glances at me and whispered comments. I wondered if you could drown yourself in a glass of Dubonnet wine.

After twenty minutes, Mrs. Roosevelt put an end to our imbibing, saying, "Now, my dears, I think we must go in to dinner. We just can't wait for Polly. If we don't eat now, the children will be late for the theater." I almost expected her to clap her hands. As we filed down the hallway, I vaguely wondered who Polly could be. Elliott was still on the telephone, so Mrs. Roosevelt started to walk with me, saying, "Come, dear . . ."

At that instant, the door flew open and in floated one of the most vivid creatures I have ever seen. She had bright purple hair with a deep widow's peak painted on with eye shadow, and a complexion paper-white. Her 4-foot, 9-inch frame was wrapped in an ancient chinchilla coat. Her thin arms and hands were alive with bracelets and rings of diamond, sapphire and jade. One dinner ring on her right hand had a diamond the size of an egg. Beneath the fur she wore a gold-colored blouse and red velvet pants, all held together in the back by a pin of diamonds and sapphires. Pushed into her hair to complete the ensemble, like a crown, was a large diamond bar pin. I caught my breath. Shucking the chinchilla hurriedly, she stood there jingling and announced: "I'm sorry I'm late, Eleanor. Well, where is she?"

"Polly, my deah," Mrs. Roosevelt replied, "I want you to meet Elliott's new wife." With that, she steered me toward the tiny, seventy-four-year-old woman. This was Laura Delano, FDR's wealthy spinster cousin, the Roosevelts' Aunt Polly. A pair of piercing eyes examined me, and the thin slash of a mouth snapped: "Well, so you're the latest one, are you? What have you got to say for yourself?"

Titters broke out around me. The titters swelled into laughter. Discretion was gone. I flushed and looked her full in the face. "Yes, ma'am," I said, "but I'm the last one and the best one."

With that, Aunt Polly threw her arms around me and whooped, "By God, Eleanor, I think he's finally got a live one."

After that, dinner was a blur. Mrs. Roosevelt had set two tables in the tiny dining room and placed me on her right. Aunt Polly switched the place cards so she could be on my other side, and sat down chatting amiably. By now, even I could sense a sourness in the lingering laughter of the others. Laura Delano was, after all, the grand dame of the clan, heiress to part of the Atlantic Coast Line Railroad fortune and owner of a fabulous home overlooking the East River in New York, on Sutton Place. She also had a splendid 200-acre country estate at Rhinebeck, New York, where she spent her summers, owned a kennel of fine long-haired dachshunds and Irish setters, and one of the finest private collections of jade in America. Everybody hoped that when she died she would leave them her fortune. They chafed to see her cotton to a stranger.

Dinner conversation was a drag. It would brighten considerably, I was certain, when we had left. For now, there was a perceptible boredom at being at Mummy's again for dinner.

From the meal itself, some of this was understandable. I had assumed that dinner at Mrs. Roosevelt's would be an elaborate affair. Instead, the fare tended to be plain: soup, pot roast, vegetables, salad. The salad dressing, to my dismay, was of a particular orange-colored commercial variety that I despised. I later learned that Mrs. Roosevelt was probably one of the world's worst cooks, and seemed disinclined to even hire someone who could prepare exotic meals. From lifelong habit of thrift, she also measured everything so that guests had one serving and there were no leftovers. The china, too, was a variety of unmatched sets and odd pieces.

During dinner, her aloofness toward me remained. It was an unspoken kind of thing, noticeable more for what was unsaid than for what was said. Talk was rambling and dull. Elliott had joined us with the soup course, and sat across from me offering encouraging winks, eyebrow waggles and grins. My disappointment in Mrs. Roosevelt's attitude must have shown. I felt like blurting out that she really needn't expect to be hurt over her second son any more; that Elliott would not be hurt either, and that we truly loved each other and could make a life together. What I did not know was that this evening was equally unpleasant for her, that the task of accepting still another new wife had put her in a mild state of shock.

Looking around me, I could see that this evening was an all-too-familiar pattern in the ill-starred domestic lives of FDR's sons and daughter.

There was Anna, strong-willed, detached, a sharpness to her features. Eldest of the five, she then lived with her third husband, the physician Jim Halsted, in Lexington, Kentucky. Her first marriage in 1926, to New York stockbroker Curtis B. Dall, had ended in divorce. Likewise the second, to newspaperman John Boettiger, a tragic figure whose publishing business collapsed in bankruptcy. Following his divorce from Anna, Boettiger flung himself from the upper window of a New York hotel.

There was John, tall, husky, capable of great charm but with a strong character. Youngest of the family, he married blond Boston socialite Anne Lindsay Clark in 1938. The marriage lasted twenty-seven years but finally ended in 1965 when John, a Wall

Street broker, got a Mexican divorce. A week later he married divorcée Irene Boyd McAlpin of Memphis and New York.

Charming, convivial and bearing a striking resemblance to his father, Franklin Jr. had a winning way about him that made him a natural politician. But his private life, too, had been marred by domestic troubles. He and his first wife, Ethel du Pont, were together twelve years before his interest in politics, which she abhorred, cracked the seams of their marriage and she won a Nevada divorce. Ethel, like John Boettiger, also was destined to die a suicide. After Franklin was elected to Congress from New York, he married Suzanne Perrin, a trim blonde whom he had met in Long Island society. Franklin's political ambition was to carry him into an unsuccessful bid for the New York gubernatorial nomination.

Jimmy, the only one missing from this family gathering, was the tall, baldish eldest son, whose three marriages equaled Anna's trips to the altar. His first, to Betsy Cushing, went on the rocks in 1940 after ten years; his second, to nurse Romelle Theresa Schneider, lasted until 1955, just prior to his election to Congress from California. In the summer of that year he married Gladys Irene Owens, a receptionist in his business office. Jimmy later resigned his congressional seat to become U.S. representative to the United Nations Economic and Social Council.

Had I known at that time that both Franklin and John had received their first nuptial blessings from my cousin, the Reverend Endicott Peabody, perhaps we could have established a rapport—still it was even then too late to mention those times with all that had gone on since in all of our lives.

Although neither FDR nor Eleanor Roosevelt ever interfered with the private lives of their children, Mrs. Roosevelt was obviously deeply concerned about her family. Big divorce settlements, too, were eating into the fortune. Now, in the last years of her life, my presence at her table proved that domestic upheavals were still in progress, and Elliott's financial disaster had been the worst of all.

"Children," she said at last, "is everyone having dessert?"

After the main course, I was sure that this agonizing meal would at least end with some dignity of flavor. We were to have strawberries Romanoff, one of those whip cream, ice cream goodies I can never resist. This one I could have resisted quite well. Instead of fluffy, it came out runny. The ice cream fell onto our dessert plates in a mass of reddish goo. Gratefully, we all pushed back from the table.

Then, with a flurry of good-byes and handshakes, the four of us—Elliott and I and the Coombses—bundled into our coats to go to the theater. Just before leaving, I heard a jingling beside me. Aunt Polly's hand touched me lightly on the arm.

"Come and visit me tomorrow for tea," she said.

My first impression of the theater in New York was a dreadful disappointment. I had expected Arabian opulence and found rather tawdry worn trappings. We were ushered to our seats in grand style however, as Mrs. Roosevelt had made the ticket requests—and she would be given only the best. The house lights dimmed and I was transported into another new phase of life. I floated as would Guinevere in the arms of King Arthur through the delightful play, *Camelot*. Not so my friend husband—when the house lights went on, I was returned to earth with a thump to see Elliott sound asleep next to me. Again I had forgotten that these new "firsts" for me were somewhat tarnished for him. I revived at Sardi's after the play.

Laura Delano's home at Sutton Place is, I am sure, one of the picturesque houses of the world. Overlooking FDR Drive on the East River, it strikes your eye as a kind of structural cameo, five stories high. A front door of Chinese red distinguishes it from other homes in this highly exclusive pocket of New York. I arrived in a taxi and was met at the red door by Delia, her Irish maid.

Aunt Polly was ensconced in her second-floor sitting room, all but buried in a chaise longue. Beside her stood a round marbletop table bearing what appeared at first glance to be a bundle of rolled-up brown monkey fur, but on closer inspection proved to be a spoiled and exceedingly ill-tempered Pekingese. Everywhere else in the room, on tables, on shelves, along the mantelpiece of a marble fireplace, were displayed pieces of fine jade and ivory. There were jade ash trays, cigarette boxes, statuettes, vases, snuff boxes, paperweights and cigarette holders and exquisite figures of animals and birds. Some pieces were inset with diamonds and other precious stones. Elliott had described glowingly the magnificence of Aunt Polly's collection, but his words did not prepare me for this. I entered the room and stifled a gasp. From the chaise, a thin, pale hand flashing huge diamonds motioned toward a low table laden with liquor bottles, mixers, magnificent decanters of leaded crystal, a silver ice bucket and fine-wrought tumblers of crystal. There was rum, scotch, bourbon, gin, vodka . . .

"All right, what will you have?" came the voice from the pillows. "After that ordeal last night I'm sure you must need something."

Aunt Polly's "tea," obviously, would be 80 proof.

I asked for scotch, which Aunt Polly poured with a heavy hand. On the table beside the Pekingese, Ming, sat a tumbler of her own favorite drink, a ghastly concoction of rum, sugar syrup, and lemon juice. Each time she reached for it, the dog growled. Her hand was incongruously etched with white scars. To my horror I quickly learned that, to Aunt Polly, this was a mark of love on Ming's part. "But he is my lion," she would proudly announce! "I love it when he's fierce and untamable. It's part of his heritage." Further discussion brought out that to comb the little beast required a straitjacket for his head, made out of a linen towel. Poor Delia, who was given the task of caring for him, was also a mass of scars.

On my way in, I had noticed that the house seemed to be filled with dogs, as well as jade. There were three long-haired dachshunds and an Irish setter. Now, two of the dachshunds came padding in and flopped down at my feet. Aunt Polly attached a cigarette to a long jade holder and lit it from a silver lighter. Inhaling quickly, she said, "Well now . . ." and the voice came out on a cloud of blue smoke. The grilling began.

"I noticed that you have good table manners. Did your family have money? . . . Who is your family, my dear? . . . Where did you go to school? . . . Did you go to private school or ordinary public school? . . ." It was rapid-fire, blunt, no-nonsense questioning. I had the impression my answers were being recorded on a mental computer tape, there to be sifted and analyzed; ultimately an invisible card would be stamped "Approved" or "Disapproved" and placed in her memory file.

How did I meet Elliott? Was it true we lived in sin in Mexico? "No? Well, I didn't think Elliott had that little sense."

Nervousness had made me thirsty. The scotch was buzzing in my head, because I had gulped it down. Now I hoped it would not thicken my tongue or my judgment.

"I am very fond of Elliott," she was saying. "He's my godson. He is really the dearest to my heart."

Then abruptly the quizzing stopped, the conversation took another tack. She began to tell me about what I could expect from others in the family.

"It isn't going to be easy for you, Patty. Be on your guard. This is an extremely jealous family, and jealousy is a terrible thing, a terrible thing. Keep an eye on your flanks."

The small, crowded room had been oppressive at first, with its *objets d'art*, its two couches, its French provincial chairs with their spindly legs, and Aunt Polly in her bracelets and rings and, today, a tweed skirt. But the oppression, I realized now, had been in myself, and suddenly here was warmth and welcome from a valuable new-found ally. Tension evaporating, I smiled, relaxed and enjoyed the feeling of scotch. "A good drink is good for you," Aunt Polly said. "It will help bring your blood back to normal."

She told me there was a challenge to living as a Roosevelt, and that I could expect the others to toss me off as another of Elliott's mistakes. To make matters worse, there were people in all walks of life who would despise me, for no other reason than that my name was Roosevelt. This was part of the hidden legacy of the man who had been President at a time of great crisis; whose works had won for him not only the adulation of millions of ordinary Americans, but also the bitter enmity of those relative few who came to regard the New Deal as a bureaucratic cancer on the U.S. body politic.

We had been talking for an hour and a half when Elliott arrived. There was worry in his face. A disaster was in the making in Sheldon, Iowa. He said, "I've got to fly out tonight, Patty. You go on to Washington with the Coombses and I'll meet you there in time for the inauguration."

Aunt Polly expressed her concern for my future in the Roosevelt melee. "Elliott, she is not like the rest of you. She is guileless. She talks honestly. Don't let her say what she thinks."

"She can take care of herself," Elliott replied.

"No I can't, honey," I said. "I thought they would all want to make friends, and they really don't. I'll just keep on being hated—a fifth wheel on your wagon—I can't take care of myself any more."

"Of course she can't, Elliott," Aunt Polly said. "She is just a child. She won't be able to defend herself."

Elliott drank and looked thoughtfully at the window.

"I understand this divorce cost you a lot of money," his godmother said. "How much do you owe?"

"Over six hundred thousand," he replied heavily.

She pursed her lips, said she had been horrified that he would be foolish enough to take on another wife and four children with everything in such a mess.

"But if you can make it with anybody, you will with Patty. She's full of beans, Elliott. I'd say you have a better than 50–50 chance."

Elliott finished his drink and we stood up to go.

"I think so too, Aunt Polly," he said.

The inauguration of John F. Kennedy turned Washington topsy-turvy. Bitter cold had swept down from Canada packing a blizzard. Visitors streamed into the city by train, plane, bus and jitney, bringing their best clothes and jamming every available hotel room. When the city could hold no more, the overflow spilled out into surrounding Maryland and Virginia. For the nation, which had elected its dynamic young President in the most exciting, closely fought campaign in United States history, this was the grand climax, the great celebration, and there had never been anything like it before. The parade for the new President would be the biggest of its kind, ever; the capital would swirl with inaugural balls and parties, bringing new vitality and glamour to a Washington long jaded by the drab officialdom of the Eisenhower period, and before that, the Kansas City style provincialism of the Trumans, and before that, war.

Snow choked the streets. The freeze covered main thoroughfares with sheets of glass. Adding to the confusion was an unending series of minor collisions. While frustrated traffic cops blew the silver plate off their whistles, stalled motorists swore and radiators came to a slow boil. It took Harry and Ginny and me four and a half hours by taxi to go from the Union Station to our hotel. Meanwhile, before we arrived, Bill Roosevelt's wife, Karyl, went to Jimmy's office across town to get our parade tickets and never got back. Elliott was late coming in from Sheldon. Snowbound in the hotel, I watched the parade on television. Elliott arrived as it was about half over. Bone-tired from his trip, he fell into bed and took a nap.

That night, Elliott put on full-dress, complete with white tie, top hat, silk scarf and rows of medals, to take me to the inaugural ball at the Armory. I wore my new gold and white brocade dress and mink coat. Elliott's son David, on vacation from Culver Military School, was our driver. We pulled up to the Armory entrance just ahead of the Kennedys and walked into a mad-house.

The place reminded me of the San Francisco Cow Palace, gigantic and filled with a seething mass of revelers, television crews, police, celebrities, and politicians. Dancing was all but impossible. People swigged champagne in paper cups. Waiters scurried away for ice and set-ups and never returned. Everyone was smoking. I felt closed in, trapped, swallowed up. Just breath-ing was a chore. TV cables and electrical wires were everywhere, and periodically, the camermen splashed huge areas with their blinding lights. The band blared madly on, and my beautiful dress and shoes were being ruined. After twenty minutes, I tugged at Elliott's sleeve, "Oh honey, let's go. Let's get out of here."

"What are you saying?" he said.

"Please, darling, Harry and Ginny Coombs want to go too."

"Okay."

On our way out, we walked around the Armory toward the Kennedy box, hoping we might get to say "hello." A stretcher went past us carrying Jimmy Roosevelt's wife, Irene. In the crush, she had fainted.

Well wishers and curiosity seekers made a tight throng near the presidential box. Secret Service men were everywhere, rec-ognizable by their little lapel buttons. We made it through and were permitted to greet the Kennedys. The buoyant President smiled broadly at Elliott and shook hands. Recognizing me, he remembered in this hour of triumph the oddball nature of our first meeting many months before at the Democratic Convention in Los Angeles. Then he showed me a memento of that chance meeting, and won for himself another lifelong admiration.

Elliott had gone to the Los Angeles convention as a member of the Colorado delegation. Since we were not married at the time, I went from Phoenix with friends and met him, with the Justices from Dallas, each day at the convention hall. One day Jack Kennedy was to speak to the delegation at a luncheon, with Mrs. Roosevelt as a special guest. Elliott's mother was late. As the noon hour approached, he asked me to go to the phone in the lobby and call her. Mrs. Roosevelt was leading the Adlai Stevenson forces, and had been delayed in a meeting. Posing as a secretary, I reached the Stevenson headquarters and waited while someone went to find her. While I stood with the receiver at my ear, a man walked up.

"You going to be on that phone long, sis?"

The face looked very familiar. Trying to place it, I said "No." I was trying to get a message to Mrs. Roosevelt. Where had I seen that man before?

"I'm Jack Kennedy," he said. "Weren't you with Elliott Roosevelt last night?"

I almost dropped the phone. "Yes," I said. "Gosh, Mr. Kennedy, I hope you win." I told him I had gone to the Sacred Heart Convent in Seattle, the same school his sisters had attended in Boston and Europe. Juggling the phone on my shoulder, I rummaged in my purse for a small medal of St. Madeline Sophie which I always carried. "This is my lucky medal, Mr. Kennedy," I said. "I'd like to give it to you." He grinned and pinned it onto his lapel.

Now, at the inaugural ball in Washington many months later, the new President of the United States leaned toward me and flipped over his lapel. "You see, Patty, what we did?" There, pinned to the underside, gleamed my medal.

At the crowded entrance we waited until the Kennedy family and friends had left in chartered buses before David could ease our car into traffic. A man and woman in the driveway asked us for a lift into town and slid into the front seat. Along the way, they pointed out places of interest. They did not know who we were.

"I lived through the greatest era of our country," the woman said. "I was president of the Women's Democratic Club when Eleanor Roosevelt was in the White House. Have you ever been to Washington before?"

"Quite often," Elliott said.

The woman said she had met FDR and Eleanor Roosevelt many times. We drove past the White House. "There," she announced, "is where they lived." Elliott, for whom the White House had been a second home, peered out. "That so?"

We dropped them off, still unintroduced.

"Thanks for the ride," the woman said.

Elliott smiled. "Don't mention it."

9

Blizzard, Bands, and Bankruptcies

Marriage to Elliott Roosevelt began to resemble a celluloid epic, in wide screen and color. Our lives together defied pattern, or sometimes even rationality. Things had a way of mushrooming. When a crisis came it had to be a big one. Somehow I had become the wife of a Jolly Green Giant. Looking back now, I must have spent those first months with a silly glassy stare, never quite knowing where the next thunderbolt was coming from. I certainly did not expect it to come from Sheldon, Iowa, nor did I dream that during four short months we would be caught up in a major banking scandal involving a two-million-dollar embezzlement and the collapse of a booming enzyme feed enterprise.

The Sheldon episode began quietly enough less than six weeks after we had set up housekeeping as newlyweds in the Versailles Apartments in Denver. Through a promoter he knew, Albert Heyutin, Elliott met Etienne Perenyi, president of the North Denver Bank and a man of many business interests. Among them was the Northern Biochemical Corporation, a firm in Sheldon, Iowa, manufacturing a new enzyme product for feeding poultry and livestock. It was headed by a personable, thirty-five-year-old business whiz named Harold E. Kistner, Jr., who wanted to borrow money from the Denver Bank for expansion. Perenyi needed a livestock and financial consultant to look over the operation. "Elliott, you've had a lot of experience in ranching and agriculture," he said. "I'd like you to talk to this boy Kistner and see if there's any merit to this thing."

The effect of enzymes on the quality of beef is nothing new. For years, cattlemen have given their steers shots of enzyme for tenderizing while pen-fattening them for slaughter. Now, by a process so secret that even technicians in the Sheldon plant were kept in the dark, Kistner and his father had perfected a revolutionary new process for including enzyme in the regular diet. They had formed two companies, Bio-Zyme, Inc., which manufactured the enzyme ingredient, and Northern Biochemical, which mixed it with feeds for poultry, cattle, hogs and other stock.

The growth of the operation had been incredible. From a tiny beginning with four employees and $8000 capital, young Kistner —a newcomer to Sheldon who had just married Harriet Smith, a hometown girl—built Northern Biochemical in less than two years to where it had a fleet of twenty-seven company cars, four twin-engine planes worth $40,000 a piece, four offices in Sheldon and nearly one hundred and fifty employees. Nobody knew where the money was coming from; but whatever the source, it was never-ending.

As the bank's adviser, Elliott met with young Kistner in Denver. The enzyme entrepreneur was slender, bespectacled and brimming with energy.

People who met him could not help but be impressed. Elliott, too, was impressed, for he saw immediately the tremendous potential of this new enzyme feed and how it could be marketed throughout the world. Kistner suggested that Elliott join the firm as a vice-president and adviser on national marketing and distribution. The salary would be $2500 a month, a windfall in the existing state of our finances, and he would have the use of a new twin-engine Cessna 310. With the bank's blessing, Elliott agreed, and it was arranged for us to fly to Sheldon on December 9.

Before Elliott could make the trip he had to be checked out in the Cessna, a task which fell to his pilot-son Bill. My husband, who had had 13,500 hours flying time logged in everything from P-38s to jets, scoffed at the idea. "What do you mean, check me out?" he said to Bill. "I've got more time in the air than you've spent on the ground."

Regulations are regulations and up they went, Elliott nursing a head cold, while I sat in the Federal Aviation Agency control tower at the airport listening in on their radio talk. Elliott's cold had clogged his ears and stuffed up his nose. At 10,000 feet it caused him to lose consciousness. Bill's voice came crackling over the radio: "Pilot Roosevelt has blacked out. This is co-pilot William Roosevelt. I am taking the controls." I could hear Elliott wheezing and moaning. Bolting from my chair, I tried to seize the microphone from the air traffic control operator, shouting, "What's the matter? What's happened up there?" The man held on grimly, "For Chrissake, lady, please sit down." The plane was met by a rescue wagon and stretcher. They carted Elliott into the pilot's lounge, where he quickly recovered, got to his feet and said to Bill, "Well, let's take off." That afternoon he received his check-out in the Cessna, and the next morning we left for Sheldon in a snowstorm on a scheduled two-hour flight that was to stretch into nine.

Elliott Roosevelt's joining the firm was a major coup for Kistner, who now set out to reap maximum publicity from it. At 10:00 A.M., when we were due to arrive, he had a large part of the town (population 4251) at the airport, with the welcoming committee bearing roses, gladioli and ferns, ribbons stretching gaily into the one-room terminal, and the high school band going oompa-oompa in the cold and snow. At the time we were supposed to land, our little plane was circling the perimeter of a blizzard and Elliott was cursing eloquently. Finally we had to land at Des Moines and wait five hours. By the time we touched down at Sheldon at 7:00 P.M., the winter night had closed in, the glads were frozen, the crowd long gone and band mustering a dispirited hum-hump-de-hump. The ribbons drooped tiredly in the snow.

The following morning, Sunday, Elliott was out early to shake hands with the leading townspeople. Sheldon, Iowa, gave warm greetings to the Roosevelt who was joining an industry which overnight had become their pride and joy. To those who knew Sheldon, the success of Northern Biochemical—or NBC, as they called the company—was fitting reward for a town built on honesty, hard work and thrift.

Civic leaders were quick to fill us in on the characters of this prairie community sitting in the middle of northwest Iowa's

rich soybean and corn country, whose storage silos rose on the
landscape as monuments of diligence and enterprise. Established
in 1876 and populated by the hardy German, Irish, and
Pennsylvania Dutch, Sheldon had a dozen churches and two
banks, including the fifty-five-year-old Sheldon National Bank.
Folks said of Sheldon: "If you can't make a living here you
can't make one anywhere." Sheldon National boasted that none
of its depositors had ever lost a dime.

One of our first stops was at the home of Sheldon's leading
female citizen, Mrs. Bernice Geiger. She was the assistant cashier
of the Sheldon National Bank and daughter of the eighty-four-
year-old president, W. P. Iverson, who liked to say that he ran
the most conservative bank in Iowa. Her husband, Wallace
Geiger, was a respected hardware merchant. She was also treasurer of the Congregational Church, Sheldon's most fashionable,
and taught Sunday school there. Her good works and many
gifts to the poor had won her the nickname of "Lady Bountiful."

Lately ugly rumors had been whispered about Bernice, but
people shrugged them off as malicious gossip. After all, in her
dedication to her town and her work as the bank's bookkeeper,
she had never even taken a vacation in thirty-five years.

We arrived at Mrs. Geiger's home shortly after she had wheeled
her new Buick into the driveway, returning from church. I
noticed that the coat she removed was a vicuña, and her clothes
of expensive, if conservative, cut. She was medium height, stout-
ish, with grayish-brown hair, a pale lipstick and kindly, trustful
eyes. Her hands were expressive but she talked little, preferring
instead to draw us out.

Her house was a showplace, with brick outside and tasteful,
superbly matched furnishings, floors burnished to a lustrous deep
polish and Oriental scatter rugs on the interior. Left to the
Geigers ten years before by Wally's father, a contractor, the house
was square brick and frame with a screened-in porch and a feeling
of space and comfort. It was the kind of house which, in summer,
would catch the cool breezes and provide a perfect backdrop for
a garden party. People didn't ask how the Geigers could afford it,
but it was said Bernice had brought down a decorator from Des
Moines to plan the interior, and the remodeling had taken six

months and cost $20,000. The rugs were deep, the draperies velvet, and there was a costly hi-fi and an electric organ.

We had a pleasant Sunday morning visit and a lunch of sandwiches and coffee. Somehow I felt overdressed when I donned my huge mink coat, size forty-four, which Elliott had bought me with money from his mother for the gift. (My reasoning had been that a size forty-four mink coat costs no more than a size twelve, and that I might cut off part of the fur for a stole as well as a collar and cuff set.) Mrs. Geiger's eye flicked coolly over the coat as we said good-bye, but she made no comment. Little did I realize that later I was to become a familiar woebegone figure in Sheldon, trudging through snow in forty below zero weather in that coat, my head and face covered by the huge collar, while the town sank into an economic traumatic shock unmatched in its history.

The next morning, Harold Kistner, Jr., and his wife, picked us up in a Lincoln Continental and drove us to the plant. It was an enormous quonset hut structure, piled all around with snow drifts. A three-foot path was cleared to the door. As befitting his position of corporation president, Kistner's was the only office with carpeting. He also had a public address system which could monitor conversations throughout the plant. After we had been introduced to the various department heads and foremen, I whispered to one of the women, "I need to go to the ladies' room."

"We don't have one," she said.

Elliott had overheard. "You don't what?" he asked.

"Well, the men have an outhouse in the back, but I don't think you'd want to go there."

So Elliott and I trudged a block and a half to a service station, and already I was having qualms about Sheldon, Iowa. My husband got his feet wet.

Next day I broke out in hives. I kept wanting to scratch, muttering, "This damn mink coat."

"I thought you always wanted a mink," Elliott said.

With that he sniffed. The sniff became a cough. The cough developed swiftly into a head cold and fever. We went to Kistner's house and he called a doctor. The physician was friendly. He seemed to want to draw Elliott aside, and kept dropping hints that we might not like Sheldon. In the kitchen, Elliott bent over the table, unbuckled his belt and received a shot of penicillin in the hip. The doctor then shut his black kit, shook his head meaningfully one last time, and was gone.

We flew back to Denver. Soon Harold Kistner arrived and Elliott set up feeder lot operations, to test the enzyme feed. Two weeks of tests on cattle showed startling results. Joe Bloes brought a crate of eggs for tests. In our apartment we cracked eggs and lifted out the yolks, which did not break. We broke and tested three dozen eggs, tossing them all in the garbage can. It seemed a terrible waste. Elliott would stand at the sink breaking eggs, with Kistner peering over his shoulder at the results and saying, "Break another one, Elliott. See how firm those yolks are? Now that's a firm yolk." Crack, squish, another egg.

Hating such waste, we sought the aid of the chef at the Cosmopolitan Hotel. "Sure, I'll cook 'em, ma'am. But that's a lot of eggs." Joe Bloes, the company treasurer, carted in some more, the chef fried them, scrambled, baked, shirred, and broiled. Then, we ate eggs three meals a day until my stomach flipped at the thought of a soufflé. As a result, to this day, I will eat eggs only under protest.

They also brought in some enzymed chickens, which Kistner took to the Cosmopolitan chef. We had a fried chicken banquet and invited banker Perenyi and Bill Roosevelt.

Kistner decided to take the penthouse apartment in the Versailles Apartments, and asked me to complete the furnishings.

I went to the Denver Dry Goods store and bought electric blankets, towels, sheets, and other household items.

The expansion-minded president of Northern Biochemical, meanwhile, still needed more expansion money. It was decided to tap the resources of Walter Heller & Co., a Chicago firm that made loans against inventory in a process called factoring. The plan was for Heller to keep a sealed warehouse of enzyme feed, which it would release—and take repayment—as the supply was sold. Elliott, Kistner, and I flew to Chicago to make the arrangements, but when the time came for our meeting with Heller & Co. officials, Kistner failed to show up. This left only Elliott to negotiate with the firm, on the basis of his records and those of the bank. Without the corporation financial statements no deal could be completed. Later we found Kistner at the hotel. He said he had gotten lost.

As the Christmas holidays neared, the corporation president announced that he planned to spend them in Honolulu and take his relatives along. They flew out, nine in all.

Elliott was flabbergasted. But since we were caught up in our own plans for spending our first holiday together, and then taking a trip to New York and attending the inauguration of President John F. Kennedy in Washington, Sheldon tended to slip temporarily into the background.

It exploded upon us in mid-January when Elliott, at his mother's apartment in New York, received a long-distance telephone summons from the board of directors of Northern Biochemical urging him to hurry back to Iowa. The company and the whole town of Sheldon were in deep financial trouble.

Normally, at this time of year, the icy winds howl down from the Dakotas, sending the thermometer plummeting to forty below and locking the towns of northern Iowa in snow and ice. But this January 16 came on mild.

The Sheldon National Bank was a narrow two-story building of yellow brick at 308 Ninth Street, its name spelled out in block letters over the front door. Farmers and businessmen went to W. P. (Bill) Iverson, Bernice Geiger's father, for their loans. Despite his eighty-four years, Bill Iverson did business every day at his desk upstairs, while Bernice handled all the accounts in her pink-and-green basement office. She could be counted on to arrive at twenty minutes of nine, and this day was no exception. It had been so for forty years.

Bernice kept the books in longhand, for she did not trust machines. She also did the accounting for her husband Wally's hardware business across the street. He suffered from stomach trouble and emphysema. One wondered what other interests she could possibly have time for, since she always seemed to be slaving at the books. One day a woman customer, seeing Bernice starting down the steps toward the basement, joked: "Do you live down there, Bernice?"

"Yes," Mrs. Geiger replied, with a sweet smile.

The customer turned to Bill Iverson. "Does she behave herself down there?"

"Oh, yes," Bernice's father said proudly.

Despite Bill Iverson's conservative banking practices and genial, person-to-person way of doing business, he had been worried lately because deposits during the past year had dropped off about $900,000, while the rival Security State Bank picked up $300,000. In any other bank they would suspect embezzlement, but with Bernice seeing to all the accounting the Sheldon National president knew this could not be the cause. Still, he had expressed his concern to a director, Ralph Hollander, who ran a store next door and whose father had once been president of the bank. Hollander and his wife joked about it at home, saying Bernice fitted the classic pattern of the embezzler but he didn't see how she could steal from her own bank. The idea kept nagging at his mind, however, and finally Hollander made a plane reservation for Chicago, where he planned to attend a merchandise show and maybe have a chat with some federal bank officials about Sheldon National. The reservation was for January 16, but Hollander never made the trip.

Waiting for Bernice Geiger in the basement office that morning was National Bank Examiner M. B. Moon, down from Sioux City to make his semiannual inspection of the books. Moon's function consisted mainly of checking the arithmetic. If the books added up, he was not expected to probe any deeper unless something aroused his suspicions.

Working from ledgers taken at random from a pile, the examiner ran down a column of figures in the quiet office. Suddenly, his eye caught an apparent error. There was an $8000 discrepancy in one of the books. Almost apologetically, he took the ledger to Mrs. Geiger. Had she entered the amount accidentally in the wrong column?

Bernice did not bother to look at the ledger. "It's no use," she said, "the books won't balance." Then, quietly, competently, she proceeded to tell the astonished bank examiner how she had stolen $2,126,859.10 during a period of thirty-five years, keeping track of every penny in her careful longhand math.

It was one of the largest bank embezzlements in the history of the United States.

Moon, feeling a little shaky, went upstairs to inform Bill Iverson. Cashier Fred Pylman hurried over to Hollander's store to begin summoning the directors. Bernice, meanwhile, came up to her father's office. Her face was a sickly gray, her eyes dry. Asked the total amount of shortage, she replied, "Two million dollars." Iverson, who was hard of hearing, asked, "What did she say?" The figure was repeated. The old man slumped in his chair and burst into tears. "My God, that's more than the bank is worth."

The hurriedly summoned directors had to consult their bank handbook to find out what to do. It said they should take a vote to call in the FBI. Hollander made the motion. It was seconded by the assistant cashier . . . Bernice Geiger.

To avoid a panic, the directors agreed that the theft should be kept secret as long as possible. Thus during the remaining few hours of that strange day, business went on as usual in the Sheldon National Bank. Bernice managed to get off to herself long enough to make one phone call, to Harold E. Kistner, Jr. The young president of Northern Biochemical told his general manager, Orville Ohlen, what her message had been: "It's all over. Leave town." Kistner vanished.

Bernice Geiger, it was revealed, had been Northern Biochemical's biggest single investor. Her 130,000 shares represented about one-third of the stock. Investigators from Des Moines and Sioux City were already swarming into Sheldon, and they would have a lot of questions about Mrs. Geiger's interest in the enzyme firm and her business relations with the young Kistner.

That night the news was out. Fred Pylman called Claire L. Schneider, president of Sheldon's other bank, Security State, to alert him against a possible run on his bank. Even as the astonished Schneider was being given the full story, an FBI car sped away from Sheldon carrying Bernice Geiger to jail in Sioux City. Next morning, depositors found the door locked at the Sheldon National Bank, and a typed notice stuck to the glass: THIS BANK CLOSED BY ORDER OF THE BOARD OF DIRECTORS. M. B. MOON, NATIONAL BANK EXAMINER IN CHARGE.

Even before the shock waves began to spread, Elliott had flown to Sheldon and taken charge of Northern Biochemical, in the absence of Kistner. Following an eight-hour huddle with the board of directors, Elliott called a midnight news conference. He reported that Mrs. Geiger had been buying shares at from $1.08

to $1.16 each since February 1960, eleven months before. By a strange coincidence, this was also about the time that the Kistner enterprise began to show such phenomenal growth. There was confusion about the actual number of shares outstanding in the company. Although the last statement had listed 199,000, Kistner insisted that there were 350,000. Elliott discovered that Northern Biochemical, although capitalized at $500,000, had not made a dime in fourteen months.

As the story unfolded in headlines across the nation, townspeople reacted with stunned disbelief. They saw their savings locked up tight, one hundred fifty jobs in the enzyme industry in jeopardy, and the town's hopes for a thriving future seemingly spiraling down the drain. The place was alive with FBI men, auditors of the Federal Deposit Insurance Corporation, press, radio, and television.

Mrs. Geiger, probers learned, had started siphoning off the funds by a twist of irony. When she came to the bank in 1922, she discovered that a $75,000 shortage already existed, apparently the work of some sharp-penciled predecessor. She covered it up and continued the thievery. When bank examiners showed up periodically, she closed out enough depositors' accounts to match the shortages, carefully keeping all records in triplicate. By 1959, she had filched one million dollars. Nobody knows where all the money went. She gave heavily to her church, even donating hymnals with her name inscribed on the back of the book, and a new public address system. She had sunk $100,000 into stock and grain speculations, losing about $1000 a month. She spent liberally on clothes, and was said to own one hundred pairs of shoes.

She gave generously to needy children and to people who worked for her. Interestingly, her doctor reported that she never had an ulcer.

The financial plundering had stepped up sharply after Mrs. Geiger became interested in Northern Biochemical. Kistner had begun selling stock around the country, much of which he failed to register with the Securities and Exchange Commission.

With Mrs. Geiger's support, he also devised a complicated "time-check" method of taking payment for shipments of feed. Under this scheme, the company sold feed to a distributor and received a postdated check in payment. The distributor then took a postdated check from the dealer, and the dealer worked the same arrangement with the consumer. Eventually these checks trickled back to the Sheldon National Bank, where Bernice Geiger discounted them at eighty percent of face value. This enabled the company to receive three discounted payments on one shipment of feed.

With the money pouring in, Kistner once appropriately described Mrs. Geiger as the "Fairy Godmother" of his operation. During the first eight months of 1960, approximately $400,000 of bank funds were absorbed into Northern Biochemical Corporation. Then the flow increased until more than $900,000 in company checks had cleared through the Sheldon Bank, not even covered by the time-check method. Bank auditors found that Kistner had cashed about $25,000 worth of personal checks over a seven-month period, which were not even charged to their account.

Less than twelve hours after Elliott's first news conference, another disclosure shook the company. Records in the county attorney's office revealed that in 1958 Kistner had pleaded guilty in Buffalo County, Nebraska, to improper selling of securities in an oil company and had drawn a year's probation. Two other counties in Nebraska had lodged similar charges against him.

The Northern Biochemical president insisted he was innocent of wrongdoing in the Sheldon case and had no part in the bank embezzlement. "We borrowed a lot of money from a woman who just didn't have a lot of money," he said. "We sold her some paper that did not go through the bank."

With charges being drawn up against him, Kistner holed up in his parents' home in Sheldon, while Elliott tried to bring some semblance of order to the mess. Elliott made it plain to the board of directors that he wasn't going to become enmeshed in it without having a thorough examination of the books by competent Certified Public Accountants.

The company filed for bankruptcy and an Omaha accounting firm, Arthur Anderson & Co., offered as a public service to try and straighten out the tangle. Elliott was appointed president pro tem, with the job of preserving the assets until a receiver could be named in behalf of the board of directors. Before assets could be preserved, however, they had to be found. There was also the matter of discharging, where possible, the company's most pressing obligations, especially debts to the hometown people of Sheldon who had placed their faith, as well as their funds, in the enzyme operation.

Young Kistner was arrested on a federal charge of aiding and abetting the embezzlement, but the charge was dismissed on January 26 by a United States Commissioner in Sioux City. Kistner's lawyer argued there was no evidence of wrongdoing between his client and Mrs. Geiger. In four months, however, he was to be convicted along with two aides for selling unregistered stock in violation of federal laws and sentenced to eight years in prison.

Even amid the disaster, Elliott's enthusiasm for the enzyme feed was undimmed. The results of the tests, he believed, were undeniable proof that here was a tremendously salable product. He hoped to buy the company out of bankruptcy and get it on its feet again. But, of course, this was impossible without the formula. The elder Kistner, who had developed it, sat on the secret and refused to budge.

Elliott moved his headquarters from Denver to Sheldon and I soon joined him, establishing temporary diggings in a $60 a week motel. Not long after that I went to Mrs. Harold E. Kistner, Sr., and tried to talk her into giving us the enzyme formula. By resuming operations, I argued, we could afford to get her son out of jail. She refused to discuss it.

The cold of Sheldon, Iowa, seeped into my bones. The wind blasting off the prairies brought with it a peculiar grain smell from the storage elevators outside of town. I pitied the terribly isolated existence of farmers and their families in those little farms scattered across the bleak landscape of this corn state. It was impossible to understand how they and their forebears had thrived in such a life which to one born and bred to city comforts, seemed as harsh as existence on the far side of the moon.

Life in the motel was miserable. I missed the children. After a month we rented a two-bedroom house on, of all places, Roosevelt Drive. I sent for Ford, Gretchen, and David in Denver (Jimmy was away in school). The house was not large enough for the children and us too, so we rented a fifty-foot housetrailer which we parked in the backyard on concrete blocks. Elliott and I moved into the trailer while the maid and the children had the house.

Housetrailer living is fine for some people, but not for the bulky, comfort-seeking likes of Elliott Roosevelt. His 6-foot, 3-inch frame wouldn't fit the three-quarter bed, and the Roosevelt heels hung over the bottom; he chafed over low ceilings and narrow hallways, and disliked the stingy heating capacity of the kerosene furnace; the Roosevelt head was forever banging into something, bringing a hearty "Goddam!"

As the board of directors' trouble shooter, Elliott felt a keen responsibility for the people who had invested in Northern Biochemical. Some of them held time checks given by Kistner, and now to their dismay found the paper worthless. There were debts owed to people who could ill-afford to write them off. One morning an old man came to the door of the trailer pleading for payment of a $48.50 delivery bill which the company owed him. Elliott dug into his pocket and counted out the cash. I started to protest, for our finances were at rock bottom, but swallowed the words when I saw my husband's face. As the old man went away, happily expressing his thanks, Elliott stood there smiling as if it was he who had collected the debt. I began to understand more clearly what it meant to be a Roosevelt. It meant believing in people, especially when they believed in you. He was the son of famous parents and had to uphold what they had done. That night, we talked late in the darkness. "Here they are and here we are, doll baby," Elliott said. "If anybody needs help, if an Eskimo needs help, I've got to do my best to provide it."

At 6:30 each morning Elliott went off to work in a drafty little office in town. With two accountants from Denver, he prowled through ledgers and accounts and old check stubs, trying to follow the twists and turns of Kistner's business dealings. The only heat came from one sputtering little stove. It was a frustrating, tedious business, and when he came home his face often sagged from fatigue. But there were no complaints. When the chips were down, I was finding out, Elliott Roosevelt could be like a rock.

Our personal finances were in a sorry state. Elliott worked now at a small weekly salary, and we complemented this as best we could with commission money which continued to trickle in from my past real estate ventures in Phoenix. Our maid, the loyal employee who had been with us in Denver, received $40 a week and room and board; then there were the routine living expenses to be met. I did not know how to budget, and Elliott was not accustomed to scrimping. This and the cold and a perceptible growing hostility among townspeople of Sheldon put a steady drain on our spirits.

Frequently, Elliott had his business conferences in the trailer, and more often than not they were disheartening sessions. People were broke, and Elliott would continue to buy their feed for the company and give them a note.

A Denver bank, meanwhile, was trying to repossess the three company planes. They were parked at the Sheldon airport, which was run by an ex-mechanic who also had a lien on them for repairs. Each time a man from the bank showed up, the airport operator would remove a part from the planes so they would not fly. It got so that airplane parts were stashed all over town, while angry repossession notices arrived with practically every mail.

By early February the blizzards struck in earnest. Each time you stepped outdoors, icicles formed on your nose. My huge ranch mink coat was the only suitable coat I owned for such weather, but other women of Sheldon seemed to resent it. I would walk along muffled in mink and crunching over the snow in a little pair of fur boots Elliott had bought for me in New York my greetings of "Hi!" to passersby bringing nothing but icy stares. Before long, I was despising Sheldon, Iowa, with an intensity I had never felt before about any place or anybody.

David came down three times with double pneumonia, and each time had to be admitted to the small Sheldon hospital.

Neighbors complained about our housetrailer in the backyard.

One Sunday morning we awoke to find the trailer teetering crazily on a twenty-degree slant. During the night we had had a slight thaw and one of the concrete blocks slipped down. We had to walk uphill to get to the kitchen. The water slipped out of the bathtub. Repairs required equipment we did not have. Nobody would come to help on a Sunday. We lived that way for twenty-four hours. That night Elliott rolled out of bed.

Crash.

"Goddam!"

For our maid, life in Sheldon was even worse than it was for me. Locked in a prison of snow and cold and racial barriers, she had no one to talk to but the children and me. If there were any other Negroes in Sheldon besides our maid, I never saw them. Walking to the grocery store together, we made a curious pair. I was all but lost in the mink; she wore a white coat of simulated leather and white knee boots. From neck to toes, only her brown knees were exposed.

After a while, she showed signs of being moody and depressed. I asked what was troubling her, but she only shook her head. Finally, one day Gretchen came to me crying and said our poor maid had been receiving threatening phone calls and notes. Quietly, Elliott began to investigate. When the phone rang, we would pick up the extension. "We don't want colored folk here," a man's voice would say, "you'd better get out of town, or next time you go to the grocery store you might get hit by a car."

Our maid began to complain of headaches. One day I walked into the kitchen and found her sitting there, holding her head and crying.

"What's the matter?" I said.

"Nothing, ma'am, nothing at all. I got my monthly headaches."

I said, then, that we knew about the phone calls. She burst into a fresh flow of tears and told me about some calls we had not heard. I felt a chill.

"Don't let them scare you."

"I'm not scared for me, Miz R. I'm scared for those children," she said. "I want to go home. I've got people in Louisiana, and I want to go back there."

She packed, and I asked Elliott's assistant, Jack O'Connor, to drive her down to Denver to catch a bus. So my faithful servant, who—besides Elliott and the children—had been my only close friend in Sheldon, left the little prairie town. In six short weeks, so much had happened here to so many people. I stood on Roosevelt Drive and watched until the car was out of sight.

With our maid gone, I turned to cooking, sewing, and cleaning. Elliott and I played gin rummy. I made snow cream for the children. More snow fell. It covered the windows. It covered the world. Sheldon, Iowa, closed in around me, silent and white and cold.

Sometimes I felt like screaming.

By early March it was apparent that any plans Elliott had for reviving the company out of bankruptcy were washed out. When Northern Biochemical went into the hands of a receiver, there was nothing left for Elliott in Sheldon.

The experience had not been a complete loss. During his tenure as the head of the firm Elliott had become a close friend of Dick Johnson, managing partner of Arthur Anderson & Co. in Omaha. Through Dick, he had met a group of bankers in Minneapolis headed by Carl Pohlad of the Marquette National Bank. Pohlad asked Elliott if he was interested in doing some public relations work. One weekend he sent his plane to Sheldon for us and we were flown to Minneapolis. We stayed at the beautiful Raddison Hotel, and Elliott was introduced to a number of prominent businessmen. Among them was Elliot Hoffman, who published a police journal distributed throughout the country as a state publication for police chiefs, and also had begun a travel service club. Hoffman made us a very attractive proposition. Clearly, there was opportunity in Minneapolis. As we returned to Sheldon to clear up our personal affairs and move, I was almost giddy with relief and excitement.

There was no regret at closing this chapter in our lives. It was tragic, though, that one which had opened with such bright promise should come to such a dismal pass. As we left Sheldon, the play and its leading characters had gone through all the acts.

Harold E. Kistner, Jr., was awaiting trial in Sioux City.

Wally Geiger, the hardware merchant, one-time bit player in Hollywood and husband of a sweet-faced woman who had a way with figures, would soon die a bitter, broken-hearted man.

Sheldon National Bank had closed its doors forever.

And Sheldon's "Lady Bountiful," Bernice Geiger, was already beginning a fifteen-year term in the Federal Prison for Women at Alderson, West Virginia. She would be up for parole in five more years.

As we put Iowa behind us, Elliott rubbed one hand over his brown hair, glanced at me and grinned.

"Honey," he said, "I think you're going to like Minneapolis."

10

The Land of Sky Blue Waters

Minneapolis is industry, culture and a restless, burgeoning spirit. Its people, deep-rooted and sociable, spend much of their lives in heavy clothing. The winter cold is numbing and dry, and seems to last forever. Streets turn glacial, perfect for sledding; skaters skim across frozen ponds and rinks; elders gather in warm taverns behind the frosted windows for companionship and beer, or go to concerts performed by their own symphony orchestra, one of the nation's best. And then one day the air changes, the sky takes on a richer blue and flower buds poke through the thawing ground. Spring suffuses the city with a balm only people of the north can truly appreciate. For it promises summer, and summer gives Minneapolis an astonishing amount of greenery, turns the lakes blue and flecks them with boats and sails and white wake; summer puts buoyancy into peoples' lives. To us, newly out of Sheldon, Iowa, this city was pure enchantment, even in the cold of March.

Elliott was enthusiastic about prospects in Minneapolis. His employer, Elliot Hoffman, a short, energetic entrepreneur, wanted him to promote a new motorists' organization patterned along the lines of triple-A. His main job would be to promote an assortment of special benefits the members could enjoy, such as special prices on service and accessories, insurance and lodgings.

Elliott was to be paid $12,000 a year and have an option to buy stock.

We moved into a suite in the Raddison Hotel, a quiet, commercial establishment downtown. When he used the sitting room for business conferences we put the children in a bedroom with the TV. One of our first visitors was Elliott's boss. Somehow I could not feel at ease with Hoffman, a squat, muscular man with dark hair and a fondness for pin-stripe suits. He painted a glowing picture, however, of the travel business and Elliott's future in it. "You're going to do great in this thing, E.R.," he declared. "It might seem small at the start, but remember money isn't everything."

Six weeks at the Raddison gave us a liberal dose of confined living. With no yard, no playground, not even a nearby park, it was especially hard for the children. To avoid disturbing other guests I limited them to three trips downstairs each day. The hotel staff took pity on them. A bellhop smuggled in leftover ice cream and cookies. A woman elevator operator invited nine-year-old Gretchen home to play in her yard.

One evening Elliott received a telephone call from a radio newsman we had met in Iowa. "It's important that I talk to you," the man said. "We can't discuss it on the phone. This thing is too big." The proposition, he hinted, was an offshoot of the Sheldon business. He arrived at 10:30 P.M., a strange hour for a business conference. Wary of me, he spoke to Elliott behind his hands.

A kingpin in Minnesota vice circles was in trouble with the Justice Department. Would Elliott use his influence in Washington to get him off the hook? There was money in it, perhaps $25,000 in cash.

By now I had had enough of dark glasses and bulging briefcases. Twenty-five thousand was a fortune to us, but I wanted none of it. "Elliott, you can't afford to get mixed up in anything like this," I snapped. "Sir, we are not interested. Good night. And don't let us see your face around here again." The vice lord's emissary left, in a pout.

Hotel life wore rapidly thinner. With our funds near zero we could not afford to buy a house. Renting with three children was not an easy matter either. But finally, with the help of a real estate woman, we found an English brick home on a hilltop overlooking Minneapolis. The owner, a wealthy widow, was going abroad and would rent it to us for six months, furnished. We were delighted.

Elliott's work was going well. The magic Roosevelt name opened doors everywhere. Soon, however, frustrations began to develop. My husband, accustomed to being his own boss, found it difficult to work for another man with his own decided views on how things should be done. We were also expected to undertake a heavy schedule of social activities, which ate into our free time. Evenings and weekends often found us at parties hobnobbing with prospective business contacts. We were also invited regularly to a country club for Sunday night buffets.

In the everyday world of Minneapolis, we were discovering, one never knew when he was about to step into social quicksand. It was quickly apparent how the political land lay. This was a stronghold of the GOP, and to some people the name Roosevelt was more to be spat than spoken. The sentiment was evident everywhere.

At the staid Minnekada Club, the hostess for a luncheon in my honor introduced me to the ladies by saying, "Patty's different. She is not like the others."

The League of Women Voters was so anti-Democratic that I was never invited to join. I was tempted to lodge a complaint with the national organization, saying that the Minneapolis Club should call itself the Republican Women Voters instead of the League of Women Voters.

One evening we were invited to a party in conjunction with the annual Minneapolis Symphony Ball. Our hostess took us around for introductions. Among the guests was a retired businessman and investor. When we were introduced, he peered into Elliott's face and snarled, "I don't care to meet any son of that terrible man! Roosevelt, I spent half a million dollars trying to have your father impeached."

These brushes were only warmups, though, for our biggest test, a weekend at the rabidly Republican Woodhill Country Club.

Our invitation came at 12:30 one morning with a phone call from a woman asking to speak to Elliott. He was asleep, and I refused to awaken him. The next morning he returned her call. She was Mary Jim Bagley, widow of Senator William H. Smathers of New Jersey, and now the wife of Ralph Bagley, a Minneapolis businessman. They had a home on Lake Minnetonka, ten miles west of Minneapolis. We were invited to visit them that weekend.

Mary Jim and her husband were an incongruous pair: she, a Democratic cracker from Winter Haven, Florida, with a southern drawl and a fondness for Roosevelts; he, a gut-Republican, somewhat on the stuffy side but fun-loving and a good friend. The Woodhill Club was having its annual invitational guest tournament this weekend. Mary Jim told her husband, "Rayelph, Ah'm going to have me a Democrat as a guest. Let's call the Roosevelts. They're new in town and don't know anybody."

We turned up at their pretty hilltop house on Saturday morning, bringing a ton of luggage and our golf gear. I had never met Mary Jim until a blonde came rushing out whooping, "Elliott, darling, how are you?" and planted a noisy kiss on my husband. Oh boy, I thought, he hasn't told me everything. It was soon apparent, however, that this was her wonderfully friendly and exuberant way. As fellow dinner guests that evening they had Bill and Patty Tenney, who knew practically everybody in Minneapolis. We spent a delightful social evening playing bridge and exploring each other's convictions and foibles.

The next day we took our golf bags and went off to Woodhill. If there has ever been a fortress of Republicanism in Minnesota, this was it. Snobbish and ingrown, the club had less than two hundred members. A newcomer was not admitted unless someone died. For all her vivaciousness, Mary Jim was still regarded with reservation. After all, she was a newcomer and a Democrat. Certain old line members felt that Ralph Bagley had a lot of cheek to bring her to Woodhill. To top all that, she was just learning golf. I had received the schedule of events two weeks before and had noticed that the ladies would play eighteen holes on opening day. Going out secretly to a nearby driving range, day after day, I faithfully hit two buckets of balls the way I thought I had seen it done on TV. A nice, quiet gentleman took pity on my second day's efforts. "Take the club in your left hand," he said. "Good. Now overlap your right hand, thumbs in a vertical line. Good. Now keep your head down . . ."

I did not discover my "angel's" name until we arrived at the

Bagleys. During cocktails on the porch that evening, a speedboat flipped by in front of the house. The driver waved, and our hosts motioned him on to the dock. It was my golf teacher! "Who is he? What's his name?" I gasped. Ralph replied patronizingly, "Oh you wouldn't know him. He lives out here and plays at Woodhill."

"Oh yes I do know him," I said.

Walking up to the porch, the newcomer greeted me. "Well, Mrs. Roosevelt, I'm glad you finally decided to play in our invitational tomorrow. Just be yourself and remember what I taught you. You'll be fine."

The others stood with their mouths open. My "angel" of the driving range had turned out to be Sewall Andrews, a stanch Republican.

The following morning we teed off for the ladies' round. Patty Tenney was a smashing golfer, with sizzling long drives, deadly chip shots and unerring putts. All year round she commuted forty miles to St. Paul for lessons from a golf pro. I plodded along miserably, digging up sod and whacking the ball into the trees. Uphill, downhill, uphill, downhill. By the time we got back to the clubhouse I was ready to fold up. In the ladies' locker room I overheard a tidbit of conversation between two other women:

"Do you know who Mary Jim is with?"

"Yes. Isn't it just terrible?"

"And Ralph Bagley, he is actually playing with Elliott Roosevelt."

"What in the world is happening to this club?"

Mary Jim and I watched the men tee off. Elliott and Ralph played for two days and finally won in their class. When they were not on the links, the four of us clustered together like chickens in an incubator. Ralph had been among these people all his life, but very few came to greet us.

Winner of the weekend play was Jack Nicklaus, then a brilliant amateur. It was one of his last such matches before turning professional. Just before the awards presentation an official walked past me carrying a trophy. I asked if it were the one that would be given to Elliott Roosevelt.

"I don't know any Elliott," he sniffed, "and I certainly don't know any Roosevelt."

We took the trophy home with us Sunday night.

Eventually we were to work our way into the hearts of the Woodhill people and make some lasting friends, but it took the better part of our nearly three years in Minneapolis.

Life with Elliott Roosevelt could be exhilarating, tedious, uproarious, heartbreaking, or just plain pathetic.

Since the earliest days of our marriage, Elliott had made plans to legally adopt the children and give them the Roosevelt name. In May 1961, in a moving and unexpectedly hilarious episode at the Minneapolis City Hall, the adoption became a reality. From plan to completion, the adoption took seven months and in the course of it my husband demonstrated a decisiveness and initiative which made an enduring impression on me.

The idea of adoption first came to Elliott while we were living in Denver. Before making a move, however, he wanted to talk it over with my former husband Milt. "It isn't fair," he said, "to take the children out from under him without at least giving Milt a chance to discuss it." During the Christmas vacation we flew to Phoenix, in the twin-engine Cessna, taking along Jimmy, sixteen. I called Milt and asked him to meet with Elliott at our hotel. I assumed they would talk in the lobby or the cocktail lounge. "Nonsense," Elliott said. "We will do it right here in the room."

This was the first time I had seen my ex-husband since marrying Elliott. Milt had remarried too. His appearance surprised me. He had lost weight and was deeply tanned, making his brown curly hair and dark eyes seem darker still. He wore a black golf sweater and a pair of slacks. As he walked in, a silly womanish notion flashed into my mind: my nightgown was next to Elliott's pajamas in the dressing room, our toothbrushes hung together in the bathroom. Blushing from embarrassment, I rushed out, scooped up the articles and dumped them into a drawer out of sight. Both men could see me. Neither spoke. "Now we're not going to bring up any unpleasantries," Elliott had warned me, "just discuss the welfare of the children."

Facing Milt, he calmly began to talk about what was best for

Jimmy, Ford, Gretchen, and David. They were going to grow up with us, he said, and it would be difficult for them to carry one name and their parents another.

It lasted an hour. By then I had a sinking feeling. Did I have the right to deny the children their natural father? What, after all, was their birthright? My thoughts whirled as the talk went on. Jimmy was in the next room, out of earshot, waiting. We had discussed it with him before, for he was the eldest son. He seemed content with the idea of taking the Roosevelt name. Then it occurred to me that you don't win the love and respect of a child simply by giving birth to him. You have to earn that love and respect. Milt was indeed the natural father of those children. And now Elliott had won their affection and ultimately would provide them their strength and courage as it came time for them to take their place in the world. Children want someone to lead them, and I could not do this by myself.

It ended with Elliott making the decision for us. The adoption would proceed. When my former husband left, I was emotionally and mentally drained.

The formal adoption in Minneapolis proved to be far more complicated than I had imagined. First, it required the changing of their birth certificates, putting in Elliott's name as the father and his occupation at the date of birth. (On Jimmy's, he was a general of the Air Force: on David's, a rancher.) The State Welfare Department sent a social worker to interview us, to determine if ours was a proper home. By law, the children could be adopted without the consent of the natural parents, thus, Milt had no say-so once the formalities had been completed. Elliott insisted on calling Phoenix to tell him the adoption proceedings had begun, "I'm sorry," Milt said, "but I can't let you adopt them." Elliott told him that we would go through with it. "We are filing the papers in three days." And that was that.

On the morning of the hearing, the six of us dressed to the teeth, arrived at the courthouse nearly an hour early. The lawyer met us carrying a very official-looking briefcase. While he went into the judge's office to find out when our hearing was to begin, we stood in the lobby drinking machine coffee. After a while Elliott said, "Well, honey, while we're here let's get a license for Duke." Marmaduke was the newest addition to our household, a boisterous great Dane pup. The lawyer joined us, still clutching his briefcase, and we all trooped to the second floor office of the city clerk.

Everyone was splendidly attired: David in short pants, and sport coat, an Eton shirt with a bow tie and the collar pinned together, Gretchen in her best dress, Jimmy and Ford wearing suits and ties, me in a black and white suit. Elliott and the lawyer wore business suits. We filed into a small office and lined up along the wall facing a counter and a sign reading LICENSES. The lawyer snugged up his briefcase and looked solemn. Elliott stepped forward and announced to the clerk, "Sir, we would like to buy a dog license, please."

The man stared at him, "A dog license?"

Holding David's hand, I spoke up behind Elliott. "While we're here why don't we get married?"

Heads turned in the office. Secretaries stood up and peered.

"Honey, please now," Elliott laughed.

The clerk looked at me. He looked at the children. He looked at the lawyer. "A dog license?"

"Yes."

"What kind of a dog?"

By now other people were clustered around the clerk, listening and looking.

"We have a great Dane and his name is Marmaduke," Elliott said. He handed over Duke's papers. The clerk gave him a card to fill out, and Elliott wrote his name as the owner.

"You sure this dog ain't Falla?" the man said.

The other office workers were laughing and asking for autographs. Marmaduke's license probably took longer to process than any dog's in Minneapolis that year.

The judge's office was crowded. In the hallway outside, men and women waited their turns for hearing on straight-back chairs. Many couples had a child by the hand, or carried a baby. For the most part the youngsters were up for adoption but in some cases they were being given up. Ours was the only large family group. It was an odd feeling, to think that most people adopted one child at a time but here was Elliott adopting four. Little David, in his glasses and pinned-together Eton shirt with the bow tie, clutched first Elliott's hand and then mine. Across the room people whispered and gestured toward us, just as we were whispering about them. The byplay reminded you of a game, to be performed by people waiting in hallways. Our attorney steered us into a secretary's office, where a young man ran his finger down a paper and said, "Oh yes, sir, yes, yes, I have you down, you go right in . . ." His only information about us was an entry on the docket, "Elliott Roosevelt, Adopter." With a look of mild surprise, he counted heads, "One, two, three, four, five, six. Yes."

"How do you do?" Elliott said. "I am Elliott Roosevelt, this is my wife and this is Jimmy Roosevelt, Ford Roosevelt, Gretchen Roosevelt, and David Roosevelt."

"Yes, well, how do you do?"

In the chamber, two rows of padded chairs faced the massive polished desk of the judge. Flags flanked the desk, and to its right stood a witness chair. A court reporter also sat on the right of the desk with his stenographic machine, and opposite him was a clerk, arranging manila file jackets in neat rows. The dull decorum of the room was a disappointment to me. I had envisaged something more exciting, like what you see in a television courtroom drama with a district attorney stalking about, thumbs in vest pockets, spouting sulphurous oratory, perhaps even a jury. Instead, the court reporter caught David's eye and winked.

Judge Thomas Tollakson entered the room, the clerk ordered us all to stand. Then the first witness took the chair and the judge began asking him questions.

"Mr. Roosevelt, how old are you?"

"Fifty, sir."

"Do you realize the difference between your age and the childrens', and the responsibility you are incurring, financial, physical, mental, and spiritual?"

"Your Honor, I'm sure you have the papers about this case. I feel it is incumbent upon me, it is an honor for me, to be able to adopt these children. They are my children and I want to make the whole thing legal . . ."

"Are you willing to assume their support?"

"Yes, sir."

"Are you capable of it?"

"Yes, sir."

Next he summoned me to the stand. Elliott flashed me a reassuring smile as I sat down.

"Mrs. Roosevelt," the judge said, "as the mother of these children, are you convinced that Elliott Roosevelt is the man you want to be their father?"

"Yes, sir. I have never been more sure of anything in my life."

He smiled. "Thank you."

Then, by turns, each child went to sit in the chair and answer the kindly questions of the judge.

"Jimmy? You are Jimmy?"

"Yes, sir."

He consulted our file. "You are in high school now. Do you like your school?"

"Very much, sir."

Ford's file contained a report on the accident in Denver when he had spilled hot grease down his leg. There was also his infant medical history, with details about his severe lung congestion.

"Are you feeling well now, Ford? Your lungs don't bother you any more?"

"No, sir. I'm fine."

The judge talked to Gretchen about school and pets.

"Do you have a dog, Gretchen?"

"Yes, sir. We have a dog named Duke. He's a great Dane. We just got a dog license for him upstairs."

"Er, yes, I heard about it."

David was three years old. He sat in the chair in his short pants and Eton shirt. Freckles marched across his nose. His eyes peeped out from behind big glasses. His feet dangled six inches from the floor.

"David, what do you think of your mother and dad?"

"Fine."

"What did you come down here for today?"

"I came with my mummy and daddy . . . I got a new suit."

"That's a good-looking suit, David. What are you going to do when you leave here?"

"I'm going to go and get adopted."

The judge smiled and wiped his eyes. The court reporter wiped his. The lawyer balanced his briefcase on his knees and looked away.

David returned to his seat. The judge said, "I want this in the record, what I'm about to say."

And then he told us that this was his last day on the bench before retirement, and it was fitting that this would be one of his last cases.

"I have had to see so many unwanted children brought into the world, to grow up floundering and blighted by neglect and then sent out unprepared. It is one of the great tragedies of our times. The responsibility a judge must face," he went on, "gave one an acute sense of inadequacy. It restored his faith in people to see that there were still dedicated adults in this world. Men and women determined to help right some of the wrongs—make a better place for children to live in, give them standards.

"Elliott and Patty Roosevelt, this court gives these children to you, to be their lawful parents. Guard this trust."

It was done. As a parent, I felt renewed and refreshed. There was a closeness to us now, of a kind I had never experienced before. We filed out holding hands and loving each other.

Elliott fished Marmaduke's dog license from his pocket. Walking toward the exit he began to read it.

Marmaduke was a great lumbering bulk on four feet, all frolic and clumsiness. He had come into our lives on a whim, my whim and was to go out in some disgrace. In the eight months we had him, he grew to weigh nearly two hundred pounds, wolfed down enough horse meat to feed a Siberian regiment, and had a bad habit which tested even my passion for dogs.

To begin with, I had thought it would be a clever idea to give Elliott a great Dane for Father's Day. He had told me that years ago in Texas he had owned nine of the huge dogs at one time, a male and female and their seven pups. Such a pet now would re-create for him something from the past. I schemed to make it a surprise.

On Father's Day we were invited to a party with the children at the home of Marge and Bob Wilkie, who owned a Snap-on tool company in Minneapolis. It was a gay affair in the yard of their estate outside the city. Families celebrated Father's Day with a swim in the pool and yard games and a barbecue. The guests of honor also found other forms of refreshment. One father, Franz Perkins Jeune, Jr., insisted on demonstrating his prowess on the trampoline. Jeune was an ardent skier, hiker, deep breather, devotee of yoga and eater of wheat germ. This day he had switched from wheat germ to something stronger. The result of his trampoline exhibition was a cracked head and a strained back.

The grand finale came late in the day. I sprung Marmaduke from his hiding place and he came romping into the crowd, while the children sang, "Happy Father's Day to you, Happy Father's Day to you . . ." At four months, Marmaduke was already belt high and growing fast. The other fathers laughed and slapped Elliott on the back and were vociferously glad they did not have such thoughtful wives. Elliott tried to laugh back, mouthing something between a chuckle and a gasp, and whispered, "Darling, where are we going to keep him?"

We took Marmaduke home to Mrs. Martin's house. On the way, his ungainly bulk consumed so much space the children were complaining. I had visions of a serene, happy household with a superbly trained great Dane heeling and staying and acting the perfect four-footed gentleman. But things got off to a bad start.

Elliott explained to me that if a man truly loved his dog, he slept with him. A dog and his master were inseparable. And so, Marmaduke climbed into bed between us. During the night I kept awakening on the verge of being pushed off the bed. From time to time, Marmaduke would express affection by licking Elliott's ear. It sounded like a horse drinking from a watering trough. It was a restless experience.

I assumed that great Danes were always happy and harmless. When I mentioned this theory one day, Elliott's face clouded, "Well, now . . ." he began, and told me what had happened to his nine great Danes in Texas.

One night they all got out on a rampage across the countryside and killed three calves, seven sheep, thirty turkeys and two hundred chickens before being rounded up with the help of a sheriff's posse. "Once they get the blood taste, they don't stop," he said. I turned pale.

Marmaduke was a peaceable soul. He did not want to make

trouble. He just grew. And grew. And grew. He also had a problem. Marmaduke would not be housebroken. I followed him around with a shovel. He ruined the rug in Mrs. Martin's bedroom and we replaced it at great cost. After six months he was big enough to saddle. Coming down the uncarpeted stairs, he would lose his footing and descend with a thumpity, clattery, bang ending in a heap on the landing. He'd get up, shake that great head and smile. But his problem did not improve. So we gave him a nickname: Plopaduke.

When our six months tenancy at Mrs. Martin's house ended, we found another on DuPont Street. It had a tiny yard, and no place for Marmaduke to romp and play. The weather turned cold. I took him on long walks. The neighbors peeped out from behind their blinds to see me being pulled at a trot by a chest-high dog. One day I took him six blocks to a wooded park which had playgrounds, and sat on a swing holding his leash and watching the children. Marmaduke became excited and bolted away. I flew off the swing, dropping the leash. Mothers and children scattered in the path of the romping great Dane. "Marmaduke! Marmaduke! Come back here, Marmaduke!" When finally I caught him, I was so exhausted I had to wait ten minutes on a hard bench in order to move on home.

The neighbors were not fond of Marmaduke. He bayed at night. In the mornings, he liked to go around stealing milk cartons from their front porches, bringing them home in his giant jaws. After such forays our telephone clamored with angry complaints.

After our first Christmas in Minneapolis, when Marmaduke ate all the decorations off the tree, we decided it was time to be rid of him. Elliott's brother Jimmy and his wife, Irene, paid us a visit. Marmaduke, with his fawn coat and black markings, had never looked more stately. In the evenings before dinner he would stretch before the fireplace while we had cocktails, giving the living room a touch of baronial class. Irene was enchanted. Elliott and I conspired, dropping hints that we would like to find a good home for Marmaduke.

"Wonderful animal, Irene. We sent him to training school. He will sit and stay and lie down. Fine disposition. Marvelous." We neglected to mention the shovel upstairs, or Marmaduke's nickname, or the milk cartons. The prospect of owning such a dog sent Irene into raptures. We promised to ship him to Washington.

It was a cold and cheerless night when Marmaduke left us. On the drive to the airport, he filled first the back seat, then the front and sometimes both. I was bereft. "Plopaduke," I said, "I'll miss you. I really didn't mind the ruined carpet or the milk cartons or all that shoveling." Elliott patted me on the knee and talked about what a good home Marmaduke would have and how Jimmy and Irene would love him. In the baggage room, the attendant eyed Marmaduke's bulk and scratched his head. "Ma'am, I don't know how we're gonna get all that dog into anything." It was, indeed, a struggle. Finally we tilted a traveling crate forward and Elliott tumbled the dog in headfirst, like an overlarge sack of potatoes.

The adventures of Marmaduke were not ended with his departure from Minneapolis. In Washington, Irene decided to drop by the airport and pick up the arriving dog on her way home from the beauty parlor. That afternoon she was going to a garden party for a congressman's wife. At the baggage station, she asked the man to help her open the dog crate. "Sure thing," he said.

Out burst two hundred pounds of great Dane, deliriously happy at being freed from his prison and dying to find a fire plug. Irene screamed. Marmaduke galloped across the terminal and into the passenger areas, joyously trying to give each stranger he met a friendly lick in the face. Barking, he barreled across the magazine stand. Somebody blew a whistle. Redcaps formed a cordon at the exit. At last Marmaduke allowed himself to be corralled and a choke chain put around his neck. They got him into Irene's car. When she arrived home, another disaster: Marmaduke bounded up the sidewalk and bowled over their tiny son, Del, who set up a howl. For three days, each time the two got close Del was run over. On the fourth day, Marmaduke found another new home.

Former actress Ilona Massey, the beautiful, Hungarian-born blonde, lived on a lovely country estate on the outskirts of Bethesda, Maryland, with her husband, Donald Dawson, a Washington attorney. Their house was surrounded by woods and fields.

The Dawsons loved dogs, especially great Danes. Ilona was delighted to take Marmaduke off Irene's hands.

When we received the news, I gulped. Mrs. Dawson, I knew, always gave her dogs free run of their house. She and her husband also possessed magnificent antiques, including fine Dresden and porcelains along with priceless statuary. Eventually, on a trip to Washington, Elliott and I visited them to see Marmaduke again. The house was even more unique than I had imagined, a miniature castle set in the woods, furnished like a private museum. Her collection included marble columns and busts dating back before Christ.

In the far end of the living room was a raised dais portion. Beside the landing were two free-standing Dresden hat racks, about three feet high, of priceless porcelain. As we chatted, Ilona Dawson summoned the dogs. Two canine monsters the size of ponies came pounding around the corner, skidding on the slick floor. They flashed past the fragile hat racks, but touched neither. I recognized the fawn-colored brute with black markings. Marmaduke tried to drown us with kisses.

11

A Roosevelt Houseguest

From the beginning, being Elliott Roosevelt's wife has been a process of learning and doing. Carrying a name that is so much a part of the American tradition, even when acquired through marriage, gives one a unique new set of responsibilities. The public expects more from Roosevelts, more tact, more drive, more wit, more patience, more giving of time and energy and ideas. It is unthinkable that a Roosevelt would have money worries, or feel pain, or have bad breath, or family feuds, or tired feet at a public function, or be anything less than gracious and tall and selfless. The 1961 visits by Mrs. Roosevelt to Minneapolis, Rochester, and Mankato, Minnesota, gave me rare glimpses of a great public figure's life on the other side of the handshake, the cameras, and the interviewer's questions. This, also, was the first time Mrs. Roosevelt was a guest in my house, a prospect which I had assumed would demand the ultimate from me as a hostess. Before the visit was ended, however, I was to be astonished by the almost-Spartan simplicity of her needs.

As is often the case, behind the crowds and publicity and hubbub some devious purposes were at work. In Mrs. Roosevelt's Minneapolis trip, this unseen element was my determination to recover some of the priceless Roosevelt heirlooms Elliott had lost in the divorce settlement with Minnewa. Since the financial disaster of the previous summer, when the Colorado National

Bank impounded his personal assets as collateral, I had been trying to conceive of a way to recover some of them. Locked up in a warehouse in Denver and Phoenix were enough antiques, furnishings, Roosevelt mementos, and *objets d'art* to make me agonize over the thought of losing them. Once sold on the open market, they could never be recovered. This prospect brought about many sleepless nights. Elliott, of all FDR and Eleanor's children, had such a strong feeling for family mementos. He had beggared himself many times in the past to acquire some piece of memorabilia that had belonged to a Delano or a Roosevelt. Thoughts of this gigantic loss brought much pain and anxiety to both of us.

The Minneapolis Institute of Arts had launched a series of exhibits of antiques and personal possessions from old-line families. Museum Director Carl Weinhardt and his wife lived near Mrs. Martin's house on Mt. Curve Avenue. When we moved in for the summer, the Weinhardts became neighborly acquaintances. The museum project, I realized, could be the break we needed. Casually, I remarked to Carl one day that Elliott had some superb old Roosevelt items in Denver. There was the massive desk George Washington had used as President, Franklin D. Roosevelt's overstuffed chair and his study table from Harvard, life-size portraits of assorted ancestors, and such articles as priceless silver bowls, cigarette boxes, silver-framed autographed photographs of English royalty, and numerous paintings and assorted bric-a-brac. Many of the things had been gifts to FDR and Eleanor Roosevelt from leading figures of the world—Winston Churchill, Jawaharlal Nehru, Charles de Gaulle, Madame Chiang Kai-shek. The museum director's pulse quickened. He took the idea to his board of directors. Some GOP members resented staging a Roosevelt exhibit in a city noted for its stanch Republicanism, but even they could not deny the drawing power of such a display. Director Weinhardt won the board's approval.

For our part, I had no idea how Elliott and I could manage to regain possession of the articles once they were brought to Minneapolis. But the first step, clearly, was to get them out of Denver and Phoenix. We would cross the other bridges later. I enlisted the help of a local art dealer and Roosevelt buff, Joseph E. Walton of the Beard Gallery. Acting as intermediary for the museum, and a cover for us, Joseph persuaded the Colorado bank to ship him the collection for the exhibit, along with a consignment agreement to sell what he could. A share of the proceeds would go back to the bank to pay off debts. Another portion was to be credited to us and would be applied to our repurchase of Elliott's possessions.

The Rooseveltiana exhibit was scheduled to open on a Thursday in June and continue for three months. To give it a proper launching, Elliott invited his mother to be the guest of honor. When Mrs. Roosevelt agreed to take part, the museum arranged an opening night dinner and private reception. Dinner would be $100 a plate; those museum supporters desiring to attend the reception only, and tour the exhibit on the opening night, would pay $25 a head. Regular admission to the public, then, would be one dollar. (In three months, the museum was to make $60,000.)

Then somehow, the shipment got lost on the way from Denver and all points west. Frantically, we burned up the telephone lines to the bank, and sent out tracers. Finally located, the van did not roll into Minneapolis until Friday night preceding the opening. I rushed down to help the museum staff unpack, sort, polish silver, clean and label each item. Friends were enlisted to assist. The labeling proved a frustrating task. Someone would unwrap an oil painting or a vase, asking, "How should this be identified, Mrs. Roosevelt?" Usually I didn't have the foggiest idea, and had to run to Elliott for help. One of the items I found was a photograph of Minnewa and Mrs. Roosevelt, which did little to provide a tranquilizer for me. That evening at home, Elliott asked pleasantly how things were going. "Terrible," I said. I was appalled at how some of the items had been abused. Two magnificent Sèvres vases, dark blue with gold trim, contained a litter of cigarette butts, chewing gum wrappers, and paper scraps. An old French vitrine cabinet of mahogany and heavily leaded crystal which had been the repository for Elliott's war medals, came to us with six inches slashed from the delicately wrought legs with their bronze inlays. The medals were among the missing. Evidently they had been mislaid or disposed of by some insensitive person.

Few are aware that Elliott had entered the service, volunteering for the Air Corps, long before our country became fully involved. In spite of all the hue and cry of "I want to be a captain, too" and "How come Roosevelt's son gets all the honor and glory," the medals that had been displayed in the case were small tokens of Elliott's participation—from captain through brigadier general—in the maelstrom which was World War II. He had been the recipient of the Croix de Guerre, Distinguished Service Cross, Air Medal with twelve oak leaf clusters, Commander of the Order of the British Empire, to name but a few. A Purple Heart with three clusters signified each of the four times he was wounded. War indeed had not been for him a time of glory and excitement.

To give us financial padding, the Beard Gallery arranged to sell two items then in the exhibit, a five-foot rosewood grandfather clock which had belonged to FDR's mother, Sara Delano, and a huge silver tea service which had been made for the Theodore Roosevelt family by Kirk Silversmiths of Baltimore, in the latter years of the eighteenth century. The service was very unusual in size and design—most of the pieces were two feet in height—and had proved more functional than decorative during President Roosevelt's tenure of office. Elliott also owned a matched pair of pistols, supposedly belonging to Jesse James, which we gave to the Beard Gallery for sale. Crowds flocked to the attractive window display where the pistols lay, resplendent on black velvet. They brought a price of $2500.

The George Washington desk and other FDR furniture pieces were among the hits of the exhibit. Another was a 300-year-old Italian dining room set of black oak which Sara Delano had given to Franklin and Eleanor Roosevelt as a wedding present (Minnewa had had it stripped and bleached blond). There was furniture manufactured in Mrs. Roosevelt's factory at Val-Kill, near Hyde Park, during the '30s; a small oil painting of Elliott Roosevelt, Sr., brother of Theodore Roosevelt and father of Eleanor Roosevelt, on a fox hunt; an enormous carved wooden jewelry case which had belonged to Mrs. Roosevelt; massive silver candelabra; a pair of delft tobacco jars from Holland; a silver bowl presented by King George VI and Queen Elizabeth after their visit to Hyde Park; a Daniel Huntington oil portrait of Theodore Roosevelt, Sr., and life-size portraits of Dr. and Mrs.

Edward Ludlow, relatives of the Delanos. Mrs. Ludlow's portrait hung for twenty-five years in New York's Metropolitan Museum of Art as an example of the finest early American primitive style of portraiture.

Appraisals had been made by the Denver bank, valuing the collection at approximately $100,000. We also asked a friend, Victor J. Hammer of the Hammer Galleries, New York, to make an appraisal; and Joe Walton made one of his own for pricing purposes. The Beard Gallery director shared our reluctance to see the heirlooms leave the hands of the family. In months to come, he was to keep them on consignment in order that we would have ample opportunity to buy them back as our finances improved. Happily, the stock Elliott was buying on option in Motor Travel Service, Inc., at $1.10 per share fluctuated as high as $12. In a year he made $50,000, enough to recover the collection—at Joe Walton's price—and to buy our first home together.

Any compunctions I might have had were salved by the knowledge that the bank really could not care less who bought this collection or what sentimental value was attached to it. A tiny rocking chair I found among the pieces, for instance, had little cash value to anyone else, but to us it was beyond price: it had been Elliott's, as a baby. There was a bronze figurine of a mare and colt, similar to those you can buy in most bric-a-brac stores, but this one FDR had bought for Elliott in Paris for his birthday, and brought it back in the diplomatic pouch.

Such knowledge made the business at hand doubly important to us; and I felt that Mrs. Roosevelt, had she suspected, would give it her tacit blessing. She knew well that her visit would enhance immeasurably the prestige of Elliott and his family in Minneapolis, and boost the career of this son who had had such a series of misfortunes. With a shrewd sense of practicality about the value of a great name, this was the woman who autographed books and pictures fully as "*Eleanor Roosevelt*," even for her grandchildren. She knew that in some future time of financial need, there was no benefit to be gained from simply the signature of "*Grandmère*."

What I could show her about Elliott's new life during the brief time she would be in my home, would, I knew, go a long way toward erasing any marks left in her mind by rumors, half-truths, and malicious gossip. As her hostess and newest daughter-in-law, I was desperate to make a good impression. Perhaps I carried it to extreme.

Mrs. Martin's hilltop house had a superb setting with lovely woods all around, a fine view of the city, and a large sunken garden. In the garden there was promise of flowers, but the blooms had not yet appeared. I wanted to have a lawn party for the children of the neighborhood and their parents. "Mummy will love the garden," Elliott said. "She is so fond of flowers." Each morning I poked my head out, looking for a blossom. Nothing. Not even a dandelion. Then I had a brainstorm, went to a nursery and bought $50 worth of blooming potted flowers—asters, zinnias, mums—brought them home and planted them. They all died, in spite of my efforts with fertilizer, watering, etc. Undaunted, I trudged out again and bought artificial flowers. By this time, I had an investment of $50 below ground and $50 above ground—'C'est la guerre.' That evening Elliott was amazed at the display. "Honey, it's beautiful, you have a beautiful garden," he exclaimed. Ruefully I confessed that the flowers were artificial. Elliott's face grew long. "Mother will be crushed," he said. "She loves to go out in the early morning and pick flowers before breakfast." Thoroughly humiliated, I undid all of my handiwork and resigned myself to the fact that we would have a flowerless garden.

A large crowd gathered at the Minneapolis airport to welcome Mrs. Roosevelt. The morning was hot, and perspiration soaked the backs of official greeters as they stood in the sunshine awaiting her plane. Elliot Hoffman had a sheaf of roses and a plaque from his police journal association to present to her, and insisted that she ride in his car with a police escort. The airliner landed, taxied in, and she walked off the plane carrying a small zipper-type suitcase of blue canvas with red leather trim. She wore one of those nondescript dresses and beamed her smile at the crowd. Someone reached for the suitcase. "Thank you, no," she said. "I can carry it." The crowd pressed in close: women in big hats representing garden clubs and sisterhoods, Negro men and women, city officials, students of all ages. After greeting Elliott and me, she turned her attention to them. I tried to shield her, saying, "Don't push, now. Don't bother Mrs. Roosevelt. We have to go home so she can rest." Mrs. Roosevelt turned to me with one of those patronizing "My deah . . ." smiles. Without a word being said, I dropped back and fell silent, punctured. Then, eying the bag she carried, I realized suddenly that this was her entire luggage for a two-day trip including a formal dinner. "Elliott," I whispered, "she'll have to buy some clothes." He smiled and shook his head. On such trips, his mother carried three basic dresses, including a formal, all wash-and-wear. She had one pair of shoes, a hat, and a handbag. Period.

Elliot Hoffman was bursting with excitement. Scurrying about and shouting orders, he got us all into the Chrysler. Mrs. Roosevelt sat in front beside him, and Elliott and I took the back seat with Harriet Hoffman. The car was oppressively hot.

Mrs. Roosevelt had removed her glasses and sat with her shoulders slumped forward. Harriet Hoffman chattered gaily at the back of her head. "Mrs. Roosevelt, did you have a nice trip? . . . We certainly are glad to have you in Minneapolis . . . Everyone is so excited . . ." There was no reply. When Mrs. Roosevelt removed her glasses, she also took off her hearing aid. At the moment, our distinguished visitor was fast asleep.

Somewhere I had learned that when you entertained a visiting dignitary you prepared a schedule of activities and placed it in their room. Carefully, I had written out a minute-by-minute summary of the day. "Noon, sherry in the living room; 12:05, Ford does magic tricks; 12:10, lunch . . ." I kept misspelling the word "occasion." There were fresh flowers in her room, a carafe of water, and I had stocked the bathroom with so much of her favorite Elizabeth Arden soap, bath powder, hand lotion, and cologne that the place reeked of it. Mrs. Roosevelt read the schedule and said, "My deah, you didn't plan any time for rest."

"Rest?"

"Yes, my doctor has given me explicit instructions, and I'm afraid he would be so upset. I find that it does get me through. I must have an hour of rest in the afternoon." Actually, I had planned an hour and a half, but it was following the garden party, which would last until about five.

While she unpacked her three dresses and hung them up, I rushed downstairs, worrying.

"Elliott, do you think everything's all right?

"Relax, darling. Everything's fine."

Upon arrival, Mrs. Roosevelt had given her son the usual perfunctory buss on the cheek, more noise than kiss, and offered a handshake for me. As in New York, her manner toward me lacked warmth; it was cordial, but not warm. When she came down for sherry, the conversation was light, small.

"My deah, what a lovely home."

Ford was dying to entertain *Grandmère* with his magic tricks. His portable magic table was set up in the living room. As Elliott and his mother talked, Ford kept inching the table closer to her, hoping she would notice. She didn't notice.

The great Dane, Marmaduke, padded into the room. Mrs. Roosevelt's eyebrows lifted. Marmaduke gave her a slobbery lick on the hand. I crossed my fingers, hoping he would not have an accident on the living-room floor.

"What a lovely dog," Mrs. Roosevelt said. "But how can he run? Elliott, what do you do with the dog at night?"

"He sleeps with us, Mummy, on our bed."

I wondered if that would make an impression, knowing that in this marriage her son shared a bed with his wife as well as a dog.

"Well, deah, doesn't he harm the furniture? What would happen if he ruined this charming furniture?"

We did not tell her of the mess Marmaduke already was making of the carpet in our bedroom.

"Elliott," I whispered, "can Ford do his magic tricks now?"

"Not now, baby. Later."

Ford looked at me in dismay. Our Norwegian cateress, Julienna Nordby, came in to announce that luncheon was served. I signaled to Ford to bring his magic into the dining room.

"Honey, can Ford show his magic tricks now?"

Elliott was holding the chair for his mother. "Do we have to have it right now?" he said.

"It's the only time."

"Oh, all right." Raising his voice, he announced, "Mummy, Ford wants to show you his magic tricks."

"Really?" The head lifted, the eyes sought Ford, the face crinkled in a smile. "Magic? Well, Ford, what are these tricks?"

Calm, bespectacled, dressed in his best suit and a white shirt with French cuffs, my fourteen-year-old son proceeded to tell a story about the starving children of China. Pouring a cup of rice into a small bowl, he said that one day a magician came to the land of the starving children. "This was a very wise and powerful magician." He poured a cup of water into another bowl. "Seeing their plight, he decided to use his magic powers." Ford covered the bowls with a cloth. "He said a few magic words, passed his hand over the magic scarf, and . . ." He flicked it off. Rice poured everywhere. It filled the bowl to overflowing. It filled the cup and a pitcher, it spilled over the table. It spilled over the floor. "There was plenty of rice for everybody." And now we, too, had rice everywhere.

"Ford!"

"Oh, oh," said Mrs. Roosevelt, "did you see what that boy did, Elliott?"

Then Ford brought in his guillotine trick. This was the one I hated. The guillotine was four feet high, and appeared disturbingly real. Speaking a line of patter, he placed a bundle of carrots on the chopping block and sent the blade crashing down, slashing the carrots to bits. Then his assistant for this trick, David, put his head in the slot. Again, the blade crashed. David's head pitched forward. Then he lifted it again and grinned at us, with all those gaps in his teeth.

"My word," Mrs. Roosevelt said.

After lunch, about twenty neighborhood children came to the garden with their mothers to meet Mrs. Roosevelt. Shortly after 2 P.M., we prepared to leave for a full-scale society garden party at Mrs. Alice Martin's summer home on the lake. Outside, another police escort was waiting for us. The sun was beating down. An odor of fresh asphalt, laid the previous day, rose from the street. As we walked toward the car, someone shouted "Eleanor, Eleanor. I got to talk to you." Across the fresh pavement came a large Negro woman. Suddenly I remembered the telephone call I had received at seven o'clock that morning. It was from the dispatcher of a cab company. "Mrs. Roosevelt," he had said, "do you know an Emmy Lou Bider?" I told him no. "Well, she's been here at the office pestering me to death. Says she's got to see Eleanor Roosevelt. Wants a cab to drive her out to your place, but she doesn't know the address. I figured I'd call first." I told him to send the woman to the Minneapolis Institute of Art tonight. Apparently, however, she had found our home address.

Mrs. Roosevelt left us and walked across the asphalt to meet the woman in the middle of the street. There, while their heels sank into the soft pavement, the two women talked. In 1935, it seemed, Mrs. Bider's husband had received a letter of congratulations from FDR for a civic service. The letter had been destroyed in a fire. The husband was now dead. Still, that letter had been the most proud possession of this family. Now Emmy Lou Bider wondered if a copy existed, so she could pass it on to her children and grandchildren when she died. "Why certainly, Mrs. Bider," Eleanor Roosevelt said. "I am sure there is a copy in the archives at Hyde Park." She took the woman's name and address. A few weeks later, the copy was sent out from the Roosevelt Library.

Police sirens screaming, we roared to the garden party. Mrs. Roosevelt had changed to a lavender-and-white afternoon dress and wore her small flowered hat. Five hundred of Minneapolis' top society had turned out to greet her and drink punch and nibble cookies, standing on the dark green lawn which swept down to the lake. Elliot Hoffman had brought his forty-five-foot cruiser into service to shuttle people back and forth from a parking area across the water. He wore a white cap with gold braid and bore a faint resemblance to Admiral Chester W. Nimitz. Swiftly, amid polite small talk, Mrs. Roosevelt took command. With her hostess, Mrs. Martin, she greeted people in the front of the house for a while, then announced, "Well, my deah, I think it's time we went to the garden." The garden party was clearly hers, now. Calm, perfectly at ease, outgoing, she stood for two hours shaking hands. Seen turned on full, the Roosevelt charm was awesome. People remembered her from past affairs, when to Mrs. Roosevelt, they must have been blurred faces and quick handshakes among hundreds. One woman said she had met Mrs. Roosevelt at a Wellesley College graduation, many years ago. "Yes, I do indeed remember that graduation," Mrs. Roosevelt said. "Wasn't that a beautiful day?"

All the while she kept me near her. "This is my daughter-in-law Patty, who is Elliott's wife." Appearances, I was learning, were important. She wanted us to appear close.

Guests had been invited in shifts, and represented the leadership of the Minneapolis financial, business, industrial, social, and cultural worlds. By turns, boats arrived from across the lake, nudging into the dock to discharge men and women. The women wore hats and gloves and light, colorful dresses, tending to accentuate the plain but functional attire of the guest of honor. You could tell without looking when Elliot Hoffman's boat arrived with another load, by the sound of its banging into the dock. There was no question about when the party came to an end. Precisely at 5 P.M., Mrs. Roosevelt looked at her hostess and said, "Well, Mrs. Martin, it's time for us to go or we'll be late for the art museum tonight. Thank you so much. It has been a delightful party, perfectly delightful . . ." And with that, she headed for the car.

By now, the split-second timing of things had begun to affect me. When we arrived home, I automatically dashed up to her bedroom, drew the blinds and turned down the bed. Then while she rested, I joined Elliott downstairs and we each had a quiet relaxing cocktail. That made us feel better. And now, we discussed the thing that had been troubling us for days. My husband and I were bursting with news. Added to the fact that Elliott had adopted my children was another equally wonderful development. I was pregnant, and we were both so happy.

We wanted to tell his mother everything, and didn't know how.

The discovery of my condition had come a few weeks before, in an offbeat kind of way. For months, since Sheldon, I had suffered from a persistent cough. Combined with it were frequent spells of low-grade temperature. Finally, I went to a doctor for a check-up. He found a spot on my lung. "Histoplasmosis," he announced. I told him I also had heartburn and general listlessness, which was unusual for me.

"Doctor, I think I might be pregnant."

"You couldn't be pregnant. How old are you?"

"Thirty-nine."

"And Mr. Roosevelt, how old is he?"

"He's eleven years older."

The doctor took a blood sample and sent it off to the lab for testing. To avoid attracting attention to the name, he simply noted that the sample belonged to "Mrs. Buttons."

The laboratory reported back: "Positive, Mrs. Buttons."

A nurse, having only Mrs. Buttons' name, and with it my address and phone number, called me. "I'd like to speak to Mrs. Buttons, please," she said.

I didn't know about Mrs. Buttons either. "There is no Mrs. Buttons here," I said.

"Well, this is the doctor's office. We have this number for Mrs. Buttons, and I was calling to tell her she is pregnant."

Imagine being pregnant and having histoplasmosis! Elliott was ecstatic. He whooped and danced around. He wanted to call his brothers and tell the world. He refused to let me carry a magazine across the room, and frowned at my lifting anything heavier than a cigarette lighter.

Next day he came home with a yapping black poodle the size of a water glass. This, he declared, was Mr. Buttons. Then, to explain to the children where a poodle with such an unlikely name came from and why, we had a formal family dinner, with wines and much festivity.

We felt that Mrs. Roosevelt should not be told about the pregnancy without also being informed of the adoption. The question was, how best to broach the subject. The task was clearly Elliott's. Keeping such happy news from her this long had been a chore for him.

By evening, I was beginning to wonder about my mother-in-law's physical stamina. Already her day had involved a long airplane trip, a noisy airport welcome, two and a half hours of standing and shaking hands at a garden party, and several fast, hot motorcades. I was nearly forty years younger and feeling the strain. But she came downstairs smiling and freshened from her hour-long nap, fully prepared to formally open the museum exhibit.

After still another pell-mell auto ride that sounded like "Gangbusters," we arrived at the art museum. Two hundred guests had made their reservations for the private dinner. They were mostly the leading patrons of the museum. Mrs. Roosevelt sat at the head table. Afterward, we formed a receiving line which included Mrs. Roosevelt, Director Weinhardt, Elliott and me, to greet the opening night guests.

Three thousand of them filed past, and we shook hands with every one. Such a turnout astonished even the most optimistic of the museum directors. It demonstrated beyond question the heroic stature of this woman, whose presence transcended the bounds of political affiliations. Amiable, gracious, strong, she stood beside me shaking hand after hand, exchanging pleasant greetings, passing them on. Many people unthinkingly would plant themselves solidly before her, only to find they were being pulled along toward the next outstretched hand by the surprising grip of this stooped, elderly woman. "Yes, how delightful it is to see you tonight. This is my daughter-in-law, Patty . . ." I became so fascinated watching her that I missed some of the hands.

For that evening, I had slipped a dinner ring onto my right hand, and wore a pale chartreuse linen dress. After more than an hour of handshaking, I glanced down and noticed spots of blood dribbling down the right side of the dress. My ring finger was bleeding. Mrs. Roosevelt noticed too. She whispered to me: "Don't ever wear a ring on your right hand, dear. Then always take their hand, don't let them take yours . . ." People were still coming through the line. I was trying desperately to remove the ring and wipe off the blood. Still they came. It was like a bad dream. Finally, I gave up and held my handbag over the blood spots, and continued to shake hands. Fatigue and pregnancy joined forces. I became lightheaded. My feet were throbbing. I did not see how Elliott and his mother could go on. They stood there, knees slightly bent, weight evenly balanced, and never moved their feet. At this time, Mrs. Roosevelt's feet and toes were badly drawn by arthritis, which made even walking an agony at times. If she felt pain, her face never betrayed it.

A line of Italian throne chairs had been placed at some distance behind us. I whispered to Elliott, "Honey, I'm tired." He nodded, shook another hand and murmured to Mrs. Roosevelt: "Mummy, I think we should sit down now."

It was after eleven o'clock when we got home. I had been looking forward to preparing a good breakfast for her: eggs, bacon, toast, coffee. For some reason I decided to bring up the subject. "What would you like for breakfast, Grandmère?"

"Metrecal, my dear," she said. "Chocolate Metrecal."

The Norwegian cateress was waiting as we walked into the house. "Mrs. Roosevelt," she said, "you haven't had your desserrrt yet. I fix fine desserrrt and you don't eat it." She brought out a great wedge of chocolate cake, placed it before our guest and shook a Norwegian finger beneath her nose. "That is my special Norwegian cake, and I want you to eat that, good ladeee." Then she sat down next to Mrs. Roosevelt, in her uniform to wait while the delicacy was consumed.

After that, Elliott and I went out to find a 7-11 Store that sold chocolate Metrecal. Dick Johnson, the accountant for Arthur Anderson & Co. in Omaha, whom we had known in Sheldon, went with us. Dick had flown up for the Rooseveltiana opening and afterward joined us for the cake-eating ceremony.

"Do you really think she'll want any breakfast at all now, Elliott?" he said.

Mrs. Roosevelt left the following morning to fly back to New York. We took her to the airport behind another noisy police escort. I was tired of hearing sirens.

The Rooseveltiana exhibit was a smashing success. On weekends Elliott gave it a boost by personally taking crowds through, explaining the various pieces. A favorite of the public's was his story about a small portrait of a Chinese merchant, in a gold leaf frame. It had belonged to Sara Delano. She had received it as a gift from a Chinese businessman who for years sent her tins of tea at Christmas. Elliott called his little speech "The Story of the Chinese Gentleman in the Opium Trade."

"This picture," he told the crowds, "is a portrait of the man who was head of a tea firm in Canton, China, when great-great-grandfather, Edward Delano, first went to China with Russell & Co. of Boston in 1817.

"In Canton, Edward Delano was told by the Russell & Co. agent there that he should try to buy fine tea from this merchant, and arrive at the best possible price. He went to the merchant's house, was duly ushered into the gentleman's sitting room and offered tea. Edward, who was seventeen at the time, preferred to come right to the point. 'Mr. Merchant,' he said, 'I am here to see if we can agree on a price for a shipload of tea.'

"The tea merchant promptly ordered him out of the house.

"Back at the office of the agent, the flustered Mr. Delano reported what had happened and said, 'What did I do wrong?' The agent blanched. 'You are never supposed to bring up business,' he said, 'before observing the amenities of a Chinese gentleman's house. When drinking tea, one discusses his host's health, his family and the state of their health, anything but business. You violated one of the basic rules of Chinese etiquette.' Edward Delano was thoroughly contrite. He asked the agent how he could make amends to the merchant. 'The only thing to do now,' the agent replied, 'is to go to the gentleman's house and sit down next to the door leading into the courtyard until you are invited back inside.'

"The next morning he went to the merchant's house and sat down outside. Noon came, and afternoon, and evening. He was not invited in. The second day, he returned and waited half a day. At midday, the invitation came. The merchant greeted him cordially and offered tea. They spoke of the weather, of Delano's family and their health, of the merchant's family and their health. After the tea things had been taken away, the merchant placed his fingertips together and asked, 'Now, what can I do for you, young man?'

"He began by apologizing for what he had done, saying he had been sorely ignorant of the rules of good manners and he begged the merchant's indulgence. The merchant waved off the apologies. They then began talking of price, and the merchant offered to sell him tea at a price which would make possible a fine profit on the cargo shipped to America. Young Delano came away elated. That was the beginning of the Delano fortune in the China tea trade."

As Elliott talked, people would study the meticulous detail of the oil painting and the figure of the merchant himself, standing in dark, expensive robes and looking back at them. At this point, Elliott livened up his story with hints of dark doings as the tea trade flourished.

"Later, ships of the trade often smuggled opium into the United States. This was done through the captains and crews. Westbrook Pegler eventually charged that father's fortune was based on opium smuggling, but nobody ever accused my ancestors formally of such illicit activity.

"Late in the nineteenth century, my grandmother began to receive gift tins of tea at Christmas from the grandson of the original merchant. This continued until she died. Then they sent the tea to my parents until the Japanese overran China in World War II, and the gifts stopped.

"This was a wonderful fortune, but eventually it was to trickle away. My father helped to dissipate it because he spent $100,000 a year of his own capital being President of the United States, over and above his presidential income.

"By the time Father died and we children came into his estate," Elliott concluded, "there wasn't very much left."

A month after her first visit, Mrs. Roosevelt came again, this time for a swing through Rochester and the college town of Mankato, Minnesota. At Rochester, her hosts would be a couple of old friends, Dr. Charles Mayo and his wife. This son of one of the founding brothers of Mayo Clinic had invited Mrs. Roosevelt to speak in the high school, on behalf of the United Nations Association. Again she carried only a minimum of luggage, if anything even less than before. During the three-hour drive to Rochester from Minneapolis, Elliott decided to give her our news.

"Mummy, how do you like the children?"

"Elliott, dear, they really are very nice children. Perfectly lovely. I know you must be proud of them."

"I am. I adopted them all."

His mother gasped. "Elliott, you didn't!" The three words, more exploded than said, stung me like a slap. "Don't you realize, deah, how young little David is and how old you are?"

The response was so cold, so totally unexpected, that it slammed a damper over our spirits. We decided to say nothing about my pregnancy. The rest of the drive was made almost in silence.

Mrs. Roosevelt's popularity with young people was brought home to me that afternoon in Rochester. There was a huge reception for college students active in the UN Association's collegiate program. Afterward, Mrs. Roosevelt sat down in a winged chair and the young people, boys and girls of mixed races and nationalities, gathered around on the floor. The theme of her discussion was what the youth of today can contribute to the world and its people, regardless of nationality. In response to questions, she spoke easily in that soft, quavering voice, but with an astuteness which cut through muddled thinking like a hot knife through butter.

That night, people, young and old, thronged to the Rochester high school gym to hear her speech. Without referring to notes she stood for more than two hours talking about the United Nations, its humanitarian objectives in a troubled world, and its great achievements in the face of adversity. Despite my painful resentment of her attitude toward the adoption, I was fascinated by the manner in which she handled herself in public. Again, she stood rock-still for two hours and never moved her feet.

In Rochester, Mrs. Roosevelt was the houseguest of Mrs. Howard Gray, widow of the surgeon who had operated on Jimmy Roosevelt in the early forties, removing part of his stomach. It was during this illness that Jimmy met Romelle Schneider, the nurse he later married. Charlie and Alice Mayo had a dinner for Mrs. Roosevelt in the hotel, and that night, following her speech, they invited Elliott and me to their home for a late party.

The famous doctor, son of co-founder Edward Mayo, now ran the Rochester clinic. He was a stocky, energetic man, fiftyish, with thinning brown hair and great personal warmth. His wife, Alice, was warm and delightfully flighty, reminding you somewhat of the actress Billie Burke. Their home was a four-story rambling frame in Rochester, with terraces opening off the rooms. It had a cool charm and was beautifully furnished. Joining us for coffee and conversation were two Mayo sons and the wife of one of them.

Charlie Mayo had known FDR and Eleanor Roosevelt as a personal friend. They had visited in the doctor's home while Franklin Roosevelt was President. Mayo regaled us with anecdotes, and his favorite was about his determination to loosen up the President with a drink. Mrs. Mayo had been horrified at the idea. "Charlie, you're not going to serve the Roosevelts liquor," she had protested. "They don't drink." This popular conception of a non-drinking President again proved incorrect. FDR and Dr. Mayo had two martinis apiece and enjoyed themselves thoroughly.

I was taken by this pleasant man, who talked to me like a Dutch uncle, and expressed to him my fears at coming into this clannish but extraordinary family of Roosevelts. He smiled broadly. "I'll give you one word of advice, Patty. You keep going the way you're going and you'll make them all look sick."

At eleven o'clock, Dr. Mayo looked at his watch and excused himself. "Sorry," he said with a yawn, "I've got surgery at 6:00 A.M. 'Night." We quickly said our good-byes and went to our hotel.

The following day we drove from Rochester to Mankato, Minnesota, a rural community and a college town in the heart of a rich area of truck and dairy farms. A few miles out we were picked up by another motorcycle escort, and led noisily to the town limits. There a large crowd awaited us, gathered around a ribbon stretched across the road. They handed Mrs. Roosevelt a bouquet and a huge wooden key, painted gold. The mayor cut the ribbon and made a speech. Flabbergasted, I peered around, wondering where all these people came from.

The hotel in town was old and atmospheric, with no air-conditioning. In its day it must have sheltered many a visiting lightning rod salesman. Electric fans mounted on tall metal stands blew hot air across the lobby.

Waiting to greet us was a delegation of the press from surrounding small towns, most of them representing small weekly papers or farm journals. To them this was the story of the year. Also on hand was Mrs. Roosevelt's secretary from the American Association of the United Nations, Miss Estelle Linzer of New York. Brisk and efficient, she carried a typed itinerary and was ready to ride herd on the press conference to avoid letting it consume too much time. Miss Linzer's predecessor in this job had been Pat Baillargeon from Seattle, whose sister, Jane Heffernan, was an old friend of mine. Pat's father, Cebert B. Baillargeon, was a powerful figure in Seattle and one of the respected bankers there. I was delighted to learn that Pat was a member of Mrs. Roosevelt's United Nations Staff.

As the newsmen and -women asked their questions, Estelle kept track of the time. Finally, she stepped forward with, "That's all, ladies and gentlemen, time's up. Mrs. Roosevelt . . ." Her boss nodded, smiled and went to her room to rest. Estelle turned to us and said, "Well, Elliott, what's new?"

Luncheon was served, with speechmaking and songs, in the Rotary Club dining room, after which we went to the school for

Mrs. Roosevelt's talk about the United Nations. The auditorium-gymnasium was packed. The whole town of Mankato had come to see her, along with large numbers of people from surrounding communities. Again she spoke for two and a half hours, without a note, not once moving her feet.

Afterward, we drove back to Minneapolis, discussing events of the two days but never mentioning my being pregnant.

It was a relief not to have a motorcycle escort.

12

Republicans and Roosevelts

As the summer passed, my pregnancy progressed with reasonable comfort. My friends Prudy McCarthy and Ann Watson were great aids to my disposition. Ann was a bright young matron with a gift for light talk. We nicknamed each other Pearl and Mabel. She would call me and ask, "Mabel, have you gained weight? How do you feel?" My reply was predictable: "Terrible."

Ann's family were old-time Minneapolisians and she owned a beautiful mink coat. One day she came to visit me, took the coat off and tossed it onto the couch by the stairwell—it was also near the nest of our poodle pup, Mr. Buttons. We went upstairs briefly, then returned and discovered Mr. Buttons chewing happily on the coat. Looking up at us, he spit fur and wagged his tail. I almost fainted.

Before school started that fall we decided to take the children on a vacation trip to Texas. Glenn and Martha Justice, our old friends from courtship time, invited us to stay at their ranch near Dallas for two weeks while they were away on a trip. The children rode horseback every day and swam in a dammed-up part of the creek. Elliott decided to demonstrate his prowess from his old rodeo days riding Brahma bulls and bareback broncs. Cutting a steer out of Glenn's small herd, he put a circingle on him, mounted and the animal went bucking and plunging across the corral in a burst of flying hoofs and dust. Elliott stuck to his back like a cocklebur while the beast went sliding, diving and pounding all over the lot. Fearing more for my husband's life than his bones, I stood holding my breath by the fence. Finally, the animal tired, he hopped off and came back, grinning and trickling sweat. "Guess I could still get a job bull-riding in a pinch," he said.

The nights of late August were stifling. None of the ranchhouse bedrooms were air-conditioned. One night, by mutual agreement, we all dragged our cots out onto the covered patio to sleep. Ford brought along his radio to listen to rock and roll music. About 2 A.M. I awoke in the pitch dark to see a large shape looming above me. In terror, my voice froze. The thing was some kind of a beast, hovering there, breathing. As if in a dream, I finally managed to croak: "Elliott, quick, wake up!" As I moved, a big hoof came down on the foot of my bed, which promptly collapsed. The crash jarred Elliott to his feet, shouting, "What the hell's going on?" "I think it's a wild animal," I stammered. One of the children snapped on a flashlight. There, milling around us, were several of Glenn's horses that had escaped from their pasture. The light sent them galloping away. One passing hoof pounded down on Ford's radio, crushing it like a matchbox.

Those two weeks gave us a delightful change of scene. On the way home, we stopped at another of Glenn and Martha's hideaways. This one was Lake Texahoma, about a two and one-half hour drive from Dallas. They kept a 35-foot cabin cruiser docked at the yacht club, a vessel which I am sure saw little use. Elliott decided to take it out overnight. Bringing aboard enough groceries for a month, we shoved off at sunset. Glenn had told us about a little private cove providing good anchorage for swimming and fishing. The last rays of sun cast a coppery sheen over the water, cut through by our wake of black and silver. Elliott handled the strange vessel on this strange body of water with the skill of a man who knows boats. By the time we were in what we thought was the proper vicinity of the cove it was dark. Probing the black water with the spotlight and gas pole, Elliott finally decided it would be safe to anchor. We had supper, took a swim and then settled in for the night. Ford had decided to sleep ashore, and jumped overboard with his possessions rolled in a blanket. Jimmy stretched out on top of the cabin by the mast, and had lashed his arms and legs to the railing to keep from falling overboard.

Again I was awakened in the middle of the night. This time, the disturbance was a man's voice, shouting out of the blackness, "Will you get your goddam boat off mine?" Elliott rushed to the deck. During the hours we slept, our anchor had dragged and we had bumped into the side of the other man's boat.

"I've got to start the engines!" Elliott shouted, and dashed for the controls. No keys. "Where are the keys? Who took the keys?"

"Move your damn boat, please," the stranger pleaded.

Elliott suddenly remembered the keys were in his pants pocket. "Where are my pants?" He rushed about the cabin. "I've got to find my pants."

"You put them on top of that chest."

"Well, they're not there."

"Get your glasses and you can see better."

"Never mind the glasses. I can't get my glasses because they're in my pants, too."

Finally a frantically groping hand found the trousers where they had fallen to the cabin floor.

Jimmy, meanwhile, was told to untie his arms and legs, jump overboard and retrieve the anchor, so the boat would stop drifting.

"Jump over?" he said. "What do you mean, jump over?"

"You heard me," Elliott snapped. "In you go."

"But I can't see."

"Doesn't matter."

Manfully, Jimmy squeezed his eyes shut and jumped into the darkness. He landed in waist-deep water.

It was two hours before things quieted down once more and we could go back to sleep.

The next day, we cruised the lake, fished, sunned ourselves and swam. At the Roosevelt Dam Bridge, Elliott put his tongue in his cheek and announced to his gullible crew that each time a vessel passed under a Roosevelt bridge, it was proper to salute

and blow the horn. Convinced that we were performing a solemn
custom of seamanship, the children and I stood on the bow of
the cruiser saluting stiffly, while Elliott steered slowly beneath
the bridge blasting on the horn and laughing so hard that tears
streamed down his face.

A couple of fishermen took a look at the five figures standing
at rigid attention and almost fell off the bridge.

While living in a rented home, I had been actively seeking
a house to buy. It would be a fine thing, I thought, if we could
find the home of our dreams, and move in before the baby was
born. Afterward, with the busy life of a new mother filling my
days, moving would be a chore rather than a pleasure. For the
first time in our married lives, we were also becoming financially
able to afford our own home. Elliott had cleared $40,000 by sell-
ing off his stock holdings in the travel service. Shopping for a
home and finding one, however, soon proved to be two different
things. The Roosevelt name carried a couple of built-in handi-
caps. In some neighborhoods there was such an undercurrent of
hostility among stanch Old Guard Republican families that
real estate agents would not even bother to show us available
property. When pressed for explanation, the usual comeback was:
"Oh, you just wouldn't be interested in that location." And
then there was the matter of price. Being named Roosevelt automatically tagged you as rich. The houses shown to us usually
ranged around $150,000 in price, which was three times what we
were prepared to pay.

At last, with the help of Virginia Bachman, of Carlan and
Associates, a real estate woman, we decided on an eight-room
country home on Gleason's Lake, near the village of Wayzata. It
had been one of the first I had inspected, and I had fallen in love
with the place immediately. Owned by Mary and Judd Ringer, it
was only tentatively on the market. Mary wanted to sell, but her
husband was reluctant. They owned a piece of property next
door, where Mary wanted to build a new home. After a great
deal of dickering, Judd finally agreed to sell. The only hitch in
the deal was that they wanted to retain occupancy until their
new house was finished. That meant another six months of
renting, and making the move in the dead of winter.

Elliott's excitement over the prospect of having our first home together, however, more than made up for the disappointment. "Honey, it's a lovely place," he said happily. "We can make do for a while longer. You won't be sorry."

With winter just around the corner, we settled into our second rental house to wait.

13

Livingston Delano Roosevelt

Numbing cold turned Minneapolis into an icebox. Days passed with sporadic snowfall and lowering skies, giving the city and surrounding countryside a monotony of white. Our move into our new home was beautifully timed: coinciding with the arrival of a January blizzard. Snow swirled across the wooded knoll, caking thickly the north sides of the pines and making fairyland patterns against the ivy on the house. With eleven acres of wooded land around it, the house was framed in pines and commanded a superb view of Gleason's Lake. Snow added another dimension to its country charm.

Luckily, the movers managed to do their work before the worst of the blizzard struck. Tracking snow, they carted in bales, boxes, and furniture while I sat drumming my fingers as a useless spectator, six months pregnant. When the men had finally left, after putting all our things into place, it was painfully apparent that we didn't have nearly enough furniture to fill such a large house. What we owned was positioned with loving care, and we tried not to be upset by the big empty spaces. As days passed the business of bringing order to the household chaos helped me to overcome the feeling of snowbound isolation.

Even the worst of Iowa's weather had hardly prepared us for this. Morning after morning the temperature plummeted to 47° below zero. You could not breathe facing into the wind. A brief outing left the eyes streaming and nostrils a vivid red, flecked with frost. Walking off the cleared paths was virtually impossible. Powdery drifts piled rooftop high, and each step sent you plunging up to the hips. Family life went on at its usual noisy pace, with crises interspersed. Jimmy picked this particular period to fall in love. He was seventeen now, dark-haired and handsome. A girl named Sandy batted her eyes and he was thunderstruck. Soon he was spending untold hours mooning into space, wallowing in drippy music and dallying over his meals. I'm sure Jimmy saw her as a vision of charm and beauty. My own view was somewhat different. She would baby-sit for her younger brothers and sisters and invite Jimmy over to keep her company. I used to wait up for him to come home, biting my fingernails and fearing the worst. Occasionally she would call Jimmy on the phone, an act of female forwardness which bothered me no end. It had been drummed into me from childhood that girls do *not* call boys. If a boy wanted to talk with you, he would take the initiative. Only "not so nice" girls usurped this prerogative. My grandmother used to say "Girls are like streetcars, men aren't interested, once they have caught them." This girl was on roller skates, however, the way she went after Jimmy. After a couple of telephone run-ins with me she took to disguising her voice. I tried not to harp about Sandy to my son, but maternal instinct fairly clamored for me to put my foot down. Elliott took a calmer and more sensible approach. "Patty, let it run its course," he said. "You can't be pulling strings all the time. Things will work out." He was right, of course. After several agonizing months, time and circumstances combined to cool Jimmy's ardor. When it did happen, I felt like a cliff-hanger who had at last been thrown a rope.

The move to a new home, meanwhile, had done little to relieve us of the old bugaboo of anti-Roosevelt sentiment. This neighborhood had large yards and costly houses, and behind their well-trimmed lawns and picture windows the people were, for the most part, stanchly Republican. The extent of their disdain for anything or anyone bearing the taint of FDR was soon made cruelly apparent with an example which fell upon the head of Gretchen. Fortunately, even at the age of nine Gretchen was a calm, mature-minded girl. A few weeks after transferring to St.

Bartholomew's School she arrived home one evening announcing coolly, "Mother, we're having a little problem," then proceeded to tell me that she had been blackballed from the Brownies. I felt as if I had been slapped. Gretchen kept her composure, but I could not match her spirit and I sought the privacy of my bedroom to get myself under control. It was not the first such incident and it wouldn't be the last. Carrying the Roosevelt name, I was learning the hard way, took a strong back and vast stores of fortitude and forgiveness.

Such concerns about the children helped to distract me from the weather and also from the discomforts of pregnancy. Already I had the feeling that the latter was not going well; but had I known what really lay ahead, I think I would have been tempted to walk out one frozen night and lie down in the snow. Warning signs were apparent in my fourth and fifth months. I was retaining far too much water in my system. Although my maternity wardrobe was gorgeous—Aunt Polly had sent me fifteen ensembles from New York—my stomach was growing so huge that none of them fit properly. I felt like a whale. Merely walking across the room was a chore. After the slightest exertion I would collapse into a chair, blowing as though I'd just been beached. Despite the experience of four previous pregnancies, I wasn't as alarmed as perhaps I should have been. Memory plays strange tricks, and pregnancies before this had never been pleasant anyway. During the years with Milt, they had always been the aftermath of our short-lived reconciliations. Desiring Elliott's baby as much as I did must have removed much of the anxiety which ordinarily I would have felt. Besides, our family health worries suddenly focused not upon me, but Elliott.

Gretchen's tenth birthday was March 13, and we decided to celebrate the following Sunday with an ice skating party. The day arrived with the Weather Bureau warning of another blizzard. Ten children, mostly Gretchen's school friends, were guests, and my friend Prudy McCarthy had volunteered to help. Elliott was delighted and in high spirits. Strapping an apron over his coat he went out to fix a barbecue in the snow. From the library window I watched the children skating on the lake, their happy voices drifting up to the house. Then they all trudged up the hill and started a snowball fight. Snowballs zipped across the yard and splattered against the trees. Elliott joined in the roughhouse, floundering like a big bear. I watched this interesting and complicated man I had married enter into the games of children and felt a surge of warmth. Through the frosted glass I saw him toss a handful of snow at Gretchen then suddenly stand erect, strangely off-balance. My heart tightened. As if in slow motion, Elliott pitched face forward in the snow.

I rushed clumsily out the door. Children were grabbing for his arms and legs, trying to pull him up. "What's the matter, Daddy?" Gretchen cried. "Get up, Daddy." His eyes were closed, face waxen and gray. Prudy was beside me, shouting orders to the children. "Get his arms and legs and carry him in the house. You, you, and you. Now lift." Five of them carried his arms and five his legs, in a strange procession resembling Lemuel Gulliver and the Lilliputians, and thus hauled him into the house. I was shouting and so was Prudy. "Put him down. Put a pillow under his head." "No, no, lay him flat." "Get brandy." We put him on the couch and I lifted his head to pour brandy down his throat. Prudy hurried to the library and called the doctor. The only way he could get to us was by helicopter, he said. "Well, do you have a helicopter?" "Uh, no." Finally he decided to try driving across the lake. Within an hour we saw his car approaching, a black speck in the white expanse, steadily growing larger. Then he came trudging up the slope, a squat, gray figure carrying a black bag. By this time Elliott had somehow survived my attempts to drown him in brandy and was feeling better. He was conscious and grumbling, always a good sign.

The doctor grumbled too. "Don't let him move for two days," he said. They needed an electrocardiograph and blood pressure tests. He should be sent to a hospital as quickly as possible. Elliott shook his head, No hospital, absolutely not; next day he was to go to Wichita on business, and he intended to do so. The doctor left a supply of pills and departed, muttering.

When his car had once again become a speck on the lake, I decided to take things in hand. "Elliott," I announced, trying to make my voice firm, "you aren't going anywhere. I'll hide your pants." "You hide my pants," he rumbled, "and I'll take this place apart." "I'll hide your pants," I said. And I did. Later, when he was napping, I took them all to the basement and stuffed them into a secret closet. If he left for Wichita it would be in the nude. He awoke enraged. The Roosevelt invective went rolling through the house. But in the end he agreed to remain in bed one more day, no more. I said that after that the trousers would be returned but I intended to go with him to Wichita. A grin spread slowly across his face. "Okay," he said.

But it wasn't to be. Even as we talked, I was less than three days from the beginning of the worst ordeal of my life.

Elliott left the house early Tuesday with plans to meet me at noon in Charlie's, a popular luncheon spot in the city. We ate there often and usually they gave us a table in the middle of the dining room. I arrived about ten minutes before the hour, feeling strangely lightheaded and queasy. Most of the morning I had been out of sorts and the mood did not improve even after Elliott arrived at the restaurant. Something told me to take a table by the door. There, we practically inhaled a stout martini, then I sat back and my eyes grew big as saucers. "Oh, no," I said. Elliott leaned toward me. "What's the matter, darling?" I put a hand on my abdomen and glanced around, whispering, "The baby, I think my labor has started."

Elliott led me quietly to the ladies' room. The hostess ushered everyone out and they put me on a couch. While the hostess went to telephone for my doctor, Elliott bathed my face with a cold cloth. Outside the blizzard was raging again and it was lunchtime. Doctors just weren't in their offices. Finally he called back, and the hostess explained. "Bring her straight to my office," he snapped.

Snow was falling in thick, blinding flakes. With the windshield wipers thumping, Elliott drove slowly through whitening streets between great piles of snow scooped up along the sidewalks. At the doctor's office there was no place to park. He let me out and drove around the block, looking for space. I walked slowly inside, deathly afraid, clutching the front of my huge mink coat. When Elliott burst in I was already on the examining table. "What's the matter, Doctor?" my husband asked.

"I think she should go right to the hospital, Mr. Roosevelt."

At St. Barnabas Hospital I was put to bed with orders not to move a finger if I could avoid it. The pregnancy looked as though it would be terminated two months ahead of time, but if I could postpone giving birth for another two weeks the infant would have a chance; otherwise, it would probably be too premature for survival.

Elliott remained by my bedside that day and night, and the next, and the next. Thursday night he went home to pack, having decided to make the Wichita trip the following morning. Early Friday he came to say good-bye, and then was gone. Shortly after 9 A.M. the baby started to come. The umbilical cord prolapsed. There were no labor pains. The nurse called the chief obstetrician, Dr. O. M. Robbins, who had been my doctor during the past months. He examined me and announced they would have to take the baby immediately by Caesarean section. "This will give the baby a 50–50 chance," he said. "By normal birth . . ." He shook his head. "We've got to reach Mr. Roosevelt. He must sign the papers, giving us permission to operate."

"But he isn't here," I said. "He's flying to Wichita."

"When will he be back?"

"Tomorrow, maybe tomorrow evening."

"Can't wait. We have to have written permission now. All we can do, then, is to have you sign, Patty."

I signed. The doctor left, and nurses began preparing me for surgery. They performed the usual chores, then gave me a shot and put me into a clean gown. Then the doctor returned.

"Patty, we can't give you much anesthetic," he said. "There will be some pain."

"What do you mean?"

The baby was premature and very weak, he explained. Any drugs given me now would lessen its chances of survival. "You will have to make up your own mind."

Fear welled up so strongly I could almost taste it. Memories of past pain from broken bones flashed in my mind. I had delivered Jimmy with a fractured pelvis. Now I lay shuddering and nauseous, and going through it all over again. My voice was barely a croak. "Go ahead, but can you get my son Jimmy? I want somebody here."

They called Jimmy at school. He jumped into his car and sped out onto the slick streets. A police car stopped him. He identified himself and told them what was happening, and they gave him a siren escort to the hospital. He arrived as they were rolling me into the delivery room. I reached out my hand and he took it, with a firm grip.

By now, I trembled so it was difficult to move from the cart to the delivery table. Above, the big lights looked down with an impersonal glare. Surgeon and nurses moved about the table, all swathed in green. Eyes peered at me across white masks. There was a glitter of silver tools, the clink of metal on metal. Then I was being swabbed. It was cold to the touch. Surgical soap, alcohol, antiseptic. The first needle of Novocain bit into the flesh over my stomach, and it began.

What followed was a delirium of pain. With each passing of the knife to open a layer of skin they poured on Novocain. The pain came in great, searing waves and washed me screaming into unconsciousness, only to waken again, again screaming. My own voice, as if from a great distance, reverberated through that white room. I twisted and shook, and the pain washed over me again. It took an hour and a half to get the baby. I was losing blood freely. In semiconsciousness I fought to touch the baby. The hell of this could be made meaningful only by our baby. After an eternity, I knew it was over, and he had been born, but the silence seemed all wrong. "Why doesn't he cry?" I gasped. "I can't hear him cry!" A voice came back to me. "He's fine. He's crying. Listen, you can hear him crying." "No, no, why doesn't he cry? Why doesn't he cry?" Then the baby was lying on my body, a wet, kicking life. His head rested in my hands. "I want to baptize him," I said. "Water, get me sterile water, please." It was a Protestant hospital, but one of the nurses was Catholic and brought the water. With a wad of cotton she swabbed it over the tiny head. "Livingston Delano Roosevelt," I whispered, "in the name of the Father, the Son, and the Holy Ghost." Then a deep stab of pain plunged me into blackness.

Finally, they were rolling me back to the room. Jimmy walked beside the cart, still gripping my hand. Through the entire ordeal he had held on while our fingernails bit into each other's flesh. My hands were bleeding from Jimmy's nails. Blood oozed down my fingers and dripped to the polished floor of the corridor. They had given me a shot and I drifted off to sleep, saying, "Jimmy, I want to call Bama." But the boy was already on the telephone.

I could hear him telling someone, "Yes, it's a boy. Fine. They are both fine. He only weighs three pounds, but he'll make it, I'll bet."

At about one o'clock I was awake again, and the call was through to Bama in Seattle. The conversation came as a shock to me. Mother seemed little concerned about what I had been through. "Did you baptize the baby?" she kept asking. It gave me a tremendous letdown that she would have so little confidence to think that I would let him go unbaptized. "Of course, Mother," I said, coldly. The incident put an extra chill on our relationship, which was to last for a long time.

In the afternoon Elliott finally got through by phone. They had found him in Wichita, where the blizzard still raged. His voice was taut with worry. "I'll be back as soon as possible," he said. "I'm catching a plane now." Then Jimmy put in another call, to Mrs. Roosevelt in New York. Even his awe of her was not going to prevent him from performing his duties as man of the hour. "*Grandmère*," he announced, "you have a new grandson." He did it well, and I was proud of him.

Elliott didn't arrive until 12:30 A.M. He walked into the hospital room unbuttoning his topcoat. His face was pale, and strained. We talked brief, whispered talk, and then gently he picked me up, swathed as I was in bandage and hospital gown, and put me in the wheelchair to go down the hall and visit our baby. At 1 A.M. in the silence of a sleeping hospital he wheeled me down the corridor to the infant nursery room. Little Del was rocking in an incubator. In silence we watched him through the glass, rocking, thrusting out his chin and biting his tongue, a three-pound bundle of life. "He is the image of you, Elliott," I said. My husband began to cry. "He's beautiful, Patty, so beautiful, my darling. Thank you. Thank you so much." He held onto my shoulders as I sat in the chair. Del turned his head. His eyes were tiny slits. His hands and feet moved in slow rhythm under the fluorescent lights. A quarter of an hour had passed before we turned away and Elliott rolled me slowly back to my room. "Honey, as soon as you wake up in the morning, we'll come back," he said. "We'll come back and visit our little Del some more."

Elliott wanted me to nurse the baby. It was important to him.

I knew I couldn't nurse him yet, but could use a breast pump. "Certainly, I will, my love." As I dozed off, he pulled up a big armchair beside the bed, wrapped himself in a blanket and settled down for the night.

Mrs. Roosevelt was calling at 6 A.M. "Elliott, my dear," she said, "I'm so thrilled for you and Patty. Now do you need anything? Remember I will be more than glad to share the expense." She had just received a $3000 income tax refund and wanted to give it to the baby. I told her how much Del resembled Elliott and how pleased we were. Even over the telephone, I felt a new closeness to Mrs. Roosevelt. It was as if by pain and suffering I had won a kind of acceptance; not genuine affection, perhaps, but acceptance. "If you need me I'll come right now," she said. We thanked her, and said it wasn't necessary. For always, we had each other.

The time passed slowly for us. Elliott was there constantly except for an hour each morning when he would visit the office. My room filled with flowers, from my family, all of the Roosevelts, and friends in Seattle, Phoenix, Dallas, and Minneapolis.

The baby and I made improvement for the first three days, and then the picture began to change for us both. Del's weight dropped to two pounds, then went up again slightly. But he lacked strength and vigor, and remained in the incubator. I was having problems as well. The spot on my lung which the doctors had found earlier was still there. They wheeled a portable X-ray machine into the room, took pictures and then began talking of more surgery. The spot was in the lower right lobe, and they suggested that it be removed. "No, I don't want any more surgery," I said. "You're not going to touch me. No, no, no." They went away. By now, I was in the grip of double pneumonia.

The crisis came the fifth night after Del's birth. My strength began falling away rapidly. It was an eerie sensation as if life itself was starting to go out like a match. I could hear my own voice, talking to Elliott and the nurse; but it was as if I spoke through a barrel, and there was a persistent buzzing in my head. Slowly I drifted into unconsciousness. When I awoke again, the spirit had left my body and was sitting in a corner of the ceiling, looking down. Several doctors were by the bed, and one of them said, "We can't seem to reach her, Mr. Roosevelt. We can't get to her. She is just not responding."

At 5 P.M., the baby died. Nobody in the room mentioned it but I knew. At the same time, they were preparing to pronounce me dead. I lay cold as stone. A priest was enroute to the hospital. The nurse went out to bring back the doctor. Elliott sat in his big chair, shoulders slumped, eyes shining and his face a mask of despair. I could see him, in the strange half-world into which I had drifted; I could hear myself speak, but he could not hear. "Don't worry, Elliott. I'll take care of Del. I'll take care of our baby." Elliott looked into my face and began to whisper. "Please, my darling, please Patty, don't die. I need you and the children need you. Please, please don't die. Come back to me . . ."

He stood, reached down and scooped me from the bed. Then he was in the chair with me on his lap, whispering into my ear . . . "Stay with me, baby, and help me. I need you. The children need you. Don't die. Don't do this to us. Nothing is more important than you. We'll have another baby. Come back to me . . ." Except for his words, the room was as quiet as death. A small single light bulb cast deep shadows, so that on the back wall loomed a silhouette of the big chair, the man, and the bulky, blanketed shape in his arms. Time stopped. His whispering went on. At last, I stirred. My eyes opened. Elliott's face came slowly into focus next to mine. He put me back on the bed, then, and sat beside me. I took a deep shuddering breath and then coughed. I discharged a large clot of blood. But worse, the muscular spasm of coughing broke my incision. Something hot poured across my abdomen. Elliott reached beneath the covers to rub my legs, snatched his hand back and threw off the sheet. The bed was filling with blood. All my terror of surgery came welling up again. Grabbing Elliott's shoulder, I begged, "Don't call the doctor, Elliott, maybe it will stop. Don't tell them yet." "Honey, I've got to," he said. "You'll bleed to death." He rang the buzzer.

The doctor who came was a resident obstetrician. I was trembling and bleeding, but after a quick examination he assured me that I would be all right. "We'll just take a stitch or two," he said. I shook my head and pleaded not to be removed from my room. He looked at my face and decided the stitches weren't worth the anxiety. With the help of Elliott and the nurse, he did the repairs there in the room, cauterizing the incision and dressing it with a snug butterfly bandage. The job took an hour, but when it was done the bleeding had stopped. (When the wound finally did heal I was left with two navels.)

Afterward I felt guilty about my outburst, and the knowledge that somehow I had failed Elliott for not demonstrating that stoic acceptance of pain which marked the Roosevelts. While I dissolved in grief and shock and self-pity, Elliott held my hand firmly and quietly for hours. I apologized, sniffed, then dried my eyes. "Elliott, I'm so sorry for being such a boob. Please forgive me." Suddenly, I wept afresh.

The following day my husband went quietly about the business of arranging last rites for Del. He telephoned the archdiocese and informed them that our baby had died and we were requesting burial in a Catholic cemetery. Then he selected a casket and asked our attorney, Matt Levitt, to accompany him to the funeral.

They rode through the snowy streets in a black limousine to the churchyard cemetery, Elliott holding the tiny casket across his knees. The grave was a brown cavity in the snow, banked with flowers. The archbishop stood by it in his black coat, the Book open in his hand, and spoke into the wind. His hands were red in the bitter cold. Then a workman lowered the casket. The three men walked away, unspeaking, between the headstones, toward the gate.

It was snowing again.

14

First Visit to Hyde Park

Depression settled over us like a shroud. The death of the baby, the unrelenting gray skies and snow and cold, the nagging worry over my health and Elliott's state of mind, all combined to make that spring absolutely dismal.

After eighteen days in the hospital I was allowed to go home. Mrs. Roosevelt continued to call three times a day, and we received the $3000 check. It paid for a nurse full-time at the house. Elliott insisted on changing my dressings himself, and performed this unpleasant task every morning and each evening when he came home from work.

An autopsy had been performed on Del, but I did not want to ask about the findings. Now I know that it was the same kind of pulmonary disease which claimed the life of John and Jackie Kennedy's baby, Patrick, in August 1963, I was too blue to care about the details.

Elliott, in his love for our baby and his sorrow in our loss, had given a set of the Children's Encyclopedia to the Basilica School in honor of our little Del. It is always a tragedy that the living must ease their suffering by a material gift of some kind. In this instance, he felt that other little children could learn as a result of the love and happiness we had both known in the short flame of days that Del spent with us.

Each week there was a trip to the doctor for an examination.

Finally I got up the nerve to look at the scars, and saw with dismay that my bikini days were over. The healed rupture had left a deep and ugly scar.

The only way to break this terrible mental slump was to come out of myself and again take an interest in the surrounding world. Elliott hit upon the idea of taking me to Hyde Park for Memorial Day. The prospect revived his spirits, put the spring back in his step and gave his eyes that old familiar snap. His enthusiasm infected me, and I, too, began looking forward to the trip.

For so many months my husband had talked of growing up at Hyde Park and described his mother's house at Val-Kill. From his descriptions, I could visualize the woods and fields, the rolling hills overlooking the Hudson, and the stately Dutch colonial beauty of the Hyde Park mansion.

Mrs. Roosevelt had strong misgivings about me making such a trip. "But my deah," she said in our telephone chats, "you should not be out of bed. I fear the trip will be too much for you. You know, Jackie Kennedy, too, had a Caesarean, and she stayed in bed for two months." I had the impression that even discussing this made her nervous. Knowing how upset we both were, I felt she was reluctant to chance anything which might create additional worry.

Meanwhile, there were visits from Elliott's other children and grandchildren, a well-meaning attempt to cheer us up. In some instances, because of my shaky emotions, they had just the opposite effect.

Tony called from Denver to say that he and his wife and their little girl, Laura, would come up for a few days. They stayed five. It was fantabulous. Our first experience as grandparents taught us many lessons. Laura was an adorable little miss, who at this time being an only child had found there was no such thing as "*no*." When her parents left the room she began to cry—then wail—then scream. Forgetting my own misery, I took this little "hurricane" into my lap. Suddenly I realized that for all the shrieks and noise there were no tears. I shook her for all she was worth. She kept turning blue. Finally Elliott thundered, "By God, I never thought I would live long enough to want to spank a grandchild.

The parents are supposed to do the disciplining, and we're supposed to enjoy them."

From that time on, Laura and I enjoyed a rapport. This was intensified by my feeling for her mother. I had a soft spot in my heart for Tony's wife, Joanne.

During this visit, Tony's wife was trying hard to help us get our minds off our problems; by a curious kind of reverse English, little Laura's tantrums helped.

Then the visitors seemed to arrive on each other's heels. Elliott's oldest son, Bill, flew up in his plane, but unfortunately left his wife and four children in Denver. Dick Johnson came in from Omaha. Each spent a long weekend with us. "Big" David, Elliott's youngest son, came from Texas and spent nearly a month. At Texas Christian University he was living off the campus, not too happily. He considered our suggestion that he come up and enroll in the University of Minnesota, but eventually discarded the idea.

As Memorial Day neared, life grew progressively brighter. Spring melted the last of the snow and brought balmy days and soft breezes off the lake. In woods and fields around our house, wild flowers burst into bloom, trees took on heavy green leaf and on sunny mornings the grass glistened with dew.

I was feeling better and regaining strength and weight. The last dressing came off about a week before the trip. We boarded a plane in Minneapolis more lighthearted than we had been in months.

The flight took us to Newark, New Jersey, where Mrs. Roosevelt's chauffeur, Tubby, was waiting to drive us to Hyde Park. The car was a Jaguar limousine, provided to her by Franklin, Jr., through his automobile agency. It bore her initials on the front. Tires whispering on the pavement, the car sped northward on the freeway up the Hudson. Green and white road signs flashed past, with the names of cities and towns familiar to me from Elliott's descriptions. I peered into the darkness, trying to catch a glimpse of any landmark and frustrated because I could see nothing but galloping guardrails. We turned off at Poughkeepsie. During the last thirty miles, fatigue seeped into my bones like liquid lead. Despite the tiredness, I sat bolt upright and wide awake. Near the village of East Park, we turned off the two-lane highway onto a narrow country road, graveled and chuckholed, lined on both sides by rail fences and blooming foxtails. In a few months to come, this road would be etched forever on my memory; for we were to ride along it accompanied by three living Presidents in a cortege which saddened the world. But now it was merely the final lap of a journey which, thus far, had taken me thirty-nine years to cover.

Lights streamed through the windows of the large, surprisingly plain house at Val-Kill. It was 12:30 A.M., and dogs set up a clamor as the car turned into the back circular drive. Every dog within miles was barking and howling by the time we walked up the short dirt path to the rickety porch and rang a set of hanging cowbells. The place was surrounded by heavy shrubbery and woodsy growth; ivy climbed the walls of flat gray stucco, and the porch floor creaked as a houseman opened the door.

I remembered Elliott telling me about how Mrs. Roosevelt had built this place as a furniture factory during the Depression, to provide work for the young people around Hyde Park. She had later converted it into a home. There was a much prettier cottage next door, where Johnny Roosevelt and his wife, Anne, lived. I thought perhaps we had come to the wrong place; but no, Mrs. Roosevelt was there as we entered, with a kiss and a pat on the arm for each of us. While Elliott and the chauffeur brought in the baggage, she led me to a chair and we chatted about our trip and how I was feeling. There was a new tone of warmth in her voice, which had not been there at our last meeting, when she had visited Rochester and Mankato. Ironically, physical suffering had given us something in common. When Elliott finally joined us, she said, "Now, my deahs, when you get settled we'll have Johnny and Anne here, Trude and Joe Lash and the Gurewitsches are with us, too. They want to say 'hello,' then you can pop into bed."

We were staying in a part of the house called Tommy's apartment. This was a suite consisting of a sitting room, two bedrooms, two baths and a small kitchen once occupied by Mrs. Roosevelt's devoted secretary, Malvina Thompson, who had passed away. Our room contained an enormous high-backed bed, its headboard almost touching the ceiling. As we freshened up, the house creaked as if its planks and beams were discussing our presence there. From the bathroom tap came a trickle of foul-smelling mineral water which had long since put a permanent ring around the lavatory. "Phew!" I said. "Elliott, I'll have to drink soda. I can't stand this water."

Back in the sitting room, Johnny and Anne were waiting for us with a nightcap. I was introduced to Joe Lash, an assistant editor of the New York *Post*, and his wife Trude. The Lashes were part of the constant entourage with which Mrs. Roosevelt liked to surround herself. She was forever calling such old friends in New York and saying, "My deahs, come and spend the weekend in the country," or "Deahs, do you want to go to Europe with me? I must visit France for the AAUN." Their attitude toward me had a distinct chill. I was unaware of it at the time, but Elliott's fourth divorce and fifth marriage had been such a traumatic experience for his mother that she had still not completely recovered from it. These close friends had lived through it with her, and looked upon me as the cause of an anguish Mrs. Roosevelt did not deserve. At this point, I had no one in perspective and was on the shakiest of ground.

Johnny and Anne invited us over to their house, but Elliott glanced at my ashen face and demurred. When they had gone, he rummaged in the icebox looking for milk or fruit juice. The only drink available was a vintage juice. He brought out two bottles of 1950 French champagne, two champagne glasses and carried them to the bedroom. We sat up in bed until 5 A.M., and drank both bottles, while Elliott drew vivid word pictures of the relationships between various brothers and sisters-in-law and others in the family, the back-biting and personality conflicts. We did not realize that the Lashes were in bed in the room directly above ours, and their floor was so loosely built they could hear every word. Finally we heard their beds squeak. Elliott nearly collapsed. We turned out the light, dove under the covers, and that was the end of the exposé. Next morning, breakfast was served at eight o'clock sharp. Elliott insisted that I go in first. "I will not," I said. "I just can't." But I did. Trude, a tall attractive Scandinavian girl with thick blond hair drawn back in a bun, gave me a knowing glance. Elliott finally wandered in, trying to make offhand conversation. During the meal, the Lashes dropped subtle little hints. ("My, you all stayed up late last night. We thought you were going right to bed.") I wished I could have hidden under my toast.

If there was any similarity between Mrs. Roosevelt's New York apartment, scene of my ghastly introductory dinner, and this house, it was overabundance of furniture. There were so many tables, chairs, mirrors, pictures, wallpieces, and whatnot that you thought surely she had bought up a freight sale. Every stuffed chair had two end tables, and most of the end tables sprouted lamps. Throughout the house, chests and china closets were chock full of memorabilia—medals, decorations, jeweled pieces, letter openers, cigarette boxes. Some of the cigarettes in the boxes must have been put there for Franklin D. Roosevelt twenty-five years before; they were so stale no one would have the stomach to smoke them. Mrs. Roosevelt neither smoked nor drank hard liquor, and obviously tried to discourage these indulgences in others. Thus, the only liquor on display was a bottle of scotch three-quarters empty; to get more you had to go to the cellar, and a couple of trips down there made you want to give up drinking. The ash trays she put out were so tiny one filled up after two cigarettes and you had to go and empty it. Sometimes lighting another just wasn't worth the trouble. In the sitting room was a table crowded with framed, stand-up pictures of family, friends, dignitaries such as Winston Churchill and Madame Chiang Kai-shek. Her favorite spot was a chair by the fireplace with a table on either side. Servants would bring still another small table for her coffee tray, and when she grew tired, her glasses with the built-in hearing aid would dangle from a neck chain, her head slumped forward, and she napped.

After breakfast, we spent a couple of hours watching Mrs. Roosevelt's work routine. Her office was in the library of Tommy's apartment, and here she spent each morning going over her heavy correspondence, dictating letters, writing speeches and newspaper and magazine articles. Shortly after ten o'clock she suggested that we all go outside and she would show me the property. The setting was beautiful, with towering maple trees, spruce, willow, and sycamore. Spring flowers were everywhere, and the lawn sloped down from her house and Johnny's next-door cottage to a half-moon pond which Elliott had put in years before. Ducks quarreled among the rushes. The house occupied by Johnny and Anne was compact and snug, built of fieldstone and white clapboard. It had a swimming pool built for them by Mrs. Roosevelt which was still freezing cold. We saw the dog pens and stables, and then it was time to go back into the house for lunch.

This time, the food was simple but elegantly prepared; a formal lunch, with soup, finger bowls and the ever-present Dubonnet wine. The meat dish presented was knockwurst and sauerkraut. As before, at the New York dinner, there was no surplus of food— just enough to go around. Again I was intrigued by the fact that none of the china matched; although you would imagine Mrs. Roosevelt would have everything in perfect order, her table was a conglomeration of china, mostly from broken sets. This and the furniture impressed upon me anew the frugality of this woman, who had had to practice thrift to meet household expenses even when her husband, scion of a wealthy family, was President of the United States. The paradox was even more bizarre when you realized that she earned $150,000 a year lecturing and writing, but had to give most of it to charity because of taxes. Instinctively I knew that much of her fine china and crystal had gone to help furnish the home of a new bride. With so many children, grandchildren, and uncounted nieces and nephews, her cupboard must always be bare.

Johnny and Anne came over for dinner that evening, and afterward invited us to their cottage for after-dinner cocktails and friendly talk about old times. I should have known better, but at this point I was gullible and wide-eyed. I sat there while Johnny, Elliott and Anne chatted. "Oh Elliott," Anne breathed, "you'll never guess who I had lunch with the other day." He tumbled for the trap. "Who?" She smiled deliciously. "Why Faye, of course. She looks wonderful . . ."

Feeling as left out as the fat man at a tennis match, I amused myself by examining the furniture and admiring the rich walnut cathedral ceiling of their living room. Johnny poured the drinks, the voices grew louder, the talk more pointed. Elliott had not seen Johnny for a long time and found the conversation interesting. Despite his determination that nobody was going to deliberately hurt me, he was unaware of how the "old times" talk battered my ego. At last I insisted that we go home and to bed,

and Elliott told them good night. As we picked our way through
weeds and shrubbery to Mrs. Roosevelt's house, all the dogs
started barking again. Branches slapped my face. Ducks and
chickens flapped about underfoot. It was a scene from *Ramar of
the Jungle*. I wanted to strike out and answer, "Shut up!" In
Mrs. Roosevelt's kitchen a plate of cookies and two glasses of
milk had been put out for us, which helped calm my nerves.
Again, I had a spooky feeling that she suspected I might need
calming.

The two empty champagne bottles were still in our bedroom.
Conscience-smitten now with the thought that she might have
been saving them for a special occasion, we carried them out
behind the barn. There, while I stood watch, Elliott threw them
into the woods. At that instant, every dog in the neighborhood
fell silent, and the night was broken by two very sharp and
distinct sounds: Clink. Clink.

Despite the long trip and scanty rest the night before, I slept
fitfully. All sorts of gargoyles pranced around in my head, with
bodies like ducks and faces like Roosevelts. The next morning
I had a mouthful of cotton wool, circles under my eyes and the
disposition of a steam boiler.

By rights, Anne and I should have had more mutual sympathy
and understanding. They, too, had lost a child, and had gone
through perhaps an even greater hell. In the summer of 1960,
just before we were married, their daughter Sally, fourteen, was
thrown from her horse at summer camp. She got up and walked
away, but the following day went into convulsions and died.

The following morning Mrs. Roosevelt left early for Philadelphia to make a speech, and planned that night to return to her
apartment in New York. We were to join her there. Johnny and
Anne said they were driving down and we could go with them.
Drawing Elliott aside, I tried to persuade him to make other
arrangements.

"Couldn't we go on a boat or a train or something? Couldn't
we fly?"

"No, baby, we'll just drive down with Johnny and Anne. Besides it will help our budget."

We left in the late afternoon. The sun slid behind a line of
clouds and a cold wind sprang up, making the day as cheer-

less as my mood. As darkness came, we stopped at a roadhouse called "The Bird and the Bottle." A few customers lingered over drinks, survivors of the afternoon, and the proprietor was preparing to close. Johnny wanted to go in. "You remember this place, Elliott? My God we used to go here and have more fun." Johnny banged on the door and harangued the man to let us in. "Okay," he said, "but the kitchen's closed." Johnny said we would just have a few drinks.

Elliott and the owner recognized each other. They were old friends. Soon they were all gabbing in loud, boisterous voices, remembering old times.

Someone asked Elliott if he remembered a certain woman, and dropped her first name.

"No, I haven't heard from her in years."

"Well, she was just in here last week . . . matter of fact, she left me her telephone number. Lessee. Yeah, here it is. Why don't you call her?"

The proprietor was unaware that I did not know the woman. From the remarks, I gathered she was very rich and lived in Philadelphia. While Elliott placed his call, the tavernkeeper invited me to his office, where he said I could listen on the extension phone. It was a disaster. The woman's voice fairly dripped honey into my husband's ear. Her tone smacked of old times fondly remembered.

"Elliott, why don't you come over? I haven't heard from you in years. All this trouble you've been through, I would have helped . . ."

I was waiting for him to tell her he was married again, loved his wife and had a fine family. But he didn't. He kept saying he was fine now, but no word of wife.

"Oh darling, I've missed you so much," the woman trilled. "Don't you remember how we used to call each other every New Year's Eve? . . . This year it's your turn to call me."

The conversation closed with Elliott promising to get in touch with her, but still not mentioning his marriage. I hung up. Like a zombie I walked out of the office into a dark hall. A flight of steps led upward, apparently to what had once been the proprietor's living quarters on the second floor. My heart was pounding. The walls were closing in. I climbed the stairs to a little room. Light from the road filtered in through a dirty window. Standing there in the half-dark, I burst into tears. They streamed scalding down my face, and I couldn't stop. I began to tremble all over, on the verge of hysteria.

Downstairs, the talk went on and on, and finally someone noticed that I was missing. They started looking for me and calling. They looked in the ladies' room, the office, the kitchen. I could hear Elliott's voice, "Patty, darling, where are you? Patty? Oh baby, you're so sick and so tired."

I went into another little room and closed the door. He found me there, hiding. "What the devil? . . ." Without even a sputter of warning, I blew up in his face.

"Go away from me. I never want to lay eyes on you again, Elliott Roosevelt! Go away, go away, and take that terrible brother of yours with you . . ."

"What's wrong, my dearest, my little one?"

"You talked to that woman, that's what's wrong. You didn't even tell her you were married!"

Dumfounded, he put his arm around me and, talking softly, began to restore me to some semblance of calm. After ten minutes I stopped shaking and sobbing, but my face was a wreck. In the ladies' room I looked in the mirror, and something looked back that could hardly be identified as Patty Roosevelt. The complexion was almost blue, the eyes swollen nearly shut were surrounded by a mass of mottled red. I washed my face but it didn't help. Then they put me in the car, a huddled heap of misery.

Elliott pulled me to him, burying my face in his shoulder. "Please, darling, my love . . ."

Even after we arrived in New York, I was still in a fury. "Take me to a plane," I said. "Let me go home." Johnny and Anne tried to soothe me but I would have none of it. "Don't talk to me," I snapped. "Just don't say a word to me."

Mrs. Roosevelt met us at the door of her town house. She wore a lovely blue bathrobe and her hair was down, tumbling to her waist in long, soft waves, and caught in the back with a blue bow. I remember thinking how feminine she appeared and how surprised I was that her hair was so long.

She took one look at my misshapen face and said, "Elliott, what has happened to this poor child!"

Elliott hustled me past her. "Mummy, she'll be all right. I'll just get her to bed."

The next day, I looked as though I was in the middle of both chicken pox and measles. Alarmed, Mrs. Roosevelt called a doctor, who gave me medication to reduce the swelling and put cold compresses on my eyes.

Two days later we flew back to Minneapolis. Except for Elliott, I didn't even want to hear mention of Roosevelts again. Maybe now, I thought, things would get better for us.

But our bad luck streak wasn't over yet.

15

Last Visit to Hyde Park

The spring passed into early summer. Wild flowers made a gaudy display in the woods and fields. At evening, the lake at the foot of our lawn lay glassy smooth, broken only by an occasional jumping fish. Crickets sang in gathering twilight. There was a fragrance of flowers and ivy and fresh-cut grass.

Elliott's work grew even more demanding and frustrating. His differences with Elliot Hoffman over how best to develop the travel service were clearly irrevocable. At every turn he saw himself thwarted. The thought of making a change was very much on his mind.

My own health and peace of mind continued to improve steadily. I regained strength, unfortunately put on weight, and the emotional turmoil of the Memorial Day trip soon faded out of conscious memory. I enjoyed outings with the children, playing bridge, and talking endlessly with friends on the telephone. Now, perhaps, we could look forward to a few months of pleasure and contentment. But it was not to be. In June, my terrible personal jinx popped up again.

The only relative I had at the head of the Mississippi in Minneapolis was a cousin, George Hoke. He and his wife Betsy were recently separated. One evening she had invited us for dinner at her new home, a low, rambling ranch-type structure with a circular driveway. Several other guests were present, and we enjoyed an evening of parlor games and fun. At about 11:30 we said our good-byes and walked out the front door. Misjudging the steps, I fell. One foot doubled under me. I felt the crunch of shattering bone and blinding pain. I rolled over and sat there in the gravel, moaning. Elliott came out of the house and looked around for me. "Where's Patty?" Then he saw me. "Honey, what are you doing? Get up." I told him I had just broken my ankle. "That's ridiculous," he snapped, "get up." With that, he pulled me up. I almost fainted. The whole party took part in my misery.

Another couple advised sympathetically, "What's the matter? Let's get her to a doctor."

My right foot and ankle were swelling like a balloon. Already the shoe dug painfully into oversize flesh. "It's all right," Elliott said, "she'll be fine." We got into the car and started off, followed by two other couples as we drove home. Shock waves rolled over me. I groaned with pain. Elliott lectured me all the way about not overdoing it. "Roosevelts don't feel pain," he said. At the house, I collapsed on the couch and he went to answer the door. He ushered our guests into the living room and one of the women said, "This is ridiculous. Let's call a doctor. She's in agony."

Elliott agreed grudgingly, saying it was a waste of time and money. At this time we could certainly not afford to have a broken foot. One look at my face should have convinced him that I wasn't joking. Dr. D. W. Feigal had an office in the village of Wayzata. He instructed them by telephone that he would meet us in fifteen minutes. There he and his nurse were waiting. In the dead of night, I hobbled through a back door, garish beneath the light of a naked bulb. Again I began to shake, and could hardly get onto the table. "Lie still," the nurse demanded. X-rays showed the bottom bone of the foot was broken in eighteen places. Four bones on top were fractured. The nurse took one look at the negative and her eyes widened. Her voice immediately took on an apologetic tone. The doctor shook his head and said he would have to set the bones before he could apply a cast. He had no anesthetic in his office, only a shot for pain. "Oh, no," I said. "Here we go again."

The party guests crowded around the table. Elliott's face

was a study in remorse. I grabbed his hand as the doctor went to work, pushing the toes down, manipulating bones, applying plaster cast. When it was done, the cast reached to above my knee, and I was in agony. As they carried me out, Dr. Feigal's parting words were: "I want to see her again in two days." It was two days of unrelenting pain, and no sedative was strong enough to dull it. Elliott wanted to call in an orthopedic man, but I refused, fearful of more surgery. Back at the doctor's little office again, he removed the cast, inspected his handiwork, with the help of more X-rays, and decided it would have to be done over again. He pulled the foot up and re-set it, while I screeched at the excruciating pain. I was glad Elliott was not there to see me in such a sorry state.

Ultimately, I spent the summer in a cumbersome cast. I was only allowed to move in a wheelchair or on crutches. Friends carted in jellies and custard, trying to be helpful, and as a result I gained twenty pounds and resembled a Raphaelesque matron with a stovepipe leg. Finally, when I was just on the verge of going out of my mind for something to do, Elliott suggested we drive to Hyde Park for Labor Day. We would stop to see his sister, Anna, and her husband Jim Halsted in Birmingham, Michigan, on the way. After weeks of correspondence with his mother, everything was finally arranged. One day we piled everything into our Pontiac, including my plaster burden, and headed east over endless gray ribbons of turnpike.

Elliott loves to drive. He handles the wheel with an air of ownership. Even on the longest trips he prefers to do the driving himself, rather than take turns. For him, it is a punishing grind, but this, too, is part of his preference. I was nettled with Jimmy because he was still deeply involved in his teenage romance and begged to stay in Minneapolis. Ford, Gretchen, and David, then, rode in the back. To while away the miles, we sang songs, played games and counted road signs and telephone poles. Biggest break in the monotony was an eight-mile ferry ride across Lake Michigan.

Jim Halsted was a physician with a union-supported hospital in Detroit, and Anna was on the public relations staff. They lived in a small house with a wooded yard in Birmingham. She had made motel reservations for us near their home and prepared a barbecue supper. They made a great show of welcome and congeniality for us, which took me off guard. Elliott's big sister appeared more cordial this time, in contrast to the rather cold reception I had received from her before. Sparse, tall, and angular, Anna settled back, fixed me with a half-smile saying: "Well, now, my dear, you must tell us all about your trip . . ." She and Dr. Halsted, her third husband, had a huge pair of collie dogs, and a small breakfast table where they would eat breakfast at seven o'clock each morning and listen to the bird calls. Dinner for me was a boring affair, for both Jim and Anna turned their attention to Elliott and a lengthy discussion about the good old days involving, for the most part, people and names totally unfamiliar to me. Possessed of a keen, inquiring, and highly organized mind, I got the impression that she did not condone my customary state of life, which is about as organized as a cavalry charge. In the course of the evening, Jim did manage to give me a great deal of medical advice about my broken foot, my Caesarean operation and the baby. We left clutching lunch boxes Anna had prepared for our trip next day, consisting of sandwiches, graham crackers, and some pieces of dry toast—in case of car sickness.

By the time we pulled into Hyde Park, I felt that we had been traveling all of our lives. Elliott had rolled up nearly eight hundred miles per day. Mrs. Roosevelt had asked that we try to arrive by 7 P.M., saying, "We are having a quiet family dinner; just the family for the weekend." At three minutes to seven, tired, rumpled and out of sorts, we wheeled into the driveway at Val-Kill. An old man I did not know was standing on the porch, and supported by two canes. Mrs. Roosevelt came to the door. "Hurry along, children, dinner is just about ready. Did you have a nice trip?" We all rushed into Tommy's apartment, splashed water on our faces, and hurried to the dining room. The "quiet family dinner" was for some thirty-odd people.

The old man with the canes turned out to be another of the colorful members of this family, Uncle David Gray. Courtly, tall, and pink-cheeked, he was the ninety-four-year-old uncle of Eleanor Roosevelt, lived in Sarasota, Florida, and traveled to Hyde Park each summer on the train. For nearly forty years, he had been working on an unpublished book about the Roosevelt family. He changed the title frequently, and with each change began a new manuscript and started again. On each journey to Hyde Park, Uncle David carried with him his typewriter and every scrap of his writings. All the porters knew him, and always looked after his precious papers. Once, however, a new porter forgot to take the articles off the train at Hyde Park, and Uncle David sued the railroad. He liked an occasional glass of sherry and knowing his niece's distaste for alcoholic beverage would hide small flasks of it in his canes.

In the flurry of welcome each of our children was introduced around the room. When we came out of the bedroom, Uncle David was waiting, balancing on his canes. He looked down upon our four-year-old son and, with mock severity, intoned: "What did you say your name was again?"

"David Roosevelt, sir," the little boy replied, peering up from the height of the old man's knees.

"Indeed? How do you have a name like David?"

"My mommy named me David."

It was the first of many exchanges between these two, little David's awe of his new great-great-uncle was tinged with mystery and fear. For one thing, wherever the old man walked he made a brisk tap-tapping noise with his canes on the hardwood floor. For another, Uncle David would go tap-tapping frequently to the bedroom, there to perform some solitary rite. But most awesome of all was Uncle David's strange affinity with the Monster in the Basement.

The first time David heard the odd noises from below was shortly after our arrival. It began with a whirring whine, rose to a rattling rumble, and then settled into a rhythmic *gush-gush-gush*.

In the dark hallway, little David gave a start and looked up at Uncle David. "What's that noise?" Uncle David cocked an ear. His visage grew somber. Shadows played over his face. "David, the Blue Monster is in the basement," he said. The old voice dropped to a chilling whisper. "There are *ghosts* in the basement, my boy."

Mrs. Roosevelt served dinner on her large screened-in porch, with several tables arranged in such a way that she could see all her guests. She placed Elliott and David at one table, Gretchen at another, Ford and me at still others. As usual, dinner was a rather formal affair, served by the butler and the maid. David had no one to help him cut his meat, but managed somehow— one learned self-reliance early among Roosevelts. When dinner was finished, the butler brought around finger bowls, on dessert plates, with the doily underneath, and a spoon and fork. With studied calm, David properly placed the spoon and fork on each side and the bowl and doily above the plate. Then he looked across at me and piped: "Gee, Mom, aren't you glad I know what to do with my finger bowl?" The dinner party burst into gales of laughter.

The following day we made our first tour of the Roosevelt estate, starting with the magnificent Franklin D. Roosevelt Memorial Library, an archive containing every scrap of memoranda from the hand of FDR which he ordered preserved at the outset of his public life. The library and museum is a fieldstone Dutch colonial structure designed by the late President himself, on the grounds of the Hyde Park mansion and just a few steps from his grave in the rose garden. Ford spent about forty-eight hours of his visit among the library stacks. Meanwhile, as I stumped along on crutches and Gretchen and David trotted behind, Elliott took us on a guided tour. There is a small ticket booth at the museum, and I watched, astonished, as my husband stepped to the window and paid our way, not even identifying himself to the attendant. Inside, a guard finally recognized him. "Mr. Roosevelt, how are you?" With that, other uniformed security men and a crowd of sightseers flocked around while Elliott paced past displays of photographs, clothing, souvenirs, and countless mementos of his family, telling stories about many of the items. In one large room we saw FDR's priceless collection of ship models, including the USS *Constitution*, which he refurbished himself. Lining the upper walls are the famous Roosevelt collection of naval prints, many of which Elliott helped his father to find in out-of-the-way shops and private homes around the world.

From the museum, we went to the mansion itself, past the tall spruce tree Elliott tumbled out of as a boy, up the steps and into the broad hallway with its dark wainscotting. Elliott led us to the huge library at the end of the hallway. Across from

the small office FDR used on the first floor was Sara Delano
Roosevelt's Dresden salon. Magnified by many mirrors, one could
see a world all its own. Everything here from candelabra to hat
racks, vases, plates, sconces was all delicately wrought Dresden. It
was a fairyland of color and beauty. It was a room where dreams
could come true. I only wished, but could not have, some of
this lovely porcelain in our home. Now, however, the United
States government had first claim on it. FDR, in his last will
and testament, had given everything he owned at Hyde Park to
the government. It was then made a National Monument, under
the supervision of the National Parks Service. The big house,
fully furnished, was taken over lock, stock, and barrel. However,
the children were to be allowed to retain the title during their
lifetime, should any of them care to live there and maintain it.
This right was waived immediately, as the property was too
large and costly for any of the children to carry.

Our next stop was the dining room, furnished with a replica
of the three-hundred-year-old Italian dining table and chairs we
now had in our home. We mounted the stairs, which, along with
the floors, had been reinforced to bear the weight of two hundred
thousand sightseers who trekked through the house each year,
and walked past the bedrooms once occupied by the King and
Queen of England during their visit in 1939 to Hyde Park.
Elliott showed us the bedroom his father was born in, and
then the bedroom FDR occupied as President, with everything
in place as it was on the day of his death in Warm Springs,
Georgia. Next to this was the small chamber, more suited for a
sewing room than sleeping, which was Mrs. Roosevelt's room. It
contained a small bed and beside the bed, a nightstand, with a
fresh yellow rose in a bud vase, and a few books. The simplicity
of Eleanor Roosevelt's bedroom was almost Spartan, sand-
wiched between the adjoining rooms of her husband and ma-
triarchal mother-in-law, Sara Delano. As we continued our tour,
Elliott spoke in hushed, reverent tones. "This is the room where
my father was born . . . This is the room where we played."
The laughter had gone, the house had become sterile and in-
dexed and carded, but my husband heard and felt the ghosts of
memories past. Adding to the sense of the unreal was the recorded
voice of Mrs. Roosevelt, coming over small walkie-talkie type

tape machines, available for a dollar to sightseers. On the third story of the mansion was the children's playroom, covering the entire floor. Here, too, were the cubicles the children had slept in, and a closet where Elliott once spent eight hours of terror which haunt him to this day. A nurse, angry at the boy, locked him in the closet and accidentally broke off the key. As a result, even now he is unable to remain for long in a room with the curtains drawn. He often gets up at night to turn on a light in our adjoining bathroom. Away from home, he always makes it a practice to locate available window and door openings in hotels through which we could escape in an emergency.

From the house, we went to the barn, an immaculate place with the pictures of horses on stalls they had occupied and each piece of harness perfectly preserved and labeled under glass. Behind the barn was the steep narrow road cutting down through the woods to the river. "Here," Elliott said wistfully, "we used to ride our sleds."

We strolled the grounds as much as possible, considering the handicap of my cast. The view of the Hudson was breath-taking, a river of silver in the distance, framed in wooded rolling hills and the farther blue reaches of the Catskills. Directly opposite the Roosevelt mansion stood the castle-like retreat once occupied by Father Divine, commanding a massive bluff. Looking across at the fabulous haunt of the ermine-capped spiritualist whose gullible followers had poured a vast treasure into his coffers, I reflected upon the immense contrasts of life and humanity evident here.

Mrs. Roosevelt conducted a great deal of her personal business at the mansion, driving over from Val-Kill. In the great library room, she received dignitaries and delegations, representing everything from the United Nations to federations of garden clubs.

In the rose garden, I saw a sight which sent shivers up my spine. The garden itself was beautiful, surrounded by high hedge, clipped and arranged. In the center rested the plain block of white marble marking the grave of Franklin Delano Roosevelt. The dead President lay beneath a covering of low-growing evergreen planted over the dimensions of the grave itself. On the marble block were his name and the dates of his birth and death. An identical stone was next to his with the name of Anna

Eleanor Roosevelt, the date of her birth and . . . a space for the date of her death. "Elliott," I said, "how can your mother look at that blank space without, without . . ." A look from my husband left the sentence forever unfinished.

By the time we arrived back at Mrs. Roosevelt's house, I was convinced that I could drop from exhaustion.

My spirits were revived the next day when we met another of those delightful relatives of Elliott's. This was Cousin Leila Delano, who had married Laura Delano's brother, Lyman, and was FDR's first cousin. Her estate was a place harkening back to another time, a great old wooden house set in the middle of an enormous tract of forested land overlooking the Hudson. A tire swing dangled from a towering oak tree, and her veranda was furnished with old rocking chairs and couches with little chintz cushions, everything fresh and clean and newly painted.

Cousin Leila herself was the figure of old-world charm and refinement. With her petal-soft skin and refreshing femininity, she had finely cut features and downy white hair, done in soft waves. Her voile dress was ruffled at the sleeves and throat, and her spectacles hung from a delicate silver chain. Her shoes were comfortable and conservative, with pointed toes. We sat together, and the voice that spoke to me was full of cultivated warmth I had known since childhood. "Where are you from, dear? . . . And where did you go to school?" Gently speaking, moving slowly and by instinct, she followed Aunt Polly's form of inquiry. Hearing her, I could visualize again my grandmother at her endless games of Russian bank, talking soft, feminine talk behind the drawn shades.

When we had chatted for a while, looking out over the rolling hills of pine, oak, and maple, Cousin Leila reached for a tiny bell, whose delicate tinkle produced a maid bearing a huge tea tray and large chocolate cake, with thick frosting and marshmallow filling. Cousin Leila then invited little David to sit beside her on the porch swing to eat his cake. Swinging lustily and kicking his heels, he balanced the cake expertly on one knee while Elliott and I exchanged anxious glances, fearing he would spill something on our hostess's lovely dress. Nothing spilled. David not only knew how to use a finger bowl, he also was very good at juggling chocolate cake, especially when served on a Dresden plate.

When he had finished the last crumb, Cousin Leila glanced at the empty plate and wistful expression and exchanged dishes with him. "Now, David, I am an old lady and can't eat chocolate cake because it's fattening. So you eat mine."

Inside, the house was high-ceilinged and hung with magnificent crystal chandeliers. Priceless antique furnishings gave it the look of a museum. The servants were faithful retainers of many years service, who seemed to blend in with the wall hangings. After a quick tour, we went to the stables to see the famous strain of Norwegian ponies which her husband had brought to this country many years before. The animals were characterized by a quick, high-stepping pace and a distinctive white stripe down their backs. One pony had reached the great age of thirty years.

Major-domo of the stables was Mr. Thomas, who sat on a box chewing a piece of straw and a pipe that had not been lit for twenty years. Aged, bewhiskered, and peering out from beneath a little peaked cap, he saw Elliott coming and leaped delightedly to his feet. They pumped hands, hugged, and carried on at a great rate. The two had been friends since childhood, when FDR's children would visit and ride.

The groom led an old pony from its stall, put on a saddle and bridle, and turned him over to me. As I took the animal out into the cobblestoned courtyard for the children to ride, Thomas watched and grinned. "You know horses, girl. You got a good girl there, Mr. Elliott, any girl that knows horses." The little pony had no shoes, but his step was sure. Ford, Gretchen, and David took turns riding. I regretted having the cast on my leg, which made it practically impossible for me to mount. Our visit ended with the old groom back on his box chewing straw, and Cousin Leila waving us away with a little lace handkerchief. I felt that we had spent the afternoon going far back in time.

Two days later, we went to New York. Elliott was having some discomfort with his left foot. We checked into the Roger Smith Hotel, and the next morning he awoke in agony. The foot was swollen. He could not put his shoe on without help. The throbbing brought tears to his eyes, but he set his jaw and refused to admit pain. I kept thinking, maybe Roosevelts don't acknowledge that they hurt, but Peabodys do. I was sure he had somehow broken the foot, and now we would stump around on matching casts, but the ailment turned out to be gout. Elliott had to go to Washington on business, and he mustered enough determination to go limping away to catch a plane. Ford and I, meanwhile, headed for Jones Beach, where we were to meet Peggy and Jack Lydon. She was an old friend of mine from Seattle. Unfamiliar with the freeways, I made a wrong turn and got lost in a Puerto Rican suburb where the people were celebrating the Festival of Guadalupe. When we finally arrived at Jones Beach, it was raining and blustery, and bugs had gotten into Peggy's beautiful picnic lunch. We remained two hours and then returned to the city, a thoroughly dispirited group.

The next day, David had his first luncheon with New York society. It developed into a near-disaster.

Elliott had known Martin Jones for years. He was an elegant and fastidious bachelor and entrepreneur whose many interests included owning a theater and producing plays.

He and Elliott had been partners in Roosevelt Enterprises, Inc., which produced and syndicated Eleanor Roosevelt's radio show from New York. They also produced a thirty-minute Sunday TV show over NBC. This won the Peabody Award in 1948 as the best public service program on television. During this period John Roosevelt's department store in Beverly Hills went out of business. Elliott immediately arranged for him to move his family and household goods to Val-Kill, near Hyde Park, where Elliott was then living.

Martin Jones had a town house in New York and a home in Miami Beach. For some time he had been urging Elliott to move to Florida, where tremendous business opportunities were available. I had heard a great deal about Martin but never met him, so his telephone call inviting us to Sunday luncheon came as a nice surprise.

The doorbell rang at noon sharp and in came Martin, a grayish, distinguished-looking man of the type who could influence headwaiters and wither an unwanted acquaintance with a glance. "Mr. Roosevelt, please?" he said, enunciating superbly.

I flounced up to him in my best Seattle manner. "Hi, Martin,

I'm Patty Roosevelt." He peered at me with cool detachment. "How do you do. I am Martin Jones."

David, meanwhile, came into the living room in his best plaid sport coat, white shirt, bow tie and short pants, a very manly four-year-old. Mustering dignity, he planted himself in front of Martin, fixed his eye on our guest's belt buckle and said, "How do you do, Mr. Jones, I'm David Roosevelt."

"Where," Martin breathed, "did *he* come from?"

Elliott appeared from the bedroom and the two men greeted each other cordially. After a brief conversation Martin glanced at his watch and then at David. "What will you do with him?" he asked.

"David? Oh, we'll take him with us," Elliott said.

Martin's eyebrow lifted. He examined David stonily. "To Peacock Alley?" he said.

"Sure. Come along, David."

Peacock Alley in the Waldorf-Astoria is a favorite luncheon spot for the smart and well-to-do. They go there after church in finery and white gloves to lunch on cold pheasant and white wine. The four of us marched through pillared opulence, David holding Elliott's hand, and me on crutches, to Martin's reserved table. As we went over the menu, Martin said with eloquent disdain, "I hope he doesn't spill anything on his suit."

The meal was excellent and David ate hungrily. He put away two lamb chops with mashed potatoes and gravy, soup, salad, and dessert. After lunch, the adults had a round of whiskey sours and David ate all the cherries, including Martin's. We chatted on over the drinks and ordered a second round. As if on signal, David turned a bilious green. I took one look at his face and went into action. Grabbing a handful of napkins, I jumped up and took David in my arms. Somehow managing my heavy cast and crutches, I tossed napkins over his head and made for the ladies' room. Already he was vomiting in the napkins as I pushed open the door and poured him over a sink. A quarter of an hour later, we emerged with David, white-faced and weakened. But he hadn't drooled a drop on his suit. He hasn't touched a maraschino cherry since.

I should have known that David was not through yet. Big

troubles are not the only things that come in threes. So do embarrassments involving small boys.

Elliott had appointments in Washington for several days, representing a bank in Minneapolis. September is time for all good little boys and girls to go to school, so Ford and Gretchen were put on a plane for home and studies. We drove down to the capital accompanied by David. Settling into a motel on the Virginia side of the Potomac, we called Jimmy Roosevelt. Irene and Del were in California, and Jimmy invited us for dinner that evening. This meant getting a baby sitter for David. I inquired about this service with the management. They said the front desk would take care of the little boy, and we gave him instructions: "Now, David, if you get nervous or if anything happens just dial 'O' and the operator will answer. Tell her what you want." Barely had we left when he made his first call. "This is David Roosevelt. I need help. I haven't had enough ice cream." That marked the beginning of a hectic evening for the motel staff. "Please send three lunch boxes . . . I can't turn on the light in the bathroom . . . I'm lonesome . . . This is David Roosevelt . . . This is David . . ." At 12:30 A.M. we returned, and the "sitter" switchboard operator had never been happier to see two parents return home Everybody had joined in the project to keep David content. The janitor had drawn crayon pictures on hotel stationery and Scotch-taped them to the walls, the pool lifeguard had stayed overtime to cart in ice cream and lunch boxes, the maid helped, the desk clerk, the parking lot boy. Elliott was horrified. I was embarrassed. David was sleepy. "Gee, Mom," he said, "we had a good time."

The following day David explained that he had ordered two of the box lunches so that he could share them with Caroline Kennedy. He was going to invite the President's daughter, he announced, on a picnic. When we insisted we were not even going to the White House, he moped. Later we drove past it on our way to Jimmy's office. David recognized the building. "Why can't we go in there?" he said. "Let's stop and ask if she wants to go to lunch." We drove on, rapidly.

A favorite restaurant of ours in Washington was Paul and David Young's on Connecticut Avenue opposite the Mayflower Hotel. Mama Young, a bright, friendly woman speaking broken

English, was captivated by our son at dinner and kept bringing us extra cookies and rolls. When we had eaten, the brothers came to our table. Paul asked, "Mrs. Roosevelt, how are you getting around town when Mr. Roosevelt is working? We have a car and driver you can use." I told him that would be wonderful. "Fine, the car is at your disposal, anywhere you want to go." The chauffeur's name was Charles. He would have the car at our motel the next morning at ten o'clock.

Everywhere in the nation there seemed to be old friends of mine from Seattle school days. One I had not seen for twenty-five years was now Jane Ringenberg, the wife of a naval officer in Washington. She had been a doctor's daughter who lived next door to Anna and John Boettiger in Seattle. I managed to reach her by telephone. Her husband, George, was a Navy Commander, attending the War College in Washington, D.C. She sounded excited about the prospect of seeing me again. She had to go to a brunch at the admiral's house that day. I told her I would pick her up there.

The Youngs' car turned out to be a huge 1940 Rolls-Royce, all blue chromium and black leather, which they used to promote the restaurant. With the Negro chauffeur, Charles, at the wheel, it purred into the motel driveway at ten o'clock sharp. As other guests ogled, we climbed in, trying to appear nonchalant. Inside, it was like riding the bridge of the *Queen Mary*. There were little flowers tucked around and bottles of perfume, and the floor was covered by a beautiful fur rug. The upholstery had that luxury you can sink into. Tires whispering, we sped to our rendezvous at the admiral's house with my friend.

Charles obligingly went to the door to ask for Jane. She came out and her brows lifted just a trifle, then dropped again. After all these years, her greeting was perfunctory. No kiss, no hug. Climbing in beside me and David in the Rolls-Royce, she gave me a thin little smile and said, "Well, Patty, how have you been?" During the entire time we spent together, several hours, including lunch, there was no mention of the car. At noon, we met Elliott and Jimmy at the Mayflower Hotel across the street from Paul Young's restaurant. Charles was the soul of courtly obsequiousness. "Madam," he inquired, "where shall I meet you?"

I waved a finger offhandedly, "Oh, Charles, just wait across the street. We'll come to Young's for lunch."

That evening we had drinks with Jane and her husband, George, and I managed to catch his ear privately. "I can't imagine what's happened to Jane," I began. "She has changed completely. I met her with this . . ."

"Don't tell me how you met her," he laughed. "The minute I got in the house she was talking about, 'Boy, that Patty Peabody, how did she ever get a chauffeur and a Rolls-Royce?' She's been blowing her top."

I don't know if Jane ever found out it was Paul Young's restaurant car. Elliott had strong feelings about the incident, though. "Patty," my husband grumbled. "Why did you do that? I've never heard of such a dirty trick."

We returned to Minneapolis, refreshed from our vacation. But the good feelings were to be short-lived. Ahead lay an ordeal that was to test the mettle of the Roosevelt family, and reveal some cracks in its armor.

During the Hyde Park visit Mrs. Roosevelt's declining health
had been painfully apparent to us all, but no one realized the
truly grave nature of her illness. After arriving home I wrote a
thank-you note for her hospitality. Her secretary, Maureen Core,
sent me a cordial reply but made no mention of the fact that Mrs.
Roosevelt had just been admitted to Presbyterian Hospital of the
Columbia-Presbyterian Medical Center in New York. Thus, the
long-distance call from Jimmy two weeks after our return came
like a thunderbolt.

"Elliott, Mummy's in the hospital," he said. "It looks like the
beginning of the end."

For Elliott, the first reaction was shock mingled with anger
that the family had not forewarned him about his mother's condition.

The cast had been removed at last from my foot, leaving the
leg white, thin and ugly. At least, as we rushed back to New
York, I was no longer packing around twenty pounds of plaster,
although I did walk with a limp. Upon arrival, Elliott was given a
quick explanation. Mrs. Roosevelt was suffering from anemia, due
to failure of the bone marrow. About four months before this, in
May, tests showed her blood platelets had become very low in the
blood count. The platelets are necessary for clotting. To stimulate

the bone marrow and prevent bleeding, she was being treated with steroids.

The full complexity of her terminal illness was not to be revealed, however, until after her death. An autopsy would show that she also suffered a massive flareup of tuberculosis of the lungs. In a post-mortem, physicians were to agree that the steroid treatments actually "lightened up" old healed TB lesions, presumably dating back to 1919 when she had pleurisy.

From the beginning of her terminal illness, Mrs. Roosevelt was a reluctant patient. She complained so bitterly of being in the hospital that doctors finally allowed her to return to her New York apartment. She arrived home in the ambulance, face puffy and pale, hair in disarray. Somehow the news media had been tipped off, and the street was swarming with reporters and photographers. Pictures spread across the front pages next day were of a woman with just a short time to live, resembling anything but the vibrant Eleanor Roosevelt who had moved so energetically in national and international affairs. It marked the beginning of a strange six-week death watch that was to bring to the surface some of the powerful undercurrents coursing through this family.

At Mrs. Roosevelt's apartment, Anna was in complete charge of household matters. After consultation with Mrs. Roosevelt's doctors, she put out news bulletins to the press saying it was felt that Mrs. Roosevelt could be treated as easily at home as in the hospital. Treatment now consisted of almost daily blood transfusions. In a short time the patient's flesh became so perforated from injections it was difficult to find a fresh place to insert the needle.

To Eleanor Roosevelt, illness of any kind was a psychological blow. All her life she had driven herself and could revive her energies with a catnap in a moving car, or even at a banquet table. Such a steamdriver approach to life was not surprising. Theodore Roosevelt, too, had driven himself unmercifully, boasting that he never slept more than four hours a night.

In the last ten years of her life, pain had become a constant companion to Mrs. Roosevelt. She suffered severe arthritis in her feet which tended to draw the toes downward. The discomfort was excruciating when she had to stand for long hours at state functions and in receiving lines. Arthritis and rheumatism also affected the muscles in her back and shoulders, causing her to stoop and preventing her from turning her head more than 10 degrees. With characteristic stoicism she accepted these afflictions without comment, and I doubt that anyone realized the suffering she endured in daily life. In the last seven or eight years she had developed a tremor in her hands and had difficulty walking. Her handwriting became barely legible.

Until the past June, however, she had remained extremely active although obviously not feeling well. The anemia was accompanied by persistent fever and a general listlessness. By midsummer she was having to cancel most of her speechmaking, travel, and official engagements, and was spending the better part of her time at Hyde Park. In August, she began to deteriorate rapidly.

In the New York apartment, they had converted her narrow second-floor bedroom into a sickroom. The room had an airy feeling, and even though heavy red side drapes hung beside the edge of the ceiling-to-floor bay windows, it was bright and cheerful. In front of the window stood a lovely Queen Anne drop front desk where Mrs. Roosevelt often sat until late at night personally answering some of her voluminous correspondence. A large headboard framed a three-quarter bed, beside which stood her simple dressing table, crammed with pictures, mementos, and a silver dresser set. Across the room was the fireplace, and you could hear the soft tick of the gold pendulum clock on the mantel. It was a modest room, but the kind you would expect Mrs. Roosevelt to have. Her closet was narrow, utilitarian, with surprisingly few clothes. At the end of the bed stood Sara Delano's hope chest. There was an occasional chair by the fireplace and a small table beside it, where she loved to sit in the evenings reading and finalizing her busy schedules.

Elliott and I took a suite in the Summit Hotel and twice a day he walked twenty blocks to the apartment to visit Mrs. Roosevelt. I remained at the hotel taking phone calls, playing solitaire, and writing letters to the children. The beautiful rooms we were given soon became a box for me. I did not wish to intrude on the family, and Anna made every effort to shield her mother from unnecessary visitors.

Mrs. Roosevelt's sons and daughter took turns, more or less, at her bedside. With the consent of her brothers, Anna made all the arrangements, paid all the bills out of Mrs. Roosevelt's account and saw to the marketing and household duties. To help run errands, she brought in her daughter, son and daughter-in-law. She and her husband moved into the small back bedroom on the third floor.

With their own occupations to follow and families to care for, the four Roosevelt sons were unable to remain full time. Franklin, Jr., came up from Washington frequently, enroute to his home in Dutchess County. Jimmy also would fly up from Washington, when Congress was in session. Elliott and I went back and forth from Minneapolis, where the children remained. John, of course, lived in New York City, and was partner in an investment company. Anna tried to arrange times for them to visit their mother.

Elliott was terribly shaken by the ordeal. For hours he would sit at his mother's bedside, holding her hand. In the early weeks she would open her eyes fleetingly, recognize him, squeeze the hand that held hers and drift off to sleep again.

In October her condition grew sharply worse. She went back to the hospital for a few days, rallied again and was returned to the apartment. By now a grim realization had dawned upon us: Eleanor Roosevelt, realizing that she had an incurable illness and unwilling to linger as an invalid, was trying to die.

Autumn's crystalline days and long shadows came to New York. The breeze blew chilly, bringing down cascades of golden maple leaves. Late afternoon sunlight lay silver up the Hudson, cut by the black wedges of excursion steamers. Interspersed with the sunny weather were days of heavy gray skies and cold, drumming rains which streaked the windows of the sickroom. The leaves dried, died and fell, leaving black branches.

Mrs. Roosevelt drifted into a deeper coma, with fewer periods of consciousness. My husband lived in a state of suspended shock, whether beside her in the darkening room or traveling to and from Minneapolis. He begrudged bitterly, now, the years they had been apart and the words they had never said privately to each other. Adding to his frustration was the knowledge that even in these final weeks he could not remain at her bedside around the clock. And he could not shake from his mind the memory of that moment when his mother had awakened briefly with the pain of another transfusion needle going into her arm and whispered: "Let me die. Let me die."

On one of our return trips to Minneapolis a letter was waiting from Elliott's old friend Martin Jones. It urged him to think seriously of moving to Miami Beach and establish a business there. Our discontent with life in Minneapolis had been mounting steadily. Now another winter was nearly upon us.

The first weekend in November we went ahead with plans to visit Martin in Miami, if only for a quick break in our depressing routine. Even as we flew down, Martin was arranging meetings with several business and community leaders, including former Senator Claude Pepper. Within hours after we arrived in Miami Beach, however, the telephone rang at Martin's home. It was Franklin, Jr. His voice was muffled.

"I'm sorry, old man," he told Elliott. "Mummy's gone."

My husband's face crumpled. "Oh, my God," he said.

We flew immediately to New York, where the family was gathering from all points. It was decided that the following day everyone would go to Hyde Park. Preparations began for a huge funeral.

Because of the complex nature of Mrs. Roosevelt's illness, physicians immediately requested the family's permission to perform the autopsy. It was done at the Presbyterian Hospital, where the tuberculosis was confirmed. The finding automatically canceled one of the great humanitarian's bequests to help others. She had willed her eyes to the eye bank. Now they could not be used.

Immediately the family began to feel world-wide repercussions from Eleanor Roosevelt's death. Telegrams and letters, messages of condolence and grief, began pouring in from everywhere. Letters came in all shapes and sizes, many poorly written and badly spelled, from the people who remembered her humanitarianism and what she had symbolized. They saw her both as the widow of the man who had led the country out of the Depression and a woman who had herself taken active leadership in getting people back to work. Commentators and writers, representing many languages, colors, and creeds extolled the great heart which death had stilled.

Her life was chronicled in columns and columns of newspaper

space. This, they remembered, was the woman who had gone into politics reluctantly at the instigation of Louis Howe, FDR's close adviser for many years. He had urged her to become active in order to keep her husband's interest alive after his attack of polio at Campobello in 1921. She overcame an inability to make speeches and extreme nervousness in public. Her voice was unsuited to public speaking, with a high register and a tendency to quaver. Even when she became proficient at speaking, she would sometimes break into the middle of a speech with a giggle. This voice was only one of the many things that worked against Eleanor Roosevelt. As a child she had suffered an acute shyness and inferiority complex. As a teenager, she was a wallflower, by her own words. In her early married life when Franklin was Assistant Secretary of the Navy and was called upon to have numerous social engagements, she suffered an almost crippling shyness at parties. She later recalled the night she left her husband at a party, pleading a headache, took a taxi to their apartment in New York and, because she had forgotten to get the key, spent three hours sitting on the floor of the vestibule outside their apartment, in her evening gown, waiting for him to come home.

When FDR became Governor of New York in 1929, Eleanor took up teaching in a girl's school and three days a week would commute from Albany to New York City, a three and a half hour train ride. It was during these years that her life took on a tremendous vitality. It carried into the White House where as first lady she wrote the daily syndicated column "My Day" plus a monthly column for the *Ladies' Home Journal* and *McCall's*, did radio shows, traveled incessantly, and made numerous public speeches and appearances. After FDR's death, she resolved to keep her life active. Thus, in 1945, she was named by President Truman to the U. S. Delegation to the United Nations and served until the Eisenhower administration. She then became a moving spirit behind the American Association of the United Nations, the organization created to educate the public on the aims and objectives of the UN.

As a public speaker she became a professional, greatly in demand, and much of her annual income eventually came from this. In the last ten years of life she earned $150,000 annually, and gave almost all of it to her favorite charities, one of which was the Society of Friends. Although she was not a Quaker but an Episcopalian, she believed in the Society's efforts to promote missions in the backward areas of the world.

She also contributed heavily in time, effort, and money to the alleviation of the suffering of the survivors of the concentration camps of the Nazis. Later she was to crusade for assistance for the new state of Israel. Not only did she support financially organized charities, but also those organizations striving to bring about civil rights for the Negro. She was the moving spirit behind fund-raising efforts for the Wiltwyck School for Boys, devoted to rehabilitation of wayward boys from the greater New York area. Hundreds of private individuals were recipients of cash assistance who appealed to her for help in their times of trouble.

Although Mrs. Roosevelt tried to avoid doling out money indiscriminately, she did provide financial support for a great many people, many of whom became close friends. One outstanding example was Lorena Hickok, an AP correspondent in Washington who for many years had covered Mrs. Roosevelt in the White House. Miss Hickok was a diabetic and eventually became an invalid. Mrs. Roosevelt found her a place to live in Hyde Park and induced the former reporter to begin writing children's books, and helped arrange the publication of them. But even knowing all of these many facets of her life, we were ill prepared for the wave of public reaction and sympathy to her passing.

The day after her death, John summoned us all to his apartment for the reading of the will. We gathered at noon, had a round of drinks and lunch. Elliott was openly upset. The attorney arrived about 1 P.M., gathered us together, put on a pair of half-moon Ben Franklin glasses, cleared his throat and began to read the will. For all the dry legal phraseology of the six-page will, the warmth and personality of Mrs. Roosevelt came shining through in the small intimate things she regarded of value. She remembered everyone with something, including the nine godchildren and the servants.

The bequests included: "To son James Roosevelt all my flat silver EF and the old silver Lady Bell . . . To my son Elliott Roosevelt what remains of Grandmother Hall's pink china and

two silver serving trays . . . To my son Franklin, Jr., the
Japanese screen on wall of my living room in my New York
apartment and the silver tankard . . ." She left the largest cash
bequest, $10,000, to her family doctor "in gratitude for his
devoted care for which he would not accept compensation during
my lifetime." Personal items in the Manhattan apartment were
to be distributed equally among the sons and Anna. Mrs.
Roosevelt's employees received $100 in cash for each year of
service, up to $1000. Her secretaries received up to $2000.

17

"She Would Rather Light a Candle"

Preparing a funeral on the scale of Mrs. Roosevelt's was an immense and intricate undertaking. Three United States Presidents were to be present. Every formal act would be performed in the full glare of world publicity, combining spectacle with state ceremony. The variety of details demanding attention was endless. There was timing to be plotted, messages sent, protocol planned, crowds controlled; funeral dignitaries had to be transported, escorted, positioned, guarded, fed, and entertained. The task of planning and directing fell to the Roosevelt children. With the lifelong conditioning of their kind, they rose superbly to the occasion.

From New York, Mrs. Roosevelt's body was taken to Val-Kill, her country home two miles east of Hyde Park. After the reading of the will, all of the immediate family except Elliott and me made the ninety-five mile trip in Jaguars supplied by Franklin, Jr., through his automobile agency. Accompanying the others were Joe and Trude Lash, and Edna and Dr. David Gurewitsch, perhaps the family's most intimate friends. The Lashes, Anna and her husband Jim Halsted were installed in Mrs. Roosevelt's house. Johnny and family were in their fieldstone cottage next door, and Franklin, Jr., at his farm a few miles to the south. We remained in New York to have dinner with Elliott's four older children. When we arrived later, we were put up in a motel.

Anna continued to direct things for the family. Each of the Roosevelt children were given an assignment. Johnny had general charge of funeral arrangements and parking; FDR, Jr., would invite VIPs and governmental notables; Anna was to supervise correspondence and telephoning, Jimmy deal with the White House mortician and handle church arrangements. Elliott had no special function except to help greet dignitaries as they arrived. Mrs. Roosevelt's secretary, Maureen Core, was brought up from New York to do correspondence. Each member of the family prepared a guest list. About fifteen hundred invitations were to be sent by telegram, and tickets were printed for the VIP luncheon and church service. The luncheon would be at Johnny's house at noon, the funeral in St. James Episcopal Church, Hyde Park, at three.

During the three days between her death and funeral, messages of condolence poured into Hyde Park. By mail and wire came expressions of affection and grief from people to whom Mrs. Roosevelt had become, in her own right, a champion of human dignity. Some of the letters were crudely written, tear-stained or badly spelled. Some were in crayon, the work of school children. Some could not be read immediately, for they were in a foreign language. Around the world, she was revered for her work in the United Nations, to help make life better. And to the millions in America and the Western nations, she was the widow of the man who had led them out of the "Great Depression," whose ringing words had kindled hope when despairing people needed it most desperately: "The only thing we have to fear is fear itself."

But occasionally, too, the work of a sick mind crept into the bulging sacks. One I remember was an almost illegible scrawl which said, "I'm glad you're dead, Eleanor."

The Hyde Park Post Office put on three extra mail trucks, which made half a dozen trips a day to the country house. The wives were assigned to help Maureen sort through the deluge, culling out the personal and VIP messages which would require immediate reply. Nobody invited me to help, but I volunteered anyway.

The area around Val-Kill was becoming alive with people, cars, police, photographers. They clustered along the narrow country road which wound in from Highway 9 and jammed up at the gate three hundred yards from the houses. Accredited photographers and reporters gathered in the yard, trampling the flower beds. Dour security police in dove-brown uniforms appeared in strategic places. Nobody was trusted. We were issued identification badges bearing our photographs. I felt as if I were back in the Boeing plant in Seattle.

Along with the mail came a rising tide of flowers and food. People carted in cakes and pies and sandwiches, jugs of coffee and platters of potato salad. Finally, Anna had to post a policeman at the door to turn away gifts, dispatching floral offerings either to the church or the graveside at Hyde Park, depending on their quality.

Mrs. Roosevelt's plain oaken casket, covered by the family's white floral blanket, rested in state in the small parlor of her house. The shades were drawn and small lamps lit, casting deep shadows in the room. At the head of the casket was displayed a picture of FDR. For two days, friends came and went, paying their respects. They stood in silence, singly and in groups, at the casket and some prayed. The house grew close with the odor of flowers and too many people.

That evening Elliott and I knelt by the casket and said the rosary together. My husband's face was sickening. There was nothing I could do to ease his grief but be present, stay close to him. This seemed to be all he expected, or needed, for his mourning was something apart from our experience together. Elliott's feeling for his mother had great depth; his sense of loss was the more acute for the worry he had always caused her. I thought of Mrs. Roosevelt's anxiety for Elliott, the boy punching cattle in Wyoming and riding broncs in the rodeos; for Elliott, the brash wartime pilot; for the business risker who twice went to the brink of financial ruin, for the dashing romanticist with four marriages that failed. In his adult life, they had never had enough time together, alone, to talk of important and personal things. Elliott hungered for the stability he felt she could help him achieve. He had always said that both of his parents had died too soon, with too much work left undone. Now, he accepted with humility part of the mantle of responsibility that was left to the children. Perhaps he could finish in some small measure the work left undone.

In the dim light, he appeared ashen and drawn. I kept silent, and he slipped his rosary beads beneath the floral blanket.

Later, someone found the beads and threw them away. They also discarded a small bouquet of gardenias and violets which Laura Delano, our beloved Aunt Polly, had sent down. Aunt Polly, the peppery, eighty-year-old first cousin of FDR, never got over this.

On the eve of the funeral, the Roosevelt offspring gathered in the dining room and sitting room.

I assumed that this night someone would sit up with the body. When my Grandmother Peabody died, the family took turns on watch throughout the night. Elliott was prepared to do this by himself. At 9:30 P.M., however, everyone rose and it was agreed it was time for the family to retire. "We will have a hard day tomorrow," somebody said. "Everybody off to bed." Elliott was astonished, and said he wished to sit with the casket. "Don't be ridiculous," came the reply. "We don't need any of that nonsense. There is nothing we can do for her now." And with that, the parlor door was locked.

I should have expected as much. This would not be my first taste of detachment. There had been, for example, the episode of the previous evening during a family get-together at the home of Franklin and Sue. They live in a large colonial farmhouse on a hillside, commanding a view of the rolling pastureland where Franklin raises pure-bred cattle. The house contains a spacious and seldom-used living room, a homey library, and an office adjoining. They had dinner for about forty people, members of the family and close friends. During dinner, someone announced that color-coded tickets would be handed out for the funeral. "Red tickets for the VIPs," he said, "green tickets for the semi-VIPs, blue tickets for the no 'IPs.'"

I left the table.

After dinner, they decided to call top governmental figures, particularly the President and ex-Presidents, with personal invitations. To make myself useful, I volunteered to place the long-distance calls. Others would then do the talking. At first I suffered a twinge of nervousness. "I am calling President Kennedy, this is Mrs. Elliott Roosevelt speaking . . . This is Mrs. Elliott Roosevelt. I'd like to speak to President Truman . . ." I called the White House, Independence, Gettysburg; I placed calls to Dean Rusk, to Robert McNamara. Each time, it was strangely elating to sense the power of the Roosevelt name. Magically, it opened doors closed to other people, including Patricia Peabody. It was as if, suddenly, I held a passkey to the world.

When, at last, the telephoning was finished, Franklin, Jr., announced, "We should all thank Patty for what she has done tonight. I am very proud of the way you handled this, Patty, and how you said, 'This is Mrs. Elliott Roosevelt,' instead of simply 'This is Mrs. Roosevelt.' A lot of people here wouldn't have done it that way."

"Well, I am Mrs. Elliott Roosevelt," I said.

He gave me an enigmatic smile.

The day of the funeral arrived with cold morning drizzles and skies the color of slate. A chill breeze whipped up from the Hudson, rustling the bare branches. In the woods around Val-Kill, evergreens formed somber ranks, and dead leaves made a spongy carpet underfoot. The half-moon lake at the foot of Mrs. Roosevelt's yard was a dingy smear on the landscape, populated by a clutch of miserable-looking ducks. The waterfowl had been brought in by Johnny for shooting, and they all had names. The rushes and foxtails, which had bloomed so riotously lavender in summer, stood now as brown weeds.

The dove-brown uniforms of police were everywhere now, at the doorways of the two houses, along the split rail fences on the road, melting in with the landscape.

Johnny's house, a picturesque colonial cottage of fieldstone and white frame, tops a small rise overlooking the narrow rock-and-asphalt road which winds through the countryside off Highway 9. Heavy screening of trees and shrubs separates it from Mrs. Roosevelt's home fifty yards away. The road crosses a small bridge, then slices eastward through woods of maple, spruce, and syca-more, but a gravel spur loops around and makes a circle behind the two houses.

The cottage of Johnny Roosevelt is tidy and charming. Its living room is small, with a high-beamed ceiling of rich woods; there are leaded casement windows, a stairway leading to an upper balcony above the living room, a tiny kitchen, a glassed-in porch on the ground floor. Somehow, into this house we were to pack two hundred fifty people for a VIP luncheon, including John and Jacqueline Kennedy, Harry and Bess Truman, Dwight Eisenhower, Lyndon and Lady Bird Johnson, Adlai Stevenson, notables of the FDR administration, the United Nations, the consular corps and some dignitaries. I visualized them stacked up and hanging from the ceiling—which, as it was to turn out, wasn't far wrong.

During the morning, servants put out fresh flowers everywhere and gave the furniture one last wipe with the dustcloths. Anna paced, making frequent trips outside to peer at the leaden sky. The elements, at least, would not be cowed. There were numerous whispered conferences with John, speculating over whether or not it was going to rain again.

My spirits took an upturn with the arrival of Aunt Polly, a short human dynamo with her purple hair, dressed in a simple black suit and suitably adorned in mourning weeds. Shortly before noon, she and I took seats on the sun porch so we could watch the limousines arriving along the narrow road. Aunt Polly eyed the swarm of waiting photographers and pursed her lips. "What nonsense," she said. "Eleanor would have hated this display. When I die, I want them just to put my bones in the ground and leave me be."

The first car to appear was a huge gray Cadillac driven by a chauffeur. It came rocking down the road, splashing muddy water in the chuckholes. In the back seat sat a man in a Homburg. "I don't recognize him," Aunt Polly said. "Go see who it is." I walked out to the driveway as the chauffeur was opening the car door. Pushing aside a gray wool lap rug, the man got out, a figure of Pickwickian elegance. He wore morning clothes, soft gray gloves, a topcoat with velvet collar and carried a walking stick. I made discreet inquiries, then returned to Aunt Polly. "Nobody knows who it is, Aunt Polly." She squinted, studying his face, and at last came a spark of recognition. "Why that's Langdon Marvin," she said. "Very distant relative. I haven't seen him in years." Cousin Langdon, I learned later, liked to do things in style. The Cadillac and chauffeur had been hired in New York.

More limousines moved slowly up the road, lurching like tanks over the ruts. As each arrived, it was met by the brothers in the circle driveway and the dignitaries ushered into the house. The Kennedys—Jack and Jackie, Bobby and his wife, Ethel—came in a black Continental with a phalanx of Secret Service men and mobile telephones in the cars. As usual, the President was hatless and wore no topcoat against the cold. Jacqueline wore a two-piece black suit with a small hat of dark mink. Their arrival electrified the place. The JFK charm radiated all around. In the small living room, he was all gracious sociability, but at the same time kept a perceptible restraint proper to the circumstances of his visit.

The President greeted Elliott warmly and grinned.

"Elliott, Ike's going to be here, isn't he?" he said.

"Yes, I think so."

"I'll bet you twenty dollars that in five minutes he'll have me backed against the wall giving advice about how to run the country, and in three days, he will be at the White House with some more ideas."

Barely were the words out of his mouth when Dwight Eisenhower arrived. The former GOP President came without Mamie. Ike shook hands all around then made straight for President Kennedy, steering him into a corner. Jack finally signaled for help. Jimmy and John caught the sign, joined the two men and maneuvered President Eisenhower into another room.

Each of the Roosevelt women were assigned a top VIP to make certain that glasses were filled, comforts seen to and conversation kept flowing. Johnny's wife, Anne, a Republican, was hostess for President Eisenhower; Irene, Jimmy's wife, had Harry and Bess Truman; I was to help entertain the Lyndon Johnsons. Aunt Polly made her own selection; she was captivated by New York Governor Nelson Rockefeller.

As the VIPs flocked in and the clock passed noon, the yard and road became glutted with black limousines, onlookers, major and minor functionaries and security men. With so many Presidents present, plainclothes agents were tripping over one another. Irene received the biggest shock of the day. She went to the bathroom, glanced at the window and shrieked. There, peeping in, was the face of a Secret Service man.

Shortly after the arrival of the Trumans, the three Presidents and Vice-President Johnson were given a chance for some rare private shop talk in a small library off the living room. After more than a quarter of an hour had passed, Mrs. Truman said to Irene, "Would you please go in there and get Harry? He has been at it long enough." Irene opened the door and said, "Mr. President, your wife would like to see you." Three heads swiveled. "Which President?" Truman burst out laughing. "Oh my gosh, it's Bess, I'm sure. I can just hear her saying, 'You old fool, you've been in there talking long enough.'"

Dwight Eisenhower's presence at the funeral won him extra regard from the family. Upon assuming the Presidency, Ike had not reappointed Mrs. Roosevelt to the United States delegation to the United Nations. A story had trickled back to General Eisenhower that Mrs. Roosevelt had been critical of his wife, which was not true.

After the breakup of the Presidential bull-session in the library, President Eisenhower wandered about at loose ends, a Republican in a hotbed of Democrats. Gathering courage, I planted myself at his elbow and announced that I had always admired him and back in Seattle had been a leading young Republican for Eisenhower. Soon we were busily chatting about his favorite hobby, cooking, and exchanging soup recipes.

I reminded him of an impromptu meeting he had had with me and our son, David, three months before in Minneapolis. We happened to drive up the school football field where Mr. Eisenhower's helicopter was about to land, bringing the former President for a speech. David and I got out of our car and strolled over to the landing pad where an official greeting party had gathered. David, then four years old, was bundled up in a camel's-hair coat and jaunty little cap. The propeller blast of the descending 'copter sent the officials scurrying back holding their hats. David and I were left standing in front. As Eisenhower stepped down, I whooped, "Hi, President Eisenhower, I'm Patty Roosevelt." He remembered the incident and laughed. "So you're the woman with the little boy in the camel's-hair coat?"

My first attempt at conversation with Vice-President and Mrs. Johnson was a dismal failure. He was so busy looking around to see who was present that I don't think he heard much of what was being said. Lady Bird, too, seemed preoccupied. I groped for some topic of common interest and could think of nothing but horses. What I did not know was that as the wife of Elliott Roosevelt, I had as much common ground with the Johnsons as practically anybody in the room. For Elliott had performed a favor that helped launch LBJ's political career. The man who in just thirteen months would be thrust by national tragedy into the Presidency had never forgotten it. The Vice-President finally sat down with Elliott's children, Chandler and Tony, Chandler's husband, Henry Lindsley and me, and told the story.

During FDR's first term in the '30s, he recalled, the President went down to Texas on a fishing trip. Elliott, at the time, was raising cattle and Arabian horses near Fort Worth and was president of the Texas Young Democrats. One day, Lyndon Johnson called him and said, "Elliott, ole boy, you could really do me a favor if you would just get me on your father's train going back to Washington. It runs right through my district." Elliott made the arrangements. FDR met the young Texan, took a liking to him, and stopped the train in Austin and Johnson City to appear with Lyndon on the platform and wave to the crowds.

Tony and Chandler enjoyed the story. They had known Lyndon Johnson for years and liked him. During the campaign prior to the Democratic convention, Tony had worked hard for the Senator in Dallas and Fort Worth.

As we chatted, Jackie Kennedy sat regally on the couch nearby, listening with cool unconcern to the scraps of talk floating about her. Tony and another of Elliott's sons, David, could not keep their eyes from the beautiful First Lady. With an elegant gesture, Jackie took a cigarette from her purse and held it for a light. The two young men were too mesmerized to react. They stared. Jackie balanced her unlit cigarette, waiting. They stared. Jackie waited. At last, with a resigned sigh, she drew a match from her purse and lit it herself.

In the midst of this byplay, a telegram was delivered to Elliott from our four children. WE ALL WISH WE COULD BE WITH YOU NOW, it said. WE ARE ALL SHARING YOUR SORROW AND KNOW HOW YOU FEEL. LOVE TO YOU AND MOM. It was signed Jim, Ford, Gretchen and David. Elliott read it, standing with John Kennedy,

Governor Rockefeller and Aunt Polly. When he finished, there were tears in his eyes.

Lunch featured turkey, ham, and molded salad. To serve it, practically every dinner plate, coffee cup and piece of silverware in the Roosevelt family had been brought out. All the in-laws were asked to help. The affair was a mass of confusion, with two hundred fifty people looking for places to eat in close quarters, balancing plates. There were occasional spills, and Elliott went dashing around with a sponge helping to clean up. People munched turkey in the living room, the library, on the porch, in the bedrooms.

When the last mouthful had been eaten and it was time to go, Elliott took each of the Presidents to the kitchen to meet the servants. Then we all filed out to the cars, touching off a new scramble of photographers through the flower beds. Johnny, in his quest for perfect organization, had come up with another brainstorm. Each car was numbered, and members of the funeral party assigned corresponding numbers. About fifty cars made up the motorcade for the five-mile drive to St. James Episcopal Church, where Mrs. Roosevelt's casket had been taken earlier that morning. As usual, there were mixups. Aunt Polly had stuck beside Nelson Rockefeller during the luncheon. She clung to his arm as they walked out to where Johnny was directing the loading of cars.

"John," she said, "which car am I to ride in?"

He glanced at Aunt Polly. "Don't worry," he said, "we've taken care of it."

Actually, Miss Laura Delano, first cousin to FDR and stubborn champion of Eleanor Roosevelt, had been overlooked. Governor Rockefeller looked down and said, "Miss Delano, I would deem it an honor if you would accompany me in my car."

Aunt Polly smiled quizzically. "I accept with alacrity, sir," she said. They marched out, and were not seen again that day.

The order of precedence in the funeral procession had presented a sticky problem in protocol. The question of who should go first, the Presidents or the family, had touched off a lively discussion the night before. Someone said we should follow the Presidents; Elliott was just as strongly against this. "It is our mother who died and not the Presidents' mothers," he protested.

"We should be in the first mourners' cars." Elliott's arguments prevailed. So the first two limousines bore ushers and honorary pallbearers; the third carried Johnny and Anne, Franklin, Sue and Adlai Stevenson, a man whose face sagged with grief and who had barely been able to carry on a conversation during lunch; and Elliott and I were in the fourth car with Jimmy, Irene, Anna, and Jim Halsted.

The roads were lined with people. They clustered along the unpaved secondary road to the highway, and on both sides of the highway to the church; people heedless of the cold and wet, people with tears in their eyes and Brownie cameras. There were shouts of recognition as we rode past, and for the three Presidents who followed. In places the onlookers stood three and four deep. To my horror, I saw a placard hoisted by one nondescript man: "We're glad you're gone, Eleanor." The police arrested him.

Rain sluiced down as we arrived at the church, a small, ivy-covered structure of cut stone set back from Highway 9 amid soaring pines and spruce trees. Across the highway is the fabulous Hudson River estate of Frederick Vanderbilt, which FDR turned into a national monument. Behind St. James is the graveyard, where rest generations of Roosevelts.

The sanctuary is long and narrow and red-carpeted, with an arched high ceiling of walnut and a small organ loft. Each walnut pew is closed off from the aisle by a small gate bearing the nameplate of a family, and is furnished with red velvet seat cushions and kneeling hassocks. The three front pews on the left are the Roosevelt pews, a few feet from the marble font at which FDR and his children were baptized. Before the font stands a brass lectern, its top in the shape of a spread-winged eagle; to the right is the walnut pulpit from which Franklin Roosevelt, as senior warden of the church, once delivered a sermon.

As Elliott helped me from the car, I saw a Catholic priest and Dr. Gurewitsch and his wife standing to one side. The priest smiled and nodded. Dr. Gurewitsch, an avid photographer, was busy snapping pictures. The Presidents and Vice-President filed into the chapel, where ribbons in various colors marked off who was to sit where. The place quickly filled and the crowd spilled out into the churchyard.

With the stained-glass windows shut tightly against the cold, there was an odor of stale cigarette smoke and wet fur coats, exaggerated by the number of people wedged into the small church. Mercifully, the service was brief and unemotional, and soon we were filing out again past the grim-faced state troopers at the front doors. We climbed back into our numbered cars for the short drive to Hyde Park and the dismal graveside service in the rose garden.

While we stood solemnly laying to rest one of the greatest women of our times and a nation formally mourned her passing, someone quietly left the ceremony, and upon the instructions of Mrs. Roosevelt's legal advisers went straight to Val-Kill to padlock every door of Mrs. Roosevelt's house. We did not discover it immediately. Following the funeral, we drove back to John's house to discuss plans for memorial services for Mrs. Roosevelt in New York and Washington, D.C.

That night, we went to Franklin's house for dinner. Franklin and Elliott are very close, and they sat up until 3 A.M. talking. The family decided that Johnny and Anna would have charge of the New York memorial service in Episcopal Cathedral of St. John the Divine, and Franklin and Jimmy would direct another service in the Washington Cathedral of St. Peter and St. Paul.

On November 15, five days after her funeral, more than one thousand people gathered in Washington for a hushed silence, and a eulogy by Secretary of State Dean Rusk, who described her as "a woman who had no capacity for hate but much for indignation. Her compassion led her to passionate words and deeds against poverty, disease, exploitation, prejudice, fear, and oppression. . . ."

Two days later came the shining tribute from her old friend and stanch ally, Adlai Stevenson. In the vast New York Episcopal cathedral on Amsterdam Avenue, the United Nations Ambassador mounted the pulpit wearing a scarlet academic robe and spoke with deep emotion to the hushed throng of ten thousand. Eleanor Roosevelt, he said, was one of the greatest figures of our age, "whose lucid and luminous faith testified always for sanity in an insane time and for hope in a time of obscure hope

—a woman who spoke for the good toward which man aspires in a world which has seen too much of the evil of which man is capable . . . Her life was crowded, restless, fearless. Perhaps, she pitied most not those she aided in the struggle, but the more fortunate who were preoccupied with themselves and cursed with the self-deceptions of private success.

"She walked in the slums and ghettos of the world, not on a tour of inspection nor as a condescending patron, but as one who could not feel contentment while others were in distress. Today, we weep for ourselves. We are lonelier because someone has gone from one's own life who was like the certainty of refuge; and someone has gone from the world who was like a certainty of honor. She would rather light a candle than curse the darkness."

To the world, Eleanor Roosevelt was all the things Adlai Stevenson said she was. To my mind, in the time I had known her, she had become many other things as well. Since one etches from his or her own impressions and experiences, each picture a human draws of another is different from anyone else's, and so was mine. After the memorial services, I tried to knit my impressions together.

Mrs. Roosevelt's personality, seen close up, had had an immensity about it, and you sensed her tremendous inner power. Her will was all the stronger for having been forged in a lifetime of overcoming personal handicap and disillusionment.

Basically, she had created her own image. As a teenager with buck teeth and stringy hair, she was a wallflower, acutely shy, a poor creature of unsureness and distress. This she turned to an advantage of sorts, for in deciding to overcome this, she made up her mind to do what she must do, when she must do it. The agony in early marriage of being relegated to an inferior position in the Hyde Park household—caught, as it were, between the doting and powerful mother-in-law and the pampered son—cut and shaped and tempered her even more. Thus, when FDR was felled by polio and she took on the rebuilding of a cripple into a man, she was prepared.

The woman I knew had strength and decision, and with it, peace. She created, willfully, I think, the aura of tranquillity and power which the public saw. It was a product of experience and breeding.

Yet the little asides I saw convinced me that it was a mistake to accept fully this public personality. Coming from a strong-minded family myself, I had bred into me some of the strength necessary when one has to face the firing squad.

Thus I caught glimpses of a Mrs. Roosevelt who could be brusque and indifferent, a surprising contrast to what I had read and been taught to believe. Though never deprecating or patronizing, she was quite capable of holding herself aloof. You sensed that this aloofness, too, was a calculated thing. She could turn it on and off, especially when displeased by the turn of a conversation or backed to the wall by a question from a newsman.

Hers was a superb mechanism for self-protection. I think she had built a shell to survive and always kept it handy, like the hermit crab. She preferred to steer the course of conversation, made the opening and closing statements, picked the time and place and circumstances, made her own judgments of people, and was not above brushing off those whom she disliked. One example of this in the family was her treatment of Aunt Polly. Although a woman of pronounced eccentricities, Aunt Polly was Eleanor's social peer; she doted on Mrs. Roosevelt, seldom failed to support her in anything, but was never close to this enigmatic woman. Long after Eleanor's death, however, Aunt Polly still champions her.

With her own family, Mrs. Roosevelt was loving, protective, not terribly demanding but, I think, had an intense desire to give them a closeness and unity which she herself never had. Mrs. Roosevelt was enthusiastic about family meetings, family dinners, children and grandchildren. To some extent, she was thwarted by all the divorces, but even made an effort to keep in touch with the former wives.

Ironically, even the name Roosevelt tended to work against her efforts. Her children had been offered the world, and in so many instances, it turned out to be a balloon, popping in their faces. They were, and are, naïve—Jimmy is perhaps the least gullible—and have all been hurt by opportunists, battered by people who were their father's enemies, villified and spat upon. To this day, it is difficult for a Roosevelt to make a strong personal friend, and part of this is because so many times in the past, they have found that people who professed to desire their friendship actually wanted something else, prestige or advantage or financial gain.

Seeing this, and sensing some of Mrs. Roosevelt's frustrations, I have become even more determined that my children should have a chance for permanence and security. At the dinner table of Franklin D. Roosevelt, the talk was of objective things: ships, stamps, governments, naval history. In our family, the talk more often is of personal things and personal problems; for where else can the children find a sympathetic forum?

Mrs. Roosevelt was troubled over the failure of Elliott's four previous marriages. She knew he needed stability, and hoped that he would find it. Given this, he can believe in what he does, and accomplish practically anything. Her death came after we had been married but a few years, but in that time, she and I had made progress from being two wary strangers to friends with the beginnings of a mutual regard.

The death of Elliott's and my child touched Mrs. Roosevelt deeply, and she gave me to understand that she knew what I was suffering. She recognized, too, that it was Elliott's good we were both striving to achieve; Elliott's fulfillment came first, rather than mine or hers or the baby's. I discovered in this tragedy that when you needed her strength, you could draw upon it, but not always in the way you expected. I also became aware that in those first painful months of marriage, when I was an outsider thrust into the Roosevelt hopper, she understood from her own socially tormented girlhood what I suffered; but I would have to fend for myself and learn to stand on my own feet. She would not prop me up.

Because of this, I doubt that I will ever again need such a prop.

Eleanor Roosevelt was dead. For the great family which I had lately joined, it was the end of one era and the beginning of another.

18

Roosevelt "Per Stirpes"

Death disrupts the order of families. When a dominant figure
dies, the lines of influence which once passed down from that
person become severed and hang as useless tendrils. There were
those in the family who had depended on Mrs. Roosevelt for
their own strength. Now cut adrift, they had alternatives of
floundering, or attaching themselves to another strong personality,
or developing a new resourcefulness uniquely their own. But
great families such as the Roosevelts have more to orbit around
than the presence of a strong parent. They also have a broad and
lasting heritage. What they do and how they present themselves
to the world reflects upon this heritage, and it upon them. Thus,
while most family units could expect a certain degree of disin-
tegration, the offspring of Franklin and Eleanor Roosevelt could
close ranks to the world on this rich and common ground. Their
differences were kept scrupulously shielded from outsiders because of family pride and by tacit agreement.

Perhaps most shaken by events of the past two months were
those who lived on the periphery of the inner family, the in-laws,
grandchildren, assorted cousins, the newcomers, children of previous marriages, and those adopted children born outside the
bloodlines of the Roosevelts. For in this family blood, not love or
marriage, was the criterion for full acceptance. In legal terminology it was called *per stirpes*, or inheritance through the

bloodline. Since the reading of the will, *per stirpes* had become my personal overdone bugaboo. It meant that Elliott's children by previous marriages, Chandler and David and Tony and Bill— all heirs, or potential heirs, to fortunes through their mothers— would also share in the Roosevelt family estate; but our four children, now legally his by adoption and morally his through love, were excluded.

Franklin Delano Roosevelt's estate had been valued at about $1,250,000, and had been left in trust to his children, with the income going to Mrs. Roosevelt as long as she lived. During the balance of her lifetime, the estate grew in value to $2,400,000. When Eleanor Roosevelt died, half of this was distributed in cash among the five children. Elliott's share, $240,000, went directly to the Colorado National Bank to help pay off his divorce settlement. We never saw a penny of it. The other half of the Franklin Delano Roosevelt estate, $1,200,000, went into a trust fund for the natural offspring of the five Roosevelt children. Thus, upon the death of, say, John Roosevelt, one-fifth of the remaining total estate would be distributed among his surviving children by blood.

In the course of burying and memorializing this great woman, however, there were also other revealing incidents showing the delicate interplay between members of her family and my relationship to them. One occurred during the memorial service in New York, following her funeral.

It was a rainy, blustery day in the city. All morning it poured down from a gray and cheerless sky. The streets were black and glistening, and the spires of New York towered above us like wet tombstones.

Cousin Leila Delano had a luncheon for the family and close friends prior to the service. Then again came the sad procession of rain-spotted limousines with their thumping windshield wipers, again the numbered cars and numbered seats, the red tickets for the family, green tickets for VIPs and blues for the crowd. The Cathedral of St. John the Divine filled with the musty odor of wet furs as Ambassador Stevenson stood haggardly delivering his eulogy. A shiver went up my back as he hurled his words at the walls, crying that Eleanor Roosevelt would rather "light a candle than curse the darkness." And then we filed back to the limou-

sines again. I sat on the back seat between Cousin Leila and
Aunt Polly, while Elliott rode up front with the chauffeur. The
car eased out into the street between cordons of police and
pressing crowds, and then we drifted into the mainstream of
traffic picking up speed.

Cousin Leila leaned across me to speak to Aunt Polly. "Laura,
did you see Faye Emerson?"

I jumped as though I had been shot. "Who?"

"Indeed I did," Aunt Polly replied. "Hasn't she gained a little
weight?"

They were speaking quietly, like parlor gossips, and Elliott
could not hear. I nudged Cousin Leila and winked. "Say it
louder."

Cousin Leila obliged, in a voice like a train announcer at
Grand Central Station. "*LAURA, DID YOU SEE FAYE
EMERSON?*"

Elliott's ear perked up. When the entire exchange had been
repeated, Cousin Leila nudged me and whispered, "Now, does
this make me your favorite cousin?"

That afternoon we were summoned by the executors of the
estate, Franklin and Johnny, to appear at Mrs. Roosevelt's apartment and pick out those of her possessions that we wanted. Each
of us was given a mimeographed list of what there was to choose
from.

Again I rebelled at what seemed to me a barbaric custom.
"They divided my garments among them and upon my vesture
they cast lots"—I knew this performance was necessary but how
dreadful to face especially for us. Elliott was torn with grief, and
certainly not in the mood for such things. Taking me was a
waste of time as I couldn't and wouldn't speak up. I didn't even
know really what had been in her apartment. The mimeographed
lists were a blank to me.

We got the Reedy Western prints for Chandler and gave them
to her. The only things I wanted were carpets, rugs, curtains,
and linens to help furnish our new home in Miami Beach.

When the shipment arrived in Miami Beach, the crate yielded
very little that was usable for our large floor space and many
windows. We did select, and receive, some very valuable books,
an old icon with an enamel face, and a precious painting of the

Madonna. We were also sent a rug which had been given to Mrs. Roosevelt by an Episcopal minister. When he found out what had happened to the rug, he asked that it be given back to him.

The Washington, D.C., memorial service also had provided me with fresh glimpses into how this family lived and thought.

As Undersecretary of Commerce, Franklin, Jr., had a lovely home in Washington. He and Sue traveled back and forth to their farm in Dutchess County, New York, usually in a private plane owned by his Roosevelt Motors firm.

Franklin's plane, like Franklin's boat and Franklin's farm, was one of the important things of life. Franklin enjoyed doing things with style. I had never seen the aircraft, but imagined that it must be a stunning sight. So when Elliott and I were invited to fly with Franklin and Sue to New York, I looked forward eagerly to the trip.

Franklin's secretary met us at the airport with a great accumulation of letters to be signed. In the waiting room, Elliott's brother sat down and began scribbling his signature, scattering letters all over the settee.

In midsignature, up strode an elegant figure resembling a cross between a Knight Templar in full clambake dress and the captain of the USS *Constitution*. He wore four gold stripes on his sleeve, gold spaghetti on the bill of his cap, gold epaulets and a glittering pair of aviator's wings. The man snapped Franklin a salute. His employer acknowledged with a nod and a curt, "Very well, Captain, we will be with you in a moment." My, I thought, what an important brother-in-law I have. When the signing was completed, the captain led the way and we set off toward the airplane parking ramps. I felt that the U. S. Marine Band should be playing *Stars and Stripes Forever*. We passed a big privately owned jet. (Nope, not that one.) We passed several handsome DC-3s. (Not one of those, either.) We walked along a line of somewhat smaller but no less elegant planes. (Well . . .) At last, we halted at the nose of a spunky little twin-engine Cessna, the kind that had bounced Elliott and me all over the skies of Colorado. My expectancy deflated like a six-ply tire. The captain removed his gold-trimmed coat, took off his gold-braided cap and wrapped it neatly in a cellophane bag, then tucked the bundle into a back compartment. "Franklin, you ought to be ashamed of yourself making that pilot walk around under such a load of gold braid," I said. "He'll have a breakdown."

Apparently my chiding remark turned out to be more prophetic than funny. Not long after this, a hired pilot took off in Franklin's plane and was gone for weeks, while his angry boss swore out warrants and combed the countryside.

As time passed, however, I became more and more aware that one could make warm friends even without being a member of the family's inner sanctum, that *per stirpes* had nothing to do with whether or not a child could be happy and properly disciplined. These points were brought home rather emphatically during our next trip to the nation's capital.

Three months after the death of Mrs. Roosevelt we went to Washington for the presentation of a commemorative stamp in her honor by President Kennedy. Prior to a reception and ceremony at the White House, we were invited to a coffee in the Mayflower Hotel. The place was teeming with dignitaries. I sat on a couch sipping coffee and trying to recognize faces. Across the room came a tall slender blonde, sophisticated and businesslike. Without bothering to introduce herself, she queried, "Have you seen Adlai Stevenson?"

I almost choked on coffee. "Who?"

"Oh for heaven's sake," she fumed, "you know, Adlai Stevenson."

"Well, I haven't seen him. I don't think I'd recognize him if I did."

Flipping open a formidable notebook, she peered down upon me and said, "For heaven's sake, who are you?"

"I'm Patty Roosevelt."

The notebook snapped shut. She slipped it back into her purse. "Oh you are, are you? Then precisely which one are you?"

"I'm Elliott's wife."

"Certainly, I know that, but *which* Elliott's wife?"

A flush of anger came to my face. "I am Elliott Roosevelt's wife. Period."

"Well, I am Betty Beale. You have no right to talk to a reporter like that."

"I'm sorry," I replied, "I don't know you. Are you a reporter?"

The well-known woman columnist had her turn to flush now. In Washington society, matrons clucked and cooed over Betty Beale. She sputtered and huffed a few times, then sat down beside me, smiled and said, "You know, you're different from the rest."

As we chatted, Elliott and Franklin, Jr., walked in from another room, saw what was going on and sucked in their breaths. "Elliott, do you see who Patty's talking to?" Franklin said. "It's Betty Beale. My God, let's get over there."

From long experience and many misadventures, the Roosevelt brothers had grown suspicious of the press generally and columnists in particular. They knew Betty for a hard-working newswoman who didn't let anybody scoop her. Elliott feared that she would be tricking me into some juicy off-guard comment. I saw them bearing down on us and smiled.

"Well, well, well," said Elliott, in a tone half conciliatory and half mock concern, "Patty, you must be tired, wouldn't you like to go freshen up a bit before . . ." Then, pulling me aside, he whispered that this was Betty Beale and I should be careful.

"Elliott, I think she's divine. Let me talk to her."

There wasn't much he could do. From that afternoon on, Betty and I were fast friends. Afterward, she visited us from time to time in Miami Beach and I came to have a great affection and admiration for her.

The stamp ceremony involved the presentation by President Kennedy of a special album to the family. Designated to receive it in our behalf was Jimmy and Irene's five-year-old son, frecklefaced, red-haired Del. Wearing a sky blue suit he arrived at the White House with his father and other members of the family.

While the dignitaries gathered at the reception and JFK chatted and swapped jokes with us, Del wandered away through the office wing of the White House. At the desk of Mrs. Evelyn Lincoln, secretary to the President, he spotted the box of candy which Mr. Kennedy always kept handy for young Caroline and John. Del's father, then congressman from California, found him attacking the chocolates with both hands and stuffing them into his mouth.

"Del," said the father. "Del, honey . . ."

"Keep still," little Del mumbled, stuffing in another chocolate.

Jimmy smiled indulgently and waited. When Del had finished he strolled into the marine trophy room. Suit, hands, and mouth were smeared with chocolate. Pausing at a display, he grabbed a ship model and fingered it with chocolate.

"Del, honey, put that down," said Jimmy.

"I won't."

The ceremony took place in the rose garden. A sizable crowd gathered with the family around the President for the presentation, including assorted cameramen and members of the press. Del, standing with his German nurse who had managed to clean off some of the chocolate, suddenly burst into tears and wet his pants.

President Kennedy, smiling gamely, patted the little Roosevelt on the head saying, "Del, come on, son, don't cry. Don't cry, honey." (*Pat, pat, pat.*) "Be a big boy."

I had a feeling the President would have preferred patting another extremity, with vigor.

19

Miami and Elliott Roosevelt International

It was time for a change of scene. Life with Elliott was a glorious and exciting thing, but the past year had brought too much tragedy and too many tears. Sometimes I had the feeling we were on a never-ending emotional binge. The thing to do was cast off the immediate past, pick up new threads for our lives, make a fresh start.

Elliott's old friend Martin Jones had plugged energetically the possibilities in Miami. It was a busy, burgeoning metropolitan city, a natural economic gateway to Latin America, a modern and promotion-minded area where there also happened to be a magnificent climate. "Reorganize your business, Elliott, and move down permanently," Martin urged.

Our good friend, the showman and entrepreneur, was particularly intrigued by the startling growth of Latin American trade. With the Alliance for Progress and such U.S. programs as Agricultural and Industrial Development turning the nation's attention toward Central and South America, opportunity for private initiative was endless. Latin businessmen, industrialists, and investors were eager to secure U.S. backed loans. Interest was keen in the availability of financing and technical assistance emanating out of Washington. And while our government cranked out various programs to help spur the Latin economy, there existed a communications gap between American agencies

and the very people they were created to help. A shrewd and
knowledgeable business consultant, based in Miami and working
as an adviser and intermediary, could do quite well. A man with
the name Roosevelt, a son of the FDR whose Good Neighbor
Policy had cemented enduring friendship with Latin America,
could do quite well indeed. Roosevelt was a magnetic word.

But it was a big move. It meant breaking off from the friends
we had made in Minneapolis, pulling up our roots, transplanting
the household and children, and going through a thousand details and minuscule harassments. We put the question to a family
conference. The four children could not have been more op-
posed to a move, palm trees or no palm trees. Jimmy had his
sweetheart, Ford was in the first year of high school, Gretchen
had met many friends and hated to leave them, and David was
looking forward to another winter of snow, sledding and fun.
"We don't want to go to Miami," they chorused. Well, at least
we had tried. Now it was up to Elliott and me to make the
decision on our own. A few trips to Miami were enough to
convince us. With Martin's help, he began establishing the office
of Elliott Roosevelt International in downtown Miami, while
I undertook the chore of finding a house. It was on one of these
trips that I met a vivacious blond real estate woman, Freddie
Peterson, who was to become one of my closest friends. Together we prowled the neighborhoods of Miami Beach, a fairyland city of lush, year-round vegetation, lovely winding streets,
watery vistas and tropical flowers. We inspected magnificent
homes, mostly beyond our reach. It soon became apparent that
some of the larger old homes were more reasonably priced than
smaller new ones.

We brought David down on one of the trips and planned to
leave from Miami to join Jimmy and Irene in Acapulco, Mexico,
for a week's vacation. Jimmy had received an unexpected contribution for his congressional campaign and sent us three round-
trip tickets. Instead of staying with Martin Jones as usual, we
spent that visit in an apartment in the Sea View Hotel, provided
by friends from Minneapolis, Dwayne and Inez Andreus.

To my dismay, little David was sick most of the time, suffering
a reaction from his vaccination. Freddie helped me obtain a
baby sitter who would stay when we could not take him out with

us. It was during this trip that I got an inkling of how nervous the rest of the family was becoming about the possibility of my writing this book.

Franklin, Jr., arrived in Miami for a meeting with his Fiat and Jaguar dealers from the southeastern United States. He invited us to attend a dinner with them at Tony Sweet's Restaurant, a posh establishment in Bay Harbor Islands. A dozen men gathered for the dinner with Franklin, Elliott, and me.

My brother-in-law was in rare form. Franklin, Jr., has an abundance of the Roosevelt wit and charm, and bears a striking resemblance to his father. With an easy good nature, he began to spin yarns about his prowess in the business and social worlds. Franklin's laughter is infectious, and when the joke is on him he will roar longer and louder than anyone else. In passing, he mentioned several rollicking adventures of the heart that brought shouts of laughter from the rest of us. I remarked gaily that I would have to remember them for my book. I might as well have dashed Franklin with ice water.

"Now Patty, behave yourself," he said, "you're not going to write a book and you know it. There have been enough books written about the Roosevelt family, and we should be allowed to live our lives in peace."

I insisted the story of life with the Roosevelts was too good to be left untold.

"All right," he said, "I'll tell you what I'll do. If you promise not to write the book, I will give you a new car."

"Then I'll go you one better," I laughed. "I will characterize you as a white knight on a white horse and give you first right to read the manuscript, providing you defend me as a lawyer against the rest of the family's lawsuits."

He laughed heartily and we shook hands in mock solemnity.

Franklin was sitting beside me at the table. A moment later, my silk purse slid off my lap. Reaching over to retrieve it, I bumped heads with my brother-in-law, who had bent to help me. "What's the matter?" he asked. "Can I get anything for you?" I told him no, I could manage for myself, and groped for the purse.

"What are you doing under the table?"

My mind took a fiendish turn. Smiling like a vampire, I said: "I'm only turning over the tape on my recorder."

Franklin was not amused.

After dinner, the three of us went to the apartment and Franklin and Elliott settled down for one of those marathon brother-to-brother talks they're so fond of having. I asked Elliott to bring David in to meet his uncle. He came in from the bedroom carrying a small, tousle-haired boy, heavy with sleep. I made the introduction, and David managed to get his eyes open long enough to mumble, "Hi, Uncle Franklin." Then his head lolled back and he was gone again.

Elliott, Franklin, and I spent five hours discussing everything that had happened since we had last been together. Again the question of the book came up, and I assured Franklin it would be written. The brothers smiled at each other. "Oh, well, you'll never really do it, so we shouldn't waste time worrying." We promised to meet Franklin the following day for lunch.

After weeks of hunting, we found a house that suited most of our needs. It was on North Bay Road in a well-to-do, but not exclusive part of the city, and had a back patio and swimming pool overlooking Biscayne Bay. There was also a boat dock. In the front it had a circular driveway, high hedges for screening and a columned portico. There were ten bedrooms and ten bathrooms, and an inside courtyard with eight doors leading into various rooms and parts of the house. The property had been woefully neglected, however, and its previous owner had painted everything in livid pastel hues, predominantly pink, which had faded with time and the elements. Walking through all those rooms of purple and yellow, blue, pink and green, I had an urge to start throwing things. It would be living in a bowl of tutti-fruiti ice cream. Elliott, however, saw tremendous possibilities with a little paint and repair. The next day we returned with Martin Jones and Mrs. Claude Pepper, vibrant and enthusiastic wife of the Florida congressman and one-time senator. Mrs. Pepper had a deep affection for the Roosevelt family and a great desire to help us get settled. Years of convent training had taught me to address anyone older than me as Mr. or Mrs. She disliked this formality, insisting repeatedly: "Call me Mildred." She said it so often that eventually I came to think of her as "Call me Mildred."

As we all stood in the 40-foot living room viewing the disaster of purple and lavender, I asked the real estate agent, Paul Wimbish, what he thought it would cost to recover the whole house with white paint. He mentioned some meaningless figures, took another look around at the ghastly spectacle, and his voice trailed off into monosyllables. That morning, to my chagrin, there had been a full-page advertisement in the Miami *Herald* announcing the opening of a new Faye Emerson paint store. "Oh well, darling," I remarked, "maybe we can buy our paint wholesale from Faye Emerson." Mildred Pepper shook her head disapprovingly, as if to say that this was not how Elliott Roosevelt's wife should talk.

Elliott had to make a business trip and left me in Miami to close the final details on the home transaction, then meet him two days later in Mexico City. Martin Jones invited me to dinner and said he would have another guest there to meet me. "It will be nice for you to get to know Phoebe Morse. She knows everybody who is anybody in this town."

It was chilly in Miami. Having no woolen dress or suit with me I wore a pair of silk dinner slacks, blouse and matching sweater, covering the entire ensemble with my huge mink coat. All I needed to be the typical New Yorker visiting Miami Beach was a pair of high-heeled gold slippers. David in tow, I arrived at Martin's lovely little house, to be introduced to one of the lionesses of Miami society.

The following day David and I left for Mexico City. Elliott met us at the airport. He was a welcome sight for I was not accustomed to traveling by myself in foreign countries with only a little boy for company. We flew directly to Acapulco, to be welcomed by Jimmy, Irene and their friends, a rich, gay crowd living it up at the peak of the season.

I was introduced to a world of unbelievable luxury, basking in sunshine and drenched with money. One of Jimmy's friends was Teddy Stauffer, once married to Hedy Lamarr. His private club featured a bar in the middle of the swimming pool, where guests could refresh themselves while splashing about. From a terraced restaurant, we watched the famous Acapulco divers poise on the lip of their cliff, then knife out and down into the abyss of rock and undulating tide, brown bodies glistening in the moonlight. The performance took on the trappings of a religious rite, with prayers at the statue of the virgin and solemn pronouncements over the loudspeakers that one small miscalculation in the flow of the tidal swell below, and the diver would be dashed to death among the sharp, wet rocks. The next day, for comedy relief, we watched a donkey guzzle beer then stagger off to lie down under a tree and sleep it off.

A friend of Jimmy's gave him the use of his sailing sloop, and we spent days swooshing over the dazzling blue waters off Mexico, bow-knifing into the water and throwing up a white wake. Salt spray stung our faces, and we would come back to shore in high spirits, deeply tanned.

David was mature to the point of being precocious. With such capacity for learning, he was soon picking up enough pigeon Spanish to order meals and ask for services to be performed. By the time we were ready to return to Minneapolis, David was a pint-size caballero.

We celebrated the Christmas and New Year's holidays facing the prospect of making the move. It brought about mixed feelings, a dread of leaving all our friends and familiar associations and an undercurrent of excitement concerning the future. There was a round of farewell parties. I remember most vividly the one given by Rosalie and Wayne McFarland, who had become friends of ours in the neighborhood around Gleason's Lake. They invited the Bagleys and the Tenneys, and the eight of us spent a grim evening reviewing all the unpleasant things that had happened while we were in Minneapolis. Elliott grew emotional, thinking about the past three years. It was difficult for him to relax and clear his mind of frustrations. During dinner we delivered pointed and brutally honest toasts about each other, so candid that Ralph Bagley took notes and filed them away for future reference, he said, when Elliott would need a poke in the ribs.

New Year's Eve was celebrated with the Bagleys, and I discovered the custom of toasting the New Year by jumping off a chair with a glass of champagne in one hand, making a wish before my feet hit the floor. Our impending trip to Florida reopened Ralph Bagley's long-standing jealousy of his wife's former life there. He had urged her for years to break those ties of the heart she had for her home state. This year for Christmas he had been even more pointed than usual, giving her a sun lamp and a steam cabinet with the note: "*Merry Christmas, this is your Florida vacation.*"

On January 3, Elliott and I took off from Minneapolis and flew to Miami with a cargo hold full of luggage and our two black poodles, Buttons and Bows.

Martin Jones asked us to spend the first night in his house on Hibiscus Island, a lovely place with a view of the water and distant, multicolored lights of the city. That evening we walked outside in the warm breeze, looking up at a full moon over Miami and silhouettes of leaning palm trees. "Elliott," I said, "we made the right choice. This is a heavenly place." "Yes," said Elliott. "My darling, this is where we will live and die. Our lives are now channeled in the right direction and I think we're going to make it." I had such a warm happy feeling at his words. My man had come into his own at last, my heart told me.

The next morning Elliott took the rental car and went off to his office in Miami's DuPont Plaza, a magnificent ultra-modern downtown building overlooking the Miami River and Biscayne Bay. We depended on Martin to get me to our new house.

As usual, Elliott's old friend obliged. I had brought old clothes for cleaning. I piled mops, brooms, cleaning powders, disinfectants and the two poodles into his elegant Jaguar and we drove off. Back in Minneapolis I had purchased two long chains for the poodles, and as soon as we arrived at the house they were tied. After ten minutes of howling and baying, however, they were released. Noisy dogs, after all, did little to make an impression on new neighbors.

The drapes were ghastly. I promptly took them down and hid them away in storage. Even as this was being done, Martin left me, saying he was going home to call the employment bureau for a painter. For the sake of sanity, we agreed it was best to cover the atrocious candy-stick colors on the walls as quickly as possible.

Changing into my work clothes, a bathing suit and skirt, I attacked various sinks and bowls with cleansing powder and went at the corners with a broom. After an hour of scrubbing, I cooled off by taking a swim in the pool. It was littered with debris and algae, but the water was wet and felt good. Then I went into the only clean bathroom, took a shower and gave myself a shampoo. We were going out to dinner that evening, so I put my hair up in curlers. I had just finished when the doorbell rang.

It took a while for me to even find the front door. Peering through one of the small windows in the door, I saw the face of a man, clean-cut but with eyes that were a trifle bleary and hair a trifle unkempt. From his work clothes and equipment I recognized him as the painter Martin had summoned. I opened the door, conscious of my head full of hair curlers, introduced myself and led him into the living room.

Depositing his ladder, drop cloths and brushes in the middle of the room, he looked at me unsmilingly and said: "Lady, how much am I getting paid?"

"I really don't know. My friend Mr. Jones made all the arrangements. You are just supposed to start work. He will be here soon with the paint. Why don't you begin by scraping the walls and getting them ready?"

He did not bat an eye. "No ma'am," he said, "definitely not. I'm not moving till I find out how much I'm getting paid."

Five minutes of argument convinced me that I could not win. Finally I went back to my toilet bowls and showers, muttering, "Pretty dumb kind of painter."

Martin soon arrived laden with gallons of white paint and toting our lunch in paper sacks. "How's it going?"

"It's not going at all," I said. "The man's sitting there in the living room on his ladder and won't budge until I tell him what his salary is."

"A dollar and twenty-five cents an hour," Martin declared, "and not one cent more."

"I don't think he'll work for that, but you try to change his mind."

Martin went into the living room and accosted our surly prospective employee. "Why haven't you been preparing the walls?" he said.

"I'm not moving until I know what you're going to pay me."

Martin's voice went out of control. "A dollar twenty-five an hour," he shouted. "And that's final."

The painter sneered, turned on his heel, hoisted all of his

paraphernalia and started for the door. Over his shoulder, he snapped, "I ain't worked for that kind of money since I was an apprentice."

I hissed at Martin, "For heaven's sake, if we have to pay more we will, but stop him. We can't let him get away."

Martin ambled after him. "My good man, we have decided we will pay you a dollar and seventy-five cents."

The painter turned and said, "My name is Art Garrett, and I'll take the job."

Art was to become a regular part of the household. After he had applied several coats of paint on the house, we discovered that he also had talent in plumbing, wiring, carpentry, and assorted other handiwork, including barbering the boys' hair.

As the painter spread his drop cloths and began mixing, Martin turned his attention to me. "You look tired. I brought two folding chairs. We can take them out beside the pool and have lunch. You need some rest."

I was still padding around in bathing suit and curlers, looking like a fugitive from Thursday afternoon at the supermarket. Martin accepted my apologies for my state of dishabille. Soon after we settled down for a leisurely lunch, I noticed a large triple-decker tourist sightseeing craft, bearing the exotic name *Dreamboat*, rounding the point of a nearby residential island and churning toward us. She was packed to the gunwales with tourists, awash with cameras, binoculars, and brochures. The ship, faintly resembling something left over from the Mississippi of Mark Twain's day, eased alongside our dock and a deckhand threw a line onto one of our pilings. The mate stepped jauntily ashore and sauntered around to where we were sitting.

"Say, mister, is this the house Elliott Roosevelt just bought?"

Martin snorted. "*Who* bought?"

The mate looked at me. "Lady, we heard down at the docks that Elliott Roosevelt was moving to Miami Beach and they described this as his house. Who are you?"

Flustered, I managed to stammer, "I'm the maid. Somebody hired me to come and clean the house, but I don't know whose place it is."

Martin had regained his composure. In a voice dripping icicles, he intoned, "Would you please remove yourself from the premises?"

"Surely," the mate said, then waved at the decks filled with sightseers, "but all these folks here want to come ashore and take pictures and get autographs."

Martin puffed up like an adder. "Get off the premises immediately or I'll call the police. This is private property."

Muttering about our inhospitable attitude, the mate retraced his steps, climbed aboard, and *Dreamboat* shoved off in the whirr of movie cameras and click of flashbulbs. I flopped limply back into my chair.

"Whew, that was a nightmare."

The children were coming in from Minneapolis in four days. We worked frantically to get the house ready. On that first day I borrowed a neighbor's phone to call for some rented beds. Abbey Rents, Inc., provided what we needed. Martin wanted us to spend another night with him, but Elliott and I were anxious to spend this very night in the new house by ourselves, to wander through all those rooms smelling of fresh paint. The house had a large upstairs area which we claimed for ourselves, consisting of two bedrooms adjoined by a large double bathroom with two commodes. On one side of the dual arrangement was a huge bathtub, fully six and one half feet long, three feet wide and four feet deep. The previous owner, Ira Randall, had reconstructed all the plumbing in the house along with the installation of this out-sized bathroom for himself. A heart patient, he required regular treatment in a Jacuzzi whirl bath. Eventually we were to transform the second bedroom into a combination library and office.

Randall had a passion for bathrooms, and had even converted several closets into small baths. As a result we had the ten bathrooms and ten small closets. My one objection to this was that we were cramped for closet space. Not everyone has to use a "John" at the same time, but everyone must have a place to hang their clothes.

We always spent the night upstairs on our rented beds and awakened the next morning feeling exuberant. Elliott went briskly into his half of the dual bathroom to shave, and in so doing peered out the back window toward posh Sunset Islands

1 and 2. His shaver whirred in midair and he announced, "I don't believe it."

"What's the matter, darling? What happened?"

He stood transfixed at the window. "Patty, do you see that boat down by the bridge between the islands?"

"Yes."

"I'm sure that is the house that belonged to Minnewa when we were married. Yes, it is. That's where we were married."

Afterward, I made it a point always to look out the east windows of the house, away from Biscayne Bay.

After the death of Mrs. Roosevelt, we had made arrangements to hire her servant couple, Les and Marge Entrup. Despite the fact that all of their people lived around the village of Hyde Park, the disagreeable treatment they received from the Roosevelt family made them anxious to move away. The prospect of coming to Miami with us delighted them. Before Christmas we had paid their plane fare to Minneapolis to help with the packing. During our trips to Miami to establish a new home and office, they took care of the children back there. Now they brought Ford and Gretchen on the long drive from Minnesota in a car packed with blankets and luggage. In addition to bedclothes, to provide some creature comforts in the event the furniture had not yet arrived when they did, they also brought silverware, a few pans, ash trays, towels and other necessities. Pat Gundy, who had worked for me years before in Seattle and Phoenix, also made the trip from Minneapolis. They pulled into town twenty-four hours ahead of schedule, but luckily I had stocked the kitchen with turkey, roast beef, ham and other foods from the Epicure, a Miami Beach market and catering service which provides some of the tastiest food obtainable anywhere.

That same day Franklin and Sue called with the announcement that they were in Miami Beach and wanted us to join them that evening for dinner. We invited them to the house for a cocktail first, and Elliott led us all on a guided tour of the empty rooms, many of them still in their garish original colors.

"Well, how do you like it?" we asked proudly.

"Very unusual. Er . . . do you plan to have furniture, or just camp?"

Five days later the furniture arrived from Minneapolis, along with a large number of unwanted odds and ends. In their zeal to bring everything, the movers had carefully loaded garbage cans full of garbage, outdoor clothesline poles in heavy globs of uprooted concrete, broken pieces of fence, and assorted skis, sleds, ice skates, snow tires, and chains we had intended to leave behind for friends in Minneapolis. I remarked to Elliott that never in history had they had snow in Miami Beach. "Patty," he observed wisely, "there's always a first time for everything. It pays to be prepared."

As the days passed, Art Garrett continued to slap white paint on the walls. The boys were enrolled in St. Patrick's School, just eight blocks from home. Gretchen was admitted to the Convent of Sacred Heart in Coconut Grove, a southern section of Miami. This new school had just been established by the world-famous teaching order of nuns, Mesdames of the Sacred Heart. Gretchen thus became the fourth generation of my family to attend the Sacred Heart convent, the others being my grandmother, my mother, and myself. The convent was a picturesque place, once the estate of Alton Jones, president of Cities Service Oil Company, whose widow sold the property to the nuns.

Organizing Elliott's office in Miami's downtown DuPont Plaza building occupied most of my time. Later we would move it to Miami Beach, but for now it seemed the proper thing to be centrally located in Miami itself, the main sister city across the bay. Sam Kipness, owner and proprietor of DuPont Plaza, gave us the kind of enlightened co-operation that gets things done. What began as a two-room suite of offices soon enlarged to five as Elliott's business immediately began to blossom.

Our real residence, of course, was Miami Beach and not long after we settled into our bayside home the time came when we were to be introduced to Beach society, which is unlike any other in the world. There is no city in America more predominantly, and proudly, Jewish than Miami Beach. More than ninety percent of the population is Semitic, and a very large proportion of these are foreign-born. One of the big perennial events here is the Israel Bond Drive. When we lived in Minneapolis, Elliott had been asked several times to speak before these huge bond dinners, and the fees had helped immeasurably to enrich our bank account. One of his first speaking invitations in Florida, then, came from the bond organization. This time the affair was a women's organizational luncheon meeting in the plush Fontainebleau Hotel.

Elliott and I spent an hour and a half in a receiving line shaking hands with the guests. Each person seemed to have a story relating to his mother and father, and their welcome for us was genuinely affectionate. In the excitement, I often forgot Mrs. Roosevelt's practical advice about receiving lines, "You take their hand, dear; don't let them take yours." By the time the handshaking was done, I was a wreck.

Dr. Aaron Kahan, Florida director of the organization, took us into a corner. "I'm sure, dear friends, you would like a little cocktail," he said. Earlier, I had turned down several offers of sherry, which I found heavily sweet and unpalatable. His offer sounded like music.

As we sat taking deep breaths, a little old Jewish lady approached us. In a dialect straight out of *Abie's Irish Rose*, she began speaking to Elliott:

"Mister Roosevelt, my husband Sam and I have for many years been buying Israel Bonds, and every year for five years we go to Israel to make a visit to the country. This year was the fifth year, and this year was the first that we saw what our Israel Bonds are doing. The sight was overwhelming this year.

"Sam and I went to Israel. We saw the Negev green, we saw the cotton blowing in the fields and we saw the water flowing through the desert. We were so excited we went back to our hotel that night and I sat down to write a letter to my daughter in Miami.

"'Daughter,' I wrote, 'Poppa and I are so excited because now we know where our money is going for the Israel Bonds. We saw the Negev green, we saw the cotton blowing in the fields and the water flowing in the desert. We even saw the cotton being taken to the mills. Really, daughter, I never saw so many cotton-picking Jews in my life.'"

Elliott and I stood paralyzed. Our little friend's eyes twinkled and she said, "It's okay, you laugh."

Elliott told this story many times at bond dinners.

The purchase of a new home and costly repairs took a heavy toll on our bank account. It gave us a helpless feeling, then, when we received formal notification that Johnny and Anna intended to auction off Mrs. Roosevelt's personal belongings. The two of them had discussed this shortly after her death and made arrangements with Victor Hammer, an old family friend and owner of Hammer Galleries in New York, to conduct the sale.

Despite our financial condition, I shared Elliott's tremendous desire to buy as many of his mother's possessions as we could beggar ourselves to pay for. We arrived in New York determined to go into debt if necessary to accomplish this.

To anyone who had known and loved Eleanor Roosevelt, the list of articles offered for public auction was heart-breaking. It included a mahogany breakfront, $850; a gentleman's umbrella, $15; pair of silver-mounted wood coasters, $100; six pewter mugs, $20 each; silver relish fork, $20; porcelain breakfast set, $750; oil painting of a woman counting money, $300; a wing chair, $150; mahogany bed, $500; pair of carved tusk figurines, $60; traveling chess and checker set, $25; silver presentation cup with fluted rim, $125; toy stuffed dog in the image of Fala, $25; blue leatherette and gold photo album, $15; United Nations Emblem pin, $20; silver-plated buttonhook, $3.50; black sealskin wallet, $75; a watercolor, "Robbers of the Plains," $300; and pince-nez eyeglasses, unpriced. Most of these were personal items, accumulated over many years and added to the comfortable clutter of her surroundings.

I will never forget the poignancy of seeing Mrs. Roosevelt's tortoise shell comb, the one I had seen her use many times, for sale for $15. It was one of the first articles I set aside.

Elliott and I purchased $7000 worth of the things said to have belonged to Eleanor Roosevelt and used extensively by her. The money was hard to come by, but we would cherish each item, confident that she would have been pleased that we would use pieces that she treasured.

20

"Mucho Gusto" Señor Roosevelt

One important client of Elliott Roosevelt International in the fall of 1963 was the government of Colombia in South America. In October, President Guillermo Valencia and his Minister of Public Works invited Elliott down for a round of conferences. Involved were sensitive negotiations with the U.S. to secure for Colombia Federal Aid Funds to develop housing and public works. It was arranged for me to go, along with George and Ethel Kennedy, George being a business associate in Elliott Roosevelt enterprises.

Casually, almost as an idle comment, the Colombian Public Works Minister, on a visit to Miami Beach mentioned to me that "El Presidente" was an ardent hunter. All his life His Excellency had desired to own two fox hound Hortons. I took the hint and telephoned the American Kennel Club of New York. Where could I buy a pair of these dogs? The AKC didn't know. They had never even heard of fox hound Hortons.

In years past, I had bred and trained Chesapeake Bay retrievers in Seattle. I knew something about dogs, particularly off-beat bloodlines, bred carefully to select quantities for strength or endurance, for cry, speed, definition, color or a combination of these, and they aren't always AKC registered. I continued the search. Several days later, by tracking from one dog expert to the other, I found the breed "El Presidente" prized, in the hill country of eastern Virginia. They weren't indeed fox hound Hortons, but plain "coon country" hounds bred by a Mr. Horton. The Colombian Minister also had let it be known that he, too, was a dog-fancier. His heart's desire was a really good English setter, preferably liver and white in color. Contacting Mr. Horton, I ordered all three dogs sent to Miami Beach, collect. The bill would come to $800.

If I had known what to expect, perhaps I would have substituted a less troublesome gift for the Colombian dignitaries; say, a brace of Everglades wild hogs.

The dogs arrived by train in miserable condition. For one thing, through a mixup in routing they had come to Miami from Virginia by way of New York City. Then there were the crates: to make certain the dogs would be securely penned, the Virginia breeder had built traveling cages of timber from piano crates, one for each animal. The crates alone weighed near one hundred pounds each. To top it off, they were mangy, tattered, dirty and half-starved. Our hired man, Art Garrett, drove a car to the station, took one look and called me.

"Mrs. R., we can't even get the dogs out of the crates. You're going to have to hire a truck to haul 'em to the vets."

"What do you mean, a truck? Can't you just load them in the car?"

"Ma'am, these crates are as big as your living room sofa."

Transporting the dogs, in crates, to the veterinarian on Miami Beach cost $50. That included a truck, workmen, and dismantling the side of each crate to let the animals out. The veterinarian had instructions to give them the required shots, plus de-fleaing, if needed. He called me.

"Mrs. Roosevelt, these are the mangiest animals I've ever seen. They're fierce, snarling, probably diseased. I've got them in isolation. We had to tranquilize them to get them out of the crates."

"I'll be right down."

"No, no, don't come near here. You'll catch some disease."

Remembering my sleek, well-fed Chesapeake Bay retrievers, I couldn't conceive of a breeder sending such dogs for $800 and figured perhaps the good doctor had been sampling his medicinal alcohol. We had planned a farewell luncheon and were expecting about a dozen guests for lunch. Taking David and Gretchen along, I hurried to the animal clinic.

Everything the veterinarian had said was true. The three beasts, subdued by tranquilizers, reminded me of children's Iggy dolls which had been left out in the rain. They were indeed mangy, rangy and cowed, their toenails long and broken, their coats splotchy. They stood quivering, tails tucked, and occasionally mustered up a bark. Pity welled in me. For some inane reason, I decided it would be a good idea to take them home with us.

A romp and some tender loving care might do the trick. Lacking collars or leashes, we attached a length of hemp rope with a slip knot around the neck of each dog and somehow, over the veterinarian's protests, got them all into the car. Ten minutes later, David, Gretchen, and I walked into the living room of our home leading the dogs, to greet our guests.

The setter took one look at all those strange feet and backed under the sideboard, piddling on the Oriental rug. The two fox hounds tucked their tails and began to bay. One of the ladies, deathly afraid of dogs, raced to the back door, threw it open and dashed out to the patio. By some simultaneous reflex, David, Gretchen, and I let go of our rope leashes all at once. Suddenly the living room erupted in scurrying women and leaping, baying hounds, each trying madly to get away from the other. All three dogs galloped out the back door on the heels of fleeing guests. One dog skidded into the swimming pool, another plunged into the bay, and the third took off over a picket fence into a neighbor's yard.

Elliott stood transfixed in the living room with his mouth hanging open, "For God's sake," he managed to stammer, "what have you done?"

"Well, I felt sorry for the . . . Elliott, the poor little dogs. I thought . . ."

"Poor little dogs! Those are the raunchiest hounds I've ever seen in my life."

Several hours later we had them all in captivity again, and the following morning the veterinarian took them to the airport for the flight to Bogotá. I still couldn't stand the thought of the animals being crated up with no attention, so once again,

Gretchen, David, and I went out carrying new collars and leashes to walk them around the lower ramp area. A dog from the country hills just isn't attuned to howling jets, clattering carts, tow-cars, and acres of concrete. They quivered, bayed, wet and refused to eat their Doggie Treats. David and I force fed them tranquilizer pills. By now, I was convinced they would arrive in Colombia raging canine psychotics. Back in the comparative quiet of the cargo room, however, and provided with deluxe traveling cages by Braniff International, the hounds quieted, dropped their heads and peered wearily out through the wire mesh, as if resigned to the fact, that their hectic lives couldn't get any worse.

Braniff's flight to Bogotá, by way of Guatemala and Panama, took off from Miami at midmorning. Jet trips always thrill me, and even as the Boeing 707 taxied toward the runway I couldn't pull my eyes away from the window. The huge silver aircraft received final tower clearance for takeoff, turned into the wind, rumbled down the tire-streaked concrete and hoisted its nose skyward. Trailing black exhaust, the 707 cut steeply for altitude, gathering up its heavy undercarriage and glinting against the clear Miami sky. Below, the subtropical city swept away, bone-white and pastel, a tableau of concrete, rising blocks of buildings, streets thrusting to the horizon, the broad blue expanse of Biscayne Bay and beyond that Miami Beach, a glittering strip of metropolis hugging the Atlantic, its beachfront crowded with baking tourist bodies.

As usual, I had brought enough clothes to open a store. The luggage was buried somewhere in the cargo hatch, along with three very unhappy hounds. The only article I had carried aboard was my cosmetic case containing the usual beauty supplies, and a small suède pouch of jewels. This was to be a costly mistake. Having few really good pieces of jewelry perhaps I was more conscious of what I did carry. There was an opal and pearl pin in the shape of a fleur-de-lis, given to me years ago by my grandmother; some pearls from Elliott; my former wedding ring, which secretly I had had made into a dinner ring, a wide gold band with a flanged side, set with diamonds and rubies; and a bell-shaped rose and yellow gold watch fob bearing the Roosevelt crest. The crest was carved onto a 30-carat white

sapphire and bore the motto, "Sic Plantum Hoc Vitum," mean-
ing "He Who Plants, Reaps." This crest, the only memento from
the family that we possessed, had been given by Elliott's ex-wife
Minnewa to his daughter Chandler. After Elliott and I were
married, Chandler let him have the crest to use in the Rooseveltiana Art Show in Minneapolis. Elliott decided we would keep it.

Panama was hot and sticky, in the full humidity of the rainy
season. We stayed long enough for George Kennedy to buy
several quarts of liquor, then took off again. The trip, I could
see, was a tonic to Ethel, his wife.

We landed at Bogotá at dark, in a driving rain.

President Valencia had ordered a VIP reception at planeside.
His personal representative, Oscar Iragorri, was on hand to greet
us along with an assortment of ministers, palace guards, and a
25-piece band. The band was drawn up in the rain in full
uniform and gold braid. It struck up the Colombian National
Anthem, the drummers making splashes with each beat. Naturally,
the formalities soon became thoroughly confused. Although the
band was playing at the plane's front exit, somebody decided to
take us out the back. Then Oscar rushed up in high excitement,
whispering, "Elliott, Elliott, you must hurry. The Presidente is
waiting at the palace. You must hurry."

In the rush, I left my cosmetic case, containing the jewels,
under the seat. Not until we got to the VIP lounge, the
equivalent of two city blocks away, did I miss it. I tugged at my
husband's sleeve as he exchanged greetings with assorted Colombian functionaries. "Elliott, my traveling case. I left it under the
seat." He hushed me and mumbled something about not making
a scene. "Well, I *am* going to make a scene, I want those jewels."

"Hush, Patty."

"Ah, Señora Roosevelt, *buenas noches.*"

"I want my jewels."

"Hush, Patty."

"Oscar, my jewels are on that plane."

"El Presidente, he is waiting, señor . . ."

"I want that cosmetic case."

At last, escorted by one of the aides, I returned to the airplane
and found to my dismay the opened cosmetic case in the aisle.
Gone was the jewel pouch, along with such other oddments as

my toothpaste, mascara, deodorant, and soap. Dejected and wet, we tramped back to be greeted by a smiling, optimistic Oscar.

"Do not worry, Mrs. Roosevelt, we get it back in the morning."

A motorcade suitable for a state visit rushed us to our hotel, where we were politely informed that there was not even time to change clothes. So at 11:30 P.M. with the rain still pouring down, our limousine turned toward the archway of the presidential palace into a cobblestone courtyard. An elevator lifted us two floors, and we walked out into a broad open terrace, to be confronted by two animal cages containing three wet, hungry, and scrambling hounds. I sympathized, for we humans, too, were travel worn and tired. My white gloves had a soggy feeling, my hair was a mess. The only thing fresh about me was my lipstick.

Our Colombian hosts were pacing around the dog cages in the rain, admiring our gifts to "El Presidente." Notably absent, however, was "El Presidente" himself who, we were informed, was still in his apartments. The cages were unsheltered from the downpour and the hounds were baying at the sight of the crowd. I went to the cages, knelt down in my vicuña coat with its soggy mink collar and stroked noses. They knew my voice by now. "Patty," said the others, "come in out of that rain. You'll be soaked."

Presently we were escorted into a magnificent room with crystal light fixtures, ornate mirrors and fine overstuffed furniture, for drinks. They were served in exquisite crystal and stemware. I was handed a Haig & Haig from a pinch bottle, with a dash of water and one ice cube; sort of a scotch on the rocks, without the rocks. I suppose protocol requires that you take your drink and like it, but I blurted out, "I want more water." Elliott frowned and whispered that he would ask Oscar.

Now, I noticed a distinct change in the treatment of me as a woman. Oscar, with whom I had been chattering freely earlier in the evening, became stiffly formal, speaking in Spanish and only through an interpreter. At 12:30, still no Presidente. Oscar entered the room bowed and announced: "El General, El Presidente, informs me that you are staying for dinner tonight."

"Dinner?" I said. "Oscar, what time is dinner?"

Elliott looked hurt. "Patty, please."

Oscar, somewhat dismayed, rattled off more Spanish to his interpreter.

"Well, Elliott, just tell Oscar we can't come to dinner. We're all tired and we want to go back to the hotel and go to bed."

"Oscar says El Presidente will be very angry," Elliott said. "You should accommodate him."

"Accommodate him? He should accommodate us. We're tired. I've lost my jewels. Those poor dogs are out in the rain . . ."

At 1:15 A.M., El Presidente made his entrance, a smiling rather attractive Latin. He wore dinner clothes, but was not as splendidly dressed as were his aides. Although his command of English was quite acceptable, he did not choose to use it. So in a supreme effort at direct communications, I unlimbered my pidgin Spanish. *"Magníficos perros!"* I announced, gesturing toward the distant sound of hounds, baying. The effort, rather than shocking our hosts, delighted them. We all went out to inspect the dogs. The Presidente was so excited he danced a little jig. Then we returned to the reception room for more drinks from the pinch-bottle Haig & Haig.

At 2:15 A.M. we sat down to dinner in the baronial dining room of the palace, attended by waiters in livery and maids in black uniforms with fluted caps and white aprons. The long table was afire with fine crystal, polished silver, and crested dinner plates so delicate they had a quality of transparency. For me, the aura of splendor lasted just until I discovered that the menu was to feature squid soup and Rocky Mountain oysters, El Presidente's favorite dish. My stomach did a flip. I called down the table to Oscar, "I can't eat these things." El Presidente lifted his eyebrows and summoned a liveried waiter for whispered conference. The man departed, and everyone settled back to await the main course. We waited, and waited and waited. Talk subsided, chairs shuffled. Occasionally someone cleared his throat. At 3:30 A.M., the main course was finally served: Rocky Mountain oysters for everybody else, chicken and rice for me.

A late arrival at the table was a beautiful young woman with lustrous dark eyes and skin like cream. She was pregnant. This was El Presidente's daughter. George Kennedy boomed a remark down the table intended as a fine compliment: "Gee, Your Highness, that daughter of yours sure is a beautiful babe!"

El Presidente smiled, nodded, and turned to address me in English for the first time. "Babe? Madame, what is a babe?"

"Well, sir, it's . . . it's . . . George, what's a babe?"

"Uh, well . . ." George fumbled, and tossed it to Oscar. "Oscar?" Oscar rose to the occasion brilliantly. Unleashing a fine stream of Spanish, he went into raptures defining for El Presidente the wondrous qualities of American women lucky enough to be called babes. When it was done, we all eyed Oscar with new respect, and El Presidente's daughter was averting her eyes, behind a pleased blush.

At 4:30 A.M. we had worked our way at last through coffee, liqueurs and dessert, and pushed groggily back from the table. It was 5:30 when we tumbled into bed.

All through the night I had attempted to tell El Presidente about my jewels, but Oscar obviously was so shaken by the prospect that I desisted. As it turned out, a cleaning man had rifled my cosmetic case, and could have been caught if the alarm had been spread promptly. The jewels were never recovered. When he finally found out about it, El Presidente was furious at Oscar.

That morning, everybody but Elliott slept off Haig & Haig and squid soup. My poor husband, however, was up and shaved by 7:30 A.M. and shambled off, pouchy-eyed and dyspeptic, for a round of meetings with President Valencia's top ministers, to discuss public works projects and how to secure U.S. loans to help finance them. At 10 A.M. the phone rang and a male Latin voice announced that he was my escort for the day's activities and would pick me up at noon. "Oh, no, you don't," I said. "I'm sleeping."

"Madam, you will have a lovely afternoon. We are going to Bogotá Country Club. I peek you up at twelve o'clock sharp."

Misery loving company, I roused George and Ethel. George had discovered that papaya seeds were good for his stomach trouble.

At noon my bachelor escort arrived, a handsome young Colombian whose easy smile and impeccable manners soon brightened my spirits. I took along my golf shoes in a plastic bag and a gold putter Elliott had given me when I first took up golf. Set in the top of the putter was a diamond (". . . to keep you encouraged," Elliott had said). My escort informed me that I had a special treat in store. American television crews were at the country club filming *Shell World of Golf*. The star this week was Julius Borros, the great Fort Lauderdale pro. Gene Sarazen was there, too, as master of ceremonies.

Ever since arriving in Bogotá we had been wheezing from high altitude. For Ethel, who suffered most, we had brought along a 90-pound bottle of oxygen. Trudging toward the club-house of the Bogotá Country Club, I took great gulps of air, wishing for a whiff at that bottle.

The setting of the golf course is breath-taking in itself, high, rolling fairways, a brilliant green, lined with pines and flecked with yellow sand traps. The thin air had a crisp bite, and the sky was a deep blue dotted with puffs of clouds which made slow-moving shadows on the fairways.

On the highest point stood the clubhouse, a magnificent struc-ture of exposed beams, glass walls and balconies, overlooking the first tee and its steeply dropping fairway.

The television crews were set up at the first tee, along with some Shell Blazers and a clutch of nervous executives. Gene Sarazen was there in his plus-fours. I said something to one of the officials in my terrible Spanish, and a TV crewman asked: "Where are you from?"

"I'm from Seattle."

"Seattle? Seattle, Washington, U.S.A.?"

"Sure."

He was overjoyed. "Great," he said. "Great. You're the first American outside this crew that I've seen in a week."

In a few moments I was introduced to Julius Borros, one of my matinee idols of golf. I burbled pleasantries with him about Fort Lauderdale and Miami Beach, mentioned that I'd brought my putter and golf shoes, and asked if I could walk around the course with him.

"Certainly," he said.

In the excitement, I had forgotten about the probable effect on my breath of a "walk" at 10,000 feet. With each step, es-pecially uphill, I felt like I had just run the mile for NYU. But

I played nine holes with him using his clubs with the mink covers on the woods. With masterly patience, Borros instructed me on playing the traps. Forgetting about his game, he would spend twenty minutes demonstrating how to blast out of sand, saying: "Patty, this can be the most important shot in golf. You get in here and you're dead." When I would start to speak between gulps of air, he cautioned me, "Don't talk. Save your breath."

That round with Julius Borros was the most rare and instructive that a fledgling golfer could dream of making. Since then, I have never again seriously dreaded dropping an approach shot into sand.

During the ten days in Bogotá, I practiced my Spanish with a dictionary in hand and more persistence than skill. To Elliott's surprise, I was able to order our breakfast each morning from the menu, madly thumbing through the dictionary while I propped the telephone on my shoulder. The room service operator was patient, and somehow we always got what I ordered. One morning, however, I began the ritual. "*Por favor, dos tostadas . . . cafe . . .*" and the operator interrupted me. "Say, lady, wouldja' mind speaking English. I can get it faster." This wasn't the same operator. "Where's the other girl?" "She's off today," came the reply. "I'm the relief."

"Oh."

It was deflating.

As the days passed, George, Ethel, and I spent time sightseeing and shopping for colorful Colombian blankets and conquistadore boots. George spent money freely, buying practically anything that caught his fancy. Elliott was busy every day with Colombian officials. He had hired a contractor from Marathon, Florida, Alonzo Cothron & Son, to work with the Colombians on road projects, subdivision developments, and sewer extension programs, along with an engineering firm from Jacksonville. The Colombians were enthused about taking on their own projects under the U. S. Agriculture and Industrial Development Program, an important form of self-help in Alliance for Progress which utilizes American know-how without the stigma of Yankee control.

Socially, we managed to demonstrate gringo ingenuity in other ways as well. One party we attended featured a contest in which you drank wine from the opposite rim of the glass. The man who spilled had to submit to having his necktie snipped off at the knot. Elliott and George were the only ones to go home with their neckties intact.

As usual in our lives, there was trouble brewing somewhere. This time it was about to pop up on two fronts, in Miami Beach and Seattle.

A few weeks before leaving for Bogotá we had hired a marvelous female cook named Sylvia. She quickly ingratiated herself to the family and showed a fine knack for whipping up quick hors d'oeuvres, excellent meals for unexpected guests, and serving efficiently and well. One day she talked Elliott into employing her husband, too, as a butler. He was a dashing fellow, even though he had no front teeth. We didn't know that he drank.

During our absence, we left the children at home in Miami Beach. Our handyman, Art Garrett, and his family, moved in to help take care of things.

From Bogotá, I called home one night and reached our son, Ford, who began to tell me about the wild things that had been going on. The butler had gotten drunk and beat up Art. He had also caught a fish in the bay and put it, live and still flopping, in the refrigerator. We fired the couple over the telephone.

After a week, we left Colombia and flew to Guatemala. At the hotel desk a message was waiting for me to call home again. This time it was Jimmy with news. In Vancouver, my father was to undergo surgery the following day. I called his wife and she told me it was cancer of the colon. Frantically, we began making arrangements for me to go to Vancouver, and I got a morning flight. It turned out to be a journey of agonizing frustrations because of the inefficiency of the Latin who booked my trip and I was bumped off the plane at each stop. Finally, fidgeting and grinding my teeth, I recognized a familiar head toward the front of the plane. It was C. R. Smith, Board Chairman of American Airlines and an old friend of Elliott's. I hugged the poor man and poured out my flight troubles. When I got bounced again in Mexico City he stayed over to straighten out the snarl, accompanied me to Los Angeles and, there, put a small company jet at my disposal for the flight to Vancouver. Then it ultimately happened that I would arrive in Vancouver after the 8 P.M. closing of Canadian customs. Even C. R. Smith's pleadings to the American Ambassador and the Prime Minister couldn't bend the regulations. So I flew as far as Seattle and made the rest of the trip the next day.

At the Vancouver hospital, Daddy had already undergone surgery.

October was closing in on the Northwest, with cool days and drizzles. I remained in Vancouver long enough to catch a terrible cold. I arrived at my mother's house in Seattle with a fever and runny nose. Mother and I had made peace by now, and used this visit to mend the rest of our fences. My cold got progressively worse, causing an ear infection, and the doctor advised against my taking a plane trip for a few days.

Elliott returned to Miami Beach from Guatemala and was calling me long-distance several times a day. Mother still had not accepted him fully as a member of the human race. When he called, she would answer with a cold "Hello?" then, holding the receiver as she would a dead rat, announce: "It's for you, Patty."

Despite my temperature and ear trouble, I delighted in seeing old friends again and was invited out to dinner for three nights straight. Each time I walked out the door, Elliott would call, his patience thinning, fuse sputtering. "Where is she?" he growled at Mother. "Well, you tell her to come right home."

Each time I talked to him, he accused me of going out on dates. I named the couples I was with, but not knowing who was married to whom, he only grew more jealous. "If you're well enough to do that you can damn well come home," he snarled.

The third night, I went out to dinner again and the phone started ringing immediately. When I got home, Mother was distraught. "Patty, that man has been calling every three or four minutes. Every time he calls he gets madder. I wash my hands of this whole thing. You handle it."

My ear was still swollen and inflamed. The doctor had given me shots and instructed me not to fly yet. I was miserable. Mother pitied me. "Oh, all right," she said, "if he calls again I'll tell him you're in no condition to fly, period." He called.

This time he was screaming into the phone. "Either you get on that plane tomorrow or you can just stay in Seattle."

Thoroughly frightened, I gathered up my things immediately: my putter, my golf shoes, huge garment bags, two suitcases, cosmetic case. I got a cab, reached the airport at 2 A.M. and sat for five hours so I wouldn't miss the seven o'clock Northwest Orient plane for Chicago.

During the flight, my right eardrum ruptured. Blood poured. They took me off the plane in Chicago. The passenger representative of Eastern Airlines drove me in his car to a doctor, who gave me penicillin and codeine. They called Elliott and told him what had happened, then put me on an Eastern plane for Miami. By special arrangement with the Federal Aviation Agency air traffic control centers, they made the entire flight below 10,000 feet, climbing and descending gradually to avoid rapid pressure changes. It slowed the trip by two hours.

We landed at Miami International Airport to be met by a shaken and contrite Elliott Roosevelt. In the car he had brought pillows, blankets, a hot water bottle, and a supply of pills. "Baby, I'm sorry," he said, fussing around with the pillows and insisting that I lie down in the back seat covered by a blanket despite the 80-degree heat. "I never dreamed, darling, I just didn't realize it was so bad. I'm sorry. I'm sorry."

It was three days before the pain subsided and the ear began to heal.

21

My Roosevelt Goes National

Politics in Florida can be as shifting and uncertain as the sand. For one aspiring to public office, surprise becomes a way of life— and for some, so do upset stomachs and sleepless nights. The electorate of the Sunshine State has tricky characteristics to confound the unwary. One is the phenomenal growth of Florida, another is its geographically split personality, still another is the questionable amount of weight carried by voluble special interest groups.

Since World War II, Americans have poured into Florida in a steadily rising tide. In recent years the influx has swollen to more than thirty thousand families annually. Today it is one of the fastest growing states in the nation. These newcomers form a heterogeneous mass having neither local political allegiance nor cohesive social and economic views. They represent, then, a constant unknown quantity.

Add to this the split personality of Florida's established electorate. Few states have such contrasts. In the sprawling urban areas of the southeast coast, from Miami to Palm Beach, the population tends to be big city liberal. Most people come from big cities of the North and East, from New York and Boston, Philadelphia, Chicago, and Detroit. Their political sentiments are of a kind. About a third of Florida's voters live along this rich, tourist-oriented southern Gold Coast. But move northward, up the lean back of the state, and both the political climate and voter prejudices undergo startling change. North Florida is red dirt, red neck and yellow pine country, and its people, still overwhelmingly Democrats form another extreme of political sentiment. Called Crackers, from the whip-cracking wagoners of old, they are shrewd, conservative, race minded, and southern. The country around Tallahassee, capital city of Florida, is in reality a southern extension of Georgia and Alabama.

As if these imponderables were not enough, the politician is frequently at a loss to know which voices of special interests it is most practical to heed. From all sides factions bend his ear and woo his promises, but many carry more volume than voting power. Hundreds of thousands of elderly people, for example, flock to Florida to bake their bones in sunshine and spend time in endless debate. Some of the loudest, however, are not even registered to vote. Similarly, candidates have found themselves basking in warm support from Cuban refugees, only to awaken on Election Day to the realization that you could fill a football stadium with refugees and not have a single vote.

Elliott's interest in politics runs in strong, deep currents. Since first serving as a page in 1924 at the Democratic National Convention held at Madison Square Garden in New York he has taken active part in all the party's national conventions, usually as a delegate. Fascinated by the subtleties of political power, he knows intimately how great decisions can hinge on the whispered word, the last-ditch compromise, or a sudden burst of leadership in the smoky caucus room. "I learned my politics," he is fond of saying, "at the feet of a master." And yet in forty years of active political life, he never ran for elective office.

His first attempt began as a surprise and progressed fitfully through stages of disappointment, grueling efforts, party infighting, and heady triumph. Before it was ended, Elliott was to learn sad truths about the worth of political promises. He would also find himself engaged in an intra-party tag match, battling not only its powerful state leadership but also a platoon of candidates thrown deliberately into the race in an attempt to sandbag his campaign. Ironically, all the sound and fury was over a job offering no salary, although the committeeman does wield influence in distribution of patronage from the national party.

Florida is one of only five states which elect their Democratic
National Committeeman and Committeewoman by popular vote
of the party. In other states, national representatives are chosen
by the State Executive Committees. They sit in the highest council of the party, and decide basic policies that Democrats will
follow.

The invitation for Elliott to make the race came quietly in
November 1963. George Kennedy, Elliott's business associate,
suggested that he have lunch with Robert Morgan, an accountant, then the chairman of the state racing commission and influential man-behind-the-scenes. A quiet, amiable pipe-smoker
with a penchant for gray suits and drab neckties, Morgan headed
one of the state's most successful accounting firms. Much of the
business involved handling accounts and audits for local governmental agencies. Morgan also worked tirelessly as finance chairman for numerous political campaigns.

The influence Morgan commanded in state politics was rather
like an iceberg, the bulk of it beneath the surface. He performed
diligently such party chores as heading up a Governor's Committee to bring the Democratic National Convention to Miami
Beach in 1964 (it went to Atlantic City), and serving as chairman
of state fund-raising dinners for John F. Kennedy in 1962 and
Lyndon Johnson two years later. His quiet words not only carried great weight of their own, they also represented the thinking
of those who guided the party from within.

Lunch was at the Miami Club, an exclusive downtown room
where top men talked matters of business, finance, and politics.
Morgan wasted little time on preliminaries. Barely had they
buttered their rolls when he said, "Elliott, now that you're living
here in Florida you ought to get active in state politics."

"Well thanks, Bob, but I've only been here a year and that's
hardly enough time to become established as a political figure."

Morgan smiled and pierced a bit of fish with his fork. "We
feel that you can perform a service to the party," he said. "You
see, we need a top-flight Democrat to run for National Committeeman. I don't think you'll even have to campaign for the job,
Elliott; declare early and it will scare everybody else out of the
race."

Elliott mentioned the demands upon his time of his management consultant business, and made it clear he did not relish the idea of a statewide battle royal. "Suppose the incumbent declares for re-election?"

The accountant brushed this aside. "There won't be any opposition worth mentioning."

"Well, I suppose I'll have to go around the state and get to know the leaders."

"Maybe you should make a swing around the most important counties. For the most part it can be a direct mail campaign."

"I can't afford to make the race on my own," Elliott said.

Morgan and Kennedy assured him money would be no problem; moreover, Morgan could handle the direct mail effort efficiently, especially among the CPAs he knew around the state.

Elliott came home with mixed feelings. He was happy over being asked to run. "It's a great honor, Patty." At the same time he had misgivings about our short length of time in Florida, and how this might affect his candidacy.

I had another reason for skepticism. Money. By now, life with a Roosevelt had taught me you don't always count even the bird in the hand.

"Elliott, I don't see how you can possibly run unless you know the money is there, on the barrelhead. We can't afford it. We simply can't afford it."

He assured me that Morgan's promises were solid. The party needed him. For too long, the committeeman's job had been dormant; nobody of any consequence in national party circles had ever held it before.

As is frequently Elliott's way, the matter dropped from further discussion. Christmas came and went, and for all the talking we did about running for committeeman, you would have thought the idea had been wiped from his mind. But then, in January, Elliott called a press conference and formally announced his candidacy.

It was time, he said, to strengthen the Florida Democratic Party, bring unity to its ranks and authority to its voice in national political councils. Moreover, he thought that he, Elliott Roosevelt, could persuade the National Party to hold its convention at Miami Beach.

After the splash of publicity, we sat back to watch how the

ripples widened. Deadline for filing as a candidate with the Secretary of State in Tallahassee was February 12. It was rapidly becoming apparent that Elliott would not be in the race alone, and the field might even become crowded. There were also indications that the money and support promised by Morgan and Kennedy might not be so readily available after all.

"Honey, they're going to come over in the next few days and take care of everything," Elliott assured me.

On the last day for filing, Elliott officially registered as a candidate for National Committeeman. The move, as we had feared, touched off a rush for Tallahassee. By closing, other candidates also had filed. They included some unexpectedly formidable names: James (Jimmy) James, a bus bench advertising man from Miami; Rex Sweat, former sheriff of Duval County (Jacksonville); Richard D. Barker of Jacksonville, a fifty-seven-year-old real estate broker who had been Committeeman two previous terms, and Grover Cleveland, John J. Kennedy, and Napoleon Bonaparte Broward. From the names alone, it was obivous that some of these candidates were thrown in deliberately to siphon off Roosevelt votes. Cleveland was a retired barber from Punta Gorda, who believed he was distantly related to the one-time President; Kennedy was a retired attorney from St. Petersburg, and Broward a son of the late Florida Governor N. B. Broward, who served in 1905–09. Election Day was May 26, and we were becoming painfully aware that ahead lay a tough and uncertain three months of campaigning.

Jimmy James, the thirty-one-year-old bus bench baron, had the support of the chairman of Florida's Democratic Executive Committee, Bradenton lawyer Warren Goodrich. James, we were assured, would mount an aggressive, well-heeled campaign, with a concentration of newspaper, radio and billboard advertising, bumper strips, and a blizzard of direct mail flyers and candidate cards. With Goodrich's backing, James also gathered in pledges of support from most of the State Executive Committee, consisting of a committeeman and -woman from each of the sixty-seven counties. Elliott launched his campaign without a single committee member's pledge.

With Morgan incommunicado and Goodrich deploying his forces for an open drive to elect James, Elliott's spirits sank. We appealed for help to two other prime movers of the party in south Florida. Would they work as co-chairmen of the Roosevelt finance committee? "Sure, Elliott," they said, "we'll be glad to help." They provided a list of about two hundred fifty likely contributors, suggesting that we invite them to a reception and cocktail party to kick off the campaign at our home. The co-chairmen assured us these people would be prepared to put up an average of $100 apiece. We should send out invitations, and they would also call each one personally.

For three days I slaved to get ready for the party. I made hors d'oeuvres and canapes, stuffed tomatoes with Roquefort, spread peanut butter and bacon, sliced cucumbers and made cheese puffs. Trays filled with snacks, I ordered extra ice, soda, and liquor, prepared a huge buffet of turkey and ham, hired a strolling accordion player and rented one hundred folding chairs from a funeral home. A Republican friend of Elliott's, James Dickey, offered his houseboat-yacht for the occasion, and brought it to our dock bedecked with two twenty-foot banners reading ELECT ELLIOTT ROOSEVELT YOUR DEMOCRATIC NATIONAL COMMITTEEMAN. By the day of the party, one hundred invitations had gone out, my fingers were sore from spreading peanut butter and bacon chips, we had carted in enough ice to build a ski slope, and Elliott had a case of nervous jitters.

To make contributing easy, I scattered books of blank counter checks around the house, each with its own pen. There was also a large silver bowl decorated with ribbons, for cash. And just to keep the party lively, I asked a glib local TV-radio personality, Larry King, to be master of ceremonies.

Less than one hundred people showed up.

The night was balmy and drenched in moonlight. Lights shimmered over Biscayne Bay. Jim Dickey's banner-hung boat nudged our dock. People wandered around the back patio and swimming pool, looking out over the bay. The accordion player played to ranks of empty chairs, stenciled RIVERSIDE FUNERAL HOME. In the dining room, platters of turkey and ham awaited absent diners. Candles sputtered, the ice melted, and crackers grew soggy. A fat, chatty woman dripping diamonds backed me into a corner, her eyes shining with anticipation.

"Now, you are the fifth wife of Elliott's," she said. "Who were the other wives? And whose children are these?"

It was too much. "I'm sorry, madam," I snapped. "I don't know your name and I hate to be rude, especially in my own home, but our private lives belong to us and not to the general public. I prefer not to continue this conversation. Now if you will excuse me . . ." Later I learned that she was a wealthy matron who had a mansion on Miami Beach's ultra-fashionable Star Island and was the widow of a prominent tycoon.

To get the contributions started, I had considered enlisting the help of some friend to act as a shill by loudly offering $1000 for the kitty. But I discarded that idea, attempting instead to get across some broad hints. "Now there are plenty of check-books, so don't be shy. If you run out, we'll just go for more." Nothing happened. The party broke up early. George Kennedy, as if to make amends, slipped me $100 cash, but it was done so furtively no one else noticed. The silver bowl stood empty, ribbons sagging. There wasn't a mark on a checkbook. And when the last of them had bowed out, smiling and shaking hands, we had enough turkey, ham, and hors d'oeuvres left to feed a horse platoon. The party had cost us $750 including hiring the accordion player. Kennedy's $100 left us $650 in the hole, and the campaign had not even started yet.

"Elliott," I said, flopping down onto the couch like a sack of bricks, "I think we're in for another dreadful spring."

After this, our co-chairmen were no longer available when Elliott called, although each did give us a $50 token donation.

In our disappointment, we failed to reckon on the magic of the Roosevelt name. It wasn't long before Elliott began to receive letters and a few checks from stanch old supporters of FDR around the state. Men like State Senator Verle Pope of St. Augustine expressed interest in his campaign and soon became active backers. J. B. Hodges of Live Oak, Florida, a power in Florida politics, came forward; his father had been a Democratic National Committeeman during the Roosevelt administration and once said the job cost him $100,000 a year in expenses. C. V. Griffin, a citrus mogul from Harvey In The Hills, near Orlando, threw in his support, as did Francis P. Whitehair of Deland, who had been an Assistant Secretary of the Navy under FDR and his campaign treasurer. A cadre of campaign workers took form, quietly but with steadily increasing weight. From Pensacola came a ready-made organization for northwest Florida. Jim Larkin, executive of a contracting firm and a sophisticated political organizer, had built a group to work for gubernatorial hopeful Fred O. (Bud) Dickenson; when Dickenson lost in the primary, Larkin needed a means of keeping his organization together and put in with Elliott. From Fort Myers, on the west coast, we enlisted Barry Williams, a land speculator who had once been an ardent supporter of Senator Estes Kefauver. At Fort Pierce, Elliott's candidacy drew the backing of a tomato packer named Sheffield Abood, who became invaluable as state co-ordinator and organizer of the Atlantic seaboard counties.

These were strong men for the most part, but with widely divergent backgrounds, personalities, and motives for supporting Elliott. They did not all come directly to us, but were oftentimes enlisted by me or Elliott after we gave them a selling job. As names of likely backers were mentioned, we would write or call. Invariably, those who had been enthusiastic for FDR also looked kindly upon his son's efforts to win the election, especially against such odds.

Sheffield Abood was an open-collar man, hefty, rough, and swarthy with the bold features of a Syrian. By hard work and shrewd dealing he had made a success of wholesale produce, and now he liked the limelight of politics and tossed big Washington names around like he was spitting seeds. "Orville Freeman looks to me for a lot of advice on agriculture, and I was saying to him, 'Orville, what you need is . . .'" Abood's reason for backing Elliott was his strong personal dislike for Jimmy James, and his resentment at being ignored by Warren Goodrich and others of the State Democratic Executive Committee.

Barry Williams also had a hatred of the state Democratic bigwigs, and saw in Elliott a chance to beat them. His interest in the Roosevelts was historical, and in Kefauver had amounted to hero worship. Barry liked to tell of how he and his twin brother Billy voted four times for Roosevelt in their hometown back in Tennessee until the sheriff finally sidled up beside him and said, "Barry, didn't I see you in this line before today?"

Barry said no, it must have been Billy. "Well," said the sheriff, "then what's he doing behind you?" Unwittingly, the twins had blundered into the same line at the same time.

Disenchantment with the Democratic powers-that-be also infected C. V. Griffin. In his heart, the crusty citrus man hoped a Roosevelt-type political vehicle would begin rolling again. We met him through Francis Whitehair, and his first check for the war chest was for $300. Later, when we became good friends, he would drawl, "Ellyet, y'all wanna be Mayor, I'll make you Mayor." His secretary, Elsie Smith, lived in his shadow, ready to take notes at the drop of a word. (Later, Elsie underwent a serious operation and C.V. called upon Elliott to help boost her morale. "Ellyet, that good girl Elsie is goin' to surgery, and I sure would appreciate it if y'all would send her some flowers.")

Florida is 1500 miles long, from Key West to Tallahassee. A statewide campaign requires a hefty treasury just to meet travel expenses. The best way to cover it, of course, is by airplane. We made most of it by car, putting 17,000 miles on my Lincoln Continental from April 3 to Election Day, May 26.

On the first day, we struck out from Miami for Fort Pierce, 230 miles due north up the Sunshine State Turnpike, laden with campaign literature and politicking zeal. Atop the car we sported a big stand-up sign plugging Elliott's candidacy. In weeks to come, the thing would blow off with maddening regularity each time we hit a turnpike.

Our baptism of campaigning was at a Fort Pierce shopping center. Swallowing nervousness, we struck out from the car with a load of leaflets. Instinctively, I began shaking hands. "How do you do, I'm Patty Roosevelt and I'd like you to meet my husband, Elliott, who is running for Democratic National Committeeman. We would appreciate your vote." Elliott, smiling and nodding, padded along behind me. As I introduced shoppers, he exchanged pleasantries with them and spent hours giving autographs. After a time I grew tired of grabbing hands. "Elliott, why don't you take over now, and I'll follow you?" He blanched. "Oh now, I couldn't do that, Patty," he said. "I'd be too embarrassed." This was the man who had taken the Colorado Democratic Convention at Durango like a one-man cavalry troop. My mouth dropped open.

The launching of our campaign coincided with outbreaks of racial strife in St. Augustine. Elliott knew that the press, as well as his political enemies, would try to wring from him a comment on civil rights. He vowed to stick to the moderate approach where his personal convictions lay. At such a time the less said the better. The night before our scheduled arrival in St. Augustine, Mrs. Malcolm E. Peabody, mother of Massachusetts Governor Endicott Peabody, was jailed following a demonstration. Mrs. Peabody is my cousin.

At 7 A.M. we arrived at the Monson Motor Lodge for Elliott's appearance before five hundred persons at a breakfast rally, to be greeted by a nervous Senator Verle Pope. "For God's sake, Patty," Pope pleaded, "don't tell them your maiden name or who your relatives are." I took his advice. Tension coursed through the city like electricity. Upon entering the hotel we saw a policeman stationed at the front door with a trained attack dog. The manager steered us into his office for a quick explanation. "We've been having a lot of trouble at this hotel, with Negroes trying to register for rooms and asking to be seated for a meal. I hope your visit will be without incident." There were none.

Elliott's speech was well received. As usual, he made it without notes, stressing the need for Florida to have a voice in the national party and enjoy a larger share of projects from the Democratic administration. In recent weeks there had been speculation that the U.S. space complex at Cape Kennedy might be phased out and its operations moved to Houston, Texas. "I will work to see that this vital installation remains on full operational status in Florida," Elliott told them. The address, and Pope's backing, won him solid support in the nation's oldest city.

As weeks passed, the pace of campaigning quickened until Elliott was making three or four speeches and at least two handshaking tours a day. I worked at planning what his next activity would be, calling ahead to alert the press and arranging TV and radio interviews. Wherever he appeared, there was a corps of local newsmen waiting for interviews and pictures.

Again the name "Roosevelt" plagued headline writers trying to wedge it into thirty-six point Bodoni type. Stories and pictures were plastered across front pages, while opposition candidates tried desperately to get just a few lines.

To accomplish this, attacks on Elliott grew bitter. Candidate Leon Whitehurst blasted him as "the California interloper" and said the only thing he had in his favor was his last name. Jimmy James brayed "carpetbagger." Others implied that Elliott was trying to seize control of the party as a kind of front man for Senator George A. Smathers. Actually, Smathers kept himself icily aloof from Elliott's campaign, sensing in it a threat to his own political position. Indirectly through the Junior Senator, we did have occasion to learn something of the pitfalls of political correspondence. At Christmas I had sent out holiday greeting cards in Spanish. *Merry Christmas* the cards read. Three months later a card of acknowledgment duly arrived from Smather's office. It was addressed to Mr. "Feliz Navidad."

As the campaign grew, so did the wear and tear on nerves, muscles, and spirit. Speechmaking was a horror to me. I'm one of those people who has to take a Miltown just to second a motion from the floor. One morning in north Florida, getting dressed before speaking to a ladies' *kaffeeklatsch*, I was so nervous I sprayed my hair with deodorant. Sometimes just smiling was an ordeal; I wore a grin for so long my face felt congealed. There were episodes to try the best of humors. In Pensacola, a woman gushed at Elliott, "Oh, Mr. Roosevelt, I'm so glad to see you. I knew your brother." Elliott said that was wonderful. Which brother? "You know, the one who married Faye Emerson."

Life lost its focus on the road. Days, events, faces and handshakes all ran together in an animated montage. Weeks passed in an endless succession of interviews, teas, luncheons and plates of chicken and peas.

At Fort Pierce, a Cadillac and Pontiac dealer named Reed Houghton took a liking to us and detailed one of his salesmen, Jake Walker, to drive us around the state. Jake was a big, friendly Irishman with deep-set eyes and a ruddy tan. At the end of a day of driving, shaking hands and changing clothes I would flop down so tired you could have wrung me out and poured me into a bottle. Jake bought some oil to rub my feet.

I told Elliott, "This is wonderful, honey. Why don't you let

Jake rub your feet?" Elliott scowled. "Don't be ridiculous," he said. "I couldn't imagine such a thing."

Elliott's campaign style was easygoing, friendly, patient. Everywhere people crowded in to see the son of FDR, usually offering some anecdote of their own about the late President. Elliott listened attentively, dropping little comments, "Oh, wonderful. I never knew that." His easy way crossed the barriers of language. Once, at four in the morning, he went out to shake hands with Spanish-speaking cigar rollers in Tampa. Unable to understand anything they said, he just stood there smiling and muttering the only greeting he knew, "*Mucho gusto.*"

In Tallahassee, Jimmy James was declaring: "It will be a sad day for our party if our voters see only the Roosevelt name on Election Day and overlook the fact that Elliott, unlike his illustrious parents, promises much although he has been unable to do anything of consequence for himself in fifty-four years of life."

A few days later, in a hot little restaurant at the town of Monticello, county seat of Jefferson County, we sat down with Eno Stark, an elderly veteran Democrat who was committed to vote for his old friend from Jacksonville, Rex Sweat. His daughter had been a Democratic Committeewoman and was now county campaign manager for Jimmy James. "I always was a great admirer of your father's," the old man said. "I don't know you." We talked, drank coffee, talked. His daughter joined us. More talk. More coffee. When we walked out together, they had both switched to the Roosevelt side.

The strategy of Warren Goodrich's forces had been to lard the committeeman race with local favorite son candidates to skim off hometown votes. Old line politicians quietly tried to persuade Elliott to heed their advice, in exchange for support, but he set his jaw and shook his head. "I'm running this race my own way." Private polls taken around the state gave Goodrich's people confidence to discount Elliott as a serious threat, and as the fight wore into May, we worked harder and harder for votes. In St. Petersburg, for the opening of a new seaquarium, Elliott was asked to pose for pictures feeding the porpoises. Lugging a briefcase bearing a gaudy red, white and blue VOTE FOR ROOSEVELT sticker, I climbed with him onto a platform over the water, from which he could feed the leaping fish. The water boiled with porpoises; their great shiny bodies leaped high for Elliott's fish. As they plunged back into the tank we were showered with spray. Then we fed the whales, dropping fish into their tank while standing in a big bucket suspended from a crane. Off to one side a herd of sea lions balanced on large rubber balls, barking and flapping. While cameras snapped, Elliott bent down to be kissed by a sea lion, beaming the great Roosevelt grin.

"Honey, you get a kiss now," he shouted.

I took one look at the slick, homely face of a sea lion and replied, "Are you crazy?"

The punishing grind of campaigning made both of us wonder if it was really worth it. Had it not been for the advice of another old campaigner early in the game, I might have been tempted to ask Elliott to throw in the sponge. The shrewd assessment of politics generally, and this race in particular, had come from none other than Harry Truman. Early in March the former President and his wife, Bess, had visited Key West on vacation. While there, he called Elliott. When they came through Miami on their way back to Independence, we met them at the airport.

I was distraught. "Mr. President, please tell Elliott not to run for this stupid office. If he does win, what does he get?"

Truman grinned. To his eye came the glint of the old Kansas City ward boss who had learned politics from the ground up. "Patty, every state in the union has to search out its best candidate material in order to become a stronger part of the Democratic Party. The only way state organizations can become real, live members of the national party, is to have the leadership of men like Elliott. Now, in politics and out, a good wife has to help her husband. I know you're a good wife."

"But, frankly, I don't think I can stand the gaff," I protested. "People say such nasty things about Elliott. They villify him."

"Listen, sis, you know what I've always said, if you can't stand the heat then stay out of the kitchen."

I looked at him wide-eyed. "Oh, but Mr. Truman, I like to cook."

Our campaign fund, if you could call it that, did not allow much cash-and-carry buying. Lacking the services of a professional publicity man, I wracked my brain for publicity gimmicks.

President Kennedy had initiated the Eleanor Roosevelt commemorative stamp. We arranged for the stamps to be issued from the Miami Beach Post Office (it is now the only post office in the United States still selling them) and designed a small sticker to go just beneath the stamp, which read: *In a Great Tradition, Elect Elliott Roosevelt Democratic National Committeeman.* We used them on all business and election correspondence. In fact, the use of the stamp and sticker caused so much comment that one of the more prominent columnists remarked in his column one day, "I'd like to see Jimmy James put his mother's face on a stamp and try and mail a letter."

Singer Eddie Fisher, meanwhile, was booked into Miami Beach's Deauville Hotel. I had called every entertainer I knew, asking if they would give us a plug. Backstage at the Deauville, I asked Eddie if he would wear one of our campaign buttons. "Sure," he said. I handed him a large homemade job. Actually, it was an old Avis Rent-a-Car button, and I had painted over the slogan, *We Try Harder.* Now it sported Elliott's name. Eddie Fisher wore it in every performance for ten days.

One night in the popular "Boom-Boom" Room of the Fontainebleau Hotel, a night club photographer, Bernice Scheib, came to our table. "Take your picture? Take your picture?" I replied that I would give *her* a picture instead, and handed over one of Elliott and his father.

"Oh, Mrs. Roosevelt," she gasped, "I'm so glad to meet you. My girl friend is the cigarette girl. Could we help you in your campaign?"

From then on, during the final weeks of the campaign, the two girls spent their days riding Jim Dickey's boat up and down Florida's Inland Waterway, live models drawing attention to the huge ELECT ELLIOTT ROOSEVELT banners. While doing this they continued to work all night in the "Boom-Boom" Room.

An artist friend of ours, Mr. Van Der Gaast of Star Island, contrived a light-up sign by cutting letters into an aluminum pie pan. Battery operated, it was activated by a pocket button. When we had guests at home, little David would stroll in poker-faced, wearing the sign on his back, turn around and blink:

ELECT ELLIOTT ROOSEVELT DEMOCRATIC NA-
TIONAL COMMITTEEMAN.

As Election Day neared the pace grew even hotter and so did
the wordplay between candidates. In the voters' eyes the national committee fight was a sideline activity, the main bout
being a bitter runoff battle for the Democratic gubernatorial
nomination between Haydon Burns, Mayor of Jacksonville, and
Robert King High, Mayor of Miami. Their race was to end with
Burns victorious, but he would occupy the Governor's chair for
only two years before losing to High in a bruising primary rematch.
Then, in a smashing upset, High was defeated in the general
election by Republican Claude Kirk.

The rift between Elliott and the state party chairman, Goodrich, grew steadily wider. It broke dramatically upon the public
just four days before Florida's Democrats were to go to the polls
May 26. Elliott took the first public swipe, saying in a speech
that he did not intend to "take orders from a state chairman who
might take a walk or turn his back on the national party ticket."
On May 22, Goodrich fired back from his hometown of Bradenton. Elliott, he declared, was a "divisive, irresponsible campaigner." Goodrich called himself an "enemy of opportunism,"
said Elliott had taken out his driver's license in Florida only
twenty-three days before, and added: "I think all Democrats will
be the enemy of an irresponsible campaigner who has done nothing in his lifetime to add to the luster of his father's name." From
the field of candidates came a new hue and cry. "Roosevelt is trying to cash in on his family name!" declared Joe Carrin, a Tallahassee real estate man. J. B. Rodgers, Jr., the former state senator
from Orlando, questioned Elliott's knowledge of Florida problems
because of his short length of residency in the state. Rodgers admitted, however, that he himself had been asked to get into the
race because Elliott was running.

But in Tampa, candidate David Gill withdrew from the race.
Tears streaming down his face, he told an audience in the heavily
Spanish section of Ybor City that he was doing it in favor of
Elliott Roosevelt.

There was no way of gauging how effective our campaign had
become. Clearly, the professional politicians disliked Elliott and
were prepared to write him off. Nobody liked him, it seemed,

but the public; the public had a strong store of affection still for the memory of FDR, but its weight at the polls would be a questionable quantity.

In Key West, local campaign chieftains for gubernatorial aspirant Burns staged a big free fish fry on the day we arrived for a speech and handshaking. In the Roosevelt state of tight-belt campaign financing, everybody paid for his own lunch. We were mobbed, while at the Burns' affair tubs of leftover fish grew aromatic and the politicos tried fitfully to make conversation among themselves.

On the other edge of the state, north of Clearwater, a Roosevelt enthusiast presented Elliott with a thirty-year-old souvenir of tragedy and terror: a gray fur lap rug, stained with blood. The blood had spilled from the body of Chicago Mayor Anton Cermak, mortally wounded in Miami's Bayfront Park the night of February 15, 1933. The bullets had been intended for Elliott's father. They were fired from the crowd by a crazed anarchist, Giuseppe Zangara, as FDR sat in an open-topped car. None struck the President, but four other persons, including Cermak, were wounded. The lap rug was placed over Cermak in the presidential car and FDR held the Chicagoan as they sped to Miami's Jackson Memorial Hospital. Behind, in a scene of wild disorder, police hauled Zangara off to jail screaming, "I hate all Presidents . . . I hate all officials and everybody who is rich." Cermak died a few days later. The wild-eyed little Sicilian who had attempted to assassinate the nation's newly elected President with a cheap pawnshop pistol was doomed to the electric chair. All these years the lap rug had been kept by this man, who had been a Pierce-Arrow automobile dealer in Miami and provided cars for the FDR motorcade. Elliott accept the gift with deep emotion.

We spent Election Day in Miami, most of it at Elliott's office. As the returns came pouring in that evening, I let out a wild whoop and we hugged each other and danced around the room.

Elliott Roosevelt was elected by a runaway, piling up 100,000 votes over his nearest rival, Richard D. Barker of Jacksonville. The Goodrich forces favorite, Jimmy James, finished a lame third.

We tallied up accounts. The campaign, which we had been assured would be fully financed, had cost us $40,000. James, in defeat, reportedly spent more than twice as much. We spent three years paying off all our debts. However in the intervening years Jimmy James has become Elliott's biggest booster. He is now one of our favorite friends.

22

The Return of the Prodigal

The frantic pressures of campaigning had wound me up like a clock. Now came the letdown. In the aftermath of triumph, my mainspring snapped and I let go, whipped. It was time for some relaxation.

A month before, in the heat of our electioneering, my mother had suffered a stroke in Seattle. The word came in a long distance call to us in Gainesville. My sister Lee said not to worry. Her condition was critical at that time, but everything would be all right.

I had an agonizing choice: leave Elliott at a crucial time in his political career, when he needed me the most, or not go to see my mother. I chose to remain with my husband. At this painful moment I knew that my marriage had reached a point of strength and maturity where my own allegiances to Elliott came before those I owed to anyone else.

This was doubly important to me in the light of a new spirit of warmth between Mother and me, and a mending of fences with my sister Lee.

This had been the outgrowth of a surprise visit they made to us in Miami Beach in March, not long before Mother's illness.

Her decision to make the trip to Florida had caught us by surprise. Dropping everything, including the campaign, we had gone on a housekeeping binge. As the date of her visit neared, Elliott grew more and more nervous. Two days before, he was so tense, he fell asleep repeatedly, and constantly chewing his lip, he asked, "Honey, what am I going to call your mother? I can't address her as Mother."

"The children call her Bama."

"No, I won't use that either. She doesn't know me and can't stand me. I'll just call her Mrs. Peabody." Only he gave it the Boston pronunciation, "Mrs. Peabuddy." This, I knew, would upset her. Mother believed that when in Rome—burn. Elliott was more New Englander than Roman.

Mother and Lee arrived at Miami International Airport, tired from the long flight and faintly perspiring in their heavy clothing. Despite my feverish excitement, I could see they were not in the mood to throw their arms around us.

Elliott smiled his most winning smile. "How do you do, Mrs. Peabuddy?"

Her response was wintry. "How d'you do, Mister Roosevelt."

While they settled into their rooms at the house, I paced the living-room floor with vigor. "Elliott, I'm just absolutely so excited and nervous I can't think. Isn't it wonderful? Isn't it just wonderful?"

He looked sleepy again.

"Oh, darling . . . Please, love, don't go to sleep!"

After dinner, we settled into the living room for conversation and Elliott asked, doubtfully, if they would like a demitasse of coffee.

"I never drink coffee before bedtime, Mister Roosevelt," Mother said.

"Well, could I fix you something else? A little something to . . ."

"I'll have bourbon and water," she said.

"You will?"

Spirits lifted, Elliott mixed drinks, and then some more, and soon he was regaling them with stories about his bareback bronc riding and the summers he worked on a Wyoming dude ranch. Suddenly we were all trying to talk at once. The long freeze melted, as if in warm sunshine. Mother, the woman who had so thoroughly despised Elliott Roosevelt that she would not even acknowledge his existence in the human race, laughed now from deep inside. This time it came from her heart.

The following morning after Elliott had left for the office she came into my room and shook her finger under my nose. "Patty," you know it is none of my business, but do you realize, *do you realize*, how lucky you are to have a husband like Elliott Roosevelt who is such a perfect father to those children?"

"Yes, Mother," I said, straight-faced.

"Well, I should hope so. You ought to get down on your knees and thank God, every day of your life."

"Yes, Mother."

That visit had made a big breach in the barriers between us. Now it was time to send all the barriers crashing down. In July, with the campaign two months behind us, we packed up the children, a Spanish maid, and about six tons of luggage and flew to Seattle to spend a month. We rented a lovely house with a huge lawn, immaculately cut, and spent our days sleeping late, playing golf and visiting friends. Elliott had always been bored by vacations and, unfortunately, he thought he had to make two business trips to Miami and Bermuda during the month. However, he did manage to spend a great deal of time with us. My mother's sister and brother-in-law, Agnes and Walter Tracey, now lived in Seattle and she proved to be a great help in my golf game. Agnes, a former northwest amateur champion now in her seventies, would take me to the front lawn each day for golf lessons. Elliott pretended he was not interested, but later would sneak out and practice the techniques he had seen her teaching me.

The most important new experience for us in Seattle was not better golf, but a six-foot, three-inch figure of muscle, confusion, and sloppy grooming named Harpur Evoy, my favorite nephew.

Harpur was eighteen, the eldest son of my sister Lee and her doctor-husband, Matty. They lived in Kirkland, Washington, outside Seattle. Already Harpur had attended seven different high schools. He drove a dilapidated old Ford, a thing of muddy windshield and gutted muffler, and slouched around unshaven in a dirty sweatshirt and jeans. But behind the bravado lurked a basically friendly soul desperately in need of attention.

The main difficulty lay between Harpur and his father, a fine surgeon with such a demanding practice that he had little time to devote to his son's upbringing. Harpur had always endeared himself to me, perhaps because he sensed that I was a fellow outlander. The day we arrived in Seattle he came blasting up the driveway and skidded to a halt, throwing gravel. A day-old stubble made a dark smear across the bottom of his face and he hadn't been near a bathtub in days. "Hi, Aunt Patty," he whooped. I wanted to grab this roughneck and kiss him, but I didn't. He needed more love than that.

"Harpur Evoy, how dare you think you can come into my house looking like a bum. You can't meet Uncle Elliott in this condition. Now you go home and change, this minute."

The smile left his lips. A sullen glaze came to his eyes.

"I can't go home," he said.

"Why not?"

"Dad won't let me in the house."

This had been another of their periodic rows, ending with Matty ordering his son out bag and baggage.

"Do you have any clean clothes?"

"Yeah, in the car."

"Get them and go up to Jimmy's room. You can shave and take a bath there. You're disgraceful."

"Can I kiss you, Aunt Patty?"

"Not until you get cleaned up."

"Aw gee, I haven't seen you for a long time."

"I'm ashamed of you, Harpur. I don't want Uncle Elliott to see you like this."

"Heck, who wants to meet Uncle Elliott anyhow?"

Elliott had heard about Harpur. Every time I had told him of the boy's troubles, I could see a softening in his face. To my husband, Harpur was a familiar tortured youngster—a rough renegade not unlike he, himself, had been years before as the maverick second son of a President. FDR also had had little time to talk about affairs of children and family.

Harpur shaved and changed clothes, slicked back his hair and came downstairs to meet his uncle. I could sense from his swagger that a test of wills was in the making.

"Hi, Mr. Roosevelt."

"How do you do, Harpur?"

As the handshake met, I could see Harpur trying to get the first grip but Elliott's hand was an eyelash faster. They squeezed, Elliott first and then Harpur. The pleasant smile never left Elliott's face. It did leave Harpur's. When their hands parted again, the sullen glaze had left his eyes and was replaced by a spark of respect.

"I'm glad you cleaned up before you came into the living room," Elliott said.

The mask dropped again. "Well, I just came in to say hello to Aunt Patty." With that, my nephew turned on his heel, stomped out of the house, and his car blew out of the driveway.

"That boy," said Elliott, "needs help."

As the weeks went by, we saw Harpur from time to time, and Elliott could not erase from his mind the look of defiance in that young face. The night before we were to leave Seattle, Elliott made up his mind. "Patty, we need to bring that boy home with us."

We had talked with Lee and Matty about Harpur and his problems. Elliott had not pulled any punches with my brother-in-law. "This is a good boy, Matty. He needs your time. You can handle him. These big, overgrown boys need a special kind of treatment. You have to be tougher than they are."

Even golf was becoming a problem between father and son. Matty had played golf for years and was accomplished at the game. But now, Harpur, a natural athlete, threatened to surpass his father.

On our last evening in Seattle, we had planned to go out to dinner with the family. I was excited about going home to Miami Beach, but regretted, too, leaving our picturesque little vacation house. It was made of English brick, and the yard sloped down to a lake. As we dressed, I was thinking about this and the cross-country flight home when a loud commotion erupted in the yard. Jimmy and Ford were in a fight.

Our two eldest sons had been picking at each other for weeks. I was sick of hearing the shouting matches, the screaming insults. "I can beat you up." "Okay, step outside and take off your glasses." Now I heard it again, from the yard. "This time you're gonna get it, buddy!"

I rushed out to find Jimmy and Ford stripped to the waist,

lunging at each other, while Elliott and Harpur stood to one side, refereeing.

"Elliott, stop them, stop them this minute! They'll kill each other!"

Both boys were weeping with rage, grappling, cuffing, kicking and rolling in the grass. As our neighbors came out and hung over the fence, watching, Jimmy—older and heavier—was pinned down by Ford with his knees. Harpur shouted encouragement to Ford. Jimmy, turning his wrath against his cousin, jumped up and dove for Harpur, who flicked him off and sent him spinning down the yard. When the fight ended, Elliott drew Harpur aside and told him he would give him $175.00 to pay his way to Miami Beach. Harpur did not seem particularly surprised.

I didn't know how Matty would take this, but I knew that my sister wanted us to try and help Harpur. Lee had said, "Patty, see what you can do for Harpur. It would be so wonderful if he could live with you and Elliott." Now, faced with making the decision himself, the first thing that popped into Harpur's mind was his car.

"Uncle Elliott, I want to bring my car. I want to drive down."

Putting aside his own misgivings, Elliott finally agreed to this. We left Seattle the following day. Harpur was to follow three days later.

Driving in the heat of August, with worn tires and an exhausted engine, Harpur's old Ford got as far as Pocatello, Idaho, before the tires went flat and the motor sputtered ominously. A used-car dealer offered him $25 for his heap. Instead, Harpur put on dark glasses, bought a big cigar and hung a sign on the Ford: MOVING TO FLORIDA, WILL SELL CHEAP. Four Mexicans pooled their money, and gave him $100.

He arrived in Miami on a Greyhound bus, wearing Levi's, thongs, a T-shirt and, of course, needing a shave. Three bottles of shaving lotion had broken in his duffel bag, giving the entire bus a sickeningly sweet odor.

On the way into Florida, the bus had passed a huge billboard left over from the campaign: ELECT ELLIOTT ROOSEVELT DEMOCRATIC NATIONAL COMMITTEEMAN. This was our only billboard, and donated at that by a friend in the outdoor advertising business.

ing of LBJ emblems, Harpur also poured out his story to Annette Baker, Elliott's counterpart as Florida's Democratic Committeewoman. Then, he walked out of Convention Hall and disappeared. We searched most of the night without success. Twenty-four hours later he turned up again, looking like a survivor from the Western Front and muttering a stream of apologies. He had spent the night being well entertained by many delegations.

After Harpur's rather undignified appearance at the convention, I went into the VIP lounge with two friends from Lakeland, Florida, David and Martha Prosser. Lady Bird Johnson and her daughters came into the room. Without thinking, I jumped up and rushed toward them, saying, "Hi, Mrs. Johnson." Suddenly my way was barred by two taut-faced Secret Service men with suspicious bulges, who informed me that only those cleared for security were allowed to speak to the President's wife. I made it back to my chair and plunked down into it, shaken, while David and Martha convulsed in laughter beside me.

Franklin, Jr., meanwhile, was hoping desperately to receive Johnson's nod as his running mate, and his friends were having banners and placards printed. They organized parades in his behalf. At any time of the day or night, we could look out the hotel window and see supporters marching along the boardwalk carrying signs proclaiming: ROOSEVELT FOR VICE-PRESIDENT. It was a spooky feeling. Although Elliott and I were sure that Franklin was not LBJ's choice, I told my husband we should certainly try to make his brother feel that his own family was behind him. To help spur Franklin's enthusiasm, I took some of the stationery the children had "borrowed" from the White House, marked simply *The White House, Washington, D.C.*, and enclosed it into a gift-wrapped package. When Franklin dropped into our room for a chat with Elliott, I handed him the present, saying, "I want you to be prepared when you become Vice-President." He removed the wrapping and grinned delightedly, confident of our support. Elliott entered fully into the spirit of the thing.

Before we left Miami, Don Pettit, a veteran Florida newsman and later key aide in several political campaigns, asked me to take along a tape recorder to Atlantic City. He was especially interested in securing taped interviews with leading women of the caliber of Mrs. Johnson, Mrs. Hubert Humphrey, Mrs. George Smathers. Never having operated a tape machine before, I asked if someone from the Florida delegation would work it for me. "Don't worry about a thing," I was told, "there will be somebody at your disposal all the time." Naturally, there was not.

So it happened that one day, totally unfamiliar with the machine, I found myself in the apartment of Mrs. John Bailey, wife of the Democratic National Committee Chairman. The plan was for me to record her comments then go to the nearest telephone and try to play it long-distance to Miami. Barbara Bailey had a grinding schedule, but graciously allowed a thirty-minute interview. I thanked her and went dashing down the hall to our suite, proud as a female Huntley-Brinkley. I burst in and announced to Elliott that I had just finished the most remarkable interview in the history of tape-journalism. "Wonderful, darling," he said, "let me hear it." I plugged in the machine, turned it on and . . . silence. I had a full one-half hour of silence. Nothing like not threading the tape.

Undaunted, I decided to tackle Perle Mesta. The famous hostess, with her usual good humor, said I could bring the recorder to one of her parties. She had rented a house in Atlantic City for the convention use as an entertainment and social center for VIPs. This time, the three boys came with me to carry the recorder and help with the engineering. The party was well under way when we walked in, and the only place convenient to do the taping—which would last about ten minutes—was a downstairs powder room. There was no plug in there, so Ford rigged an extension cord that trailed from the bathroom through the hall and into the kitchen.

Perle and I shut the door. The bathroom was very small. She sat on the water closet, and I perched on top of the radiator thrusting a little plastic microphone into her face. The house was old and the pipes leaky. Mrs. Mesta's taped interview had strange background sound effects of trickling water, gurgling pipes and, from some source we never did figure out, hissing.

Next I decided to tackle Mrs. Hubert Humphrey. The wife of the Vice-President has a friendly, folksy charm. Much has been made of her being the daughter of a butter-and-egg man, and wife of a one-time pharmacist. Muriel Humphrey, blonde, trim and beautifully tailored, gives you the feeling of a next-door neighbor dropping in to borrow a cup of sugar. While scores of professional reporters representing millions of readers and listeners cooled their heels in the hall, I was escorted promptly into the Humphrey suite, a succession of rooms making up a large part of the hotel floor. I found her in a small back bedroom, talking on the telephone trying to bring order into the chaotic events of the night before, when her husband had received President Johnson's blessing as his running mate. We sat on an unmade bed with the tape recorder between us while I fired a barrage of questions at her. When my time was up, gleefully I hoisted the recorder and went flying back to our rooms to again give Elliott the first earful of my newsy interview.

Quickly we plugged it in and pushed the buttons. We listened to fifteen minutes of questions and answers, both mostly provided by me. Of the entire quarter-hour of tape, Muriel's voice could be heard for no more than three or four minutes. Elliott laughed heartily. "But honey, when you interview someone, you ask the questions and let them give you the answers."

"I know, Elliott, but I was so afraid that she would not answer or somebody would call and interrupt us that I tried to make it easier by helping with the answers."

Needless to say, none of the intended radio tapes was ever aired in Miami.

The Florida delegation was seated on the convention floor directly behind California. Jimmy Roosevelt occupied the last chair on the row of the California delegation, and Elliott had the first seat in front of the Florida group. This arrangement made them convention mates, of sorts.

One evening as the session was in progress, we received word that President Johnson had invited all the Roosevelt boys and their wives to visit him in his box. I was ecstatic, telling everyone who would listen, "Be sure and watch up there. In half an hour I'll wave to you."

We were escorted to the balcony and our identification badges carefully screened for security. Then we were asked to sit in a row behind the presidential box until other visitors now with the Johnsons had left. The building and fire inspector of Atlantic City had issued strict orders that not more than twenty people were to be in the box at one time for fear it would fall. This gave me no great feeling of security. The thought of crashing to the floor of the convention hall with President and Mrs. Johnson was an honor I would just as soon avoid.

For this evening, I had put on a favorite old basic black fringed dress purchased twenty-two years before in Seattle. At the time I had been pregnant with my son Jimmy and could not try it on. Its sale price was so ridiculously low, however, that I could not let it go. Now, two decades later, I sat in it waiting to go into the box of the President of the United States. On my right, a man was looking oddly at me. Finally, he said, "Excuse me, ma'am, but where did you get that dress?" The question came out in a soft southern drawl.

"I got it in Seattle at John Doyle Bishops store twenty-two years ago," I replied, in surprise.

"My wife has one just like it."

"Who is your wife?"

"Well, ma'am, I'm Dale Miller and my wife is Skooter. We are close friends of the Johnsons from Texas." He added that he would tell his wife about this, and he hoped someday she and I would meet at a party wearing our basic black fringe dresses.

At long last we filed into the Johnson box, and Elliott whispered that we should remain in the background.

"But honey," I protested, "I won't be able to see anybody."

"That's all right, Patty, I don't want to push up to the front just now."

As it turned out, he had no reason for concern. Jimmy, Irene, Franklin and Sue scurried ahead of us into the front row seats. There was no place for Elliott and me, but in the back. Undaunted, I went to the railing of the box several times and waved to our friends in the Florida delegation below while Elliott yanked frantically at my fringe. There was no conversation with the Johnsons for us. When the prescribed number of minutes for our visit had expired, we were politely shown the door leading downstairs. I felt like saying, "The King has spoken. Long live the King."

Even though the tape recordings had flopped, I rated a press badge as a woman reporter from Miami. This enabled me to attend a women's press breakfast with Betty Beale, my new columnist friend from the Washington *Star*, and Perle Mesta, who was semi-qualified as press because she was writing some articles for *McCall's*.

We arrived at 8:30 A.M. and were promptly assigned to numbered tables. Nine women and one vacant chair were placed at each table. The vacant chair was explained when the first ladies trooped into the dining room, Mrs. Johnson and her daughters, Mrs. Humphrey and daughters-in-law, trailed by several wives of cabinet members, Mrs. Orville Freeman, Mrs. Stuart Udall and others. For an hour they circulated throughout the room, stopping for five minutes at each table. I left the questioning to more experienced heads, but could not help asking Luci what her most exciting experience had been in Atlantic City.

She chirped, Luci fashion, "Oh just when I am being myself, and having fun naturally."

"Would you give us an example?"

Luci giggled and batted her eyelashes. "Yes, the time I went to the clambake."

I cringed, thinking of my fearless nephew lurching after her shouting, "Hi." But Harpur was not on her mind.

It was such fun, she said, to take her shoes off and go romping through the surf, while all those photographers splashed along behind, snapping pictures.

Politically, this Democratic National Convention marked a crossroads for three of FDR's sons. For Elliott, it was his debut as an active participant in the national political scene. At the same time, Jimmy and Franklin, Jr., were nursing high hopes in California and New York, respectively. There were many straws in the wind for Elliott in Florida; for the other two, it turned out, they were not blowing nearly so strong.

Their varied approaches to the opportunity at hand was significant. While all three gave fervent lip service to Johnson, Humphrey, and party unity, Jimmy and Franklin also furthered personal causes by reaping publicity and having their pictures taken. My husband, however, bent his energies toward building a solid political base for Florida in the national party, a base upon which his future aspirations would stand. The events of succeeding months showed how profitably they had spent their time.

Jimmy ran for mayor of Los Angeles and lost. A several-time loser, his political career by November was heading for the ash heap.

FDR, Jr., could have become mayor of New York, but chose not to run. As an aftermath, he declared himself a candidate for the Democratic nomination for governor. With his political future hinging on how big a vote he could poll as a loser, he came in third. Elliott, the neophyte in politics, the one the rest of them ignored, would soon run for mayor of Miami Beach against entrenched opposition in a bitter campaign, and win.

16. December 1964. Elliott and our daughter Gretchen doing the "Mashed Potato Charleston" in preparation for the Christmas holiday parties. The mahogany bookcases in the background are from Hyde Park. (*Photo by Arnie Barnett*)

17. January 1965. A great day and the visit of a great lady to our home. This was taken at the "kick off" luncheon for the March of Dimes *Gold Coast Capers* which was held in March 1965. Mrs. Joseph P. Kennedy flew from Palm Beach with Mrs. Laddie Sanford to be our honored guests. From left to right: Sergeant Jack Allen of the Dade County Sheriff's department; Mr. Sol Silberman's chauffeur; Mrs. Joseph P. Kennedy; Mr. George Pulles of the Fontainebleau Hotel catering staff; the author; young David Roosevelt and Mrs. Laddie Sanford.

18. February 1965. A day at the races with Peter Duchin next to Elliott and Eddie Fisher on my left. Mrs. Fred Hooper was the hostess for the "March of Dimes" race at Hialeah Race Track and had a luncheon honoring Mr. Duchin and Mr. Fisher before the event. (*Hialeah Race Track Photo*)

19. March 1965. "Miss Dinette," one of the door prizes awarded for the *Gold Coast Capers*, reviews the audience. On stage the lucky winner, Mr. Murray Candib. Mrs. Perle Mesta, our honorary hostess, is next to Miss Dinette's former owner who is shaking hands with Bob Hope, our master of ceremonies. (*Rel-Be Photographers*)

20. March 1965. "March of Dimes Day" at the Doral Country Club. The stars (from the left) Doug Sanders, Jackie Gleason, Bob Hope and "Gentleman" Jimmy Demaret, talking to Elliott and me as co-chairman before the tee off. Jackie won and Bob made a generous contribution to the March of Dimes. (*Doral Beach Hotel Photo Studio*)

21. March 1965. Mother's Day is a good time to kick off a campaign especially when you are a mother with a very famous mother-in-law. We felt humble in the face of the ovation that poured from our constituents when her picture was unveiled.

22. June 1, 1965. We've finished the "last roundup." Victory night for Elliott and me shared by Gretchen and David who were too young to vote for the new Mayor of Miami Beach. (AP Wire Service)

23. Same night. Beverlye Keusch is reading off precinct results to Constable Leonard Weinstein and Elliott, the "about-to-be" Mayor of Miami Beach. Beverlye was our campaign manager in this spectacular political race for the leadership of Miami Beach. (Miami Herald, *photo by Bob East*)

24. June 2, 1965. "From one Mayor to the next"—I now present you the gavel that supposedly brings order out of chaos. Former Mayor Melvin Richard hands the token of authority to his successor Mayor Elliott Roosevelt. Councilman Joe Malek (far right) and Vice Mayor Robert L. Turchin observe. (*Miami Beach Photo Lab*)

25. July 1965. Miss Universe of 1965–66. Elliott Roosevelt in his "debatable" red bow tie and cummerbund. The Miss Universe ball at the Deauville Hotel was the beginning of a new business, Formally Yours By Elliott Roosevelt, Inc. (Miami Herald, *photo by Bob East*)

26. July 1965. All of the Roosevelt family takes part in any of the mayor's official entertaining. Some of them do more eating than entertaining, David among them. (Miami Beach Sun, *photo by Janet Chusmir*)

27. August 1965. The Mayor of Dade County, the Honorable Chuck Hall, joins Elliott, David and me at one of the Miss Universe pageants. There has been a pleasant working relationship between these two community leaders, which has made Elliott's job easier. (*Miami Beach News Bureau, photo by George Hamilton*)

28. August 1965. "Sailing, sailing" over the Biscayne Bay. One of the rare times that our family can make time for an outing together. (Left to right) Ford, David, and Gretchen, along with our poodle "Beau" join Elliott and me for some much needed relaxation. (Miami Beach Sun, photo by Ted Press)

Harpur was to remain with us thirteen months. In that time, he would help his uncle win another bitter political fight, one fought with smear and vicious personal enmity. He also would learn hard lessons about becoming a man, and in the process cause us headaches, sickening worry and some loss of sleep.

It was quickly apparent that the committeeman's race had made Elliott a prominent public figure in Florida. You could almost gauge his notoriety by the annoyances that suddenly popped up to plague us. One evening, for example, a hapless taxi driver appeared at our door with a $45 delivery of food from a Chinese take-out restaurant, C.O.D. We had not ordered it. "But lady," the man said, "what am I gonna do with all this chop suey?" I told him to take it back. Suddenly we began receiving long-distance calls, collect, from strangers needing help, saying they had known his father or mother. In most cases, the callers were sick or drunk, or both. When Adlai Stevenson, then Ambassador to the United Nations, paid us a visit in Miami Beach, we incurred the wrath of every right-wing group in town having a special hatred for the world organization. Politically, it was soon apparent that now that he had won the ball, he was also going to have to carry it.

The Democratic National Convention for 1964 was held in Atlantic City, New Jersey. The day before it was scheduled to open, Elliott's predecessor, Bob Johnson of Jacksonville, abruptly resigned, thus saddling Elliott with the work of organizing the Florida delegation.

We arranged for the three boys, Jimmy, Ford, and Harpur, to drive my Lincoln Continental to Washington, D.C., where we would meet them for three days of touring before going on to the convention. Heat hung over the nation's capital, and the humidity rising off the Potomac made it difficult to breathe. To make our visit easier, I called my friend Postmaster General John A. Gronouski, who arranged for tickets and an itinerary that included the White House, the Lincoln Memorial, the Justice Department and FBI buildings, the Washington Monument, the Capitol, and other important tourist haunts.

In the FBI headquarters, we were shown the target range where Mrs. Roosevelt had once taken pistol practice. As First Lady, the Secret Service had deemed it mandatory that she carry a small pistol in her handbag on her many visits to isolated areas. The only place she ever shot it was on the FBI target range.

Franklin, Jr., was then Undersecretary of Commerce. The boys nosed around until they found a secret door opening directly into the adjoining office of the Secretary of Commerce, Luther Hodges. As the panel slid open, Hodges and two other men in conference with him looked up, startled. "Who are you?" the Secretary asked. "I'm Ford Roosevelt," said Ford. "Who are you?"

Franklin offered us the services of a chauffeur, a genial man intimate with the streets and short-cuts of Washington. He never hesitated to park in a No PARKING zone when it suited his fancy. One day when the boys had romped out to see another government edifice and I had completely collapsed, feet throbbing, in the back seat, the chauffeur grinned. He watched the three vanishing backs, and said: "Mrs. Roosevelt, you got yourself some real cats there."

They showed their colors at the White House. Wandering through the public rooms, they stuffed their pockets full of souvenirs—matchbooks, pencils, a White House memo pad from Lincoln's old desk. Shortly after our arrival, we ran into Luci Baines Johnson. As I introduced the President's daughter, Ford, Jimmy, and Harpur all thrust out their hands at her at the same time. Luci jumped back in mock fright. Then, shaking each hand in turn, she gave them all a ladylike, "How d'ya do?" The drawl and affected manner left the boys with a slight chill.

We climaxed their visit to Washington with them climbing the stairs of Washington's (*pant, pant*) Monument. This time I went to sleep in the car.

Upon arriving in Atlantic City, Elliott established an office for the Florida delegates. Ford and Jimmy were put to work as pages, and their time was promptly filled with running errands and seeing that all of the delegates had the proper credentials. The famous boardwalk resort city was alive with people and politics, bunting, signs and wheeler-dealers in smoky rooms. Our two sons adapted quickly and eagerly. With Harpur, it was quite another matter.

My darling troubled nephew had had a difficult first week. To begin with, Elliott and I had begun working on him immediately to try to reshape this brooding, defiant personality into a semblance of order. Elliott had sent me to Miami's Jordan Marsh department store with a blank check to outfit him properly, from the ground up. Now, seen close up, the similarity between these two, uncle and nephew, was even more startling than that which I had seen in Seattle. Harpur was the maverick, running away from home, defying authority, playing the rakehell. It was the young Elliott all over again. My nephew was eager to learn and quick-minded, but the targets on which he set his sights were of a pattern. He wanted to make money, he said, and buy a yacht, a pad, women and whiskey. Now, in Atlantic City, we tried to fit him into the busy swirl of a national convention. We put it to him in the language he seemed to understand: "Harpur, you'd just damn well better get off your fanny and start to work. We didn't bring you up here to do nothing. We brought you to help out."

One of my nephew's greatest prejudices was that against walking. He refused to walk across the street, if it could be avoided. I had many friends working in the convention's various services: transportation, tickets, floor projects. I decided the best place for Harpur was the motor pool, as a driver. It was not a wise choice.

The second day of his duty as a chauffeur, Harpur was sent with a Chrysler limousine to pick up a baldish, impeccable dignitary and drive him to a clambake farther up the beach. My nephew did not know his passenger, Adlai Stevenson, from Casey Stengel. A nineteen-year-old, part-time beatnik's interest did not run toward those prominent in the higher circles of government and politics.

A huge section of public beach had been roped off for the clambake. The bulk of the crowd was made up of delegates, their wives or husbands, guests, and friends who had been met the night before. Sprinkled around, to give it prestige, were assorted big names, such as Ambassador Stevenson, in a sport shirt, Interior Secretary Stuart Udall, and Luci Baines Johnson in gingham. The beer was in kegs set up on sawhorses, and the clams and fish were covered and baked in the sand on hot coals. Elliott and I did not attend. We had been invited as guests on a luxury yacht to a party in honor of Franklin. Ford and Jimmy had other plans too. Harpur was left alone in his official capacity as a chauffeur from the car pool—driving Ambassador Stevenson to the clambake, etc. His temper had not been sweetened by the recent tongue-lashing I had given him for being so lazy. Soon he was swigging—which he was not accustomed to—beer and flexing his muscles.

The only attractive girl around was Luci Johnson. Harpur, emboldened, sidled up to Luci, saying "Hi, remember me?" With a toss of the head and a cool, "Well, really," Luci dismissed him. But Harpur does not dismiss easily. He hung around her entourage for the better part of an hour. Then, when Luci grew skittish and a corps of photographers began chasing her through the surf, popping flashbulbs and drenched to their waists, Harpur joined the running horde, bellowing like a water buffalo. Ambassador Stevenson had a difficult time finding his driver, and when he did the youth was half-drenched. For all his exertions, Harpur managed to maneuver the Chrysler through the streets of Atlantic City and deposit the UN Ambassador safely back at his hotel.

For the social Huck Finn of Seattle, the clambake was merely the beginning. By nightfall, hotels along the boardwalk were roaring full-blast with parties, and their lights splashed gaily down the beach to reflect in the flying surf. It was enough to make a young man's head whirl with excitement. With an open-house everywhere and no credentials needed, he worked his way progressively from party to party. Finally, after sessions had opened in Convention Hall, he found his way to the entrance where several groups of civil rights demonstrators were picketing. "Here, whadaya tryin' to do? Break it up," Harpur said, and waded into the ranks. A small Negro man grabbed his arm, spun him around. A voice cried, "Hit him!" A fist cracked into the side of my nephew's face. The fist was decorated with brass knuckles, which brought a gush of blood. Harpur shook his head and lurched away. Another whop of the knuckles and several spectators carried him into the Red Cross first-aid station. Harpur soon left there and arrived on the convention floor, to confront Robert King High, Mayor of Miami, whose recent campaigning for Florida governor had drawn heavy support of racial liberals. "Dirty crumb hit me," Harpur said. "Nobody understands me." Face and shirt smeared with dried blood, bedecked with an array of Florida convention badges, as well as Elliott Roosevelt buttons, to say noth-

29. September 1965. One of our favorite VIP guests on Miami Beach is the Honorable Hubert H. Humphrey, Vice-President of the United States. We have presented greetings to this distinguished visitor to our city many times during Elliott's term of office. (*Miami Beach News Bureau, photo by George Hamilton*)

30. September 1965. Life with the mayor opens up all kinds of doors— however it is sometimes difficult to walk into the next room. This is true for me when I find myself on the dais at the microphone and Elliott is listening. On this occasion Whitney Young, president of the Urban League, was also listening as I addressed their annual convention. (*Miami Beach News Bureau, photo by George Hamilton*)

31. November 1965. Theodore Roosevelt said "Charge!" Franklin D. Roosevelt said "The only thing we have to fear..." Elliott Roosevelt says "Come on down, the water's fine." The author and "Big Bear." (*photo by Annie Barnett*)

32. December 1965. "Merry Christmas to all" … Our favorite time of the year and it was fun to open our home to Elliott's compatriots on the council along with their wives. (Left to right) Councilman and Mrs. Malvin Englander, Councilman and Mrs. Paul Seiderman, Elliott and me, Vice-Mayor and Mrs. Robert Turchin, Councilman and Mrs. Joseph Malek. *(Miami Beach News Bureau, photo by Don Duffy)*

33. August 1966. A delightful assortment of "Per Stirpes." Little grandchildren who make life more exciting for Elliott and me. Little Chandler "Jr." is not in the picture which was taken on a family vacation in Connecticut last summer.

23

Marching Dimes for FDR

Sleek and gray, the Lincoln Continental limousine purred around a long curve and out onto the multi-laned straightway of the Julia Tuttle Causeway. Behind, Miami Beach was a retreating skyline of bone white buildings, waterfront mansions, palm trees, and hibiscus blossoms in splashes of red and pink. In midday sunshine, the bay spread away on both sides, magnificently blue. Ahead and to the south lay Miami itself, blocks and spires of pastel color rising from a sweep of blue and rich green. At fifty miles an hour, the car flashed across the two big causeway bridges, man-built hills of concrete and steel, over the tri-level maze of the 36th Street Interchange and onto the expressway to Miami International Airport.

Alone in the huge back compartment, a place of thick pile rugs and plush upholstery complete with air-conditioning and telephone, I stared through the glass divider at the back of the chauffeur's neck and wondered why he wasn't perspiring too. I was on my way to meet Mrs. Joseph P. Kennedy, mother of the slain President, to launch a brazen money-raising project called *Gold Coast Capers of 1965* for the National Foundation—March of Dimes. For the next three months, I would have a tiger by the tail. And suddenly, I wanted to hide.

"Patty," I said out loud. "Have you lost your mind? What are you doing here?"

It had begun innocently enough. Just a month before, in December 1964, Elliott was asked if we would serve as chairmen of the Heart Association ball, one of the top social events of the season. "I'll talk to Patty and let you know," he said. Five days later a letter arrived thanking us for accepting. We hadn't, but it was too late to back out now. Talking over the project with the association's executive director, Miss Adelita Quejado, I recalled the old Junior League Follies in Seattle—variety acts, dances, comedians, always a money-raiser. Miss Quejado's interest quickened. "I'll check with the board," she said. The Heart Association then asked me to come up with some firm ideas.

I called producer Jerome Cargill in New York for help. He had long been the entrepreneur for Junior League events throughout the country. I also began drumming up estimates from Miami Beach hotels on costs of food, availability of space for a production, and how much help we could expect. At Miss Quejado's request, I went before the Heart Association's board to outline what I had in mind. "An amateur musical revue, flashy costumes, lots of big names in the cast." The forty-member board seemed impressed. Then three days later, another call from the executive director: "Don't make any more plans, Patty," she said. "Some of the members have had second thoughts. They've decided this kind of show would be a bit gaudy." One of the top executives of a large firm in town also had a personal objection. He did not want his wife flouncing around on stage in a *Folies Bergère* type production. The board would prefer to raise $5000 in sedate fashion than $100,000 with a splash. I sent them a brief letter of resignation and gave a relieved sigh.

That same afternoon I had another call. Mrs. Betty Lou Randolph, executive director of the Dade County Chapter, March of Dimes, wanted to know if I would help generate interest in the Mothers March on Polio. "Certainly, Betty Lou," I said. "By the way, what would you think of staging a *Gold Coast Capers?*" . . . Before we hung up I was back in show business.

Once more, ideas spun in my head. The more they spun, the bigger they grew. March of Dimes had been created, after all, by Franklin D. Roosevelt to combat polio. Now it was extended to a wide range of congenital diseases. I could be audacious. Nothing was impossible. Nothing.

"Patty," said Elliott, "now simmer down, honey. You're steamed up like a percolator."

"Elliott, I am absolutely wild with excitement."

He patted my knee.

It wasn't long before the wind died and my smile went slack. All it took was my first meeting of the Women's Committee for the *Gold Coast Capers*. There were twenty names on the list. Seven showed up. We fumbled around in a welter of indecision. It would take them all afternoon just to decide when to have the next meeting. When the last lady had departed, trailing perfume, I turned to my friend, Freddie Peterson, and threw up my hands. To get this one going, we would have to light a fuse.

"Freddie, we need to get these women on the stick. A name, that's what it will take. A big name. Somebody like Mrs. Kennedy. Her daughter, Rosemary, was retarded, you know. Somebody like . . ."

I snapped my fingers. "Rose Kennedy is in Palm Beach, Freddie. I'll just call her."

There are few women with such warmth as Mrs. Kennedy. Even on the telephone, it pours out and gives you a good feeling. When she turns you down, it is done with grace and charm.

"No, Patty, I just can't do it," she said. "I don't even do this type of thing for my own children in their fund raising. And Joe has not been well, you know. I don't like leaving him."

For two weeks I kept calling her Palm Beach residence. Each time, she politely declined. Finally I sought the help of an old friend of the Kennedy family, the international socialite, Mrs. Laddie Sanford. A strong supporter of the National Foundation, Mrs. Sanford prevailed upon Rose Kennedy to make an exception, just this once. At last, she agreed to help.

My idea was to have a "kickoff" luncheon, with Mrs. Kennedy as honor guest. I set it for January 14, and plowed through the Social Register, club rosters and personal phone books to compile a guest list of forty to fifty of the most prominent women. From among them, we would form committees to do the heavy work of this benefit. The show itself would be in March.

Things began to roll. Jerome Cargill cut his prices to the marrow, and agreed to provide a director, scenery, costumes, and skits: I even persuaded him to buy two $100 tickets. I had never met him except by phone. One of the producer's top men, Brooks Russell, was assigned to direct the show. There were meetings with state and local leaders of the National Foundation, who expressed serious misgivings about such a huge production. Brashly I charged ahead, thinking big in the daytime and going sleepless with worry at night. Nobody but Freddie Peterson would even offer to toss me a life preserver if I sank.

To secure a solid base of prizes and donations, I began drumming up a list of "angels." First target was Saul Silberman, owner of Miami's Tropical Park race track. He donated a box at the track as a door prize, then agreed to buy a $1000 table at the *Gold Coast Capers*. There was one more favor I needed from him. "Mr. Silberman, you have the most gorgeous car. I love your Continental limousine. As you know, Mrs. Joseph P. Kennedy is coming down in two weeks, and I thought it would be nice . . ."

By now, I was riding in his car over the Airport Expressway to meet the arriving Mrs. Kennedy and her party. They were being flown down from Palm Beach aboard a plush DC-3 provided by another generous Miami man, restaurant owner Art Bruns. At the moment, fifty women representing top local society were waiting back there in my living room, fresh flowers were everywhere, luncheon was ready and the press had been alerted. Airport authorities had given me permission to drive right to plane side to greet her. Surely, now there could be no complications, and we would soon have the show on the road.

The Continental whispered around the huge Miami terminal building and onto the field. Ahead of us stood a man in the uniform of a county deputy. His sleeves were adorned with oversize gold sergeant stripes and from a shiny black holster protruded a magnificent pearl-handle pistol. Nearby was a long gray limousine identical to the one in which I was riding. The man waved both arms for us to stop, his sergeant stripes flashing in the sunshine. I rolled down the window.

"Officer, I am Mrs. Elliott Roosevelt and I'm here to meet some friends who are flying down from Palm Beach."

"I don't care who you are, lady. This concourse is closed for full security. I'm out here for the mayor to meet his guests."

"But . . . but I'm Mrs. Roosevelt and I am here to meet some guests."

"Those are my orders, ma'am."

My mind was in a whirl. At this moment, Art Bruns' plane was making its approach to Miami. It carried, in addition to Mrs. Kennedy, Mrs. Sanford, Mrs. Earl E. T. Smith, wife of the former U. S. Ambassador to Cuba, and Timothy and Katherine Smith, Miami socialites who had agreed at the last minute, along with Joan and Gene Caldwell, to make the flight to Palm Beach and back when it developed that Elliott could not go.

"Sir," I asked, "whom are you expecting?"

"The mayor told me to pick up Mrs. Joseph P. Kennedy and take her to his luncheon."

At the moment I did not even know which mayor he was talking about. Greater Miami has twenty-six municipalities, plus a mayor of Metropolitan Dade County, Chuck Hall. The sergeant, it turned out, was Jack Allen, driver for Mayor Hall. I told him there were fifty women waiting at my house for Mrs. Kennedy. Where did he intend to take her?

"To a luncheon at Mr. and Mrs. Timothy Smith's," he replied.

At that moment the plane taxied off the runway, gleaming yellow and white in the sunshine. The sight cheered me, but I had faint suspicion of a double-cross in the making. The suspicions were quickly proven wrong. Timothy and Katherine Smith stepped off the plane first, and he inclined his head and said, "Patty, have you met Mrs. Kennedy?"

Rose Kennedy, smiling, warm, vital, appeared with both hands outstretched. She wore white gloves, a light-colored dress in neat uncluttered style and a single strand of pearls. Her hair, a dark reddish brown, was upswept. The smile she gave me was sincere, filling the eyes as well as the mouth. "Patty, my dear, I'm so glad I could come down and help you with your drive to aid the unfortunate," she said. The words had that familiar clipped accent that sent a little chill down my back. "I must be back in Palm Beach by four o'clock. Joe is not at all well."

Timothy had hoped to drive our guest to my house in Mayor Hall's limousine. I steered her instead to the car I had commandeered, and on the way back to Miami Beach filled her in on the luncheon and what to expect there. If I had had any nervous twinges, they were dispelled the moment she stepped into my living room. That crowd of sophisticated women responded instantly to the Rose Kennedy charm. Immediately I saw the amazing similarities between this slender, erect woman and Eleanor Roosevelt. They both took immediate command of a situation and established their own ground rules.

Rose Kennedy to me was a miracle, an outgoing, kindly woman who kept her radiance despite years of awesome personal tragedy in a family which seemed to be living a jinx. Such women experience the strong, hard edge of life: they are loved and envied, they bear children, meet problems head-on, suffer the deaths of their own, and yet show to the world a face of love and understanding.

Guests for the luncheon included actress Gloria de Haven, wive of Dick Fincher, a Miami automobile dealer and representative to the State Legislature. There was, also, Monsignor William Barry of Miami Beach, a benign and beloved Catholic who had long been a leader in the community. He was captivated by my guest of honor. Reporters threw questions at Mrs. Kennedy and TV cables coiled across the living room like blacksnakes, plugs festooning every outlet. She fielded each question easily, with the style of a smooth campaigner.

Barely had Rose Kennedy waved good-bye at the airport and flown back to Palm Beach when wire stories were chattering out on teletype machines across the nation. To reap maximum advantage not only from her visit but also to provide complete coverage for the *Gold Coast Capers*, I retained as publicity chief Tony Kucherak, a shrewd, capable public relations man who recently had handled a successful United Fund campaign in Miami and had contacts with press, TV and radio. Soon we were drawing column notice about the *Capers* from people like Betty Beale, Susy Knickerbocker, Cobina Wright and Earl Wilson. The New York *Times* sent its women's editor, Charlotte Curtis, to investigate. The Associated Press assigned Jean Sprain Wilson, a woman's feature writer, to do a piece on the *Capers* from Miami Beach.

With the help of Elliott, Tony, and two secretaries I contrived every possible gimmick. The National Foundation had no such

prim reservations as did the Heart Association, so we began rounding up prizes for drawings at the *Capers*. There was a bag of
Colombian emeralds, from the government of Colombia; a week
at the Jamaica Reef Hotel, three days in the Presidential Suite
at Miami Beach's swank Fontainebleau; season boxes at Hialeah,
Gulfstream, and Tropical Park race tracks; a used Mercedes-
Benz, a mink coat, a mink-covered Castro convertible bed, trips
to Nassau and a year's supply of orange juice for a family of
eight. For door prizes, I scrounged up a racehorse, a motorboat
and trailer, a trip for two couples to the Kentucky Derby.

Hialeah race track staged a March of Dimes feature. Eddie
Fisher filled the silver winner's trophy with FDR dimes. Jimmy
Durante, who was playing at Miami Beach, agreed to buy a
$1000 table at the *Capers* and, also, to help drum up donations at
a party at our home. Bringing along his show business sidekicks,
Sonny King and Eddie Jackson, the "Schnozz" knocked out
good old tunes on our piano, while well-heeled guests "bid"
cash or pledges to have songs dedicated to them.

By mid-February I was running under full steam. Nobody had
ever made $100,000 for charity in a single show of this kind.
Now that $100,000 became an obsession with me. The only way
to do it was to adopt the strategy I had used from the beginning: enlist names, big names. For master of ceremonies, I had a
brainstorm.

"Bob Hope."

Elliott was aghast. "Patty, don't be silly. You don't even know
Bob Hope. How would you even find him? Honey, I hate to
disappoint you, but you've got to go through channels on a
thing like this, his manager, his studio . . ."

"Elliott, if you let me call him, I think he will accept."

Hope always enjoyed visiting Miami Beach. For the past several
years he had been a regular master of ceremonies for another
benefit dinner and show, for Parkinson's disease. The comedian's generosity is legendary in show business. By long-distance telephone I began a search for Hope. After two hours I
finally got around to trying the place I should have called first,
his home in Beverly Hills. His voice came over the wire, crisp
and clear.

"Mr. Hope?" I stammered. Elliott and Harpur, startled and

embarrassed for me, left the room. "Bob, this is Patty Roosevelt in Miami Beach. Elliott and I are co-chairmen of the National Foundation March of Dimes benefit this year and we are having a *Gold Coast Capers of 1965* and we would like you to be our . . ."

"Whoa, Patty. It is Patty, isn't it? Now would you repeat that again? Slowly, please."

"I've never talked to you before and I'm nervous. This *is* Bob Hope, isn't it?"

I stumbled and bumbled. Through the back windows I could see Elliott pacing beside the pool, muttering to himself.

Hope said, sure, he'd be master of ceremonies. "Just send me a formal letter, for the records." His acceptance came at me through a mental fog. I blurted something like, "Thank you," hung up, and rushed outside.

"Elliott, honey, I have news for you."

I think that is when my husband felt his first touch of amazement at my incredible run of luck.

"Bob Hope will be our master of ceremonies."

Nobody believed me. The committeewomen scoffed. The officials lifted eyebrows and gave thin dubious smiles. I received pats on the shoulders, and there were whispers that I was working too hard. Inside, my mind did cartwheels. Nothing was impossible, nothing. That Roosevelt name was a talisman. If I could get Bob Hope as emcee, why not Charles de Gaulle as the mystery guest? Failing him, we would go for Hubert Humphrey. For honorary chairman, why not ask Perle Mesta? Well, why not? Again, the long-distance telephone. Into the ear of Washington's hostess, I poured a stream of gabble about publicity, good will, desperate need. Mrs. Mesta replied: "Why, Patty, it's been a long time since I have been in Miami Beach. I'd be delighted. I'll come."

But now came the toughest challenge, a cantankerous, mustachioed multi-millionaire with a waspish tongue and tempestuous diction named Ben Novack. Rose Kennedy, Bob Hope and Perle Mesta were one thing, but Ben Novack was quite another. He owned the Fontainebleau Hotel, the swankiest, most expensive and statuaried public hostelry on Miami Beach. Its corridors were lined with Italian marble figures. Its main ballroom was big enough to hold the Orange Bowl game. In the winter season rich New Yorkers paid handsomely just so they could sit of evenings on velvet settees in the lobby snubbing everybody. It was not uncommon to see the likes of Peter Lawford go padding through the corridors in sneakers and a sweatshirt. Sinatra, a pal of Novack's, had a pad on the top floor. And Ben Novack himself, major-domo, bon vivant, favored nutty sport coats and fancy foulards, strong cigars and beautiful women. How about letting us stage the *Gold Coast Capers* in his hotel? And cutting his prices $10 a head for Hope and charity?

"Hell no."

I stared at him with the expression of a blowfish. The excitement of bearding Ben Novack in his lair now set my heart to knocking against my chest. Freddie Peterson, who had come along to give me moral support, leaped to her feet.

"Patty, what's the matter? Are you all right?"

Truthfully, my heart pounded like a two-dollar drum, but it was merely a passing spasm. Squinting one eye at Novack, I could see it was having more effect on him than me. His face had gone white and his mustache twitched. A plastic-tipped cigar bobbed from his mouth. Instead of rallying, I flopped back on the settee and gasped, "Call Elliott."

Now Novack was yelling at Freddie. "What's the matter? What's the matter? I got a hotel to run. What's the matter with her? Does she think she can get everything for free? I do this for her and I got the whole town on my neck . . ."

"Freddie," (*pant, pant*) "call Elliott."

"I'm in business. I donate enough for charity. My accountants won't let me take off any more. I won't do it!"

I concentrated on making my face turn blue.

Freddie dialed Elliott while I took long, shuddering breaths and Novack paced. What a heck of a way, I thought, to accomplish a mission. Then Elliott's voice came booming through the receiver. "What's the matter, darling? What's Ben Novack doing to you?"

I managed to croak into the phone: "Call Preston Tisch, Elliott. Tell him we'll take the Americana Hotel for Bob Hope, Perle Mesta, and the March of Dimes."

The cigar blew out of Novack's mouth. His voice rose to

something between a bellow and a scream. "Now what's the matter with you, Patty? Haven't I always been a good friend of yours? What do you mean, take it to Tisch? This is a Beach affair and it belongs in a Beach hotel."

"No, it is not a Miami Beach affair," I whispered hoarsely. "It's a world-wide affair, and I am going to hold the party where we can make the best deal. We need the money desperately for the March of Dimes, even more than you need it." It was a speech worthy of the late Ethel Barrymore.

We walked out of the Fontainebleau with Novack's promises of the $10-a-head reduction on price, plus fifteen free suites for our VIP guests.

February was almost gone, and the nearing of March brought even more cause for heart palpitations, but mostly from sheer excitement.

Guy Lombardo and his red-jacketed Royal Canadians were playing at the Doral Beach Hotel, a soaring glass-walled structure overlooking the creaming Atlantic surf. With the memory of his old musical sidekick, our mutual friend, Billy Goodheart, as a key to introduction, I asked him to help plug the *Capers* by racing his hydroplane on beautiful Indian Creek, a waterway lined with mansions and posh Gold Coast hotels cutting north and south a block west of the ocean. Lombardo's eyes struck fire at the prospect. His own hydroplane, the sleek monster called *Miss Tempo* was out of commission, so the sportsman-musician had a replacement shipped in from Ohio. In the days preceding the *Gold Coast Capers*, he defied choppy water and tricky currents to bring the hydro up to racing pitch. Then, with the banks lined with spectators, Lombardo unleashed the full fury of his vessel, skimming up the waterway with a howling engine and sheets of spray, to beat his own world speed record.

Preparations for the *Capers* went on around the clock at our house as Tony and the secretaries and I scheduled rehearsals, planned the program, drummed up advertising by telephone, arranged seating, worked out travel for the VIP guests and hounded prize donors to have their contributions in Miami Beach on time. To give the event an added international fillip, I decided it would be clever to invite a few ambassadors from foreign countries. So I lined up ambassadors of Iran, Kuwait, Morocco, Pakistan, and Portugal. Having slept through all those early geography classes in Seattle, I made the glaring mistake of being a trifle heavy on Arabic nations. In overwhelmingly Jewish Miami Beach, this could be embarrassing. I really did not become aware of the error until the evening of March 10, just two nights away from the *Capers*. Elliott looked over his glasses and asked mildly, "Dear, aren't you afraid some of the Jewish people might stage a protest demonstration? They might take it as an insult that you invite representatives of their enemies' countries as guests of honor." The prospect gave my already overworn heart another spasm. I failed to reckon, of course, upon the warmth and geniality which can be displayed by professional diplomats. As it turned out, not only did the Miami Beach people take no offense, they returned in kind the cordiality demonstrated by such guests as Ambassador and Mrs. Mabmoud Foroughi of Iran, Ambassador and Mrs. Talat Al-Ghoussein of Kuwait, and Morocco's personable Ali Bengelloun and his wife, Jackie.

In the final weeks of preparation, calamity struck when one of our doors prizes died. This was a thoroughbred racehorse, donated by the multi-millionaire Miami Beach sportsman Bill MacDonald. I figured the poor thing was simply overcome by fright at the prospect of having to clomp onto a stage in front of so many people. The papers picked up our dilemma, and within a week we had not one animal but two, a filly and a colt. There were also some unusual calls.

One came from a man in central Florida. Eunice, my secretary, answered.

"Ma'am, I understand your horse died and you need another," the caller said. "Do you have to have a horse?"

"Why certainly, a horse," Eunice replied frostily. "What else is there?"

"Have you ever thought of a donkey?"

Eunice, overburdened from long hours and relentless work, replied, "Oh, thank you, sir, but we have enough jackasses around here already."

The two-year-old bay filly was donated by insurance man Edward R. Redmond of Fort Lauderdale, and the colt by Charles F. Keiser of Ocala, Florida.

With Miami Beach at the peak of its season, hotels and

lounges and clubs in full swing and lobbies swarming with mink, show people were in abundance. Almost without exception they responded zealously to my appeals for free help. Pianist Peter Duchin was playing at the Fontainebleau. Would he donate his services? "Anything I can do for the Roosevelts," he replied. "Anything." Sammy Spear, director of Jackie Gleason's Orchestra, spent hours working out our music. June Taylor, leader of Gleason's June Taylor Dancers, did choreography; Sammy Liner was our pianist. Frances Langford, whose yacht was moored in Indian Creek across Collins Avenue from the Fontainebleau, agreed to be an honored guest, so did Gloria de Haven and Hildegarde. Unfortunately, Hildegarde had the impression she would be the only professional entertainer in the show. Not until she arrived in Miami Beach did she realize that many other big names were also on the bill. "You will ruin my career," she snapped.

Rounding up and displaying flashy prizes for the *Capers'* drawings brought unexpected flareups and embarrassments.

There was the episode of the mink coat.

Tall, suave Adrian Thal is a Miami Beach furrier who oozes quality and has that look which withers slow doormen. When charities put the touch on Adrian, the usual offering was a mink stole or fur-trimmed sweater. I thought it would be nice to give him a change-up pitch. "Look, why don't you give us a full-length mink, Adrian?" Furrier Thal had just been released from the hospital and his complexion was naturally pale; but the face now took on a funereal droop and the eyebrows shot up, so I knew I had struck home. The discussion went on for some time. Finally, he agreed to ask the Emba Mink Breeders Association to donate the skins and he, Adrian Thal, would design the coat, provided we gave it national publicity, with photographs of the creation modeled by an international socialite.

Calling modeling agencies and headquarters in New York, I learned that we already had such a socialite in Miami Beach: Peter Duchin's beautiful wife, Cheray. It was arranged, and Adrian, Tony Kucherak, and I duly arrived at her hotel, trailed by a fashion photographer and his burden of cameras. There had been a mixup on time and Cheray was late. We waited half an hour in the lobby. I spent the time gushing into Adrian's ear about Cheray ". . . how elegant, how statuesque, how lithesome."

At last from the corner of my eye I saw a young blonde step into the lobby wearing a beach coat, thong sandals and no lipstick. She was escorted by a huge Labrador retriever. She approached hesitantly, asking, "Mrs. Roosevelt?"

"I'm sorry, dear, but I am busy," I said. "We're waiting for Mrs. Duchin."

"Patty, don't you remember me? I'm Cheray Duchin."

I almost fell off the couch. Adrian Thal's eyebrows shot up again. The photographer made strange noises in his throat.

"I won't allow you to wear my coat," said the furrier. "I wanted a society model."

"Your hair looks terrible," said the photographer. Then he turned to me accusingly. "I thought you said she was a model. I can't photograph this."

I took Cheray's arm and steered her into a corner. "For God's sake, Cheray, don't you have a cocktail dress or something? And can't we fix your hair? If you don't have a lipstick, use mine."

What we did not know was that Cheray Duchin was dressed at the peak of afternoon leisure wear, in the Mod fashion. She was years ahead of us. In a lilting, little-girl voice, she told me, "Patty, I have modeled in New York for years, for the Junior League, the Opera, the Symphony. I know what the magazines like. I've been in Vogue and Harper's Bazaar a jillion times."

"She will never wear this mink coat," said Thal. "This happens to be Emba Autumn Haze, and I am taking it back."

"Let's find another model," said the photographer.

I sent Cheray scurrying upstairs for a more suitable dress. While she was gone, I resumed the task of promoting her as our model. "She's young, she's beautiful, and besides, you don't just pick up international socialites wandering through the lobby of the Fontainebleau."

When Cheray returned, the transformation was stunning. She wore a short formal and beige pumps; her blonde hair cascaded in soft waves to shoulder length; she was tall and elegant and slender. Wrapped in the mink, she did things for that coat which neither nature nor the finest art of furrier Thal could fully achieve.

"Ah!" said Adrian.

"Ah!" said the photographer.

The picture became a raging success in the fashion journals. Then there was the episode of the motorboat at the Fontainebleau.

Ralph and Frances Evinrude, who have a winter home in Stuart, Florida, donated a sixteen-foot water ski boat powered by a ninety-horsepower Evinrude motor as a door prize, complete with trailer. Why not, I thought, display it in the lobby of the Fontainebleau for three weeks? We could use it as a ticket sales booth.

"Mr. Novack, you cut your prices for us, now would you do this little favor?"

Ben Novack's face turned purple. I thought he would swallow his cigar. But then a crafty look came to his eye. "You'll have to see my maintenance man," he grunted and stalked away. I could almost see him making mental notes to tell the maintenance man: "Absolutely no. Don't let that crazy woman put a boat in my lobby." But Ben forgot. Running such a lavish hotel, after all, puts a burden on a man's mind. So one evening the boat was duly delivered to the hotel. Elliott and I were at the *Capers'* rehearsal hall a couple of miles away. I received an urgent call from the hotel. They could not get the boat through the revolving doors and into the lobby because the motor would not come off. Could I send over an Evinrude maintenance man to remove the motor?

"Where is it now?" I gasped.

"It's in the freight elevator."

"Stay right where you are and we'll be over." I rushed to Elliott and told him I had to go to the hotel; there was an emergency.

"What kind of emergency?" he said. "I've had as many emergencies as a man can live with!"

"This is awful, honey. The boat is stuck in the freight elevator at the Fontainebleau and I have to get a maintenance man to get it out and set up in the lobby."

"Ridiculous," my husband snorted. "You don't need a maintenance man. I can do it. You conned me into coming to this rehearsal anyhow when I could have been in bed. Now I have to take a boat apart."

He jumped into his car and sped to the Fontainebleau. I left the rehearsal hall about twenty minutes later and drove toward the hotel. Three blocks from the Fontainebleau, I stalled in a Collins Avenue traffic jam. That was peculiar, a traffic jam in the middle of the week. I leaned on my horn, but it was another half-hour before I could move.

I should have known the cause of the jam. It was Elliott. Corraling all the parking boys, bellhops, room service waiters and bus boys, he had removed the motor, lifted the boat off the trailer, and was easing it gingerly through the glass revolving doors. Getting a large ski boat through a revolving door, it turned out, is no easy chore.

When I walked in, they had just completed the task, and Elliott stood there drenched in sweat, shirtsleeved and without a tie. Somehow, the boat looked out of place among the gilt furnishings, marble statuary, and velvet settees. Unable to think of a truly appropriate comment, under the circumstances, I said simply: "What's the matter, darling? What are you doing?"

"I am getting the goddamn boat where you wanted it in the middle of the hotel," he thundered, "and we'll probably all be arrested for disturbing the peace and quiet of the guests, to say nothing of choking traffic on Collins Avenue."

"Can I help, darling? You're all hot and tired."

"Help! The only way you could help me is to have never gotten involved in this stupid thing in the first place."

Hotel manager Harold Lieberman, meanwhile, had backed Ben Novack into a corner of the Poodle Lounge, trying to keep his boss from noticing the hubbub in the lobby. An hour and a half later the pieces were reassembled and Elliott was flat on his back in the boat, fastening the motor into position again.

During the entire proceedings, we had drawn a bigger crowd than the Friday night fights. It grew even larger when a woman came running up, yelling: "Where is he? Where is he?"

"Where's who?"

"Elliott Roosevelt. I heard he was here and I want his autograph."

Somebody shoved a pencil stub into Elliott's hand and he started signing his name, sweat dripping off the end of his nose. Not wanting to let such a crowd go to waste, I began merrily selling tickets to the *Gold Coast Capers*. Afterward, during the three weeks the boat stood in the elegant lobby, such personalities as Eddie Fisher, Peter Duchin, Guy Lombardo, Sammy Spear and Tony Martin appeared daily to sell tickets and sign autographs.

Rehearsals, meanwhile, went on at a hectic pace. Finding a centrally located practice hall had not been easy. Finally, I hit upon the ground floor of the building on Meridian Avenue in which Elliott's office was located. The entire floor had been designed for a bank, but was vacant. Harry Seeve, owner of the building, said we could use it.

Staging an amateur production is a frustrating business, even when bolstered with top volunteer professionals. Rehearsals began four weeks before the show, and to lure amateurs I dangled big personalities as bait. To help kick off rehearsals, among our guests were Eddie Fisher and the bridge master, Charles Goren. Still, the turnout was disappointing. To stage such a production, we need one hundred and twenty-five talents or warm bodies. Fifty turned up. Fisher, sporting a big cigar, quipped: "This is the first time I ever played to an audience small enough to fit into a washroom." The amateurs we had went at it grimly. Charlie Goren and Clare Weintraub, wife of a prominent Miami attorney, did a fine "Charleston," but he almost suffered a stroke. Others went home nursing aches and pains and twisted ankles. As the weeks passed, director Brooks Russell diligently strengthened the cast and whipped the show into some semblance of shape. Performers came from all walks of life, Junior League, society matrons, political and social workers, white collar girls—even Hope Pomerance, wife of the Miami Beach police chief, Rocky Pomerance. We wound up finally with a fifty-eight minute show and a cast of one hundred and twenty-eight. The one hundred and twenty-ninth suffered stage fright at the last minute and did not appear for the *Capers*.

Everything had a built-in headache, even transportation. For a time, I chafed over how we were going to haul our incoming VIPs from Miami International Airport to the Fontainebleau Hotel, especially since they were not arriving en masse but would be dribbling in one and two at a time from all points of the compass. Then Kay Hall, district manager of Avis Rent-a-Car, stepped in, putting four limousines and several staff people at our disposal. Elliott and I drew the job of welcoming most of the arriving guests. We spent the day of the *Capers* shuttling back and forth across the causeways in opposite directions, waving at each other as we passed.

Last to arrive was Perle Mesta, accompanied by her secretary. From the outset I should have known what to expect, but by now I was almost too tired from riding to care.

To begin with, I lost my driver. He disappeared just after we had arrived at the hotel bringing the Moroccan Ambassador and his wife, Mr. and Mrs. Bengelloun. Mrs. Mesta's plane was due in twenty minutes and suddenly I was without a car. A bicycle would not do. Frantically, I searched the lobby for Ben Novack. He had a lovely 1965 Cadillac. But Ben was not around. Then I bumped into Murray Candib, a friend from Massachusetts. This man possessed a spanking new Lincoln Continental limousine with all the gadgets, including a bar in the back, and he had a jolly Jamaican chauffeur named George.

"Murray, would you take me to the airport to meet Perle Mesta?"

"Sure, Patty. Hop in."

We roared away just as Elliott was arriving with the Ambassador from Portugal and his wife, His Excellency and Mrs. Vasco Vieira Garin. I waved. Elliott waved. Both waves were weak.

Murray Candib could not believe we were going to pick up the famous Washington hostess. "Perle Mesta," he breathed. "Not really Perle Mesta!" We moved onto the concrete apron just as Mrs. Mesta stepped to the doorway of the plane. She wore a large off-the-face hat and a black suit. I ran up the steps and she gave me a friendly embrace.

"Didn't you bring a friend with you, Perle?" I said. "Where is she?"

The hostess gave a tired nod. "Back there," she said, gesturing toward the rear of the plane. "She's been sick all the way from Washington. Why do I always get involved with people to take care of, when they should be taking care of me?"

The friend was weak-kneed and white of face, but managed something resembling a grin. We all climbed into Murray Candib's car, and Jamaica George wheeled out through the terminal complex toward the expressway. From LeJeune Road, we made the long, curving climb into the stream of traffic. Along the elevated speedway we passed the rooftops of the light industrial area east of the airport. Perle Mesta and her friend sat on the back seat, while Murray and I occupied permanent rear-facing seats on each side of the back compartment. Four minutes from the airport, Perle's guest gave a convulsive gasp and her hand flew to her mouth. I shrieked at Murray, "She's going to be sick."

The controls to the compartment window and communication with the chauffeur were on my side. In the middle was a small bar. Murray fumbled across my lap for the controls, wanting to order Jamaica George to pull over. I grabbed at silver tumblers in the bar, seized one and thrust it at the ashen-faced woman. She bent her head, and with great, gurgling sounds, began to fill the tumbler. Desperately, I tore open my purse and found a plastic bag. How it got there, I will never know. By now, Jamaica George was glancing nervously back over his shoulder, shuddering at the thought of his beautiful new car being desecrated by a passenger with a weak stomach. And while all this turmoil was in progress, Perle placidly looked out the window, commenting on the passing panorama of Biscayne Bay and Miami Beach. "My, how it has grown," she said. I don't know if she was ever really aware of our problems.

At the hotel, we were ushered ceremoniously to Mrs. Mesta's suite. To my chagrin, the guest's room was not yet ready.

"Just put her down in my bedroom for a while," Perle said. "She will be all right."

Now I rushed home, with curtain time just a few hours away, to give last-minute attention to hair, fingernails, and general grooming. Elliott was sitting in the living room talking calmly with our guests from Lakeland, Martha Prosser and her friend Corinne Sykorus, who had volunteered to help with last-minute details. They had had the benefit of a beautician and now appeared cool and glamorous. I looked like Houdini's assistant.

The only VIP guest unaccounted for during the afternoon had been Bob Hope. Unknown to me, he had sneaked into town the night before to get in a game of golf. I still had a volunteer hostess at the airport waiting for him. Through the grapevine at the Fontainebleau, I finally learned that he had arrived. During the reception before the show, I called his room. Hope answered. I said we were waiting for him at the reception. "Patty," he replied, "I'll be down in a little while—I'm having dinner."

"But . . . but you're supposed to draw the prizes."

"Listen, my girl, you're just wasting me if you want me to come down now. I'm more effective later, to hold your audience."

I flagged Elliott, and he took the phone. Hope convinced him. Elliott announced that he would just have to take over the comedian's chores. Then we realized that Bob Hope had the only list of dignitaries to be introduced and prizes to be drawn. Later, I discovered what had delayed the master of ceremonies' arrival. He was having dinner with one of the showgirls due to appear in the first act. The curtain, in fact, was delayed twenty-five minutes for her arrival. We bumped heads in a doorway, and she said, "Patty, I hope we haven't kept you waiting. Bob and I were having dinner in his suite." Just before the opening curtain, Hope appeared at our table. "Hi, Patty, good to see you," he beamed. But the greeting, at this stage, did not give me much solace.

Several weeks before the *Capers*, a local socialite had cut me down with a terse comment: "A politician's wife will never be a successful social leader." At the time I tossed it off, but now it stuck in my craw. It occurred to me that the lady had a lot of cheek. Despite our chilly relations, she bought a $500 table and arrived in full social glory, attended by a retinue. I took one look and my brow darkened. "I hope one of the horses makes a mess at her table," I muttered.

Elliott hadn't caught the remark. "What's that, dear?"

"Oh, nothing, darling, nothing at all."

A highlight of the show was the arrival of the horses as door prizes. They were to be walked up the aisle and onstage, there to be presented to the lucky winner. Ben Novack, chewing up plastic-tipped cigars like a maniac, had insisted we take out an insurance policy on his carpets. Then to double the protection, the hotel staff rolled out a long red canvas runner, all the way to the stage.

I had not foreseen, of course, that the animals would have a problem. The filly was in season, and the colt was, naturally, quite inquisitive. To avoid causing undue excitement, grooms insisted on hosing down the elevator after the filly had been brought up to the level of the main ballroom. This helped calm the colt somewhat. But, as luck would have it, the colt suffered a call of nature as he approached the stage. Ironically, he left his mark directly in front of the table occupied by my socialite critic. Now, Ben Novack's advance preparations paid off. When the horses had been led away again, workmen quickly rolled up the red runner, and the result of the accident.

Bob Hope, who had watched the episode from the stage with a half-smile, quipped to the crowd: "Don't worry, folks, you'll have this for breakfast, on toast."

Then he introduced himself as a Patty Roosevelt recruit. "When she wants you to do something," he said, "you move. Patty's telephone calls kept my switchboard so jammed up that last week I was placing my long-distance calls through Elliott's office."

As fate would have it, the Evinrude ski boat was won by Mrs. Bruce Knight, part owner of Atwater Scott Outboard Motor Company. She later donated it to the Humane Society for their benefit ball. The year's supply of orange juice did not materialize. The man who won it actually received a bushel of oranges, with the stipulation that he squeeze his own.

Counting the money, I found that we had about $70,000 for the March of Dimes, certainly not the least respectable sum ever raised but still short of my $100,000 goal. However, I wasn't through yet. For weeks now, even in the midst of all this turmoil, I had nursed the idea of a spectacular golf match, pitting two of the greatest crowd drawers on the American links, Jackie Gleason and Bob Hope.

There was a running grudge between the two. Hope had bested "The Great One" already in straight pool and a previous golf match four years before, for which Gleason had trained in a bar. Since then, the 250-pound Jackie had taken up golf with the seriousness of a general at the Marne. Part of the reason for moving his entire entourage to Miami Beach as a permanent base for the Jackie Gleason television show was so that he could play golf all year round. To make the course even handier, he lived at the Doral Country Club and later built a $200,000 cottage looking out onto the main fairway of the Country Club of Miami, north of the city. At present, however, the grueling Doral was his home ground, a diabolical layout of several eighteen-hole courses designated by different colors. The architectural fiends who contrived Doral built into it thirteen lakes and one hundred eight traps. Gleason had taken so passionately to golf that it was not uncommon for him to play fifty-four holes in a day.

I envisaged the March of Dimes benefit match being played on the torturous "Blue Monster" course, dotted with traps, roughs and water hazards, before a large paying gallery and a national television audience. To make a foursome I would enlist a couple of top-rank professionals, such as Doug Sanders and Gentleman Jimmy Demaret. As a starting point, I tackled the national television networks which held contracts with the comedians. Gleason was tied up with CBS, Hope with NBC. By long-distance telephone, I began beating the bushes of those vast organizations for anybody who would lend a sympathetic ear. CBS officials said they would agree to allow Gleason to appear on the same televised golf match, but I would have to get NBC to release Hope. While I was on the phone to New York, Elliott was calling CBS President William Paley, vacationing in the Bahamas. He was told the real agreement would have to come from Gleason and Hope themselves. That was quickly scotched. An emissary of Gleason's put it to me straight: "Jackie says no. You know, he likes to have everything rehearsed; no ad lib." But "The Great One" would meet Hope in the benefit grudge match. Bob agreed with relish, and the first date was set.

The dates changed five times before I could finally nail it down for Tuesday, March 30. Now the business of promoting it began in earnest. Gleason's public relations man in Miami, Pete McGovern, threw himself into the job like a first-string tackle, arranging publicity pictures, interviews, whipping up the grudge angle to the match (this gave him no difficulty at all, in the light of Gleason's dead seriousness about the game). In California, Hope's publicity man, Frank Lieberman, gave me every co-operation. We talked so often we became long-distance buddies.

The hope of a national television exposure flickered until just four days prior to the match. Despite Gleason's rejection of the idea, I felt that he might be persuaded to change his mind. The absolute killer was the red tape and massive amount of preparation required to put on such a show live. With the national networks then definitely out of it, I began calling around among local television stations. Failing a live production, I wanted to get something on tape. Finally, I located a private filming unit from New York, Winik Films, who were then shooting the dog races in Palm Beach. Would they come down to Miami and tape the Gleason-Hope match in color? Richard Winik and his son agreed to bring their equipment and do the shooting, charging bare costs. The only labor available locally was nonunion, which gave me the jitters. I had an awful apprehension that someone would recognize our scab workmen doing a show on two of the biggest funnymen in the business and create a national furor. Luckily, it didn't happen; but then, all our shooting of the golf match was to be for naught. A year and a half later, it was still in the cans, never shown.

March in Miami is not always as bright and spanking as the travel brochures indicate. Interspersed among the sunny, halcyon days are occasional spells of cloudiness and chill bluster. As if to make up for all the worry and disappointment from my failure to get national television, the day turned out to be magnificent, with a soft warm breeze, a sky of dazzling blue and light puffs of cloud. The crowd began arriving early, and by tee-off time we had eight thousand, the majority of them shelling out five dollars a head to watch the play.

Gleason, whom the sharp-tongued Hope had nicknamed "Flab Galore," arrived aboard the Goodyear blimp, dressed in a pale blue golfing outfit. His opponent set the tone of the match right away, saying: "This is the first time I ever played a blimp." Hope's words had nothing to do with canvas and gas. Jackie let it be known he was ready. "I went to bed early, at five this morning, for this one."

The golf course resembled a stage set for *Ben-Hur*. The gallery of eight thousand consisted mainly of types down from Terre Haute whose interest in golf was fleeting at best, their attraction being primarily the entertainers. Sanders and Demaret faded into the crowd scene like spear carriers. Most people in the

to Hope and said, "Aren't we going to have a little side
the folks?"

e," said Hope, "whoever wins pays five thousand to the
of Dimes."

no, you don't," said "The Great One." "Whoever loses

hat kind of a bet is that? That's not a gentleman's bet."
eason fished out a coin, they flipped, and the side bet went
way.

rom the opening shots, it was evident this would be a hectic
for golf. As Gleason piled into his golf cart and the others
off, the crowd surged down the fairway like a cavalry charge.
om then on, it was more of a free-for-all than a golf match.
Each time Hope would drive, Gleason gave a signal and a
uple of men would go after Hope's ball, ostensibly to mark its
ocation but really to give it an extra kick to a bad lie, or into
trap. Strafaci, the referee, always happened to be looking the
other way, or tying his shoe, or blowing his nose.

"Here, make 'em stop that," Hope shouted, laughing.

On the eighth hole, his shot dunked into the water.

The gallery, meanwhile, was making a shambles of the course,
trudging through the traps and digging high heels into the green.
Behind us, the beautiful Doral course was ready for planting
corn. At the ninth hole, Gleason drove his four carts directly
onto the green, a glaring breach of etiquette, and parked them
as Hope was about to make a chip shot. The ball dropped squarely
into the policeman's cart. Gleason's private cop calmly picked
it up and tossed it into a nearby trap.

"Hey, Strafaci," bellowed Hope, "what are you gonna do
about that?"

"Well," the referee said, "Mr. Gleason, I suppose you're just
going to have to get those carts off the green."

At the fifteenth hole, Gleason was four strokes up on Hope.
Referee Strafaci began waving his arms. "The match is over," he
announced. "The match is over."

"What do you mean, the match is over?" Hope said. "We've
still got four more holes to play."

"Yeah, but the boss is four up. You can't possibly catch up.
The boss says the match is over."

gallery, moreover, had little conception o
ing golf close-up. To make matters wors
force of eighty private security guards
Guard Service, in blue uniforms and wh
even less. Some of the security men were
viously wouldn't make it around eighteen h
steam. Looming over the scene as Gleason
the first tee was a huge crane donated by
Light Company, from which the Winik Film
overhead TV shots. The crane, trailing tenta
cable, loomed like some science-fiction monster.

"Boy, I hope the chef has lots of spaghetti tod
"to go with this big meatball when I send him

Gleason came equipped with a train of four ge
was to bear himself and his favorite blond compa
Merrell, another his golf clubs and several bottles of
in an electric refrigerator, still another the referee, Fra
and another a policeman-bodyguard-handyman. Glea
sonal golf cart was equipped with a mobile telephone
rangement reminded me of "20 Mule Team." Hope
cided to make the round on foot, trailed by his cart.
professionals also walked.

In the Pro Shop, I engaged in a head-to-head argumen
Frank Strafaci, the golf teacher at Doral who was also goi
serve as referee for the match. Strafaci, who was not a pro,
Gleason's regular golfing partner, and was unknown to He
Although this was to be a regular PGA-sanctioned match, Straf
and Gleason had barred PGA referees from the course. I w
angry about this and, also, at Strafaci's order that only the
players would be allowed to have golf carts. After making all
these arrangements, Elliott and I would have to walk. Unable to
budge Strafaci, I stormed to Alfred Kaskel, owner of the Doral
Club. He put up his hands. "Strafaci is running the show. I
don't know anything about it."

"Listen, Mr. Kaskel, he is not running the March of Dimes.
And I've got sore feet."

Mr. Kaskel was most understanding and graciously allowed
Elliott and me to have a cart.

As the players prepared to make their first drive, Gleason

Professionals Sanders and Demaret looked on in mild dismay. The crowd roared. Gleason loaded up his clubs, whistled for Honey, and raced for the clubhouse and a drink. The other three played out the remaining holes and arrived at the clubhouse to be greeted by "The Great One," freshly showered and shaven and waiting to receive his trophy.

"Let's go fill up the trophy with champagne and drink it," he said.

"It was a great victory for straight living and non-drinking," Hope observed. "I'd like to play the rubber match with him in California without Frank Strafaci as referee."

Gleason said he was looking forward to playing a match with Toots Shor, the 275-pound New York restaurateur. Quipped Hope: "If those two get on the same golf course, you wouldn't see anything but shadows."

Los Angeles *Times* columnist Jim Murray later summed it up with the comment, "It was hardly golf's finest hour."

The grudge match netted $33,000 for the March of Dimes, putting us over $100,000. I went home ecstatic. It was the biggest single haul the local chapter of the National Foundation had ever made.

But I was soon to pay dearly for putting myself through such punishment.

24

Where, Oh, Where Did My Roosevelt Go?

It was Mother's Day. Morning streamed into the marbled halls of Miami Beach's Fontainebleau Hotel. Long tables were arrayed with Danish pastries, coffee, and little cups. A finger of sunlight touched the life-size portrait of Eleanor Roosevelt resting on an easel behind the lectern from which Elliott was to speak.

This was to be a free Continental breakfast for the public, kicking off the campaign of Elliott Roosevelt for mayor of Miami Beach. Unfortunately, we had made the mistake of announcing it in advance in the newspapers. Elliott, who had a speech to make earlier in the Morton Towers apartment complex, was running late. The hungry constituents were early. By 9:30 A.M., half an hour before time for breakfast and the kick-off ceremonies, the place was jammed.

Hands, most of them old and gnarled, snatched at the Danish rolls, which vanished into pockets, purses, and paper shopping bags. The crowd pushed and clamored, raising a loud hubbub. Helpless waiters stood by in red jackets, appalled. The crowd obviously had come not only from Miami Beach, but from Miami, Hialeah, and as far away as Perrine. By the time Elliott arrived, even the little paper sacks of sugar had vanished, the tables were clean and the voters were angry.

"Where's our breakfast?" they shouted. "You promised us food. Where is our food?"

Elliott mounted the stage, smiling, hands up as if to pronounce a benediction, the grin reminiscent of his father.

"Where's our food? Where's our food?"

"Ladies and gentlemen, I'm sorry if you have been caused this inconvenience," the candidate said. "I'm going to make a few remarks here and when I'm finished I want you all to go down to the coffee shop and have breakfast as Elliott Roosevelt's guests. Just sign my name."

They burst into applause and cheers. My mouth dropped open and a spasm caught me in the pit of the stomach. This was ridiculous.

As in a modern parable of the loaves and fishes, the hungry multitude descended upon the Fontainebleau coffee shop and gorged themselves.

The bill came to $3000, which we did not have.

"This," I told myself, "is going to be a long, hard campaign."

Politically, socially, and economically there is no place on earth quite like Miami Beach. It is the bagel and stone crab capital of the world.

More expensive skin is baked on its beaches than anywhere in America. From a year-round population of 70,000 it mushrooms in winter to nearly 200,000 on any given day from New Year's to April 1. An estimated four million tourists pour in and out of Metropolitan Dade County annually, and practically all of them at least drive through Miami Beach. This is a city of swank resort homes and hotel bedrooms, some of the flashiest women and most light-fingered jewel thieves in the business. At the peak of the winter tourist season, even the very poor can put on a jacket, sit in the lobby of one of the plush hotels and think rich. Top names of show business, the arts, government, science, and high finance warm their bones on its golden sands. On a given night you can take in a show by Eddie Fisher; watch Jayne Mansfield create traffic jams on Collins Avenue; see the antics of my favorite "Schnozz," Jimmy Durante; swing to Eartha Kitt, Steve Lawrence, and Guy Lombardo. For the people who reside here all the time it is like living on a carnival midway where the lights never go out. The town abounds with stores and shops and stock brokerage offices and bars. There is a city ordinance against burlesque, so the girlie shows are called "burlesk." Big spenders float in on their yachts, and a shadowy segment of the business community makes a very good living keeping little black books listing available $100-a-day girls. In a single city you can find the best of everything and perhaps a little of the worst. But it is one of the most exciting places to live and work.

If Miami Beach is anything, it is contrast. North of its beltline, Lincoln Road, you find favorite haunts of the rich and well-born, where one dresses for dinner and people play golf and enunciate well. South of Lincoln Road is the large and not quite definable area known as South Beach, where thousands of old folks live in inhospitable little hotel rooms with white walls, cold floors and a hot plate. This area is ninety-eight percent Jewish, and nearly half its people are foreign born. Many of them slaved a lifetime to make their children's lives better; and after they had created doctors and lawyers, were put out to spend what remained of their years in sunshine and loneliness. A great many have property and wealth, but cling to deeply ingrained habits of thrift and self-denial, looking forward each month to the next Social Security check.

Ironically, Miami Beach, city of glamour and sunshine, has an abundance of these elderly. Its average year-round citizen is fifty-six years old. Even more ironic, the city does not have a single cemetery.

The great preponderance of foreign-born citizens and idle retired people has helped to create a political phenomenon in this city hugging the sea: an unusually keen interest in local government. City Council sessions on the eighth floor of the City Hall are invariably crowded, and on especially volatile agendas, filled to overflowing. There were frequent disputes between councilman and councilman, councilmen and the public, and the spectators themselves. Fist fights have erupted in the council chambers; people hurled sandwiches and bits of kosher pickle. On occasion, the police had to be called in to restore order.

Administratively, the city operated in the same manner as it had for fifty years. The founding father of municipal government in Miami Beach had been its original city manager, Claude Renshaw. His methods and policies were perpetuated, even though the Beach itself had grown from a bleak and sparsely settled sandspit, inhabited by rattlesnakes and a few developers, with more gumption than common sense, into a modern metropolis. In many ways, Miami Beach was out of step with modern times. Its water and sewer lines had not been improved since their original installation by the first pioneers. The fire department operated equipment dating back to 1927. Many other pieces of machinery cost more to keep operating than to replace. No up-to-date city planning existed, and relations with the modern-oriented Dade County—which in 1957 had launched the first metropolitan form of government in the nation—had deteriorated to the point where co-ordination was practically non-existent.

From a political standpoint, too, this town was colorfully unique. Traditionally the seven-man council was overwhelmingly Jewish. As a concession to the non-Jewish minority of the population the voters re-elected, year after year, the gentile D. Lee Powell, a tall, dignified-appearing man whose image had endured. When he spoke, Powell reminded everyone that he had long been influential in city affairs.

Frequently, while meetings were in progress, councilmen would send out to the delicatessen for corned beef sandwiches on rye and eat them while conducting the city's business. The chamber would fill with luscious odors, while the audience drooled.

The mayor was more of a figurehead than chief executive. His election had always been a popularity contest, with the title going to the councilman who received the highest number of votes. But now, a change was in the making. For the first time, candidates for mayor would have to run for specific office. It was a foregone conclusion that the man now holding the job, a lawyer named Melvin Richard, would have the inside track.

But that was before a Roosevelt entered the picture.

In mid-February 1965, three months before the election, Elliott was invited to a morning meeting in the office of Joseph Weintraub, Board Chairman of American Title and Insurance Company, which was the majority stockholder of the Mercantile National Bank of Miami Beach. Also present were Louis E. Wolfson and Max Orovitz, financiers and investors with combined worth in the hundreds of millions. All three men were powers in the community. They asked if he was interested in running for mayor of Miami Beach.

A group of about seven respected men were interested in finding the best possible candidate to run for mayor and the three expiring councilmen terms. Each was pledged to put up $3000, providing a total fund of about $21,000 for the campaign.

Wolfson was the spokesman. Tall, tanned, with close-cropped hair graying at the temples, he considered himself a handsome fashion plate. Known in financial circles as the "Great Rider," he once tried to wrest control of Montgomery Ward, and did gain control of several other corporations, including the nation-wide Merritt Chapman & Scott Construction Company. The others did more listening than talking. Orovitz was short, bland, and noncommittal, his financial activities including a prominent role in the General Development Corporation, and association with Lou Chesler, the Canadian financier who had been involved initially in the fabulous Lucayan development on Grand Bahama Island. Weintraub was baldish, tall, hawk-nosed, and suave, and a man of considerable banking acumen.

Wolfson showed Elliott a telegram from his brother Jimmy. At the time, Jimmy was running for mayor of Los Angeles and was a congressman from California. The message said that Jimmy would advise Elliott to heed the counsel of Wolfson and his friends, if he chose to run for mayor of Miami Beach. Jimmy added that Elliott was "a nice boy" and would do a good job if they chose to support him. Wolfson informed Elliott that he had also talked with Franklin, Jr., by telephone. Franklin had promised to get in touch with Elliott and ask him to be guided by Wolfson.

Talk shifted to Elliott's personal life and habits. "I've heard rumors," Wolfson said, "that you are a playboy and sometimes unstable." Elliott replied that if that was what Wolfson had heard, he was grossly maligned. "I'd stake my abilities and way of life against any of you in this room." The answer seemed to satisfy them. Two of these men so concerned with Elliott's personal life, Orovitz and Wolfson, were subsequently indicted by the federal government on charges of taking part in improper stock transactions. The questions shifted to personal finances. Could he afford to be mayor if he won? Elliott gave them a detailed report of his business affairs, pointing out that in the brief time he had been in Miami Beach, he was already grossing $40,000 a year above expenses.

"Inasmuch as the mayor's job pays only $3000 a year," Elliott said, "I hope you three gentlemen will steer non-conflicting business my way so I can hire more people to handle the extra load." They all nodded briskly.

Elliott left Weintraub's office assured that in a few days an account would be opened in his name at Mercantile National Bank, and that any additional funds for the campaign would be provided without trouble.

We should have known better than to hope for this.

On February 26, Elliott called a press conference at our home and announced his candidacy for mayor with a three-hundred-word statement. "The future and economics of Miami Beach," he said, "are in our hands. We must realize our potential . . . There is no place in America to compare with our city, our climate, our people." He rejected the old "carpetbagger" label, saying "I'm as good a Miami Beach citizen as anyone else," and pledged to work for federal funds to help develop the city, and to oppose legalized gambling.

The announcement was a blockbuster. It brought an immediate backlash from Melvin Richard, who made it plain that he intended to wage an aggressive campaign for re-election. "Roosevelt is a newcomer here," he preached. "He will have to stand up and be counted, and demonstrate to the people his qualifications and background. I am prepared to match my background against him."

With that, Richard trotted out the lengthy summary of his perspiring past that was to become his stock speech as the fight grew bitter in weeks to come: "My father was not the President of the United States, but has been a fine, respected resident of Miami Beach since 1924. I was not the son of rich parents. I wanted a college education and earned my way through school." During the summers, Richard boasted, he dug ditches to lay city water pipes at thirty-five cents an hour, "and a lot of those pipes are still there." As a councilman in 1951, he had taken a leading part in bringing the Kefauver investigating committee to Miami Beach, to help rid the city of syndicated gamblers and racketeers. He called himself a "seven-day, all-hours mayor," and took the first of many digs at Elliott's domestic life. "I have been married to the same woman for twenty-four years."

It soon became evident to Elliott that again, as in the national committeeman race, a considerable amount of his previously pledged support would not be available once the campaign started. After making his announcement, he called one supporter's office for a month and was able to speak to him only once or twice. "I'm having trouble reaching everybody in town," that man stammered. "Don't worry. The money will be coming . . ." Then, as time went on, the man—as had been the case a year ago—was always "out" when Elliott called. Finally, he went once more to two former angels. Again both indicated they would be glad to help, and provided the same list of names they had before. We had another reception with the same despairing lack of success. By now, I was getting tired of having a freezer full of leftover hors d'oeuvres.

During his term as mayor, however, Melvin Richard had made a bitter and implacable political enemy in the person of Bill Segal, a Miami Beach taxicab magnate who also ran a nationwide auto leasing business. Under a city franchise, Segal had established a commercial tram service on Miami Beach's famous Lincoln Road Mall to cart shoppers along the picturesque commercial route. Richard had accused Segal of making big profits on the trams and tried to hike the city's share of the revenue, or force Segal out. Now, the still-smoldering businessman came to Elliott with an offer of support. "I am not necessarily backing you, Elliott," Bill Segal said, "but I will do anything to defeat Richard." As a starter, he provided Elliott with the services of his contracted public relations man, Stuart Newman of Miami, to get the campaign launched.

Other support also began to take shape. Elliott's chances were highly regarded, since he had polled eighty-six percent of the Miami Beach vote in his smashing victory as national committeeman. Another member of the Miami Beach Council, attorney Malvin Englander, also had intended to make the race for mayor. He now withdrew and threw his support behind Elliott. News of Elliott's running for mayor flashed across the country.

The telephone rang constantly. One call was from Jimmy in Los Angeles. "What are you doing, Beano?" he laughed. "Don't you know I'm running for mayor of Los Angeles? There can't be *two* Roosevelts running for mayor." Next came Franklin, Jr., on the phone from his farm in Dutchess County, New York. Franklin had his eye on possibly challenging John Lindsay for Mayor of New York. "What are you going, Ellio?" he said. "Don't you know Jimmy's running for mayor of Los Angeles, and I'm considering running for mayor of New York City. There can't be *three* Roosevelts running for mayor. Besides, you don't know anything about politics. You could ruin our reputation." Elliott took his brothers' jibes seriously. Later, when Jimmy was overwhelmingly defeated for mayor of Los Angeles by the incumbent Sam Yorty, Jimmy offered to ship us all his old "Roosevelt for Mayor" campaign literature. Franklin, meanwhile, quietly backed off from his mayor ambitions and set his sights instead on the New York gubernatorial nomination.

Two nights before Elliott was to file in April, I was stricken with a pain in the chest and collapsed at a dinner in the Fontainebleau Hotel. Dr. Ralph Robbins, the hotel physician, sent me to St. Francis Hospital where I was soon resting comfortably. It was a mild heart condition but not considered serious. The real attack was to come nine months later. I was still in bed, however, when Elliott filed his qualifying papers.

For the politician seeking public office, and the publicity it requires, just about any and all forums will serve. So, one day Elliott found himself sitting in on a panel discussion of, of all things, men's cosmetics. Declared *Esquire* magazine vice-president Sam Ferber to a large audience of men and women: "The sophisticated man cannot live by soap alone." Elliott, who never felt it necessary to use a deodorant, winced. The crowd was also treated to the information that Napoleon used fifty-four bottles of cologne a month. Asked to comment on whether or not politicians should use make-up for television appearances, Elliott replied they should, but only to make less obvious such problems as a shiny, bald head. "You're cheating the audience if you don't show exactly how you look."

Despite Bill Segal's help, the campaign was slow to start. Our headquarters, in the same building as Elliott's management consultant business, was manned by only two volunteers, Henry Abrahams and Moe Hyman. Very little was getting done because of poor communications between us and the public relations man, Newman. Things picked up, however, one day, when Constable Leonard Weinstein of Miami Beach walked in bringing Beverlye Keusch, a red-haired, dynamic, aggressive public relations woman and promoter who was to make the difference between a lackluster campaign and a vigorous drive. After a brief conversation, we gratefully accepted assistance, not only to co-ordinate the entire campaign, but also to help us raise funds. Another interesting newcomer to our forces was Murray Goodman. He was a young, corpulent lawyer who had a wide circle of acquaintances on Miami Beach, especially among attorneys. Murray had formerly been closely associated with Ben Cohen, one-time political power in the city. In addition to the backing of Mal Englander, who was seeking re-election as councilman, Elliott also drew support from Councilman Powell and Robert Turchin, a builder.

The last day for filing was May 2. By that time, two more men—both unlikely candidates—had entered the race for mayor: Dr. Morris Zucker, a seventy-year-old retired dentist, student of philosophy and author of a two-volume American political history, and Fred T. (Fox Hunter) Hunt, Sr., sixty-one, who defies adequate description. Lean, peppery, and individualistic, Hunt was a City Hall hanger-on who usually sported a floppy, wide-brimmed straw hat and wore a tomato sauce label as his name tag. Hunt vowed that if elected he would be a full-time mayor. This would not have been terribly difficult, since he already spent most of his time in the City Hall, sitting on a bench by the elevators buttonholing passersby. Once he took up squatters' rights by moving three grocery carts into an outside trash shed. In his offbeat political career "Fox Hunter" Fred had compiled a record of sorts for unsuccessful campaigns. He had run at various times for county commissioner, Miami city commissioner, Miami Beach city commissioner, sheriff and judge, and lost them all. Hunt also had a gift for making up catchy slogans, such as "Some people are fighters. Some are lovers. I'm both.", and "Four of a kind: FDR, JFK, LBJ, and FTH."

Richard had been a member of the council for fourteen years

and just completed a two-year term as mayor. He had strong and entrenched support. Both the Miami *Herald* and the Miami Beach *Sun*, owned by executives of the *Herald*, backed him. The Miami *News* remained uncommitted to either candidate. The weekly Miami Beach *Reporter* also hung on the fence, with editor Paul Bruun editorializing that he would go to bed Election Eve not knowing how he would vote, but hoping for divine guidance when he went to the polls. The weekly Miami Beach *Times* supported Elliott, but mostly because they hated Richard. Before the campaign was very old, it was evident, too, that we would buck such so-called influential people as City Attorney Joe Wanick and Police Chief Rocky Pomerance, whose father-in-law, Al Nason, was a big gun in Richard's campaign. In the closing days of the campaign, even our early supporters Henry Abrahams and Moe Hyman would switch to the Richard camp.

By May 11, tempers were running hot. At a meeting of the Biscayne Democratic Club, noisy supporters of councilman candidate Bernie Frank jumped up, shouting, "Lift the garbage can lid off City Hall!" I watched a retired apartment house owner toss a fist at candidate Paul Seiderman, who ducked. Next day, the antagonist insisted he did not even lift his hands. "Besides," he added, "I've got a weak heart."

In his hysterical attack on the prevailing county government, Richard went so far as to join a movement to try to split off Miami Beach into a separate county, helping to engineer a bill in the State Legislature then meeting in Tallahassee. Elliott refused to agree or disagree with the separate county concept, but cautioned against bulldozing into it before a thorough study of the consequences could be made. "These men are not doing this just to create a separate county," he warned. "They're doing this to create a smoke screen. We could be cremated."

In a city so heavily populated by senior citizens, who controlled about forty percent of the vote, such issues as Medicare and Social Security loomed large in the scheme of things. Elliott's first concerted support in this quarter came from the Florida Senior Citizens League of Voters. In its bulletin, titled *Shalom*, the group urged members to work for Roosevelt because he would bring "honor, dignity, and recognition to this magic city."

By mid-May, vicious, mud-slinging aspects of the campaign

began rising to the surface. Richard challenged Elliott to a debate. Elliott replied he would be glad to debate the issues, but feared that his opponent would turn it into a name-calling contest. Elliott recalled an incident when a columnist had made vituperative remarks about Eleanor Roosevelt, who wanted to make a reply. Franklin D. Roosevelt told her: "You're not equipped to get into a fight with a skunk any more than you are to get into a fight with that gentleman. He just wants to draw you into a name-calling battle."

To this stab, Richard replied acidly: "I would not reduce myself to that level. I never talk about my opponent. I didn't even mention that I saw Roosevelt sober today . . . He won't appear with me because he says I'll reduce it to a name-calling contest, then he proceeded to call me a skunk."

At a noisy meeting of two hundred people, members of the Progressive Democratic Club, "Fox Hunter" Hunt—who insisted now that he knew in advance that he would be elected mayor through extrasensory perception—triggered an uproar. "Unlike Elliott Roosevelt," he declared, "I don't have to hide behind the skirts of my mother and father. I fear no man who walks the face of this earth."

"Throw the bum out!" cried an ardent Roosevelt supporter. Nearby, an elderly woman shook her head and observed, "Before this election is over, there's going to be some blood."

Her words were prophetic, but the blood was not to belong to either of the candidates. It would be spilled by my errant and defiant nephew Harpur Evoy, tangling with a couple of Miami Beach policemen.

From the very start of the campaign, Harpur had thrown himself into the work of getting his uncle elected with a feverish intensity. When there was someone needed to drive, or a mimeograph machine to operate, or an errand to be run, Harpur was at our beck and call. His progress as a human being, since Atlantic City, had been astonishing, and Elliott was filled with pride for his nephew. "Harpur," he had said, "I know now that you won't disappoint me further." To complete his high school education he enrolled in the Lindsey Hopkins adult education center in Miami. He was nineteen years old, stood six feet, three inches tall, and was trying very hard to please everyone.

Elliott felt that the only way Harpur could get into college was on an athletic scholarship. He had prevailed upon the boy to give up smoking. Harpur had thrown away the pack and vowed, "I'll never smoke another cigarette." He dressed well, spoke in a gentlemanly fashion and worked hard. A visit by his mother and grandmother from Seattle put a strain on him, but he seemed to be weathering it well—until the night of the party.

Harpur's best friend in Miami was Billy Guim. The boys had been invited to a party a group of Cuban refugees were giving in Hialeah. They took one of our cars, with Elliott's registration in the glove compartment, and went off for four hours of whoopee. The drink was rum. Harpur could take this as well as anything, and it made him bold and fierce. After the party, instead of coming home the two went out on the town. Billy finally had had enough. "Harpur," he said, "let's go home." Harpur told him to go jump in the creek, blew into Elliott's white Lincoln and headed for South Beach.

At four o'clock in the morning, a policeman arrested him on Washington Avenue. Ordering him out, he made him stand spread-legged with both hands against the car, frisked him and announced: "I'm taking you to jail."

"You and who else?" Harpur growled. "Where you going to get ten men in a hurry?" He swung, caught the officer off balance and knocked him down. The officer already had radioed for help. Three other cruisers poured onto Washington Avenue, and the police overwhelmed Harpur, snapped him into handcuffs and tossed him into the back of a car. He struggled all the way to the jail. At five o'clock, we received a call from a polite police officer. "Mr. Roosevelt," he said, "we have a boy down here who says he is your nephew."

"Oh, no!" I said. "No, no, no."

To avoid rousing Harpur's mother and grandmother, we crept out of the house, called an attorney and we went to recover Harpur. Shortly after eight o'clock, he walked out of the city jail. "Don't look at me, Aunt Patty," he mumbled. "I'm not worth it." He turned to his uncle a face agonized with guilt. "I'm sorry, sir," he said. "I'm really sorry."

Elliott did not scold Harpur. He smiled and said easily, "I'm glad we could help."

Harpur looked surprised. Then he smiled at his uncle. I knew from that smile that we would never have to worry about this boy again.

Within a year, he was enrolled in Bellevue Junior College, Seattle, and working part-time as an attendant in the King County Morgue. By his twenty-first birthday, my favorite nephew was well on his way to realizing his potential as an outstanding young man. But his sense of humor remained undimmed. He wrote me a letter, saying: "Aunt Patty, I'll send you a package of fried eyeballs."

Despite the lack of support from big business, big newspapers, hotel operators and, ironically, the non-Jewish element of Miami Beach, we felt that we had a chance, going into the home stretch. An unexpected blunder by Richard which brought the involvement of columnist Drew Pearson in the campaign gave us even more reason to be optimistic.

On May 8, we were invited to the Kentucky Derby in Louisville, as guests of Governor Edward Breathitt and breeder Leslie Coombs. Joining us in the box at the derby was Drew Pearson, who asked casually: "How's Mel Richard doing in the mayor's race?"

"Gosh, Drew, I wish you could write something to help us."

He shook his head, saying it was a local election and he could not get involved. "I don't know much about it. But I'll tell you what I do know. Richard wrote me a letter not long ago on the mayor's stationery, asking for all the information I might have about Elliott Roosevelt, his family, military background, and marital activities. I wrote back and told him he had best leave this alone."

When we returned to Miami Beach, Drew sent me a copy of the letter. Signed *Melvin Richard*, it read: *Dear Drew, When I saw you in Jacksonville I gave you a bronze key to the city, but promised to forward a "gold" one from Miami Beach. I am enclosing the key. You may have heard that Elliott Roosevelt, after living here less than two years, has announced that he will be a candidate for Mayor of Miami Beach against me. I understand that he has had a rather interesting career in military service, in civic and charitable endeavors, in matrimonial ventures, in numerous business activities and in education. I am very anxious, as soon as possible, to gather as much of this information as I can acquire. I would appreciate any help or suggestions you may have in that connection.*

Pearson decided he would make known Richard's efforts after all. In a radio broadcast from Washington, May 23, aired in Miami Beach over Station WIOD, the commentator observed: "The campaign against Elliott Roosevelt, to become mayor of Miami Beach, is getting more and more bitter. Mayor Melvin Richard, who does not want to lose his job, is even maligning Elliott's wife, and indirectly, his late father and mother. He says, 'Some people think they were great Americans. Let them think so.' The interesting fact is that when the Chicago underworld assassin Zangara shot at President-elect Roosevelt and killed Mayor Cermak of Chicago, in Miami, 1933, it was Melvin Richard who wrote an editorial in the University of Florida *Alligator,* urging kindly treatment for Zangara. Today, the same Melvin Richard, who went to bat for the man who almost assassinated Franklin Roosevelt, is trying politically to assassinate his son . . ." In his column, Pearson also took Richard to task (this column, incidentally, was not run by the Miami *Herald,* in which Pearson regularly appears). "Richard is using plenty of invective against Roosevelt," he wrote, "his many marriages (five), his present wife, and even the Roosevelt family." He advised that Melvin didn't know what he was up against in Patty Roosevelt.

Richard's wife, Janet, meanwhile, stepped none too daintily into the affray. In a newspaper interview, she said that Elliott Roosevelt "shows inability, in the number of marriages, in the cities he's lived in, in the number of business failures. People are entitled to know something about a man who came here two years ago and is riding on his mother and father."

With no money for printing, I rented a mimeograph machine from an office supply company. While Elliott dictated, I took down his information in longhand, then we typed up a stencil and ran off a series of pamphlets entitled: "Elliott Roosevelt says, I Believe . . ." They gave a rundown on his platform for building an attractive, well-rounded city by securing clean industry, more business, rejuvenate its residential areas, develop special research hospital facilities and an institution of higher learning; he outlined a program for senior citizens, and called for better law enforcement to reduce the rapidly climbing burglary rate.

Although the Jewish people of the Beach were strongly pro-Roosevelt—and, ironically, Richard was Jewish and Elliott was not—I felt that we were weak among the gentiles. One important stronghold of the non-Jewish vote was LaGorce Country Club. There, a caddy was fired for wearing a ROOSEVELT FOR MAYOR button on his cap. I walked in one day to find our old GOP friend, Jim Dickey, and his wife Jeanne, talking with an elderly man who was slightly hard of hearing. His name was Bill Morse, and he was a die-hard Republican. Jim Dickey opened our talk by asking how Elliott's campaign was coming along.

"It's a tough fight, Jim," I said. "Gosh, Mr. Morse, wouldn't you like to vote for Elliott Roosevelt?"

"Don't say another word, young lady," came the crusty reply. "If a Roosevelt was running for dog catcher, I'd come out against him."

"Please, Mr. Morse, Elliott will make a good mayor for our city."

"A Roosevelt couldn't be good at anything."

I stood my ground, arguing vehemently. He argued back. But there was a twinkle in both our eyes. Finally, he said, "Well, not all Roosevelts have wives like you."

After that, Bill Morse not only got up a huddle of friends at LaGorce to help back Elliott, he became a fast friend of ours. "This is the first time in my life I ever voted for a Democrat," he said, "and I'm eighty-nine years old."

May is the beginning of the hot season on Miami Beach. One sweltering night, with the two leading candidates taking turns on the same platform, it was unbearable. More than five hundred people gathered in the Sea Island Hotel. Always, when we saw Richard, he carried a legal-size note pad and spent most of his time furiously taking notes. To harass him, I not only began taking notes too, but also bought a tiny Minox camera, and would stand up in the audience in the middle of his speeches snapping pictures. The camera made a loud snick! each time I cocked it. For all his note-taking, the speeches were the same.

Richard said Elliott wanted to start his politics from the top, as mayor, instead of working his way. "I want to tell you I worked my way through school digging ditches for water pipes in this city, and all the water pipes I put in never had to be replaced." Dr. Zucker, meanwhile, had served a lengthy "Bill of Particulars" on Richard, charging that he had used taxpayers' money to wage the drive for a separate county in the Legislature. Richard shot back that Zucker was being Elliott's hatchet man.

Richard also began a series of soap box speeches on Lincoln Road Mall, in the afternoons. One hot day, as he spoke to an unenthusiastic crowd of about forty people, I went through shaking hands and taking pictures with my little Minox. Richard was hammering away at Elliott: "He says he has a right to be mayor because his father was a great man." The hawk-faced mayor went on to say that he had "never made the statement that my opponent had five wives or that Mr. and Mrs. Roosevelt are unstable and drink too much." Richard said he had been accused of saying the Roosevelts were "confirmed alcoholics," but he had never made any such public statement. I grabbed the arm of a newsman. "I hate this," I said. "I feel sick."

Meanwhile, at nearby Pier Park in the pro-Roosevelt stronghold of South Beach, Elliott was attacking the City Council for having its head in the sand and not requesting federal funds. "I don't have to live in a city for forty years to know there is something wrong with Miami Beach."

On May 26, five days before the election, they collided at Pier Park before two thousand persons. By now, I could hardly stand the sight of Richard, and Elliott was saying I took the campaign too bitterly. Richard spoke of his two-year record as mayor, denied calling names and said he was a friend of the senior citizen. Elliott tore into City Council disunity, declaring: "During the last two years, this council has presented to the world the sight of bickering and arguing, and threats by the present mayor to have the police eject a member of the council." Blasting Richard's claims of prosperity, Elliott said there were more than two hundred vacant stores in town, ten hotels in receivership, and numerous apartment house owners were complaining they could not make ends meet. He proposed, with federal help, a redesign for the entire city. In answer to Richard's charge that he lacked experience, Elliott snapped: "I got training under a very good man, who had lots of government experience."

Radio talk shows enjoy tremendous listener popularity in Miami Beach. Few cities in the world have more open give-and-take before the microphones, and you can fairly well pick your politics and point of view by the emcee. Broadcaster Allen Courtney is the conservative and highly opinionated veteran of them all. He attracts a hard-core audience and telephone callers night after night. When the guest for a broadcast does not reflect his point of view, the listeners can be merciless. Courtney had had Richard on his show, early in the campaign. The two got along well together. Elliott had steadfastly refused invitations to go on the air with this announcer. Many years before, Courtney had been critical of Franklin and Eleanor Roosevelt. The second time Richard was a Courtney guest, the two made many sarcastic comments about the empty chair, reserved for Elliott. We were listening in our living room. At last, Elliott could stand it no longer. He dialed the station and got on the air with Courtney. The announcer did not recognize his voice. Part of their exchange went like this:

Courtney: "Who is this, my friend? Who are you?"

Elliott: "If you must know, this is Elliott Roosevelt."

After that, Elliott remained on the air, by telephone, for forty-five minutes, fielding questions from Courtney's listeners. When he finally hung up, Courtney signed off the air, stammering, "Good night, folks, hope you listen again tomorrow night. This is Elliott Courtney . . . I mean, Allen Courtney, signing off."

As the campaign neared its close, we were on the go from early morning until late at night, making as many as four and five public appearances between dusk and midnight.

Election Day dawned clear and sunny. We voted early, together, at our home precinct, a nearby American Legion post, then went to the Bayshore Municipal Golf Course to play a round. Both of us played well, despite being trailed constantly by a live TV camera crew. This upset the strange couple we were paired with for the round. Back at the clubhouse, I looked down at my left hand and exclaimed: "Oh, no." I had lost my wedding and engagement rings. "Eliott, this is a terrible omen."

The caddy hurried to the eighth hole, where he thought he might find them. There, half-buried in the sand, he saw something glimmer. The rings. When I slipped them back onto my finger, I said, "Now that's a good omen." During the day, I visited seventeen precincts, each two or three times.

At about 6 P.M., we went to our headquarters in the office building on Meridian Avenue. The polls closed at 7 P.M. One of the first reports was from our own precinct, Number 108. It went to Richard, 517 to 312. My heart sank. Elliott began thinking of a graceful concession speech. It was not long, however, before the trend took a decisive change. As the big senior citizens precincts came pouring in, Elliott took the lead and his margin kept growing and growing. By 8:15, the vote was 1172 for Elliott and 583 for Richard. The headquarters was becoming progressively more crowded as supporters, scenting a victory in the making, began to gather. Many of them were old folks, wearing jaunty little straw hats bearing a paper sign: TEENAGERS FOR ROOSEVELT. My friend Murray Candib had provided 2500 of the hats, and I circulated them among the senior citizens. The crowd grew until the headquarters was packed and stifling. We pushed our way out and went to the City Hall. By 8:30, it was apparent that we had won. I hugged Elliott and kissed him. The lobby of the City Hall and surrounding streets were a scene of pandemonium. Press, radio, and television men pushed in for interviews. Calls poured in from New York, Washington, and Chicago. When the final count came in, it was 10,002 votes for Elliott to Richard's 8601, the highest number of votes for a winning mayor ever recorded in the city.

Chanting, shouting, backslapping oldsters burst into their favorite campaign song, "Happy Days Are Here Again." It took you back, with a catch in the throat, to the days of 1933, and the "Great Depression," and FDR with his cocky grin and cigarette holder. Elliott flashed a grin and a "V" sign, and said he had won it on his own. "My brother lost an election," he told newsmen, "and he was also my father's son." Fifteen hundred wildly jubilant supporters chanted, "Roosevelt! Roosevelt! Roosevelt!"

At Richard's headquarters, a spare, low-budget office, the defeated candidate sat glumly punching an adding machine and sweating under hot TV lights. "He is going to get a surprise," Richard said tiredly. "He doesn't know what is involved."

The very next morning, Elliott did get a taste of what was involved, and let it be known bluntly that he intended to be his own man. Invited to breakfast at the home of a supporter, a big-shot former councilman, he also found several other people there. The host and a couple of the others started telling him he would have to make various new political appointments immediately and change police chiefs; then they went down the list telling him which department heads should be kept and which fired. Elliott glowered and clenched his fists. "Let's stop all this conversation," he said. "I don't want to listen to you, and I'm not going to commit myself. If you think I am going to act on any of your recommendations before examining the qualifications of those people, you're out of your minds."

Elliott was accused of turning his back on his friends, who declared they had put him into office, and could kick him out.

"If I weren't a guest here," Elliott roared, "I'd ask you to step outside."

That was the first and last time anybody tried to dictate to him.

25

"His Eminence"—The Mayor

We had won! It was a smashing victory. For days I could not breathe for sheer excitement. All the world was alive with jubilant people and handshakes and flowers and ringing telephones. Telephones. Our telephone never stopped. All day and late into the night it rang, bringing congratulations and flattery and invitations. People who had never bothered to speak to us before suddenly found new interest in Elliott Roosevelt and his wife and children. Doors swung open and hands extended. The considerable fringe of society that feasts upon power now appeared, to smile and ingratiate and smile, to fawn and seek favors for friends. Now, in triumph, Elliott's ear began filling with the unsought word of confidence, the whispered suggestion of favors for favors. This was the spoil and reward of politics, and why men drove themselves unmercifully to win political gain. In America, power and respect and prestige were there for the plucking, if you had the nerve and personality to reach. But it was appalling, too, especially to Elliott Roosevelt, who had seen politics in their grandest form played by the masters, and had built for himself an uncompromising set of ideals. Local American politics is not always pretty on the inside. It can be petty and mean and cheap. In Miami Beach there was much housecleaning to do. Elliott set out to devote as much of his time as possible as working mayor of the city. I resolved not to languish on the sidelines; I was going to be a working mayor's wife.

To make the transition from private citizens to public servants, we had extra phones installed in the house, converted the upstairs library into an office and stocked the pantry for extra dinner guests. Suddenly, at mealtime, it was not uncommon to have half a dozen unexpected guests, and on special occasions, a houseful. The quickened new pace of government was most pronounced in the mayor's office at City Hall. In past years official letterheads were ordered annually in batches of five hundred. Now, this much was consumed in a week. Another three thousand vanished before the month was out. The mayor's office filled with additional secretaries and whirring typewriters. Mail poured in from across the world. Elliott and I kept dictaphones humming answering each piece of correspondence.

My first intrusion into municipal affairs involved the keys to the city, and a brush with Miami Beach's long-time executive secretary to the mayors. For more than twenty years she had carried on much of the city's business as a kind of unofficial chief executive, handling the work of mayors who did not wish to be bothered with details. One day in the office she offered me a handful of gold-colored ceremonial keys and chains to take home to the children. "A dear friend of mine, who owns a jewelry store, made me a very good deal on the chains this year," she said. I asked her why we were buying so many that we had to get a special price. "Well, darling, it's customary for the mayor to present a gold key to each contestant in the Miss Universe pageant, and I thought it would be just marvelous if they were on gold chains," she trilled. "This year one hundred sixteen young ladies from all over the world are competing. I have just finished wrapping the last of the keys and chains for them." She pointed to a large carton beside her desk filled to overflowing with little packages done in sprightly bows and bright paper. Casually, I glanced at the keys in my hand. They were inscribed, *Melvin Richard, Mayor of Miami Beach*. I gasped. The secretary read the name on the keys and turned white. "Oh, no!" She made a rush order for another shipment. For twenty-four hours the office was awash with silver paper and perky bows, as she worked frantically to swap the Melvin Richard keys for

Elliott Roosevelt keys. And they all had to be restrung on the little gold chains.

The Miss Universe pageant has grown into one of the glamorous annual events of Miami Beach. Beauties selected from throughout the world compete in a grueling week of preliminaries at the huge Miami Beach Convention Hall. On the final night, before a live audience of ten thousand, and more than sixty million television viewers coast-to-coast, they promenade in smiles and white satin, beneath playing spotlights, for the diamond tiara and prize-laden title of Miss Universe. The night after her selection, the beauty queen reigns over her Coronation Ball, a glittering affair which draws top celebrities. The 1965 winner was Miss Thailand, Apasra Hongsakula, and her Coronation Ball was to be in the main ballroom of the Deauville Hotel. For Elliott, it would be one of his first official functions as mayor. The invitations were engraved in gold, on bright blue vellum, and in the lower left-hand corner were the instructions: *Black tie, formal.* This notation left me slightly confused. To my mind "black tie" indicated a dinner jacket for the man but cocktail dressed permissible for women, whereas "formal" meant white tie and tails, and full-length evening dresses.

Some time ago I had made Elliott a bow tie and cummerbund set of bright red silk. This evening he put them on with his midnight blue dinner jacket and cut a beautiful figure. I beamed with pride at having married a man who knew how to dress so well. Arm in arm we arrived at the Deauville Hotel lobby, where hundreds of spectators had queued up to watch all the superbly dressed guests arrive for the Coronation Ball. Smiling and nodding, Elliott strolled along exchanging greetings, as supporters cheered and reached across the ropes to touch his arm. The chorus of voices swelled. "Here's our mayor!" "Hi, Elliott, hi, Patty. You look great."

Cocktails were being served in an area outside the ballroom. As Elliott prepared to shoulder in and get us a drink, a hostess came fluttering over. "Elliott, dahling, you naughty boy, you. Don't ya'll know you're supposed to be in black tie? Ya'll have to go home and change, honey. You live close by, so it shouldn't take but a minute."

Elliott's face froze. Suddenly his fine red tie seemed to droop.

Without acknowledging what the hostess had said, he turned to me and said brusquely, "Come on, Patty, we're leaving." But now more hostesses were surrounding us, emitting little shrieks of horror at that red, red tie. "Mayor, dear, you'll have to go home and change to black tie!"

"I am going home," my husband snapped, "but I'm not coming back, with or without a tie."

By now, I was shaking my head to clear it. This was all unreal. My dander was rising. Imagine them having the gall to tell Elliott he was not dressed properly when they did not even know how to print an invitation.

A new face appeared on the scene. Our old friend, David Walters, the political influence-wielder, was chairman of the Coronation Ball. Benefits were going to the fight against leukemia. Walters reached for Elliott's tie, saying, "Aw come on, Elliott, be a sport." Then, as if on cue, an unsuccessful candidate for sheriff named Floyd Miner walked up carrying a clip-on black bow tie. Several hands reached for my husband's collar and he struck them down. "Get your hands off my tie!"

Spinning on his heel, Elliott stalked back toward the lobby with me trotting after him. Several spectators set up a clamor: "Leave our mayor alone." "Don't change your tie, Elliott." "Pat, don't let them take that beautiful tie." The situation finally struck my funny bone and I burst out laughing, grabbing Elliott's elbow for a private word.

"Darling, if we go home now we are only lowering ourselves to their level," I whispered. "Don't let them do this to you. I think we should stay here and have our dinner, then leave quietly, without fuss and fanfare."

Still glowering with rage, Elliott relented and went back to the main ballroom. Dinner, however, was a dismal affair and his fine red bow tie kept mocking me. Sharing our table were several other guests who were as shocked as we at the turn of events.

The following morning, the Miami *Herald* headlined the story: THE NIGHT ELLIOTT SAW RED. Wire services picked it up, and the incident flashed around the world. Deciding this was too much good publicity to miss out on, I formed a company to make bow ties and cummerbunds in exotic shades and patterns, named "Formally Yours, By Elliott Roosevelt." Informally, it is called the Fyber Corporation. Life with the mayor was so hectic, however, that, other than the initial programing and planning, I was forced to let it lie dormant for the time being.

The burden of the mayor's duties, however, would soon cut into Elliott's private business. Realizing this, I looked around for a competent person to help us in Elliott Roosevelt International. The most likely choice was Bobbie Leonard, a clever, tactful, and efficient woman with practical administrative sense who had worked many years for Hank Meyer, the Miami Beach publicist. Bobbie was widely known in Dade County. She was not employed now, however, and insisted that she intended to keep it that way. I pleaded with her. "Bobbie, Elliott and I need you. Please go to work for us." Finally, she agreed to become Elliott's assistant and girl Friday, and both she and her husband George soon became our good friends. We have imposed upon her unmercifully and yet her bright, cheerful nature shines through all the burdens.

It quickly became apparent, meanwhile, that if we were to carry on the role of mayor in proper style we would have to do a great deal of entertaining. As a warmup, I held a reception for members of the seven-man City Council and various department heads. Everyone attended but Mel Richard, who refused to acknowledge that he had been beaten and still regarded it as some terrible mistake. This was followed by a series of social functions at our home, which came off so easily that I was soon lulled into the notion that I could tackle just about anything. This almost proved to be my undoing.

One day Mrs. Sydney Raffel, a Miami Beach social leader, called inviting me to a luncheon in her home to entertain Takako Shimazu, Crown Princess of Japan, who was touring the United States. During our chat, Mrs. Raffel expressed some misgivings. She was not at all sure her house was big enough, and besides, the luncheon was to be held on the maid's day off. In friendly fashion, I offered to lend our house for the occasion. "Wonderful," Mrs. Raffel fairly shouted. It wasn't long before I found out the reason for her quick acceptance. The luncheon had to be held on Wednesday, and this was Monday!

By Tuesday morning the guest list had grown to staggering

dimensions. I began to think I would have to rent the Orange Bowl Stadium to hold them all. Desperately, I put in a call for help to the catering staff of the Fontainebleau Hotel. The Park Department agreed to provide flowers and greenery. Parks Director John Poulos came up with two Japanese Bonsai trees, and orchids sprouted overnight, on drapery rods, lamps, and in the planter of our courtyard. Tuesday night Mrs. Raffel called to inform me that the Princess would be chaperoned by the president of the Japanese Stock Exchange. "Do we have any guests connected with stock brokerage coming?" she asked. I told her "No." "Well, do what you can, dear," she said. I put in an urgent call to Elliott's brother John, a partner of Bache & Company in New York. He suggested the president of the Bache & Company office in Dade County, Arthur Schwartz, and his wife. Obligingly, they agreed to come.

Our only contact with the Princess would be Mrs. Kenneth Oka, who was studying Japanese, and was the wife of a former mayor of Miami Beach. She greeted our guest at the door and I kept mumbling something that sounded vaguely like "Sayonara." The Princess bowed and smiled, I smiled and bowed, the Princess smiled and bowed, I smiled and bowed . . . In this fashion we made it to the living room, where there were forty guests assembled to greet her, all smiling and bowing.

Meanwhile, my kitchen began to resemble the culinary office of the Fontainebleau. Lester Paley, the catering manager, arrived, along with George Pulles, Banquet Maitre D'Hotel, and his assistants, Carlo Landi, Herman Suarez, and Cecilio Garcia. The caterers hauled in enough steam tables, chafing dishes and boiling pans to feed the 101st Airborne Division. I had ordered a typical American luncheon of creamed chicken and patty shells, peas, salad, dainty little rolls (which turned out to be chunks of French bread) and a dessert of strawberries Romanoff. Carlo insisted I come to the kitchen, where he uncovered an enormous tureen of steaming white rice. I blew up. "No rice," I said. "No rice." But when luncheon was served, Carlo appeared, bearing a small silver serving dish with rice. When I protested again, he said, "You know the Japanese and their rice." I had forgotten completely, and could not apologize strongly enough. My apologies did not go without a last word from the caterers, however.

On their way out after lunch, Carlo remarked over his shoulder, "Mrs. Roosevelt, you would probably be mean enough to take spaghetti away from the Italians." It put me in my place.

Receptions for visiting foreign dignitaries taught me other lessons as well, including one to be cautious with my praise. When the former Moroccan Ambassador Ali Bengoullen and his wife came to our home, I mentioned casually how much I admired his gold cigarette lighter. "You do, Pattee?" he exclaimed. "I am sooo glad. Eet is yours." After dinner Elliott advised me to be more careful in the future. "Certainly darling," I said, "but what a way to acquire riches."

At City Hall, Elliott undertook the task of reducing waste and increasing efficiency of the municipal government. Traditionally government in Miami Beach had been conducted by exchange of favors and cronyism. There was an overbundance of city job holders, department heads, and assistant department heads. Some of these officials seldom appeared at their offices except to get their checks. Much of the city policymaking was done at lunchtime in the back room of Mendelson's Kosher Meat Market, where certain members of the council met with functionaries on the municipal payroll and friends who enjoyed benefits of city purchases. Favors were dispensed and decisions made over corned beef and cabbage, served on paper plates.

In the early stage of his administration, Elliott's efforts were hampered by the presence of a city manager disinclined to start eliminating unnecessary jobs and cutting budgets. The manager, O. M. Pushkin, was a bald and quiet man who had risen from the lower ranks of the public works department over a period of thirty-eight years. Ponderous, sleepy-eyed and shrewd, Pushkin had friends in all the high places and enjoyed a job security which practically required conviction of wrongdoing before he could be fired. But, late one night, his car crashed into several others at an intersection, and Pushkin vanished from the scene. From a small notice, the incident erupted into full-blown scandal. Elliott summoned Police Chief Rocky Pomerance, a burly one-time beat cop, and others to our house for a conference. "I want this Pushkin thing pursued to the finish," he declared. "If he's guilty, I want him out of the city government." In the subsequent investigation, accompanied by weeks of glaring newspaper headlines and a grand jury probe, five members of the police department were accused of covering up the city manager's accident, and a veteran detective was charged with helping him leave the scene of the wreck. Pushkin eventually was convicted of leaving the scene of an accident, and the City Council fired him.

The Pushkin affair spread over a period of four months. During that time we were threatened with violence upon Elliott, his friends and family.

While the investigation was in progress, we were visited by film producer Joseph E. Levine and his wife, Rosalie, aboard their 124-foot yacht *Rosalie L.* The vessel drew so much water that it mired in Sunset Lake, behind our home. In deference to his position in films and the length of his boat, we were according Joe our VIP treatment, which consisted of a free swim in our pool and a drink at the edge when he came up. As the Levines arrived, Elliott was holding a press conference in the living room, on the Pushkin probe. Helping to field the questions were Bobbie Leonard, Elliott's right arm, and Chief Pomerance. When the conference ended, Rocky Pomerance remained with us to greet Joe and Rosalie. Rosalie decided she would join Joe for his VIP swim. At poolside, she took off a diamond ring the size of a chicken egg and placed it casually on a table. Joe was already in the water. The size of the ring gave me a start. "Rosalie, you shouldn't do that. It might fall off and get broken." Carefully, I placed it in my cigarette case and gave it to the police chief for safekeeping. Rocky was slipping it into his pocket, when . . .

Phop! Phop!

Two pistol shots rang out from the street and bullets whizzed over our heads. A car went roaring away, tires screaming, Rocky Pomerance jerked, then sprinted around the house. Joe Levine promptly sat on the bottom of the pool, his head under water. Rosalie stood with her mouth open. I didn't know what to do, so I ran to the corner of the house and peeped around in the direction Rocky had gone. There was our police chief, impaled on a picket fence. Two wisps of blue smoke were disintegrating by our front driveway.

The chief finally freed himself from the fence and came puffing back to the pool.

"Rocky," I said, "where's the diamond ring?"

Joe Levine sputtered to the surface. "Hey, who fired those shots?" Pomerance grinned at me and produced the precious cigarette case and ring. Then he turned to Joe Levine and shrugged. To their chagrin, the Levines could not escape our noisy hospitality and had to wait until high tide that evening before the *Rosalie L* would float again.

Although there was no proof that the shooting was intended to scare Elliott off the Pushkin case, he redoubled his efforts to see the investigation through. At first Pushkin steadfastly denied even being at the accident scene, saying his car had been stolen earlier in the day. Later, his lawyer altered this, saying the city manager had been unconscious following the accident and did not know he was being carried away. Pushkin adamantly refused to resign, even under pressure from his friends. The council finally voted six to one for his ouster. Hired as his successor was Robert Oldland, a sharp young administrator from Anchorage, Alaska.

Much of the mayor's duties involved hobnobbing with celebrities and pushing projects to promote Miami Beach as a tourist and fun corner of the world. A tremendous drawing card for the city was Jackie Gleason. Since moving his television production, *The Jackie Gleason Show*, from New York to Miami Beach, the rotund comic had been accorded the homage of a local monarch of show business. His every utterance made print, his moon-shaped countenance graced newspaper pages and television station breaks, and city councils quavered at the thought of his ever growing disgruntled, packing up his dancing girls and going back to Flatbush. Annually "The Great One" escaped the heat of our summers by going off to the Catskills for vacation. His trek back to Miami Beach was always by train, for he had a deathly dread of flying. And so, around the first of August it came time again for the arrival of the *Gleason Express* train at Miami's seedy Seaboard Station. Enroute, the comic and his retinue, including a sizable representation of the press, whooped it up on snacks and schnapps, arriving with a rosy glow. As in the past, the City of Miami Beach planned to receive him with imperial fanfare, but this year there was a hitch in the free dinner. Gleason had switched his residence from the Doral Country

Club, owned by the Kaskels of the Doral hotel chain, to the
Miami Country Club. The city publicity department was loath
to ask the Doral people to provide their usual "Welcome
Home Dinner" for Gleason's party. Elliott cautioned me not to
meddle. After all, he said, Miami Beach had a good publicity
man in Hank Meyer, who was paid a huge annual retainer as a
consultant. "It's none of your business, darling. Stay out of it,"
Elliott cautioned. But, as the time for Gleason's arrival drew
near and nothing was done about the dinner, I grew fidgety.
Quietly, I approached my friend Jerry Dobin, who handled public
relations for the Doral Beach Hotel. Even if Gleason had
moved, I said, why not stage the dinner for him anyway. "Sure,
Patty," Jerry said, "it's logical that we do it. I'll call you back."
A short time later, I informed the city publicity department that
arrangements had been made for the dinner to go on as usual.

To give the arrival publicity an extra fillip for Miami Beach,
I decided to go with Elliott in the city's official car, a Cadillac
limousine, to take part in the welcome. Already waiting on the
sweltering station platform were musicians, a troupe of go-go
dancers in zebra skin costumes and white boots, and dapper,
silver-haired Chuck Hall, mayor of Metropolitan Dade County.
The *Gleason Express* was an hour behind schedule. To while
away the time, the go-go girls bounced and the musicians pumped
out snappy rock 'n' roll tunes. Mayor Hall strode over to me, gave
an elegant little bow and said: "May I have this dance?" To the
delight of picture-hungry press and television cameramen, we did
a snappy dance, making up in verve for what it lacked in style.
Our children refused to speak to me for three days . . . *Mother!*
. . . Gleason finally rolled in, sporting a flower in his buttonhole
and bestowing blessings palms out. All the way home a disgruntled Elliott lectured me on maintaining the dignity befitting
a mayor's wife.

We seemed to spend half our time now trekking to the train
station or the airport. Not long after Gleason's arrival, it was
the turn of Vice-President Hubert Humphrey to come to Miami
Beach to address the Urban League Convention at the Eden Roc
Hotel. Since the city limousine was not equipped with a two-way
radio, the security committee for Humphrey's visit decided to
lease cars for his motorcade. With Elliott cautioning me to re-

main in the background, we gathered in the hot sun on the concrete apron to await the Vice-President's arrival. To keep the interior of the cars cool, the motors and air conditioners had been kept running. As the Humphrey plane taxied in from the runway, I glanced back to see six limousines belching green liquid and boiling smoke. "They left the motors running too long," Elliott whispered.

The Vice-President passed through the crowd of welcoming dignitaries, came over to us and gave me a kiss on the cheek. "Roosevelts, how's everything going?" he said. Then he was led away by Secret Service men to be confronted by the six volcanoes that had been Lincoln limousines. Without further ado his advance guard commandeered our car, and before I could light a cigarette the Vice-President was being whisked away to Miami Beach, leaving us standing there. Mayor Hall, Mayor Roosevelt, and I were wilting in the heat. "Well," said Elliott, "I guess we'll just have to take one of those bombed-out Lincolns to town."

Accustomed as we were to air-conditioning, it was a stifling ride back.

A wealthy Miami man-about-town had made a contribution to the Democratic National Committee with the understanding that Vice-President Humphrey would take a cruise on his yacht. His yacht was 120-feet long, of German design and practically brand new. It was berthed in Indian Creek, across Collins Avenue from the Eden Roc. We did not intend to take part in the cruise, but David Walters extended us an invitation to go aboard with the Vice-President. So, board we did, and bored we stayed. Because of the tides, the big vessel could not move out of Indian Creek to deep water. We sat for several hours watching waiters carrying trays of food across from the hotel and setting up an elaborate buffet in the salon. Tourists clustered around, snapping pictures, while Secret Service men tried to put some kind of security around Mr. Humphrey. Finally, without having sailed an inch, the Vice-President's party trooped ashore again and returned to the hotel.

Later that evening they were all invited back again to go on the cruise, but the Vice-President politely refused. With all that food on hand, the host entertained his assistants and some security men. They navigated successfully through Indian Creek and were nearly in open water when they went aground near the Julia Tuttle Causeway in Biscayne Bay. The next day, as we drove Vice-President Humphrey back to the airport, we passed the yacht listing on a submerged sandbar hard aport. Several Secret Service men had been among those stranded aboard.

Lack of attention to personal business was taking its toll on our bankbook. Once again, the finances were shaky. Now that he had been elected mayor, the public felt it owned Elliott's time. He gave it generously, in speaking engagements, public and private meetings and a never-ending stream of correspondence. The first eight months, he signed so many autographs that if I had a nickel for each we would be rich. Recognizing the tremendous financial burden of the campaign, a group of supporters decided to stage a testimonial dinner in Elliott's honor. The dinner committee was made up of several people in the Miami Beach public relations field, including Bill Segal, Stu Newman, Beverlye Keusch, Ritter Levenson, and some other good friends. As such things go, by the time the bills were in, there was not much left for the deficit. Since they were having trouble finding entertainment, I volunteered to enlist someone to liven up the proceedings. Soupy Sales was in town making a movie entitled *Birds Do It*. He was staying, with his wife and two children, at the Diplomat Hotel in Hollywood, Florida. Gretchen later was to fall in love with the oldest of Soupy's boys, Hunt, and drive us crazy for weeks mooning about the house.

In addition to Soupy, two other entertainers offered their talents, singer Holly Warren, and comedienne Gino Wilson. As usual, our old friend Murray Candib was in town, and he ordered unlimited quantities of champagne. Soupy Sales, for all his pranks as an entertainer of teenagers, is a master of the ad-lib. A highlight of the show for us was his crack: "We are fortunate to have Mayor Roosevelt as our leader in Miami Beach. Histories have been written about the Roosevelts. Teddy said, 'Charge!' FDR said, 'The only thing we have to fear is fear itself.' Now Elliott sends forth the message, 'C'mon down, the water's fine.'"

Elliott was spending so much time at City Hall that I found it necessary to try to keep our accounts going at the office. One day, I came home jubilant because I had landed, all by myself, an account with tremendous potential: Sheffield Hosiery Mills.

The firm, with main offices in Miami, approached me for a program to increase the number of outlets for their hosiery products, and hired me as public relations and sales adviser. A friend of ours in Minneapolis, Jim Watson, was president of the Red Owl Stores, which were scattered widely in the Middle West. I arranged for Harold Solomon, a cousin of the owners of Sheffield Hosiery, to accompany me to Minneapolis to meet Jim Watson. I also made appointments with executives of two other large chains in the northern United States.

The owner of the hosiery firm, Leonard J. Solomon, graciously presented me with a dozen pair of stockings. I did not have the heart to tell him that I had not worn hose since arriving in Miami Beach, but I did feel that I should wear them as a representative of the industry. We flew to Minneapolis on a Sunday afternoon, late in November, and stepped off the plane into cold, blustery weather. Harold Solomon lugged two sample cases, which bumped his legs as he walked. Arriving at the Radisson Hotel, which was like home to me, I could hardly wait to get to my room and rip off those stockings. After so long without the blasted things, they felt like plastic tubes encasing my legs.

It was a bare-legged, but tan, stocking saleswoman who went out the next morning, opening the door so Harold could get his bulky sample cases through. Naturally, I wore my large mink coat, as the only protection for weather. Jim Watkins' office was at Hopkins, just out of Minneapolis. He was more than courteous, inviting his sales manager and head buyer in for an hour's well-planned meeting. Fears that someone would notice my stocking-less legs soon disappeared, for I knew that a roomful of gentlemen would not inspect them too closely. I could say without flinching that these were truly marvelous stockings. "They won't rip, won't sag, never run and mold to the exact contour of a lady's leg," I said confidently, and to prove the point extended my suntanned limbs.

Upon my return to Miami Beach, Elliott received my report of the trip with mixed feelings. "Honey," he said, "what would you have done if someone had reached out to sample the stocking and touched your leg?"

"I would have slapped his face," I said. "Don't be ridiculous."

26

"Good Old Pat"

Life had shifted into still another gear, and Elliott hurled himself into the job of being mayor with an intensity I had never seen before. There were no limits to what he would tackle if it meant bringing recognition and progressive spirit to the city. He would go halfway around the world to promote Miami Beach, if necessary, leaving his private business in abeyance. This, in fact, he did in the latter part of 1965, when it appeared that the International Jaycees were about to move their world headquarters away from Miami Beach, and perhaps to another country entirely.

Wherever they come from, the Jaycees are an enthusiastic and energetic breed. It is fitting that their international center would be in a glamour spot of the world such as Miami Beach. For years the headquarters had conducted its operations quietly from modest offices. Unrecognized by most of the local populace and civic leaders, the Jaycee staff carried on a tremendous correspondence with men under thirty-five in practically every major country of Europe, Asia, Africa, and the Western Hemisphere. Every piece of mail that went out bore the Miami Beach postmark, and Jaycee acknowledged that the center of the huge organization was Miami Beach. From a standpoint of raw economics, the local benefit was incalculable; it did not take much acumen to realize that countless Jaycees came as tourists, bringing their families and spending money. Others intended to do so at some future time.

The international office was an assortment of rooms at the Miami Beach docks. The city had a ten-year lease which was about to expire. The U.S. conference of Jaycees had voted to establish permanent headquarters and construct their own building, provided the idea was approved by the international conference. The world organization was to meet in November in Sydney, Australia. Several other countries also wanted the international headquarters. Local Jaycees approached Elliott. Would he go to Australia and present Miami Beach's request for the permanent center? Gladly, he answered, but we could not afford to pay for such a trip. Would the city pay for this jaunt?

"I'll have to put it before the City Council for recommendation and approval," Elliott told them.

For months, vigorous young leaders of the Jaycees in Dade County had been pushing for some local financial help. They wanted the community to put up $50,000 in a reserve fund for the building, or donate the equivalent in land. Most of the structure they had in mind would be paid for by the Jaycees. By coincidence, the international aspect of the project was brought home by the fact that a chief local spokesman was Eddie Gong, a young Miami lawyer of Chinese descent serving his first term as a member of the State Legislature. The council backed off. It was not the practice of the city to give money to a private group such as this, no matter how laudable the project. But they did appropriate $1500 traveling expenses to send Elliott to Australia.

In the midst of the hassle, I had a sickening thought. "Honey, how long does it take to get to Australia?" He turned to me with surprise. "Well, it's halfway around the world, darling." "It is?" I said wretchedly. "Then you'll be gone for a month." He laughed. "No, no, sweetie, not a month and I'm not going without you." At the next council meeting, he announced that he was not going without his wife, and her expenses would have to be paid too. This touched off an uproar. Elliott banged his gavel. Privately, male friends told him he was nuts, and described the delights of Sydney. "Taking your wife, Elliott? That's like taking a ham sandwich to a banquet." Elliott stood firm. The council stood firm. Finally, Elliott turned to the Jaycee representatives and said: "You dig up the money to send Mrs. Roosevelt." They blanched. The international headquarters barely had bus fare to the council meetings. At last it was resolved from another direction. Miami Beach hotelmen, more aware than anyone else of the value of the Jaycees business, dug up the extra fare for both of us to go first class. The outlay came from Herb Robins of the Carillon; Alfred Kaskel of the Doral, and Ben Novack of the Fontainebleau.

Once again we climbed aboard a jet, this time for the longest ride of my life. The 707 streaked across the continent, landing us in San Francisco in time for dinner. We visited with old friends of mine from Seattle, Jane and Stan Mott Smith, then caught the plane for Hawaii. Out of the dark Pacific, off the port wingtip, rose the twinkling lights of Honolulu. I watched breathlessly. At 600 miles an hour we were racing the spin of the earth; although we had left from Miami Beach that morning and come far into the Pacific, it was still just 11:30 P.M. Through the night we flew, each hour leaping vast stretches of ocean. Fiji was a lighted runway and a clutch of hangar buildings, a brief walk in the middle of the night, another takeoff. Auckland, New Zealand, was awash with morning sunshine when we landed there, and already the streets were teeming with people on their way to work. Desperate for something to occupy my hands, I went to the airport's duty-free store to buy more film for our jinxed Polaroid camera. I complained to the clerk that we had spent more on film than the camera was worth, and still did not have a picture.

"Gee, lady, did you ever think of checking the batteries? There are batteries in the camera itself that have to be kept charged up or you don't get any results." I told him the only batteries I knew existed were in the flash attachment. He opened the back of the camera and laughed. "You don't have to charge these batteries, because there ain't none here." Moments later Elliott came toward me from the ticket counter. I aimed the camera and fired. He scowled. "Honey, you're not wasting more film now on that damn camera, are you?" I looked smug. "You just wait." Then, in sixty seconds, I pulled out a perfect picture.

In Sydney we were due for a shock. Nobody knew we were coming. Jaycee representatives from Miami Beach attending the conference had not been informed by the mayor's office. I wanted to collapse. Here we had hopped halfway around the globe like jet-set kangaroos and there was no place to rest or even change clothes. Suddenly it hurt to smile. Pan American airline executives stepped into the breach. With a few telephone calls and snapping fingers, we were whisked away by limousine to lodgings in the leading hotel. It turned out that we were given an Oriental suite which must have been designed for Disneyland, reserved only for visiting potentates. At the hotel entrance, a tired group of Jaycee officials, themselves travel-worn, made a valiant try at providing a VIP welcome.

It was quickly apparent that any thoughts of rest were out of the question. The schedule called for a meeting with international officials, then a bone-grinding business session, then visits to various delegations from far parts of the world. Elliott put on his old Durango running shoes and visited eighteen delegations before the sun went down. While he smiled, conversed, and made friends, I shopped in an Elizabeth Arden salon in Sydney. It gave me a great feeling of contact with familiar things, similar to the time years ago when I first arrived in Phoenix to be greeted by the Carnation Milk man. Even more familiar was the Sydney convent of the Mesdames of the Sacred Heart. The customs of the nuns, unchanged from one part of the world to another or from one century to another, gave me the same warmth I had when visiting them in Seattle or back home in Coconut Grove, Florida.

The general assembly of the conference was the following morning. From the standpoint of formal credentials, Elliott's presentation as mayor of Miami Beach would be weighed against some formidable competition. Shannon, Ireland, wanted the international headquarters, and its bid was presented by the Irish Ambassador. Morocco's invitation was presented by its Ambassador. When Elliott stood up and was introduced, the audience burst forth in a standing ovation. Then, in a simple, straightforward manner and without the benefit of notes, he told them of the tremendous influence and importance of the great Jaycees organization, of how the leadership of the world would come from the ranks of such men, and how Miami Beach and Dade County were emerging as the gateway of commerce and business between

North and South America. At several points, the audience again broke into the speech with applause.

It was Thanksgiving Day when we left Sydney. We had the traditional turkey dinner on the plane that night. Next morning in Honolulu, it was Thanksgiving Day again, and we enjoyed another turkey party. There was some benefit to be had, I thought, from such fast travel. But I wondered if the people going in the other direction might not miss the holiday altogether.

The Western Hotel Association, clients of Elliott's, had opened the new Ilikai Hotel in Honolulu and invited us to stay as their guests. It would provide us the first real vacation in years. As luck would have it, soon after our arrival Elliott complained of a severe earache. I had read in the paper that Pierre Salinger, who had been President Kenndy's press secretary, was in town. Despite the earache, Elliott called him, and that afternoon we joined Pierre and his vivacious French wife Nicole. They moved in a circle of jet-setters, exciting and colorful personalities who could stop off anywhere in the world and find old friends. After cocktails, we went to dinner at the elegant Honolulu restaurant of Peter Canlis, the charcoal broiler. Elliott had bought me a new dress that day, and we decided to make dinner an event. To complement the new gown he donned his white dinner jacket with the red bow tie and cummerbund.

At dinner, we were seated along the wall next to a distinguished-looking couple. The man turned to me and, in a lofty tone, asked: "And may I ask, madam, why the soup and fish?" I grinned. "We decided that since we were on vacation and did *not* have to dress, we might as well go ahead and do it." The patronizing manner softened a bit and his eye sparkled. "Do you know who I am?" he said. I confessed that I did not, but introduced myself and Elliott, who was sitting next to me holding his throbbing ear. "I am Arthur Murray," the stranger announced gravely. "Oh, Mr. Murray," I gasped, "but you look so much younger than your pictures. I have always said that before I die I would like to dance with Arthur Murray. And to think, here I am sitting right next to you!" (Not a bad comeback, I thought to myself. My chagrin was painful.) For the rest of dinner, we chatted pleasantly about a mutual friend in Miami Beach, Russell Fairbanks, who had been manager of the Arthur Murray

Studios in our area and whose wife Mildred and I played golf together at LaGorce Country Club.

When we returned to the hotel, Elliott's temperature had shot up alarmingly. The hotel sent their physician, who found that my husband had a severe mastoid infection in both ears, made worse from long flying at high altitudes. He administered a penicillin injection and left us a supply of antibiotics and eardrops. For the next three days, we treated ears and took sunbaths.

Shortly before leaving Hawaii, we were notified that the International Council of Jaycees had voted to accept Miami Beach's invitation to build their permanent headquarters. The news made Elliott's pain more bearable.

For Elliott, the Jaycees project was a personal coup. The rest of the community gave it scant notice, however, and the newspaper coverage quickly dribbled away. After seven days of travel, covering some 18,000 miles, home looked better than the finest hotel on Waikiki Beach, our own swimming pool more delightful than the whole Pacific, and dinner in bed made even Peter Canlis's cookery take second billing.

The weeks fled and Christmas was upon us. For the person accustomed to traditional Christmases, there is nothing more out of kilter than celebrating the holiday on Miami Beach. In place of snow the vista is bright sunshine and sand, and soaring ranks of bone-white beachfront hotels; in the clubs and lounges and lobbies, a common sight beside the gaily decorated evergreen is a small sign reading: *This is a Chanukkah tree.* People spend Christmas Day in the surf getting sunburn, and Santa not only roasts in his red flannel but also is perennially frustrated because there are so few chimneys.

But our Christmas was more than kind.

On Christmas morning we opened our gifts by the tree. The first package I seized upon was from Elliott. It was a bottle of Christmas Night perfume. I opened another package; another bottle of Christmas Night perfume. A third package yielded still another bottle of Christmas Night perfume. "Elliott," I said, "some blond saleswoman certainly ran you into the wall."

After clearing a mountain of wrapping paper and ribbons, I went to the kitchen to begin my annual ritual of making the Christmas eggnog, a task requiring concentration and devotion to duty. For perfection, each ingredient must be separately whipped and lightly folded together. I was on the third batch of whipped cream when Elliott came dashing into the kitchen. "Hurry darling, you have to come out in front," he said, "immediately."

"I can't leave this whipping cream. It will turn to butter."

He reached over and turned off the beaters. "There's been an accident."

My heart bounced, and I flew for the front door. There, I was greeted by the entire household and assorted guests singing, "We Wish You a Merry Christmas." Behind them, in the driveway, stood a gleaming new white Thunderbird convertible with red leather upholstery. The car was bedecked with a huge red velvet bow, which Elliott had fashioned himself. I stood in shock. "Oh no, it couldn't be. Not for me!" We piled into the car in pajamas and robes and drove up and down the neighborhood singing Christmas carols.

By noon, hordes of people were descending upon us. As each new group arrived I met them at the door offering a ride in my new car. More than two hundred city employees dropped by to wish us a Merry Christmas. Some stayed to get merrier and others simply popped in and out.

Since our move to Miami, Martin Jones had made it his custom to spend Christmas Eve at our house in order to see the children receive their presents the next morning. This year he gave them an outboard motor for their dinghy, and laboriously wrapped it in Armour meat paper. Until it was opened we thought it was a frozen turkey or a roast beef, giving off a strange odor of motor oil. That afternoon our friend John Hertz, Jr., son of the founder of the car rental business, brought over a stereo record player for each of the children.

The end of the year came, and with it a sense of mounting pressure. During the past two years I had undertaken a tremendous load of activities.

In January I paid the price. Feeling listless and out of sorts, I had lunch with a woman political leader, then I went to the office of Elliott Roosevelt International, met a client and managed somehow to mumble through our business. When the client left, I started to rise, and felt a tightening of my chest. My face numbed, my ears buzzed. I blacked out and fell to the floor.

No one knows exactly how long I lay there. Presently, one of the secretaries walked in and found me. They called a doctor in the next office. He came in and suggested they call a heart specialist. I drifted back to semiconsciousness as an ambulance arrived to take me to St. Francis Hospital. Elliott came in just as the attendants were wheeling me out on the ambulance cart. Another screaming ride to nowhere.

At St. Francis, I returned to full consciousness, and they discovered that the walls of a vessel leading to the heart had thickened. This clogging caused an insufficiency of blood and oxygen to the heart. A leading heart specialist, Dr. Paul Unger of Miami, was called in on my case. He gave me proper medication and assured me that, with reasonable care, I could expect to live happily for many years to come. I must not continue to abuse myself any longer, and rest was more than important.

The attack caused more consternation in Seattle than it did with Elliott and the children. Mother, who was not well herself, had decided she would not come to Miami Beach this year. Elliott decided he shouldn't call her the first night I was in the hospital, since my condition was improving rapidly and was not considered critical. Local newspaper accounts, however, were picked up by the wire services and the following morning appeared in the Seattle papers to be read by my family. During my two weeks of hospitalization, Elliott made arrangements for Mother to come down. "You're the only person in the world who can keep Patty quiet," he told her. "You will be helping me a great deal if you will pay us a visit." Swallowing tranquilizers to still her quaking nerves, she boarded a plane for her first air trip by herself and arrived the day before I was released from the hospital. During my weeks convalescing at home, we spent countless hours talking in the bedroom, compiling a scrapbook of Elliott's clippings and going on a Sego liquid diet.

When the doctor finally said I could drive my new car for a short time each day, I made plans to take my nurse, Miss Shirley McClure, to visit Elliott's new mayor's office. Considerable redecorating had been done which I had not even seen myself.

A chilly breeze whipped in from the ocean, but bright sunshine made the weather invigorating. Bundled in coats and scarves, we drove to the Miami Beach Auditorium with the top down. Behind the auditorium, which had been converted into a huge television studio for taping *The Jackie Gleason Show*, were reserved parking spaces for the mayor and city councilmen. As usual, I pulled up to the mayor's space and backed in. Just as I reached for the keys, a belligerent voice bellowed from behind me: "You big dumb broad, move that car." My head whirled around as if on a swivel. At my rear fender loomed an elongated limousine being rented by Jackie Gleason and driven by a temporary chauffeur. "The Great One" was arriving for a taping session.

I tried to wither him with a look. "I beg your pardon. Do you know who I am, sir?"

"I don't give a damn if you're the Queen of Sheba, get that car out of there."

"I will not." Yanking the keys from the ignition, I got out, slammed the car door and stalked into the mayor's office with all the haughty dignity that I could muster. The nurse trailed me, shaking her head. The driver sputtered incoherently, then moved on.

That evening I recounted the incident to Elliott, who promptly dashed to the telephone in a fury, dialed his executive secretary Peggy McKay and ordered her to demand a public apology.

Mother watched my husband unleashing his temper onto poor Peggy McKay and told me quietly that I should never tell him about such things. "Any time someone insults you he sees red."

"Well, I certainly didn't deliberately put myself into this position."

"No, darling," said Elliott, "but you should always identify yourself so that this kind of thing can never happen. Always identify yourself. Tell them your name."

A week later, I had an opportunity to take his advice. Thinking Mother might enjoy a taste of Miami club life, I took her to the posh Palm Bay Club, overlooking the bay just off Miami's Biscayne Boulevard. The establishment, operated by Connie Dinkler, is a hangout for visiting movie stars and internationally known as the "Glitter Bug Club." This club was something that had been needed for a long time. It would seek and find its own level in any community, any area, where the idle rich had tired of being idle. We enjoyed a unique fun luncheon and Mother was suitably impressed.

Afterward, we drove homeward across the 79th Street Causeway, winding through some of the fabulous estate areas of Miami Beach. On one side street, our way was blocked by a large city garbage truck, stopped in the middle of the road.

"What a place to park a truck," I grumbled.

Mother reminded me of the Jackie Gleason experience, and I told her that I did not intend to argue with the driver but would try to sneak around him. As we drew up even with the truck, the driver hopped out and strode toward us, the picture of a man about to blow his top. Determined to avoid an incident, I put the window down and spoke in my cheeriest tone of voice.

"Excuse me, I'm just trying to get by. I'm Mrs. Elliott Roosevelt. Would you mind if I went through?"

The man halted in midstride, looked at me with amazement, grinned and said: "Oh, c'mon, you're not Mrs. Elliott Roosevelt. You're just good old Pat."

For months to come, the garbage truck driver brought me roses or some other floral offering a couple of times each week. I have always suspected they were someone else's leftovers, but I was grateful for his thoughtfulness. Little things mean a lot.

Shortly before Mother was to return home, ending a two-month visit, an old friend of hers from Seattle, along with her daughter, arrived for a winter vacation in Miami Beach. In their honor and Mother's I planned a lavish luncheon aboard our yacht, *Big Bear*, complete with yachting outfits and china of cobalt blue and gold bearing the *Big Bear* crest. Our guest, a onetime amateur opera singer, apparently became affected by the combination of sun and motion. During the outing, she kept bursting into song, always a fraction of a note off-key.

Shortly after Mother's departure, Elliott and I made a trip to Washington, D.C., and Betty Beale offered us the use of her bachelorette apartment. She used this "pad," as she called it, as a studio for her writing. Since our first meeting at the reception for the Eleanor Roosevelt commemorative stamp ceremony we had become close friends. Betty was blunt, energetic, honest, and intensely loyal. She and I spent a delightful afternoon between the telephone and the typewriter. When the time neared for me to meet Elliott I began pulling my dresses out of the closet, looking for one that would be appropriate. Betty took a look at the first one and made a face. The next one was too dowdy for her taste, and the next. I dredged out the last dress to my name, but it was terribly wrinkled, and Betty had no iron. Remembering an old household hint from somewhere, I rushed the dress to the bathroom, hung it on a hanger and turned on the hot water, the idea being to pull out the wrinkles by dampening the garment with steam. I rushed away to put on make-up, came back in six minutes and discovered to my horror the dress floating in a tub full of hot water. With barely half an hour to go I hurried to the corner dry cleaners. They were closing. I identified myself. This time it worked! The proprietor turned his pressing machine back on, went to work on the dress and soon had it nearly all dry. Ah, that magic Roosevelt name! Still, I had to spend the evening sitting on wet seams.

Betty Beale's wit and charm are well known in Washington, and her outgoing nature is perhaps typified by the toast she once offered at a dinner she gave in honor of Elliott and me. She wanted to make sure we met all the "in" people in the new administration. Her guest list was a White House roster, Horace Busby and his wife, Jack and Mary Margaret Valenti, Congressman and Mrs. Paul Rogers from Florida, the well-known Liz and Les Carpenter of White House fame. During dessert she rose to her feet and in her direct but vivacious manner, commanded her guests' attention. "A toast," she said. "A toast to my dear friends, Patty and Elliott Roosevelt." Twinkling at our surprise, she continued:

"TO THE ROOSEVELTS
September 18, 1964

Come, my dears and gather closer,
Draw your chairs within my range
While I tell of Big Chief Elliott
'Tis a story rather strange.

By the shores of old Miami,
Stands his tepee so imposing
Greatest tepee in Miami
Run like club never closing.

Here Chief Elliott won renown
With the help of Patty Bird
Quietest squaw in all the town,
Never said a single word.

Here he heard the people beg him
'Be our boy on big committee—
Cross the state,' they did egg him
'Twas a sound mighty pretty.

So he campaigned and he won,
But alas soon there gathers
Little storm on big horizon
Could it be that fellow Smathers?

Could it be other chieftain
Getting nervous at the fame
Of this fellow, able, friendly,
Bearing greatest tribal name?

Soon the storm has fearsome aura
Florida calls it hurricane
Says it's frightening, says it's Dora
Says it can sweep whole domain.

Quiet the people sit and wonder
Waiting for a great big crash
Waiting for the clap of thunder
Waiting for the windy smash.

'Ere the quiet drives them batty
They hear soft ripple dripping.
Makes them smile, 'It's our Patty
At her usual skinny dipping.'

May the storms of hurricane belt
in the southern latitude,
Dissolve for Chief Roosevelt
And his swimming squaw in nude."

27

The Beginning of the End

On our return from Washington, D.C., I began, in earnest, to reorganize my life. The hours spent in the doctor's office were a bore. Furthermore, the heart attack had unnerved me. I soon realized that with reasonable prudence, I could expect to regain full health and vitality. But the prospect of a long enforced idleness was every bit as upsetting as the illness it was supposed to cure. My restless nature simply is not adaptable to lingering convalescences, stretched out like Camille on a chaise longue reading French novels and fluttering a fan. With Dr. Unger's warning still making echoes, Elliott insisted that I curtail my activities. His word carried more weight than all the medical profession's. When Mother left in March, I resolved to spend as much time as possible at home, taking daily naps, keeping cool. This, I thought, would be a good time to begin writing a book.

I possessed two of the necessary qualifications, the material and the drive. The mechanical skill of writing was something else again, and for this I would need a professional. For many months I had read a daily column in the Miami *Herald* written by Charles Whited, a reporter who wrote offbeat glimpses of this unique city. I called him. A couple of weeks later we began a regimen of tape interviewing and writing that was to take six months. Although neither of us had ever written a book, our joint enthusiasm for the project brought an outpouring of production. By October 1, this was whipped into shape.

During my convalescence, we had, also, limited our social and political activities. When Bess Glasser, president of the Adlai Stevenson Women's Democratic Club of Miami Beach, asked if they could hold a membership tea in our home, I agreed to act as hostess. For entertainment, the Democratic ladies had invited an opera singer. The singer announced that she would have to have a piano, she simply could not sing without piano accompaniment. Did we have a piano? I had a grand piano upstairs which I had no intention of bringing down, and a small organ in the living room. The organ would have to do. The singer was disgruntled. Trying to be helpful, I made two hundred sandwiches for the ladies to munch on while they listened to the singing and discussed Adlai Stevenson, or whatever it was they planned to discuss. On the eve of the meeting, the husband of one of the members demanded that the meeting be called off; his business partner had died. The Adlai Stevenson Women's Democratic Club obliged. I fumed at Bess Glasser. She would have to notify all those ladies, I said, and someone would have to be at the house to turn away those who did not get word of the cancellation. "Why don't you do it, Patty?" she said. I told her I had been invited to play golf and did not intend to turn down this all too rare opportunity. Arrangements were made, and I went off with my clubs. The club representatives remained at our house long enough, they assumed, to tell all those who did come that the meeting was off, and then departed themselves. Then a latecomer arrived, became furious when told by my maid what had happened, and pushed past her into our living room.

For the better part of an hour, this woman stalked around our living room, fingering the silver ash trays and Roosevelt mementos and threatening to sue us for the inconvenience she had suffered, or at the very least, report us to the governor. Gretchen reinforced the harried maid in the living room, while the intruder ranted on: "Which wife is he married to now? . . . I'll bet they're not married at all, probably living in sin . . . Who are you, child? . . ." Trudy, the maid, managed to get the visitor's address and the name of her son, which sounded Irish, and then she left. I arrived a short time later to find both Trudy and Gretchen near tears. When Elliott came home and heard the story, he thundered with rage and headed for the front door. I trotted out at his heels, still wearing my golfing shorts.

"You can't go with me," he snapped.

"Why not?"

"Because if I go and get into a fight I don't want people to know that the mayor's wife was there with her shorts on."

There was a mixup in the address, so I called Bess Glasser. "What was the woman's name?" she asked.

"Patrick," I said.

"Patrick? That's a gentile name. You're the only gentile in the club."

"I *was* the only gentile in the club."

Later, we discovered that the woman had been under a psychiatrist's care. Her family was mortified by the incident, and fell all over themselves trying to make amends.

A couple of favorite bridge partners for Elliott and me were JoAnne McAdams and her husband, Charles, president of the McNaught Syndicate. On the Fourth of July, Elliott invited them to go with us to a session of the Teamsters' convention, which he was to open with a speech in Miami Beach Auditorium. Charlie bristled. "I wouldn't be caught dead in the same room with Jimmy Hoffa." But curiosity got the better of him, and Charlie and JoAnne turned up for the session. Several dignitaries were already onstage, and Hoffa was going among them oozing charm and shaking hands. We went backstage and promptly encountered a brace of Hoffa's bodyguards with thick necks and bulges under their coats. They all looked like Notre Dame tackles. "Sorry, but you'll have to get off the stage," they said. I told them who we were, and the atmosphere abruptly changed. "Why didn't you say so, Mrs. Roosevelt." With that, we were ushered out to join the bigwigs of labor gathered on the stage. Their enthusiasm for Elliott was exuberant. Various union leaders came to shake his hand, saying that now that Jimmy was out of politics and Franklin, Jr., appeared to be making a last-ditch fight, it was up to Elliott to carry on the Roosevelt tradition. It has always been my custom to clap harder for my husband than anyone else in the room. Even though I may have heard the subject matter, it is always fascinating for me to watch this big, forceful man command the attention of his audience without a single note—his extemporaneous speeches are far better than any others prepared hours in advance. I have, also, formed the habit of counting the bursts of applause during his tenure at the rostrum. Then I gauge the reception of his listeners. Today during Elliott's welcoming speech as mayor of Miami Beach, the three thousand Teamster delegates interrupted him with applause fifteen times.

In August we took a quick trip to New York and Hyde Park.

In a rented black Cadillac, riding on its axle under a load of luggage and people, we sped northward from the city, along the Hudson. At Rhinebeck, Aunt Polly was our hostess for three days. Amid the rolling hills and breath-taking scenery of the Hudson Valley, her shingle-roofed home reminds you of a Swiss chalet tucked into a copse of evergreen trees atop a smooth green rise of hill. We rested and talked and studied this fascinating little woman who is among the last of her blue-blooded line.

As guests we had brought Freddie Peterson, Charles Whited, and his wife Dorothy.

There were formal luncheons and dinners, with fine crystal enhancing the exquisite place settings in a tiny dining room, and hours of conversation around the little coffee table laden with glasses and liquor bottles. One could find easy comfort in her cluttered living room, with its overabundance of soft rugs and cushiony sitting places and knickknacks of gold and jade. On the enclosed patio, she sat in her chaise, the tiny purple-haired spinster, and spoke of breeding and refinement and taste in a family saturated with such qualities. And at times, the thin slash of a mouth pursed, the wise old eyes looked out across the Hudson Valley to the looming blue Catskill Mountains, and she said: "I will die and the worms will eat me, and that will be that."

Franklin and Sue joined us for dinner one evening, and we could see he was obviously concerned about mustering enough support for the governor's race. The next day he would meet Dave Dubinsky and get his promise of support, but it was apparent now that Frank O'Connor's drive for the Democratic nomination would not be stopped. Franklin's decision now was whether to take it gracefully and bow out, or make the race independently on the Liberal ticket. Elliott urged him to seize the opportunity while it was there to be seized. Elliott said: "If you bow to the brush-off of Bobby Kennedy and the old Tammany Hall leadership in New York City, you are through in politics forever. Go out and get the Liberal Party endorsement and run like you did when you first ran for Congress. You may not win, but, if you poll a million or more votes in this race, you will be a power representing the Liberals of New York State in the future. If you've got the guts to fight, you might even win!"

While they talked, the Irish maid Delia, a quiet, stolid woman in heavy shoes who once won eighty-five thousand dollars in the Irish Sweepstakes, padded in and picked up the blind little Pekingese, Ming, from his marbletop table beside Aunt Polly. Delia fed Ming strips of white meat of chicken, deftly wiping his nose when he slobbered. Her arms and hands, like Aunt Polly's, were etched with tiny white scars from the teeth of the ill-tempered and pampered pet.

A cold and another ruptured eardrum kept me at Aunt Polly's for almost two weeks after Elliott and the others had returned to Miami. When I finally did make the trip back, I was accompanied by two very special gifts from Aunt Polly, a pair of champion, long-haired dachshunds from her kennel, named Carlo and Flicka. They have become the masters of our household.

In early September came tragic news from New York. Cousin Leila was dead. This dear lady with the fine skin and sweet, old-fashioned manners had suffered a stroke a year before in her New York apartment, and now the end had come. Elliott and I made plans to go up for the funeral. As it turned out, Elliott was the only one of FDR's children present. We went directly to Rhinebeck to be with Aunt Polly as we felt she needed us.

The funeral was in New York, and then the cortege was to make the long drive to Rhinebeck for the burial in the little cemetery there. In Aunt Polly's bedroom, a couple of hours before the service in the cemetery, I watched her ritual of dressing. The suit of black grosgrain was at least thirty years old, and a lizard belt wound its way through the belt loops. The pockets of the custom-made suit reached to her knees. Her hair was caught neatly in a black velvet ribbon and a black crepe veil bordered with chiffon was kept in place with a pearl-and-diamond pin. In her hair she also wore a bar pin of emeralds and diamonds. To complete the ensemble she carried a black and white chiffon handkerchief.

Cousin Leila would have loved her last day above the ground. Fall colors splashed the woods around Rhinebeck and the old cemetery which was her final resting place. The gravesite was in a secluded area at a point high above a heavily wooded ravine. It was surrounded by the tombstones of Vanderbilts, Rockefellers, Delanos, Astors, Roosevelts, and Livingstons, all of them at one time or another related by a marriage or birth. The people who would gather to mourn Cousin Leila's passing were mostly from the Rhinebeck area. Aunt Polly was grateful that Elliott and I had come. Leila Burnett Delano had been the wife of her brother and the closest person in the world to her, and though she rarely asked help of anyone she needed support on this day of loss.

We parked above the ravine and waited for the others to arrive. Aunt Polly did not wish to remain in the car. Instead, we walked out among the tombstones and talked. "You are like me, Patty, when I was young," she said, "so vigorous, so clever, cut from the same cloth. I have never told anybody about myself before, and now you know everything. I don't know what's happened to me." Again, the whimsical smile, the faraway look. In the sunlight of midday, her hair was a vivid, purplish blue.

We sat down together on the tombstone of Alice Astor. It bore the dates 1902–1956. The next tombstone bore the inscription: *"My friend and the world's best Chef, Basil Yourtchenko."*

Aunt Polly patted Alice Astor's monument. "You don't mind if we sit here, do you, Alice?" she said. She turned to me with a twinkle in her eye. "I am sure Alice would come up and join us, if she could."

28

A Roosevelt Birdwatcher

Roosevelts are strong. Roosevelts are generous. Roosevelts do not feel pain. Roosevelts can stand immobile for hours in receiving lines. Roosevelts do not acknowledge being hated, or conned, or abused, or used. Roosevelts are rich and tolerant and don't have knobby knees. First, as an outsider looking in, then for six brief and heady years, as an insider looking out, I have found that these things combine to make a composite picture of what the majority of the public sees in the name "Roosevelt." In reality, of course, the members of this magnificent American family, which has produced two Presidents and a heritage all its own, are extremely human, sometimes human to a fault. Among them there is jealousy and frustration and thwarted ambitions. The personalities which carry on the human legacy of Franklin and Eleanor Roosevelt are strong, and being strong makes them all the more prey to the capricious nature of human kind.

The public remembers Anna as the elegant, charming daughter who dwelt in the inner councils of the New Deal, and whose children Sistie and Buzzie were the playthings of a generation emerging from the Depression. It sees in Franklin, Jr., a startling resemblance to the giant of history that was FDR: head back, hearty laugh, the quick and charming wit, the patrician good looks. Elliott's voice has the timbre of his late father's. In John and Jimmy they see the scions of great tradition and lofty ideals and strength, but little physical resemblance to FDR. In Anna it is difficult to find those outgoing qualities that so endeared her mother to the public. But what are these people really? What are they like today? I have tried to bring order out of chaos in my own impressions of my sister-in-law and three brothers-in-law, projected against their exciting, and not-always-pleasant backgrounds, as people, and as living symbols of something uniquely American. Just like everyone else, they are creatures of strength, and weakness.

Anna is the enigma. She now shuns the public limelight.

Born in 1906, she was the eldest of FDR's children. Possibly because she was also the only daughter, Anna was unmistakably her father's favorite and enjoyed a unique rapport with him during his White House days. On the first campaign, it was she who rode the train, acting as a hostess to visiting politicians, along with Jimmy Roosevelt's first wife, Betsy Cushing. Eventually she moved into the White House where, tall and attractive, she entertained visiting dignitaries with a quick wit and sophisticated charm. Once, doing a snappy little dance step, she was chided by her father, who said his daughter should not be so frivolous at a formal state function. "I'm surprised," Franklin Roosevelt said. Anna laughed. "You shouldn't be," she said. "You are responsible. After all, you helped raise me."

Domestic life did not treat Anna kindly. Her first marriage, in 1926 to stockbroker Curtis B. Dall, lasted barely as long as it took her father to get into the White House. When she moved into the Executive Mansion with her parents, Anna brought along her two children, Anna Eleanor and Curtis Dall—whom the press made famous as Sistie and Buzzie. Her second husband, John Boettiger, a one-time correspondent for the Chicago *Tribune*, took her into the world of newspapers. They married in 1934 and moved to Seattle, when Boettiger became editor and publisher of the Seattle *Post-Intelligencer*. The family lived down the street from us, and Sistie and Buzzie were always trailed by Secret Service men. On Halloween they would go out and dump garbage cans, followed at polite distance by the well-dressed escorts. Her third child, John, was born to this marriage. During the war, when Boettiger went overseas, she returned to the White House, assisted her father in planning his 1944 campaign, and accompanied him to the Yalta Conference. She never made a record of those vital years. "I promised Father," Anna once told an interviewer, "that I would not keep a diary for I wanted him to have the assurance I was not making notes of all I saw and heard."

After the war, she and Boettiger returned to Seattle, where Anna took a more active role in the newspaper. They then bought into a paper in Phoenix, Arizona, which was a financial failure. The marriage ended in divorce in 1949. In 1952 she married Dr. James Halsted, a physician working for the Veterans Administration. Elliott, Jimmy, and Mrs. Roosevelt attended the ceremony. Sistie married Van H. Seagraves of Washington, D.C., and became the mother of three children. Buzzie dropped the Dall name and adopted the name Roosevelt.

The four sons of Franklin D. Roosevelt have always been in the public eye and never attempted to hide from what, for good or ill, was their lot in life. Each shouldered his responsibility in politics, either as an active supporter of parties, and candidates, or as candidates themselves. John startled the nation by becoming a Republican to support Dwight Eisenhower for President, and later became an avid backer of New York Governor Nelson A. Rockefeller.

The other three remained stanch Democrats through the years. The American public has held a fondness for all these sons of FDR, bestowing upon them warmth and prestige and acknowledgment while sometimes forgiving them their indiscretions. Franklin, Jr., and Jimmy have pursued energetic political careers as congressmen from their respective states, but neither was successful in gaining office at the city or state level. At this writing, both seem to be on the political eclipse, and John has indicated no desire to seek public office. Ironically, this left Elliott, who stayed behind the scenes, until he was fifty-three years old and then emerged with two overwhelming triumphs within the space of sixteen months, as the logical son of FDR to fulfill the prophecy of Washington seer Jeane Dixon that one Roosevelt would rise to national prominence.

Jimmy Roosevelt, tall, bald and personable, built a successful career for himself in business and insurance on the West Coast and served for eleven years as a United States Congressman from

California. One year younger than Anna, he resigned his congressional seat in August 1965 at the age of fifty-eight to become United States Ambassador to the United Nations Economic and Social Council. President Johnson, in appointing him, said Jimmy would help to strengthen the United States delegation, then headed by former Labor Secretary Arthur Goldberg, and described him as having "a passion for peace." That appointment came just five months after Jimmy suffered a landslide defeat in his race for mayor of Los Angeles, at the hands of incumbent Sam Yorty. His try for the mayor's chair marked his second major setback in sixteen years of public life. The first came in 1950 when Jimmy made his first political race for governor of California, and was beaten by Earl Warren.

Jimmy appears outgoing, friendly, and endowed with the strong family affection which characterizes his three brothers. Candidly, he admits that while as a Roosevelt he has inherited the people who hate, by the same token, the name has opened doors to him which otherwise would have remained closed. "It certainly gave me an opportunity to know people," he has said. "It gave me an inheritance of strength."

The public and the private views of Jimmy, like the others, are separate and distinct. For all his congeniality, this eldest of the brothers also has a patchwork background of domestic life, with three marriages, and a considerable share of unhappiness. He had three children by his first wife, two by his second, and one—little Del—by his third wife, Irene.

Beyond his private loyalties to family and intimate friends, Jimmy has shown himself capable of that shrewdness which politicians euphemistically term political strategy. The incident involving Pierre Salinger leaps to my mind.

At a crucial time when the former presidential press secretary was testing his support in order to decide whether to run for the U. S. Senate in California, Jimmy was to be in Miami Beach to give a speech for the Israel Bond organization. With the deadline for filing as a candidate near, Salinger wanted desperately to talk to Jimmy and ask for his backing. The first long-distance call from Pierre in Washington, D.C., came at 2 A.M. Jimmy had not arrived. I promised to give him the message, and left a note in his room: *Pierre Salinger wants you to call White House immediately.* Evidently, he did not return the call. On the next day—Pierre's day of decision—I finally tricked my brother-in-law into taking the long-distance call, saying it was his office. After recovering from the surprise, Jimmy's genial voice boomed out enthusiasm across 1200 miles of telephone wire. "Why, Pierre, hop a jet and get out there, boy. You know you've got my support!"

The next time we saw Jimmy was on nationwide television, as the early election returns came in from California, indicating that Pierre Salinger was losing. My genial brother-in-law had his arm around Pierre's opponent, Alan Cranston, who was saying: "Jimmy, I just couldn't have won this campaign without your help." Later returns swung the nomination to Pierre. He was, of course, to lose in the general election for the Senate race to his Republican opponent, actor George Murphy.

Elliott's feelings toward various members of his family make complex patterns in human relationship. One of my husband's strong characteristics, however, is his abiding sense of gratitude for past favors. Thus, Elliott has never forgotten how Jimmy gave him moral support during his personal crisis prior to their mother's death, and steered financial opportunities our way. He also talks warmly of how Franklin, Jr., came to the rescue many times with financial and moral encouragement. When Franklin lost the governor's race in New York, Elliott was terribly upset and felt he had helped influence Franklin to become a candidate. He offered many times to go up and campaign for him and made innumerable phone calls to some of our friends whom he thought would be interested in helping his brother.

The youngest of the Roosevelts, John, always the unpredictable, displayed a dynamically independent turn of mind as far back as 1940, when he quietly made it known to the family that he was thinking of declaring himself a conscientious objector. Eleanor Roosevelt, who, for a long time, had pacifist leanings, talked earnestly with John through half the night, reminding him of his unique responsibilities to the nation as the son of its President. Thus, persuaded by his mother, he went into the Navy, as an ensign, and served with valor and distinction in some of the fiercest campaigns of the Pacific.

During the years since that time, John's life continued to follow its own pattern. While the other Roosevelt sons shed wives and conducted their financial affairs with a flair for wheeler-dealing, this one worked doggedly at his jobs as an eight-to-six man, six days a week. When his venture into the department store business in California went sour, John returned to Hyde Park and New York.

His strange ways in politics became apparent in 1948, when he switched to the Republican side to support New York Governor Thomas E. Dewey. While New Dealers were shocked and dismayed, intimates of the Roosevelt family recalled that FDR himself once admitted that on occasion he had voted for a Republican. As a leader in New York of the "Committee for Modern Republicanism," John crusaded for Eisenhower so effectively that rumors began to circulate touting this GOP member of the Roosevelt clan as a possible contender for the 1958 gubernatorial nomination in New York. Speculation ended when he firmly and decisively refuted the notion.

In the 1960 campaign, he became a vigorous champion of Richard Nixon for the Presidency. At about the same time, his brother, Franklin, Jr., was stumping the coal fields of West Virginia in behalf of John Kennedy. Johnny Roosevelt was declaring: "I am convinced that Vice-President Nixon has the best training and the greatest ability of anyone in this country for the job as President. If my father were alive today, he would vote for Nixon." He was one of the speakers seconding Nixon's nomination in Chicago, and during the 1964 GOP National Convention he worked hard for the nomination of Pennsylvania Governor William Scranton. Later he was unable to give full support to Barry Goldwater because he disagreed with that presidential candidate's positions on civil rights, publicly owned electric power, and the United Nations. In the course of his work on behalf of Republicanism, John came in for his share of attack. One of the most fervent vocal blasts came from the richly verbose former Governor Fuller Warren of Florida, who once accused John of "desecrating the memory of his sainted father."

In business dealings, too, Johnny did not always endear himself to his critics, particularly the press. As an executive for Bache & Company in New York, he attended a convention of the

Teamsters in Miami, and plugged for the re-election of Jimmy Hoffa as union president at a time when Bobby Kennedy was calling Hoffa a menace to the country. Bache & Company had been advisers on investments made by the Teamsters Pension Fund.

For all of our family-type socializing, I found John the most difficult of the brothers to get along with.

One night Johnny and Anne took Elliott and me along with a Jesuit priest to dinner in New York. Elliott was helping him to raise funds for Gonzaga University in Spokane, Washington. As we sat at the piano bar, waiting for our tables, I overheard Elliott exclaim, "Oh, Johnny, for God's sake, you must be kidding." The restaurant, it turned out, was a favorite hangout of Faye Emerson. Aghast, I turned to the priest. "Father, what will I do if she comes in here?" He smiled and patted my hand. "Do nothing, my dear," he said in a kindly tone. "Just eat your dinner, and pray." Elliott's former wife did not appear.

I must admit that my favorite of the clan is Franklin, Jr. Urbane, witty, and delightfully scatterbrained, Franklin tells a joke and takes one well. By a twist of fate, he not only bears his father's name but also such a resemblance to him that people take quick second looks. Of all the Roosevelts at this writing, he has come closest to grabbing the brass ring of national politics. If his political future had a turning point anywhere along the line, it was in the first formulative days of the Kennedy administration.

The second youngest of the Roosevelt boys, Franklin was born in 1914, studied for his law degree and served three terms in Congress. He was first elected in 1949, representing New York's West Side at the age of thirty-four. From the beginning, there had been talk that this Roosevelt would someday be Governor of New York, but somehow his state ambitions were always being derailed. In 1954 he lost his bid for the gubernatorial nomination to Averell Harriman. He then ran for State Attorney General, and was defeated by Jacob K. Javits. In 1960, during John Kennedy's crucial battle against Hubert Humphrey in the West Virginia primary, Franklin took the stump for a grueling five weeks through Appalachia and was generally regarded as the pivot for JFK in that campaign. The grateful President Kennedy

seriously considered rewarding him with an appointment as
Secretary of the Navy. This had been the springboard for FDR,
but the President was deterred by Robert McNamara, who told
him he did not wish to have a Roosevelt serving under him.
Instead, President Kennedy made him Undersecretary of Commerce, at a salary of $21,000 a year. This is the only reward he
was ever to receive from John Kennedy.

A vigorous and dedicated worker for the party leadership,
Franklin, Jr., again threw himself into the campaign of Lyndon
Johnson in 1964. Wherever he appeared, crowds burst into applause at his entrance. During one such demonstration, President Johnson told a newsman on the speaker's platform: "See
that, it happens every time he is introduced anywhere." For a
while there had been speculations that he might be tabbed as
Johnson's running mate. This was not to be.

Franklin had three children by his first wife, the late Ethel du
Pont, but politics did as much as anything else to break up the
marriage. Ethel had no taste for public life, and this was given
as the main reason for her obtaining a Nevada divorce in 1949.
His second wife, Suzanne Perrin, has shown more enthusiasm in
the political arena.

As a debonair "bon vivant" Franklin, Jr., moved with the jet-
set and the inner circle of glamour society. A small flurry was
kicked up in the press in 1963, when he and Sue went on a
Mediterranean cruise with Jacqueline Kennedy and her sister,
Princess Lee Radziwill, aboard a yacht owned by Greek shipping
magnate Aristotle Onassis. However, Commerce Secretary Luther
Hodges said he saw no conflict of interest in the trip, and the
dust quickly settled. Six years before that, Franklin also drew
criticism when he accepted a $60,000 contract to work as a
lobbyist for then-dictator Rafael Trujillo of the Dominican Re-
public. He decided not to renew the contract following the mysterious disappearance of an American pilot, Jerry Murphy, and
the persistent reports of murders by Trujillo's henchmen.

Franklin's failure to win the Democratic nomination for Governor of New York in August 1966, was one of his keenest disappointments. With a kind of naïve faith in people, he had
banked heavily on winning the support of Bobby Kennedy, as
payment of the old political debt from the West Virginia pri-

mary. Kennedy, now having ambitions of his own, turned a cold shoulder to Franklin's plea, saying the debt had been paid with the appointment as Undersecretary of Commerce. Franklin felt that the governorship versus an undersecretary's post was hardly a fair exchange. It marked the first real political split between the two family dynasties, Roosevelt and Kennedy.

With Elliott's encouragement, Franklin pushed ahead to seek, and win, the support of the Liberals to run as a third-party candidate against the incumbent Republican Governor Nelson A. Rockefeller and the Democratic nominee, Frank O'Connor. For Franklin, it represented a do-or-die gamble; for if he did badly, throwing himself at the mercy of the voters, and Rockefeller won, he could be branded forever as the renegade who spoiled the Democrats' chances for winning the power in Albany. A strong showing at the polls, even in defeat, however, would repair his image and still keep him a potent contender in the New York and, possibly, national Democratic political arena.

The most family-minded and emotional of the Roosevelt children, Franklin has a special fondness for reunions. In the summer 1963, Johnny and Anne's eldest daughter, Nina, was to be married to Douglas Sigler Luke, Jr., in the family church at Hyde Park. Franklin saw it as a fine opportunity to stage a Roosevelt get-together. As was his custom, he provided each of his brothers with a Jaguar for the drive from New York City to Hyde Park, and invited everyone to his country home, at Poughquag in Dutchess County, the day after the wedding. During a yacht club reception at Rhinebeck, New York, where the bridal dinner was held, the brothers huddled and Franklin outlined his plans. The family would gather next day at one end of the swimming pool to talk family matters, while the in-laws remained at the other end. Elliott didn't like the idea. He felt that the wives should be included.

"Anyway, I'm sure Patty won't be left out of things," he said. "When we were in New York, I bought her one of those new topless bathing suits. She's going to model it tomorrow afternoon. And, I might add, she's one member of the family who can wear it."

Nervous smiles flicked across his brothers' faces, and conversation trailed away.

It was not true, of course, but they didn't know. The crafty Elliott, meanwhile, also neglected to let me in on what was to happen. Accordingly, the next afternoon, at Franklin's house, I went into Sue's cabaña and put on my favorite Rose Marie Reid bathing suit, covered by a belted beach coat.

Emerging from the cabaña, I noticed that my sisters-in-law had all disappeared, and the brothers were strangely silent. To avoid interrupting their family "meeting," I kept my distance at the in-laws end of the pool. Finally, deciding to get wet, I walked to the edge of the pool, and shrugged off my robe, revealing my perfectly acceptable, conservative bathing suit.

A male voice breathed, "Oh damn."

From the opposite end of the pool there erupted a roar of disappointment, shouts of "Big Liar," and a mighty splash as his brothers threw Elliott bodily into the pool.

In 1964, Franklin came to Miami Beach to visit us and ask Elliott to drum up some gubernatorial support for him among leaders of the AFL-CIO, who were holding their annual executive council meetings there. Included were such labor leaders as president George F. Meany, David Dubinsky of the International Ladies Garment Workers Union, and Barney Richards, of the American Federation of Musicians. Elliott invited them to a reception in our home for the main purpose of asking their individual unions to bring their conventions to Miami Beach. He warned Franklin that this was his party, and he had invited them for his own reasons, but he could give his pitch for New York gubernatorial support if he wished. Franklin was ecstatic. As the living room filled with men and women and cigar smoke, he went from group to group exuding good cheer and friendliness to organized labor.

After an hour or so, Dave Dubinsky looked at me with an impish grin and said, "Now, young lady, what are you trying to get out of me? I don't intend to support anybody for anything." I told him I was only interested in seeing that he had a good time and hoped he would return again in the near future. As they prepared to leave, he stopped, put his arm around me and announced in a booming voice you could hear across Biscayne Bay: "I don't know about the rest of you fellows, but I want to tell you that my nominee for Governor of New York is this little lady. I am going to support her, and so is my union."

For nearly two years, meanwhile, I had kept up a correspondence with Jeane Dixon, author of the best-selling book A *Gift of Prophecy*. She had told Washington columnist, Betty Beale, that one of the Roosevelt boys was going to come into prominence, but did not know which one. Now, two years later, it seemed to narrow down to Elliott. She wrote me a letter saying that a new life would unfold for Elliott and me, and that I was proving to be the pillar of strength that he needed to make the most of his tremendous natural ability.

The morning after our reception for the labor leaders, I showed the letter to Franklin, thinking that perhaps it might help him decide whether or not to run for Governor of New York. "If you feel that Jeane Dixon really has her pulse on the future, Franklin," I said, "this might prevent you from spending a lot of money on the campaign."

He read the letter once, twice, three times. Then he put it down, rose from his chair, walked slowly across the room to Elliott, bowed with solemn formality from the waist and intoned:

"Good morning, Mr. President."

Epilogue

The sun shone in full brilliance giving geometric whorls to the waters of Biscayne Bay behind our home. At last, relaxation! It had become a reality instead of a dream. My idea of complete happiness is to slip into a bathing suit, ice up some juice, climb into my floating pool chair, and float. The soft lap of the bright water is soporific. The sun bakes health into your bones. This is tranquillity that can't be found in a pharmacy.

My book was soon finished and would be in the hands of the publisher. It had been a hectic six months of frustrations, elation and I sometimes suspected, the beginning of an ulcer.

In the process, there had been numerous explosions in the Roosevelt household. Servants had trekked in and out of our employ. At last we secured the help of an excellent cook, house-man, and butler. The cook was Marie Jacobson, who had worked many years for our friend John Hertz. When she became ill, John hired another, and Marie came to our home. She brought with her Raymond, a thirty-eight-year-old son who had been in poor health most of his life. The butler was Earl Barnswell, who had once worked for General Robert Johnson, the Band-Aid king.

Now was the time to rest, rest and let someone else take over; yet our fickle minds don't always heed our physical needs. Little nudges from the brain played tricks on my weary eyes. The face of my beloved husband kept bobbing back and forth. All our years of struggle, all our joys and heartbreaks seemed to meld into one large panorama. I could feel myself drift back into the years before I had seen Jeane Dixon and held the crystal ball in my hands. What would I have done? Sometimes it's easier to get into the water if you just hold your nose and jump. Six years ago my heart took the leap and now looking backward into my own crystal ball I knew that I would travel the same path if I had it to do over again. I remembered Aunt Polly saying long ago that I would never make it as a new member of the family without help and protection. Certainly she has extended a hand to guide me, and her heart has always been ready to hear my troubles. Yet, she still made me stand by myself. Mrs. Roosevelt in her great goodness, courageously bearing the burden of her own problems, took the time to show me so much about self-reliance. She made me a part of the family in her own way, and had we been given more time to know each other, our friendship would have deepened. My husband was always the most important of her children to her. Her knowledge that our lives were becoming fruitful and productive and filled with happiness won for me her approval. Cousin Leila Delano and I became fast friends. During our life in Minneapolis her daughter, Janie, also gave me extra go-power. Janie and her husband, Bernie Ridder, lived a much different life on the other side of the river. St. Paul and Minneapolis were birds of another feather. The Ridder family were long-time members of the newspaper profession. Bernie and Elliott sparred at first from their lofty heights. But finally, the mind of each reached out to the other and their rapport was strong.

Growing up in a fishbowl family is difficult at best. This life leaves a different mark on each of the children. My feelings about them are my own. No one had influenced me, and only the various members of the family have individually created their own images with me.

Elliott is the catalyst for it all. Love is a myriad of reasons in themselves. It is quixotic, always mysterious, never completely rational. Even if it sometimes lacks luster, true love can always be strong, sometimes demanding, always fearless. A father and mother can give only so much to their children. They can breed into them understanding and love for their fellow man. But the parents must lead the way with exemplary guide lines. Only through their actions do the progeny learn, and then they are able to carry on their traditions. In the Roosevelt family these traditions are rooted in concepts of social change and human dignity of world scope. Yet, Roosevelt children are no different than others. When they cut themselves, they bleed; when they fall from a tree, they usually break a bone; if they study they may get good grades; they feed their hunger and quench their thirst. But one thing that Roosevelts never do is to cry. For this reason, sometimes I feel more like an out-law than an in-law. Their wounds may be mortal, but the world never knows their anguish. This stoicism was transmitted through generations of Roosevelts. Four ancestors came over on the *Mayflower*. In these children lie the genes of those pilgrim fathers who fought for, protected, and helped draft the principles we live by today. And, yet, heritage weighs heavy on the shoulders of those who must carry it. Franklin and Eleanor Roosevelt may have worried in private over their children's mistakes. But, was it not because more people were curious to watch and criticize? Was it not that each mistake was magnified because their parents lived in the house on Pennsylvania Avenue? And each time they tried to correct one error, were there not many hands outstretched to offer more golden baubles? This inheritance is lonesome. This fame and glory more times than not is hollow. I was once told by Franklin, Jr., that I should wear the name with pride and guard against its tarnish. I truly hope I've done this.

It takes strength, courage, and resilience to be a Roosevelt. This I know at last. But, living with a Roosevelt—loving a Roosevelt—makes it easier.

Twilight gathered. My floating chair nudged slowly toward the steps of the pool. I took a last look over my shoulder at the things that had gone. My pulse quickened as MY Roosevelt came through the door.

The Roosevelts helped elevate America and one day soon America again will elevate a Roosevelt. But now, for a short time, we were alone.

The things that are to be, we will do together.